For AQA specification A

BRIDGWATE

AS Level
Geography

Ann Bowen

John Pallister

Heinemann

Heinemann Educational Publishers
Halley Court, Jordan Hill, Oxford, OX2 8EJ
Part of Harcourt Education

Heinemann is the registered trademark of
Harcourt Education Limited

First published 2000

10-digit ISBN: 0 435352 83 0

13-digit ISBN: 978 0 435352 83 7

05
10 9

Designed and illustrated by The Wooden Ark Studio, Leeds

Printed and bound in the UK by Bath colour Books

Acknowledgements
The authors and publishers would like to thank the following for permission to use copyright material:

Maps and extracts
T = top, M = middle, B = bottom
p.9 T, p.17 4a, 4b, p.32, p.33 M, B, p.45 Bishop and Prosser, Water Resources: Process and Management/Collins Educational 1995; p.15 M R J Small, Geomorphology and Hydrology/Longman 1989; p.16, p.21 B K Hilton, Process and Pattern in Physical Geography/HarperCollins Publishers Ltd 1985; p.25 B D Waugh, Geography: An Integrated Approach/Nelson; p.26 T, 109 B M Witherick, Environment and People/Stanley Thornes 1995; p.28 M, p.33 T R Collard, Physical geography of Landscape/ HarperCollins Publishers Ltd 1988; p.28 B R B Bunnett, Physical Geography in Diagrams/Longman 1965; p.34 Daily Telegraph; p.40 World Resources Report 1998-99/World Resources Institute; p.61 The Observer 31st October 1999; p.65 B, 68, 69, 70, 72, 75, 76, 77, 85 T, 86, 89, 110, 111 T, 180 T, 197, 200, 207, 240, 241, 243, 245 M and 258 The Guardian; p.65 T, 90 Jack Williams, The Weather Book/Vintage Books; p.70 The Hindustan Times, New Delhi 2nd November 1999; p.71 The Times of India, New Delhi; p.71, 78, 79, 82, 87 B, 147, 148, 180, 205, 208, 244, 245 T, 247, 249, 250, 252, 253, 255, 261, 263, 266 The Financial Times Ltd; p.73, 121 D C Money, Climate and Environmental Systems/ HarperCollins Publishers Ltd 1988; p.85 B, p.227 B The New Internationalist; p.94, 95, 116, 117, 121 T Greg O'Hare, Soils, Vegetation and Ecosystems/Oliver and Boyd 1988; p.108 Adrian Kidd, Managing Ecosystems/Hodder & Stoughton 1999; p.110 T BBC News Online; p.111 M, B BBC News Online; p.112 T The Last Frontier: Forests, Ecosystems and Economies on the Edge/World Resources Institute; p.126 T World Resources Report 1992-93: A Guide to the Global Environment/World Resources Institute; p.127 FAOSTAT Statistical Database 1997/Food and Agriculture Organization of the United Nations; p.125 World Resources Report 1998-99: A Guide to the Global Environment/World Resources Institute; p.129 M United States Department of Agriculture, Natural Resources Conservation Service State of the Land website; p.131 Great Lakes Commission; p.133 T, 134 T Adrian Kidd, Managing Ecosystems/Hodder & Stoughton 1999;134 M Environmental Industry Development Network p.135 Eden Foundation;Collins-Longman Atlas/Harpercollins Publishers Ltd p.139 Philips Modern School Atlas/Philips; p.142, 144, 148 Collins-Longman Atlas/HarperCollins; p.146 The Independent Review; p.149, 150 Philips Modern School Atlas/Philips; p.151 D Waugh, Geography: An Integrated Approach/Nelson; p.158 T M Carr, New Patterns: Process and Change in Human Geography/Macmillan 1987; p.158, 159 M Witherick, Population Geography/Longman 1990; p.166 Understanding Global Issues: Migrants and Refugees, September 1996; p.168 The Daily Telegraph 27th April 2000: p.168 D Waugh, Geography: An Integrated Approach/Nelson; p.170 B Knapp, S Ross and D McCrae, Challenge of the Natural Environment/Longman; p.172 Geography of the Age, Geographical Review January 1994/The American Geographical Association; p.173 Britain 2000: The Official Yearbook of the United Kingdom/HMSO © Crown Copyright; p.174, 175 T, 177 T M Carr, New Patterns: Processed Change in Human Geography/Macmillan 1987; p.176 M Human Development Report 1997/Oxford University Press Ltd; p.177 B J O M Broek and J W Webb, A Geography of Mankind/McGraw Hill Book Company, New York; p.178 Wall Street Journal Almanac 1998; p.179 Regional Trends 34, National Statistics © Crown Copyright 2000; p.181 The Financial Mail/Mail on Sunday 16th October 1999; p.182 © Times Newspaper Ltd 16th January 2000; p.184 John Dickenson, Geography of the Third World/Routledge; p.203 Chiltern Railways; p.203 Barratt Developments Plc; p.212 Charles Whynne-Hammond, Elements of Human Geography/Collins Educational; p.219 M International Labour Organisation/The Financial Times Ltd 23rd August 1999; p.240 The Observer 23rd October 1994; p.253 Map by courtesy of the Penang Development Corporation.Maps on p.31, 202, 207, and 265 reproduced reproduced from Ordnance Survey maps with the permission of the Controller of Her Majesty's Stationary Office © Crown copyright; License No; 398020.

Photographs
Cover photo by Stone.

p.5 Panos Pictures/Trygve Bolstad; p.8 (top) Panos Pictures/Paul Freestone; p.8 (bottom) Ann Bowen; p.10 (Fig 1) Ann Bowen; p.12 (Fig 1) Ann Bowen; p.19 (Fig 2) Woodfall Wild Images/David Woodfall; p.20 (Fig 1) Ann Bowen; p.23 (Figs 2 and 3) Ann Bowen; p. 24 (Fig 1) Woodfall Wild Images/David Woodfall; p.24 (Fig 3) Jim Gibson; p.26 (Fig 3) Corbis/Yann Arthus-Bertrand; p.27 (Fig 4) and p.28 (Fig 1) Woodfall Wild Images/David Woodfall; p.29 (Fig 4) John Cleare; p.34 (Fig 2) News Team/Mike Sharp; p.35 (Fig 3) Barry Greenwood; p.37 (Fig 3) Panos Pictures/Trygve Bolstad; p.42 (Fig 1) Hutchison; p.43 (Fig 2) Panos Pictures/Zed Nelson; p.46 (Fig 1) Environment Agency; p.48 John Pallister; p.49 John Pallister; p.51 (Fig 2) John Pallister; p. 56 (Fig 2) John Pallister; p. 58 (Fig 1) University of Dundee; p.60 (Fig 1) John Pallister; p.60 (Fig 2) Travel Ink/Peter Murphy; p.61 (Fig 4) Associated Press NOAA; p.62 (Fig 2) John Pallister; p.63 (Fig 3) John Pallister; p.65 (Fig 2c) Still Pictures; p. 68 (Fig 1b) Popperfoto/Reuters/Jeff Mitchell; p. 69 (Fig 3) AP Photo/Karel Prinsloo; p.70 (Fig 1) Associated Press/PTI; p. 74 (Fig 2) John Pallister; p.76 (Fig 2) *The Guardian*/Graham Turner; p.79 (Fig 3) Andrea Mandel-Campbell; p.80 (Fig 2) John Pallister; p.83 (Fig 2) John Pallister; p.85 (Fig 1) John Pallister; p.87 (Fig 4) John Pallister; p.88 (Fig 2) John Pallister; p.89 (Fig 3) Environmental Images/David Hoffman; p.91 Jim Gibson; p.92 (Fig 2) John Pallister; p.93 (Fig 3) Woodfall Wild Images/David Woodfall; p.99 (Fig 3) Woodfall Wild Images/David Woodfall; p.101 (Fig 2) Woodfall Wild Images/Steve Austin; p.104 (Fig 2) Environmental Images/Vanessa Miles; p.107 (Figs 3,4 and 5) Woodfall Wild Images/David Woodfall; p. 110 (Fig 1) Environmental Images; p.111 (Figs 3 and 5) Woodfall Wild Images/David Woodfall; p.113 (Fig 5) Science Photo Library; p. 123 (Fig 4) Jim Gibson; p. 123 (Fig 5) Woodfall Wild Images; p.124 (Fig 3) Jim Gibson; p.125 (Fig 4) GSF Picture Library; p.127 (Fig 4) Environmental Images; p.128 (Figs 1 and 2) Woodfall Wild Images/Peter Wilson; p.129 (Fig 3) Panos Pictures; p.131 (Fig 4) Nature Conservancy; p.133 (Fig 2) Woodfall Wild Images/Ted Head; p.135 (Fig 4) Woodfall Wild Images/Mike Powles; p.136 (A) John Pallister; p.137 Panos; p.157 (Fig 2) Panos; p.162 (Fig 2) John Pallister; p.163 (Fig 1) John Pallister; p.167 (Fig 4) Panos; p. 171 (Fig 2) John Pallister; p.176 (Fig 3) John Pallister; p.177 (Fig 5) Corbis; p.181 (Fig 4) John Pallister; p.183 John Pallister; p.185 (Fig 3a) John Pallister; p. 186 (Fig 1) John Pallister; p. 187 (Fig 2) Aerofilms; p.188 (Fig 1) John Pallister; p. 192 (Fig 1) John Pallister; p.194 (Fig 4) South American Pictures/Tony Morrison; p.195 (Fig 5) South American Pictures/Tony Morrison; p. 196 (Fig 1) John Pallister; p.199 (Fig 2) Topham Picture Point; p.199 (Fig 3) John Pallister; p. 201 (Fig 2) Hutchison Picture Library/Leslie Woodhead; p. 202 (Fig 1) John Pallister; p.203 (Fig 6) John Pallister; p. 205 (Fig 3) John Pallister; p.206 (Fig 1) Jay Williams; p.208 (Figs 2 and 3) John Pallister; p.210 (Fig 1) John Pallister; p.211 (Figs 2, 3 and 4) John Pallister; p. 213 (Fig 3) John Pallister; p.214 (Figs 1 and 2) John Pallister; p.217 (figs 4 and 5) John Pallister; p.218 John Pallister; p.225 John Pallister; p.228 (Fig 1) John Pallister; p.230 Panos Pictures/Chris Stowers; p.231 (Fig 4) John Pallister; p.232 (Fig 1) John Pallister; p.235 (Figs 2 and 3) John Pallister; p.236 (Fig 2) John Pallister; p.239 (Fig 3) John Pallister; p.241 (Fig 4) Still Pictures; p.245 (Fig 3) Philip Wolmuth; p.246 (Fig 3) John Pallister; p.248 (Fig 2) John Pallister; p.249 (Fig 3) John Pallister; p. 250 (Fig 2) John Pallister; p.251 (Fig 3) John Pallister; p.255 (Fig 1) Corbis; p.256 (Fig 1) John Pallister; p.259 (Fig 4) John Pallister; p.260 (Fig 1) John Pallister; p.262 (Fig 1) John Pallister; p.267 John Pallister; p.268 (Fig 1) John Pallister; p.269 (Fig 2) John Pallister; p.270 (Figs 3 and 4) John Pallister

Contents

Introduction

The creation of 'AS' level, as a new intermediate level of qualification, is intended to ease the transition for students between 'GCSE' and 'A' levels. One way of doing this is by reducing the content and lessening the depth of topic coverage. Another way is to change the emphasis in examination questions away from essays and towards more structured questions with some extended prose. However, it still needs to be borne in mind that 'AS' forms the first part of an 'A' level course, which means that, compared with 'GCSE', there will be an increase in depth of study and complexity of topic, as well as a greater emphasis on organisation and composure in written examination answers. Some of the structured examination questions may not look too different from those set at 'GCSE', but greater elaboration and exemplification is expected even in short questions worth only three or four marks. The greater content means that more decisions about what is to be included in answers are needed. The total mark for an extended prose answer may be only a few marks more than for some 'GCSE' questions, but a good answer at 'AS' level is expected to be longer, better composed and more strongly supported by precise geographical information.

How to use this book

This book attempts to hit the level of detail required by the 'AS' course in one particular specification (syllabus). However, a book which aims to do this must contain more detail than a student can be expected to reproduce in any examination answer. For most of the time continuous prose is used, although this is broken up by bulleted and numbered points in places. For examination preparation, and certainly as an aid to revision, many students prefer to convert prose either into notes or into lists of factors and reasons. However, examination answers should always be written in continuous prose, except for the shortest of structured questions. The text is also broken up by Information Boxes marked by i. These have two main purposes – to highlight significant items and to embellish related points not directly covered in the text.

Case studies are also included from time to time. These vary in length to reflect their relative significance in relation to the content stated in the exam board's specification. For example, some case studies are specified, such as a cost / benefit analysis of a river management scheme under *Water on the land*, or a small scale study of a village undergoing suburbanisation under *Settlement processes and patterns*. Examination questions for these could begin with words such as 'With reference to one

example you have studied, explain....', because they are specified case studies. These are often the longer case studies. Others are used to increase depth of study and geographical understanding. They are less likely to be directly asked for in an examination, but can certainly be used in a question which includes the statement 'With the help of an example or examples you have studied, ...'. Case studies are part of established good study practice in geography as they maintain the link to real places. Relevant use of supporting case study information in examination answers, even when not directly requested by the question, is one of the main characteristics of answers from candidates who are awarded the top two grades. However, the most useful skill that you can develop in relation to case studies is selection. Be selective; don't write everything out. The ability to select key facts and basic details about causes, nature and effects is one of the keys to examination success in 'AS' geography. There is clearly a limit to how much precise information you can learn for any particular case study considering that you need to study several different ones during the 'AS' course. Also with a maximum of ten marks and twenty minutes for any examination answer, there is a limit to how much case study information you are going to have the time to use. As a first question after some of the case studies in this book, you are asked to write down the key facts for that case study. It is around these that the other information needed for examination answers can be hung. You can also generate your own case study information by use of local examples or by visiting web sites on the internet.

Opportunities for local or individual investigation are suggested from time to time among the questions which are otherwise largely based upon the information available in the figures and text. At the end of each of the six topics of study is a page of structured and extended prose questions which replicate those in the 'AS' examination. When answering the structured questions (worth up to four or five marks), short precise answers, which focus straightaway upon the question need, are expected. There is time neither to write out the question again nor to give background information, before beginning the answer proper. The extended prose questions (worth seven or ten marks) require more thought and organisation. Whilst the geographical content of these answers is of overwhelming importance in determining the final mark, you cannot gain all the marks for an answer without effective written communication.

John Pallister
Ann Bowen

Chapter 1

Water on the land

Figure 1 Serious flooding in Bangladesh happens frequently. Ironically, the young girl to the right of the photo is wading through floodwater to fetch clean drinking water in Dhaka, the capital city.

Systems and river regimes

Channel processes and landforms

Flooding as a hazard

River basin management

Systems and river regimes

- The concept of a system
- The hydrological cycle
- River discharge
- Flood hydrographs
- The importance of extreme events

The concept of a system

A system is a series of inputs, processes and outputs and it may be applied at any scale from the Universe to the Earth; from a zone of tropical rainforest to an oak tree; or from the global hydrological cycle to an individual drainage basin.

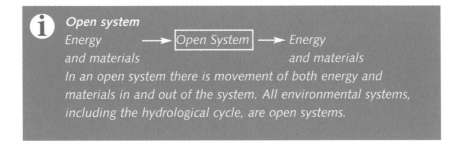

i *Open system*

Energy $\longrightarrow$ Open System $\longrightarrow$ *Energy*
and materials   *and materials*

In an open system there is movement of both energy and materials in and out of the system. All environmental systems, including the hydrological cycle, are open systems.

The hydrological cycle

The global hydrological cycle (Figure 1) is a system that summarizes the global circulation of moisture and energy between the land, sea and the atmosphere. The cycle has a series of stores in which moisture is held, such as the oceans and ice caps, and a series of transfers or flows within and between the stores, such as condensation and evaporation.

In the global hydrological cycle the water is moved between the stores. The amount of water that is held in the stores varies considerably both spatially (in different areas) and temporally (over time). All water is part of a continuous circulation, fuelled by the input of energy from the sun. There are no effective gains or losses in the cycle since there is a fixed amount of water. However, there are inputs and outputs of energy and sediments in the system making the global hydrological cycle an open system (information box).

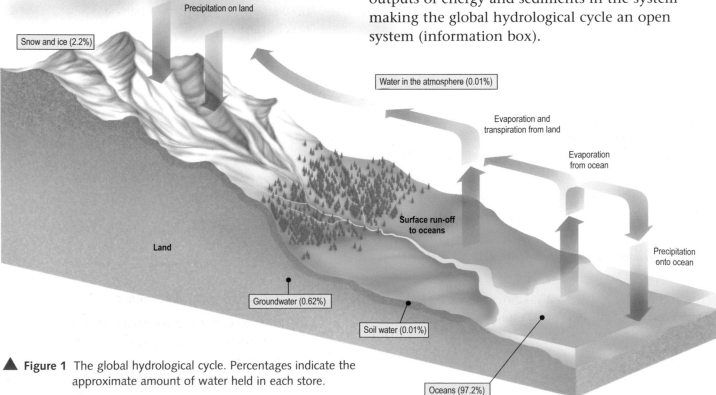

▲ **Figure 1** The global hydrological cycle. Percentages indicate the approximate amount of water held in each store.

The drainage basin hydrological cycle

The drainage basin hydrological cycle (Figure 2) summarizes the characteristics of a single river basin. It is an ideal unit of study because its boundaries are distinct with a watershed and the sea. It is an open system with inputs of energy and precipitation and outputs of water and eroded material.

> ℹ️ A drainage basin is the land area or catchment area drained by a single river and its tributaries. An imaginary line called the watershed delimits or separates one drainage basin from another. The watershed usually follows a ridge of high land; any water falling on the other side of the ridge flows into an adjacent drainage basin.

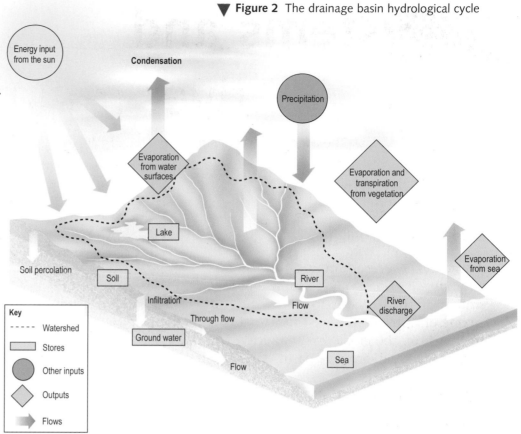

▼ **Figure 2** The drainage basin hydrological cycle

Key
- - - - - Watershed
▭ Stores
⬤ Other inputs
◆ Outputs
➜ Flows

Inputs to a drainage basin

Inputs include energy from the sun and precipitation. Precipitation is all of the water that reaches the ground surface from the atmosphere. It is mainly rain and snow falling within the drainage basin. Some precipitation may fall directly into the streams and rivers; some may fall onto the land surface or be intercepted by vegetation and make its way along a variety of routes to the streams, which run into a single stream to the basin outlet. These routes include:

- throughfall, where the precipitation falls through spaces in the tree canopy and passes quickly to the ground
- stemflow, a slower movement of the water trickling down stems and branches, and
- drip, when the water drips from leaves onto the ground.

The equivalent routes exist in urban areas via gutters and drainpipes although these flows are much more efficient than in nature.

Outputs from the drainage basin

Water is lost by:
- the river draining into a lake or the sea at its mouth
- water percolating deep underground into groundwater stores where it is effectively lost from the system
- evapotranspiration.

Stores in the drainage basin hydrological cycle

Within a drainage basin water is stored:
- on the surface, such as in rivers, lakes, streams and puddles
- in the soil
- deep below the ground surface as groundwater
- on the vegetation after a period of precipitation.

Questions

1. Explain what is meant by the concept of the hydrological cycle.

2. Using Figure 2 complete a table to show the main components of a drainage basin hydrological cycle using the following headings:
   Inputs; Stores; Flows; Outputs.

3. Using Figure 2 and your table draw a flow diagram to show the operation of the hydrological cycle.

Flows or transfers within the hydrological cycle

1 Evapotranspiration

Evaporation is the direct loss of water from the ground or from water or plant surfaces. It is greatest when temperatures are high and winds are strong. Transpiration is the loss of water through the tiny pores called stomata on leaf surfaces. Transpiration rates depend on the time of year, the type and amount of vegetation, the availability of moisture and the length of the growing season. Study the information box to see how transpiration rates vary in two different environments. The processes of evaporation and transpiration are difficult to separate so they are often referred to as evapotranspiration.

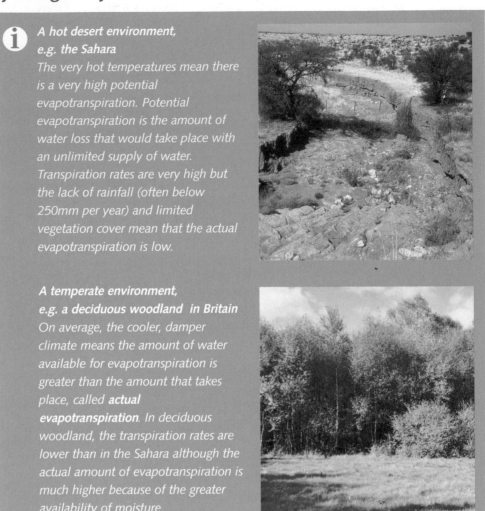

A hot desert environment, e.g. the Sahara

The very hot temperatures mean there is a very high potential evapotranspiration. Potential evapotranspiration is the amount of water loss that would take place with an unlimited supply of water. Transpiration rates are very high but the lack of rainfall (often below 250mm per year) and limited vegetation cover mean that the actual evapotranspiration is low.

A temperate environment, e.g. a deciduous woodland in Britain

On average, the cooler, damper climate means the amount of water available for evapotranspiration is greater than the amount that takes place, called **actual evapotranspiration***. In deciduous woodland, the transpiration rates are lower than in the Sahara although the actual amount of evapotranspiration is much higher because of the greater availability of moisture.*

2 Interception

When it rains moisture will collect on leaves and branches as interception storage. Research has shown that a beech woodland in Germany intercepts as much as 43 per cent of rainfall in summer. This moisture may eventually evaporate never reaching the ground surface. If it rains continuously for some time then the vegetation may become saturated and the water will begin to reach the ground by throughflow, stemflow and drip. Hence, greatest interception occurs at the beginning of a storm and is then reduced as the precipitation continues. Vegetation is most efficient in intercepting and evaporating moisture when rainfall is in light sporadic showers rather than continuous heavy rainfall. Conifers tend to intercept more rainfall than deciduous trees. Water clings to the needle-shaped leaves and they retain their needles all year round.

3 Infiltration

On reaching the ground surface water may soak into the soil pores – a process called infiltration. The maximum rate at which this can take place is called the infiltration capacity (measured in millimetres per hour). At the start of a rainstorm infiltration is often quite high because the soil is dry but as the air spaces or soil pores become filled the infiltration rate lowers to a constant value (Figure 1). Clay and silt have a much lower infiltration rate than sand and gravel due to the differing sizes of the pores in the soils. The infiltration rate is affected by the antecedent moisture in the soil, soil porosity and structure, the nature of the soil surface and the amount and type of vegetation cover. In urban areas where many surfaces are impermeable tarmac and concrete, no infiltration can occur. This may also happen in rural areas if the soil is already saturated or if the rainfall is so high that more rain is falling than can be absorbed by the soil. When the infiltration rate is exceeded then the surplus water flows over the ground surface as overland flow.

> **Field capacity** This is when the soil is saturated – all available pore spaces between the soil particles are filled with water. Any further rain falling onto the ground cannot infiltrate into the soil and forms overland flow.
>
> **Discharge** The volume or flow of water passing a certain point in a river at a particular time.

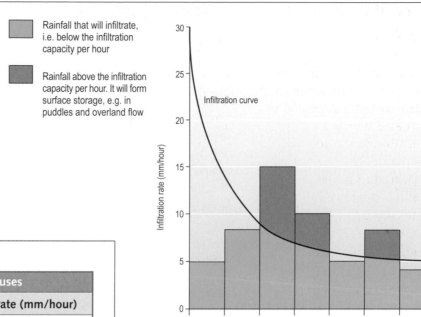

▲ **Figure 1** An infiltration curve

Infiltration rates for different land uses	
Land use	**Infiltration rate (mm/hour)**
Permanent pasture (ungrazed)	57
Permanent pasture (heavily grazed)	13
Cereals	9
Bare ground/baked hard	6

Once the water has infiltrated into the soil it may flow laterally under the influence of gravity as throughflow or it may percolate deeper into the soil to reach the groundwater stores in joints, cracks or fissures in the rocks. From here, it may flow laterally as groundwater flow (or base flow) towards the main river channel. This route is deeper and slower and there can be a long delay between the rainfall and water reaching the groundwater. The groundwater flow is continuous providing a constant supply of water into river channels. It generally maintains flow even through periods of drought and sudden rainstorms have little impact. The upper surface of the groundwater store is called the water table.

4 Runoff

Runoff is all the water which enters a stream or river and leaves the basin as stream discharge. Some precipitation falls into the river channel directly but most water reaches it by:
- surface runoff or overland flow
- throughflow
- groundwater flow.

Once in the river the water forms channel storage before ultimately being discharged into the sea and lost from the drainage basin. The channel acts therefore as both a store and a transfer for the water. During a flood the river channel is filled with water and forms a major store in the system.

Questions

1   Describe and explain how each of the following would affect infiltration and surface runoff:
- deciduous forest versus a concrete surface
- steep versus gentle slopes
- sandy soils versus clay soils
- steady drizzle versus rapid melting of thick snow
- a soil at **field capacity** and a soil after a long dry spell.

2 a   On a copy of Figure 1 add the following labels:
- Overland flow likely to begin
- Field capacity reached
- Infiltration at a maximum.

   b   Using Figure 1 describe and explain the pattern of infiltration shown.

3 a   Surface runoff; throughflow; groundwater flow – put the three flows into order according to:
- the speed of flow
- the permanence of the flow.

   b   Justify the order suggested for each one.

River discharge

River discharge is the volume or flow of water passing a gauging station in a river at a particular time. Gauging stations are found at various intervals along many rivers. They are the points where river discharge is measured either manually or using automatic gauges.

River discharge is the amount of water originating from precipitation that reaches the channel by direct precipitation, overland flow, throughflow and baseflow. To calculate river discharge:

Discharge = velocity (m/sec) x cross-sectional area (m²)

Therefore, discharge is measured in cubic metres per second (cumecs).

The amount of water in a river at any one time is affected by many factors; some to do with the physical characteristics of the drainage basin while others are connected with the climate and weather (Figure 1). Overall discharge from a drainage basin is a product of the relationship between precipitation and evapotranspiration and other factors, which control the amount of water stored in the river basin. This is called the water balance and may be summarized by the equation:

Drainage basin discharge = precipitation – (evaporation + transpiration) +/– changes in storage

▼ **Figure 1** Summary of the factors affecting river discharge

Physical characteristics

- Basin size, shape and relief
- Rock/soil type
- Drainage area and drainage pattern
- Height above sea level
- Surface water stores, e.g. lakes, glaciers

Meteorological characteristics

- Type of precipitation
- Rainfall intensity, amount and duration
- Distribution of rainfall across the drainage basin
- Prior precipitation and soil moisture
- Factors affecting evapotranspiration, e.g. wind, temperature, humidity and season

Human characteristics

- Land use
- Surface water stores, e.g. reservoirs

Factors affecting river discharge

1 Basin size, shape and relief

Size The time it takes between the water falling on to the ground and reaching the river channel is called the lag period. In a large river basin, the water has much further to travel before entering the main channel giving a long lag period. In a small basin, the water is likely to reach the channel faster giving a shorter lag period between the water reaching the ground and entering the channel.

Shape Circular river basins tend to have a shorter lag period and higher peak flows than elongated river basins.

Relief In steep-sided upland river basins water reaches the channels much more quickly than in gently sloping lowland basins.

2 Rock type

Permeable rocks allow water to pass through them. Rocks such as sandstone and chalk are porous and allow water to fill the many pores in the rock. Rocks such as carboniferous limestone are pervious allowing water to enter bedding planes and joints. These rock types have few surface streams due to high infiltration rates and limited surface runoff.

Rocks such as granite are impermeable. They do not allow water to pass through them so surface runoff is increased and there are more surface streams.

▲ **Figure 2** Part of a drainage basin in Austria. How will the physical and human characteristics of this landscape affect river discharge?

3 Soil type

The type of soil controls the rate of infiltration, the amount of soil moisture storage and the rate of throughflow. High rates are associated with sandy soils with large pore spaces whereas clays with small pore spaces have reduced rates of infiltration and throughflow encouraging surface runoff and the risk of flooding.

4 Drainage density

Drainage density is the number of surface streams in a drainage basin. High densities are found in areas of impermeable rock and clays. The higher the density then the faster the water reaches the river channel causing rapid changes in the discharge of a river. Rivers with rapidly changing discharges are sometimes called 'flashy'. Such rivers have short lag times and high peak discharges. They are therefore more prone to flooding.

5 Precipitation

Amount Long periods of rainfall are a frequent cause of flooding. The soil becomes saturated and infiltration is reduced. This generates large quantities of surface runoff causing rapid rises in the river discharge.

Type The two main types of precipitation are snow and rain. Initially, heavy snow is intercepted and stored. Over a long period, this may lead to a fall in river levels. When temperatures rise and melting occurs the water is released. This may generate large quantities of surface runoff, which reach the river channel quickly especially if the ground remains frozen restricting infiltration. Rainfall is also intercepted but may infiltrate quickly if the soil is unsaturated. The rate at which it reaches the river channel depends upon interception, infiltration and overland flow.

Intensity The intensity of heavy rain, for example during convectional thunderstorms, may exceed the infiltration capacity of the soil causing large quantities of surface runoff and a rapid rise in river discharge.

6 Temperature

High temperatures increase rates of evapotranspiration and may reduce river discharge whereas very cold temperatures may freeze the ground, restricting infiltration, increasing surface runoff and the likelihood of higher river discharge.

7 Land use

Vegetation Trees and plants help to reduce the amount and rate at which water enters a river channel by interception, root uptake and evapotranspiration. It is estimated that tropical rainforests may intercept up to 80 per cent of rainfall whereas arable land may intercept only 10 per cent.

Urbanization The removal of vegetation and its replacement by concrete and tarmac surfaces reduces infiltration to zero but the drains and gutters transport the water more quickly to river channels increasing discharge and the flood risk.

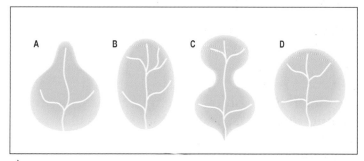

▲ **Figure 3** Drainage basin shapes

Questions

Extended prose

1   Study Figure 3.
   a Assuming other drainage basin characteristics are similar, match the hydrographs W, X, Y and Z with each of the drainage basins A, B, C and D.

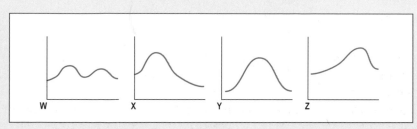

   b Justify your choice.

2 With reference to examples of named river basins, describe and explain how the physical characteristics of drainage basins (including climate) affect river discharge.

Variations in river discharge

River regimes

The **river regime** is the annual pattern of discharge by a river responding to the region's climate. The average regime is shown by the mean daily or the mean monthly figures. It is primarily determined by the climate, i.e. the amount and distribution of rainfall together with the rates of evapotranspiration and snowmelt.

Variations in river discharge

Variations in river discharge are important. They influence the energy of a river and in turn the river landforms. The factors affecting river discharge shown in Figure 1 on page 10 may produce:

Temporal variations (changes over time):
- short-term fluctuations in discharge, e.g. increased discharge following heavy rain or snowmelt. Some examples are shown in Figure 2.
- medium-term variations, e.g. seasonal variations such as less discharge when interception is higher in a deciduous forest in summer
- long-term changes in discharge, e.g. as a result of climate change or a change in land use.

Spatial variations (changes from place to place):
- rivers in different geographical locations have different patterns of discharge. The discharge is affected by the climate of the region and many other factors (see Figure 1 on page 10).

Temporal variations

Many of the world's rivers have *seasonal fluctuations* in their river discharge. They are most pronounced in climates with a distinct wet and dry season as in countries with a Mediterranean or Monsoon climate and where glaciers feed streams. Even in Britain, there is usually a marked winter maximum of river discharge and a summer minimum reflecting lower precipitation totals and higher rates of evapotranspiration in the summer. *Short-term fluctuations* of channel discharge are related to individual rainstorms or to snowmelt.

▼ **Figure 1** High discharge following continuous rainfall in the Tyrol, Austria

▼ **Figure 2** Short-term (daily) fluctuations in river regimes

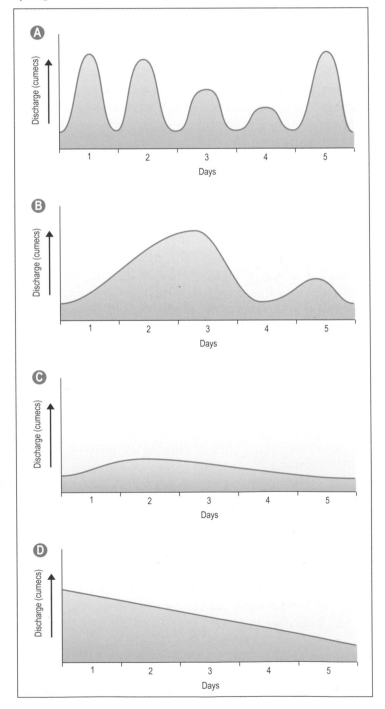

Spatial variations

There are great differences in the river regimes for different regions (Figure 3) due to the interplay of a variety of factors but especially climate and vegetation.

In areas of tropical rainforest with an equatorial climate there is considerable river discharge. This is a product of the high rainfall, often over 2000mm per year. The river discharge is high although a proportion is lost by high rates of evapotranspiration resulting from the very high year-round temperatures, often over 28°C, and the large amount of vegetation in the rainforest.

In the sub-tropical hot deserts, annual rainfall is mostly less than 250mm. There are also very high rates of evapotranspiration so there is only minimal river discharge. Most channel runoff is only short-lived in the form of flash floods following a heavy rainstorm and over short distances as the water quickly infiltrates into the sandy soils.

In the tundra regions of Northern Canada and Russia annual precipitation totals are similar to those of the hot deserts (about 250mm per year) and most river discharge takes place in a short period of intense runoff in the early summer when there is a sudden melting of the winter snow. Discharge is high at this time as temperatures are low and there is little vegetation so evapotranspiration is minimal. In addition, some areas have permanently frozen ground (permafrost) restricting infiltration. On a diurnal or daily basis, there are often short-term fluctuations. Discharges are low overnight and in the early morning because little melting takes place then. During the course of the day, as the sun melts the ice, river discharges increase to a peak in the late afternoon, only to decrease as the temperatures fall and melting ceases.

▼ **Figure 3** Spatial variations in river discharge

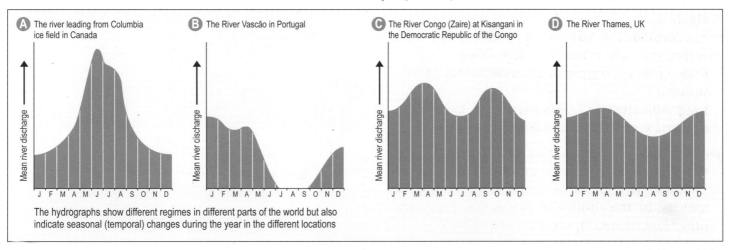

A The river leading from Columbia ice field in Canada

B The River Vascão in Portugal

C The River Congo (Zaire) at Kisangani in the Democratic Republic of the Congo

D The River Thames, UK

The hydrographs show different regimes in different parts of the world but also indicate seasonal (temporal) changes during the year in the different locations

Questions

Investigation

1 a Study Figure 2. Match each graph with one of the following statements.
  • A river in a region where there has been a long dry period and high potential evapotranspiration
  • A river where a heavy rainstorm was followed a few days later by a rainstorm of less intensity and duration
  • A river in summer that is fed by a glacier
  • A river where a single rainstorm occurred

  b Explain your choices.

  c Suggest a precise location for graph A.

  d Describe and explain the other factors that would affect the daily discharge of a river.

2 a Using reference materials (try the Internet) obtain the climatic statistics for three regions or places: a Mediterranean climate; a monsoon climate; a west coast maritime climate (UK type).

  b Construct climate graphs for each region or place.

  c Sketch a river regime graph for each area.

  d Describe and suggest reasons for the temporal and spatial variations shown.

3 a On a world map, show the locations of the countries for the four river regime graphs shown in Figure 3.

  b Explain the different patterns of discharge shown.

Flood hydrographs

A hydrograph (Figure 1) shows the discharge of a river measured at a particular point, usually a gauging station. Often, it shows the response of a drainage basin to a specific rainfall event.

In Figure 1 the graph shows the discharge of the river before the rainstorm – the antecedent flow rate. When the rain starts to fall the river discharge remains largely the same. Although some of the rain falls directly in the channel most falls in other parts of the drainage basin and takes some time to reach the channel.

Once overland flow begins (after interception storage and the infiltration rate are exceeded) and later, throughflow, the river's discharge begins to increase. This is shown on the hydrograph as the rising limb. The steeper the rising limb the faster the water is reaching the channel from the drainage basin.

The peak discharge occurs when the river reaches its highest level. The period between maximum precipitation and the peak discharge is called the lag time (or period). In river basins with a short lag time there is often a high peak discharge and the river is more prone to flooding.

The falling or receding limb on the graph shows when discharge decreases. This is usually less steep than the rising limb because although overland flow may have stopped the throughflow continues more slowly.

Eventually when all of the water from the rainstorm has passed through the drainage basin the discharge level returns to the baseflow level. Baseflow is the most significant flow over a long period reflecting seasonal changes in the climate and vegetation. Baseflow responds only very slowly during a period of rain yet maintains the flow of a river during a drought.

The language of hydrographs

Rising limb The rapid increase in the river discharge as overland flow and throughflow reach the river channel

Falling or receding limb The fall in river discharge as overland flow ceases and throughflow decreases

Lag time period The length of time between peak precipitation and peak discharge

Peak discharge The maximum flow of the river during a rainstorm

Peak rainfall The time when the maximum amount of rain was falling.

▼ **Figure 1** A flood hydrograph of the River Tees in north-east England

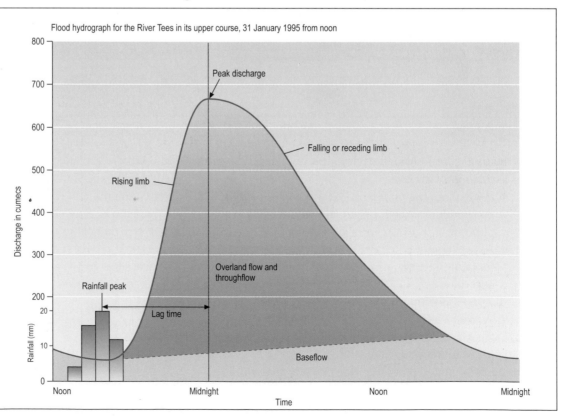

The rainfall events occurred on 30 January 1995 with 50.2mm of rain recorded at Widdybank Fell in the upper course of the River Tees.

Flood hydrograph for the River Tees in its upper course, 31 January 1995 from noon

The importance of extreme events

In any drainage basin, the discharge of the river is affected by many factors. However, many of those factors such as the relief, rock type and vegetation remain static over a period of time. The one set of factors, which is most changeable, is that of the climate and, in particular, variations in precipitation and evapotranspiration.

Periods of drought or periods of heavy precipitation are extreme events that produce the most marked changes in discharge. These changes may be recorded on river hydrographs and their magnitude and frequency may be used to help in the management of river basins for water supply and flood protection.

The graph in Figure 2 shows that there is a positive correlation between the flood magnitude as measured by river discharge and the number of years between such events. The graph can be used to predict the likely recurrence of a flood of a particular size. Figure 2 shows that a discharge of 33 cumecs is likely to occur within a 10-year period. This is called the 10-year flood. The 100-year flood has a discharge of about 80 cumecs. The use of recurrence intervals suggests that extreme floods occur less often than smaller floods and that all floods occur at regular intervals. In reality this is not the case and extreme flooding may, for example, occur two years in succession. Likewise an extreme flood may only have occurred once in the history of the river and may never occur again.

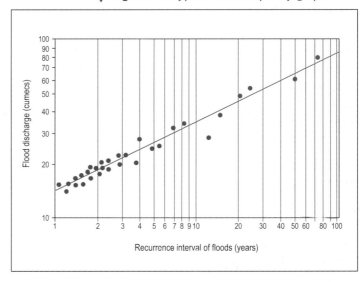

Magnitude frequency analysis
Magnitude frequency analysis is used to predict the probability of a flood of a particular magnitude happening. It is based upon the study of recurrence intervals or the return periods of a particular flood magnitude. The highest peak discharge is recorded every year and they are arranged in rank order - one for the largest, two for the second largest and so on for as many years as records exist. The recurrence interval for each flood discharge is then calculated by using the equation:
$T = (N+1)$ *divided by M*
Where T = the recurrence interval
N = the number of years of observation
M = the rank

▼ **Figure 2** A typical flood frequency graph

Flood discharge (cumecs) (vertical axis)
Recurrence interval of floods (years) (horizontal axis)

▼ **Figure 3** Two storm hydrographs

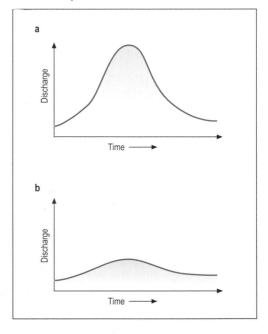

Questions

1   Figure 3 shows two hydrographs. Which hydrograph is more likely to correspond to each of the following situations? Explain your choice.
   a   A long period of steady rain and a short torrential downpour.
   b   A steep sided valley and a gently sloping valley
   c   An area with a low drainage density and one with a high density
   d   An area of granite and an area of chalk
   e   An area of mature deciduous woodland and an area of heathland in summer
   f   An area where the soil is saturated and an area which is not saturated.

The Wye drainage basin

Case Study

The River Wye lies on the border between England and Wales. It flows from north west to south east with many of its tributaries having their source in upland areas over 600m above sea level in the west. Rainfall is higher in the west while losses from evapotranspiration are higher in the east. There is therefore more water available for streamflow in the west than the east. These spatial variations of input, loss and output are similar to those in the British Isles as a whole. Figure 1 shows the annual rainfall and runoff for parts of the upper Wye. There is a winter peak of rainfall linked to the greater frequency of low pressure systems in the winter over the British Isles. During the winter runoff is also increased. The lower discharges in the summer reflect lower rainfall totals but also increased evapotranspiration due to higher temperatures and greater plant growth. Figure 2 shows the flood frequency of the Wye at Hereford between 1908 and 1999. The largest flood ever to occur was on 4 December 1960.

Within a single drainage basin there are several tributary rivers each with their own smaller or sub-drainage basins. Four of these smaller drainage areas are shown on Figure 1.

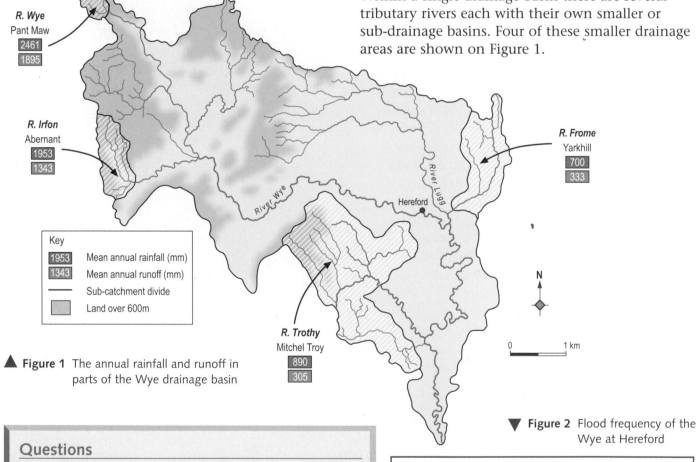

R. Wye
Pant Maw
2461
1895

R. Irfon
Abernant
1953
1343

R. Frome
Yarkhill
700
333

Hereford

R. Trothy
Mitchel Troy
890
305

Key
1953 Mean annual rainfall (mm)
1343 Mean annual runoff (mm)
—— Sub-catchment divide
▨ Land over 600m

N

0   1 km

▲ **Figure 1** The annual rainfall and runoff in parts of the Wye drainage basin

Questions

1   Study Figure 1.
   a Work out the average rainfall and runoff for:
      • the two westerly sub-drainage basins of the Wye
      • the two easterly sub-drainage basins of the Wye.
   b Describe and explain the spatial variations calculated in **a**.
   c How and why would the rainfall and runoff be expected to differ between winter and summer?

2   Study Figure 2.
   a What would be the magnitude of the 10-year flood and the 50-year flood?
   b Describe the relationship between flood discharge and recurrence interval.

▼ **Figure 2** Flood frequency of the Wye at Hereford

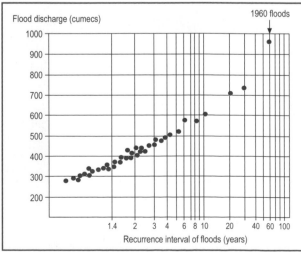

1960 floods

Flood discharge (cumecs)

Recurrence interval of floods (years)

The Nile drainage basin

Case Study

The River Nile flows northwards through Egypt eventually flowing across its delta into the Mediterranean Sea. The River Nile is approximately 6,484km long and drains an area of 2,881,000 sq km. Before 1952, when the Aswan High Dam was built, the average discharge of the River Nile was 1 584 cumecs. This discharge varied during the year. The overall variations are now much less than they used to be due to the creation of Lake Nasser. The River Nile has two main tributaries, the White Nile and the Blue Nile. The sources of the two tributaries are in two very different climatic zones as shown in Figure 3.

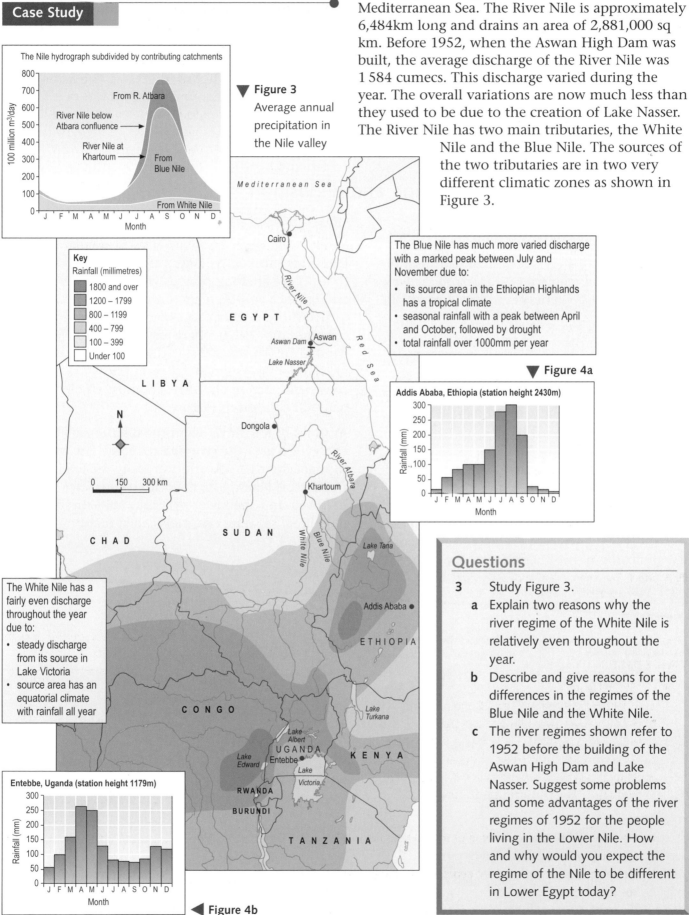

▼ **Figure 3** Average annual precipitation in the Nile valley

The Blue Nile has much more varied discharge with a marked peak between July and November due to:
• its source area in the Ethiopian Highlands has a tropical climate
• seasonal rainfall with a peak between April and October, followed by drought
• total rainfall over 1000mm per year

▼ **Figure 4a**

Addis Ababa, Ethiopia (station height 2430m)

The White Nile has a fairly even discharge throughout the year due to:
• steady discharge from its source in Lake Victoria
• source area has an equatorial climate with rainfall all year

Entebbe, Uganda (station height 1179m)

◀ **Figure 4b**

Questions

3 Study Figure 3.
  a Explain two reasons why the river regime of the White Nile is relatively even throughout the year.
  b Describe and give reasons for the differences in the regimes of the Blue Nile and the White Nile.
  c The river regimes shown refer to 1952 before the building of the Aswan High Dam and Lake Nasser. Suggest some problems and some advantages of the river regimes of 1952 for the people living in the Lower Nile. How and why would you expect the regime of the Nile to be different in Lower Egypt today?

Channel processes
and landforms

- Processes of erosion, transportation and deposition
- Landforms of river erosion
- Depositional landforms

Processes of erosion, transportation and deposition

The work of a river involves three main processes – erosion, transportation and deposition.

Erosion is the wearing away of the banks and bed of the river. The eroded material is then *transported* as the load before *deposition* of the material takes place.

The ability of a river to erode is determined by the amount of energy it possesses. Water in a river has potential energy, which is created because it is above its base level (usually sea level – see Figure 1a). The potential energy of a river is proportional to its volume and height above base level. The river also has kinetic energy, generated by the movement of the water and dependent on the river discharge. Some of the energy of a river is lost by friction with the bed and banks or through turbulence. This is particularly important in some upland river channels that have a rocky bed and many large boulders. Here, the roughness of the wetted perimeter (the area of the bed and banks of the channel that the river is in

contact with) reduces river velocity and therefore reduces the energy of the river.

Rivers are most active over very short periods of time. There are long periods when little work is taking place and there are only minor fluctuations in river flow. A river carries out most erosion and transportation when there are high-energy conditions. This is associated with large quantities of channel flow such as following heavy rain or snowmelt. Stream channels are most efficient at bankfull conditions (Figure 1b).

At times of low flow, when the discharge is low the energy levels of the river are reduced. The river loses the capacity to erode and transport the load. Deposition takes place making the channel narrower and shallower or it may split the river into individual separate channels called braiding (see page 29).

▼ **Figure 1** River profiles

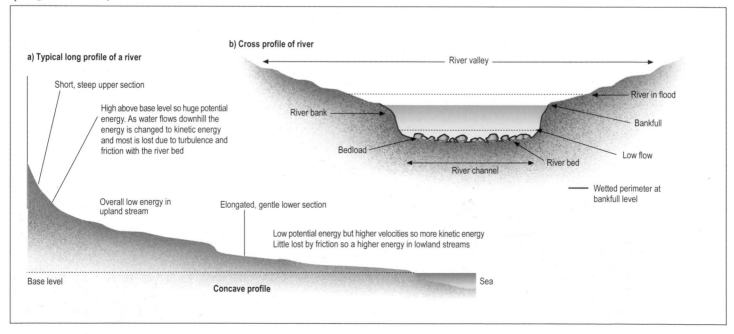

There are four main processes of river erosion:

1 Abrasion or corrasion

The most common, and probably the most effective, type of river erosion is mechanical abrasion or corrasion. It is responsible for most of the vertical erosion in a river channel.

Corrasion occurs when fragments of rock are rolled and dragged along in the river flow grinding and wearing away the bed and banks of the river. It is most effective in short, violent periods when the river is at bankfull or in flood. Then the river appears brown, charged with sand and silt that increases the rate of abrasion. At times of low flow the river carries only a small load and may appear clear. At such times the river's load is very small and abrasion is almost non-existent.

Larger particles in the load produce more rapid erosion while smaller particles tend to smooth or polish a surface. Abrasion produces very fine particles that are easy to transport.

2 Hydraulic action

Hydraulic action is the impact of the moving water and its frictional drag on the particles lying on the river bed. Under normal conditions velocities are only sufficient to move sand and fine gravel. However, the hydraulic power may be locally high especially below waterfalls and rapids where it may cause the rocks to fragment particularly where joints and bedding planes or other lines of weakness are present. On the outside bend of a river hydraulic action may lead to the undermining and collapse of riverbanks. This forms river cliffs.

3 Corrosion or solution

This is most active on rocks that contain carbonates, such as limestone and chalk and silicates such as quartz. The minerals in the rock are dissolved in water that is slightly acid and carried away in solution. The equation, which summarizes the process for Carboniferous limestone, is:

$$CaCO_3 \quad + \quad H_2CO_3 \quad \longrightarrow \quad Ca(HCO_3)^2$$

Limestone   acid water   Calcium
                                                            hydrogen carbonate
                                                            (soluble)

4 Attrition

Attrition reduces the particle size of the load. The rocks and pebbles strike one another as well as the river bed. The particles therefore become smoother, smaller and more rounded as they move along the river channel. In many rivers, the larger, more angular sediments are generally found upstream and the smaller, more rounded particles downstream. However, this is a generalization which depends on the material on the river bed, the length of time the material has been in the river and the distance the material has traveled.

Where a river flows over bedrock the erosion of the bedrock is most effectively achieved by corrasion and pothole drilling. Rivers flowing in alluvial channels are more effectively eroded by hydraulic action.

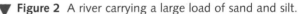
▼ **Figure 2** A river carrying a large load of sand and silt.

Vertical, lateral and headward erosion

River erosion may result in:

- vertical corrasion
- lateral corrasion
- headward erosion.

Vertical corrasion

This is a characteristic of fast-flowing rivers that are transporting a large bedload of coarse, hard particles. The particles abrade and pothole the river beds lowering them relatively rapidly. Such rivers tend to flow in deep, narrow gorges, as the resistant rocks of the valley slopes restrict weathering of the slopes either side (Figure 1).

Lateral corrasion

This occurs when a river does not follow a straight path but meanders, swinging from side to side. The strongest current flows around the outside of the bend and hydraulic action and corrasion cause the riverbanks to be undermined and to collapse. Lateral erosion is most active where a river transports a large load or during short-lived floods under desert conditions. However, as a general rule valley widening is due more to weathering and slope transport than lateral erosion by rivers.

Headward erosion

This process occurs either at the source of the river, where the length of the channel is increased or at points where the long profile of the river is locally steep, for example at a waterfall, where the gradual retreat of the waterfall takes place.

▲ **Figure 1** Vertical corrasion has created the steep-sided gorges in Watkins Glen, USA

River transportation

A river obtains its load from two main sources:

- about 90 per cent from the movement of material down the slopes of the river valley by weathering and mass movement
- the remaining 10 per cent as a result of erosion of the bed and banks of the river channel.

The amount of load transported depends upon a river's capacity and competence (Information Box). As the energy or discharge of a river increases then so does its capacity and competence. A river at bankfull stage can move large quantities of rocks and sediment.

The ability to transport depends on:

- location and supply of material
- amount of material available
- character of the material, e.g. boulders, gravel, sand, silt, clay, soluble minerals
- volume of water
- amount of energy available to do the work (greatest in times of maximum discharge or where there is the maximum flow in a river channel, e.g. on the outside bend of a river meander).

River capacity
This is the total load, measured by volume, mass or weight, that a river is able to transport at a particular discharge or energy level. A river's capacity increases as the discharge increases.

River competence
This is the maximum size or weight of material a river can transport. The River Lyn in Devon under normal flow conditions has the ability to transport only a small size and weight of load. However, in the serious floods of 1952 the river increased its competence greatly and was able to move large rocks and boulders of up to 7 tonnes in weight.

A river's capacity and competence increase downstream as the discharge and velocity of the water increases. They also increase greatly when a river is in flood although the more frequent low level floods are thought to be more effective overall in transportation.

The load carried by a river is divided into three types:

- **bedload** – coarse fragments moved only slowly and under conditions of very high energy.

- **suspension load** – particles of sand, silt and clay capable of being moved along in the flow of the water

- **solution load** – dissolved minerals carried along in the water.

The material is moved by four main processes:

1 traction – larger pebbles and boulders roll or slide along the river bed. The largest may only be moved during times of severe flood.

2 saltation – bouncing or hopping movement of pebbles, sands and gravel along the river bed. The material is picked up for a short time before being dropped again when the current falls.

3 suspension – material, often the finer sand and silt, carried along in the flow. The suspended load is often the greatest proportion of the total load and in sufficient quantity makes the river look brown. The quantity and size of the material transported in suspension increases with:

• increased volume and velocity of the river
• distance from the source.

4 solution – minerals dissolved in the water such as those contained in limestone rocks.

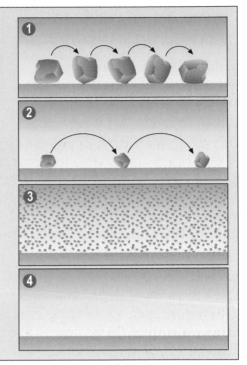

▲ **Figure 2** Processes of river transportation

The Hjulstrom graph (Figure 3) shows the relationship between the velocity of a river and the particle sizes that may be transported. It shows the critical velocity needed for the material to be moved (or eroded) and the settling velocity when deposition will take place. The area in between indicates the velocities where transportation of the material will continue to occur once the material is eroded. The graph shows that:

- sand may be eroded and transported at much lower velocities than clay or silt. Clay needs a velocity similar to that for pebbles because of its cohesive properties

- a river with high discharge and velocity increases its capacity and competence allowing increased erosion of the river channel

- the velocity needed to keep particles in suspension is less than that needed to erode them. For clay, the velocity needed to transport the particles is almost zero. This would mean that a river would virtually have to have stopped flowing in order for the particles to be deposited

- for pebbles, cobbles and boulders there is only a very narrow gap between the amount of energy needed for erosion and deposition. Therefore, only a small drop in velocity is needed to cause deposition of the larger material.

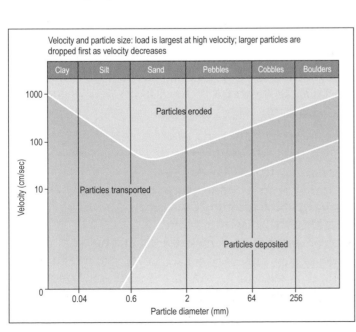

◀ **Figure 3** Graph of velocity and particle size

Questions

1   Using Figure 3 state the velocity at which particles of clay, sand and boulders will:
    a   be eroded
    b   be deposited.

2   Does Figure 3 show the capacity, competence or load of a river?

3   Describe and explain the work of a river at times of:
    a   low flow
    b   high discharge.

Deposition

As shown on Figure 3 on page 21 once the velocity of a river begins to fall its capacity and competence reduces and the load, beginning with the largest material, will be deposited. Deposition occurs when:

- discharge is reduced, such as after a dry spell
- velocity is reduced by the river entering a lake or the sea
- there is shallow water, such as on the inside bend of a meander
- the load is suddenly increased, perhaps due to a landslide into a river
- the river floods and overflows its banks resulting in lower velocities outside the main channel.

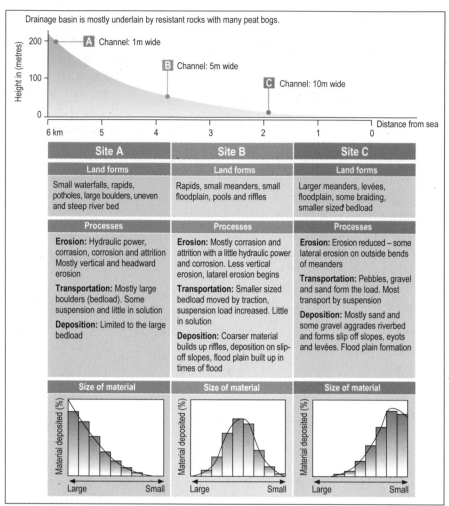

Figure 1 Glen Chalmadale, Isle of Arran, Scotland – landforms and processes at three sites

As the river velocity falls the heaviest bedload material, such as boulders, is deposited first, followed by gravel, sand and silt then the finest clay particles. The dissolved load is not deposited but carried out to sea. This pattern of deposition is reflected in the sediments found along a long profile of a river. The channels of upland streams are often filled with large boulders that increase the wetted perimeter of the stream and the turbulence of the water flow. Gravel, sand and silt can be carried further and is often deposited in the middle and lower course of a river. In particular, sand and silt are deposited on the flat floodplains either side of the river in its lower course during times of flood. The finest particles of silt and clay are deposited at the mouths of rivers. Where the river meets the sea, the sea acts as a break slowing river velocity to almost zero and allowing the very finest particles to be deposited forming mud flats or deltas.

Questions

1   Complete a table like the one below to summarize the features and processes along the River Glen Chalmadale.

	Upper course	Middle course	Lower course
Landforms			
Processes:			
Erosion			
Transportation			
Deposition			
Size of deposited load			

2   How do each of the following change downstream:
- size of the river's load
- relative importance of the processes of erosion and deposition
- type of transportation
- nature of the landforms produced?

Landforms of river erosion

The ability of a river to erode is determined by the amount of energy a river possesses. The direction of the erosion is linked to a river's base level, usually sea level. Base level is the theoretical level down to which a river can erode.

In its upper course, the river is high above its base level and the dominant processes are vertical erosion or downcutting. However, a large amount of energy is lost in overcoming friction and turbulence because of large boulders in the river bed. This leaves very little for active erosion and transportation except in times of high discharge, after heavy rain or snowmelt. In times of high discharge, the large bedload can be moved by traction and saltation which results in vertical erosion of the stream channel.

Towards the river mouth, the river is closer to its base level and the main processes are lateral or sideways erosion. Along the course of a river outcrops of resistant rock or lakes may create local base levels and over time a river will try to even out these irregularities to create a graded or smooth profile.

V-shaped valleys and interlocking spurs

In the upper course of a river vertical erosion dominates as the stream cuts downwards. Weathering and erosion on the valley sides removes material causing the valley sides to retreat forming a V-shaped valley (Figure 2). This material moves downslope and it may eventually enter the stream channel where over time the river will erode and transport it downstream. If the river removes the material transported downslope (by slope processes) more quickly than material is provided then a steeper valley is produced. The steepness of the valley sides also depends upon these factors:

- **Climate** The amount of precipitation is important in determining the type and frequency of mass movement on the valley sides. It also affects river discharge and therefore the ability of the river to erode and transport the bedload and debris which has been deposited from the valley sides.
- **Rock structure** Resistant rocks, such as carboniferous limestone, often produce gorge-like valleys (Figure 3) because of their resistance to weathering and mass movement processes.
- **Vegetation** The vegetation helps to bind the surface soil and maintain slope stability.

The streams are rarely straight in the upper course but wind around interlocking spurs of more resistant rock. There is therefore some lateral erosion taking place as well as vertical erosion. The stream works to achieve an equilibrium or balance between slope retreat, debris supply and vertical erosion.

Questions

1 a Compare the photographs shown in Figures 2 and 3.

  b Suggest reasons for the differences you observe.

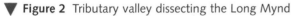
▼ **Figure 2** Tributary valley dissecting the Long Mynd

▲ **Figure 3** Watkins Glen, New York State, USA

Potholes

Active corrasion along a stream bed produces potholes (Figure 1) especially in fast-flowing rivers with strong eddying. Potholes are cylindrical holes 'drilled' into the bedrock by turbulent high velocity flow. The eddying creates a shallow bowl that may become occupied by small stones and pebbles. The constant swirling of the pebbles deepens the depression into a pothole in a process known as pothole drilling. Adjacent potholes may join together creating sudden and considerable deepening of channels such as can be seen at the Strid on the River Wharfe, in North Yorkshire.

▲ **Figure 1** Potholes and rapids in the bed of the River Wharfe

Waterfalls and rapids

Waterfalls and rapids occur where the long profile of a river is steep. This is usually the result of an outcrop of more resistant rock, often called the cap rock, overlying a softer rock. Erosion, especially by the hydraulic power of the water, is concentrated in the plunge pool at the base of the waterfall. The waterfall becomes undercut and the hard cap rock above periodically collapses resulting in the headward erosion of the waterfall and the formation of a gorge of recession. Figure 2 shows the formation of a waterfall.

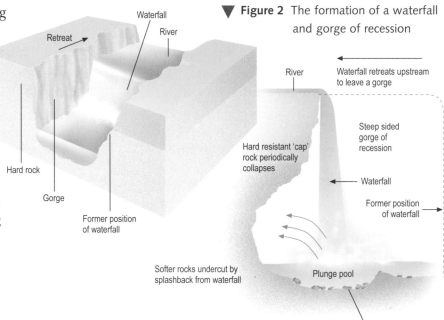

▼ **Figure 2** The formation of a waterfall and gorge of recession

Waterfall
River
Retreat
Hard rock
Gorge
Former position of waterfall

River
Waterfall retreats upstream to leave a gorge
Steep sided gorge of recession
Hard resistant 'cap' rock periodically collapses
Waterfall
Former position of waterfall
Softer rocks undercut by splashback from waterfall
Plunge pool
Fallen angular blocks

High Force waterfall, Upper Teesdale Northern England

Case Study

▼ **Figure 3** High Force waterfall

In Upper Teesdale an outcrop of an igneous rock called Whin Sill causes the formation of rapids at Low Force and the High Force waterfall (Figure 3). Whin Sill is the resistant cap rock overlying softer bands of sandstone, limestone, shales and thin coal seams. These less resistant rocks erode more quickly creating an overhang of the Whin Sill which collapses from time to time causing the waterfall to retreat. Waterfall retreat over many thousands of years has created an impressive gorge of recession. The waterfall is the tallest in England at 21m high with a very deep plunge pool.

Questions

1 a Draw a labelled sketch to show the characteristics of the river and channel at High Force.
   b Describe and explain the formation of the waterfall and gorge.

Meanders and ox-bow lakes

Meanders are bends in the course of the river channel. They often begin to appear as a river approaches its middle course and the gradient of the channel becomes less steep. They are thought to be a response by the river to the excess energy it now has having emerged from the steep gradient of the upper course.

Meanders are characterized by a river-cliff on the outside of the bend and a gently sloping slip-off slope, sometimes called a point bar, on the inside bend of the meander (Figure 4).

Meanders are a result of helicoidal flow in which the fastest current spirals downstream (Figure 4) in a corkscrew fashion. The movement results in erosion on the outside bend of the meander to form a river cliff and deposition on the inside bend forming a slip-off slope. The flow moves sediment downstream but not in a straight line. The material eroded from the outer bank of a meander will spiral downstream and be deposited on the inner bank building up or aggrading to form point bar deposits. This produces the characteristic asymmetrical shape of the cross-section of a meander.

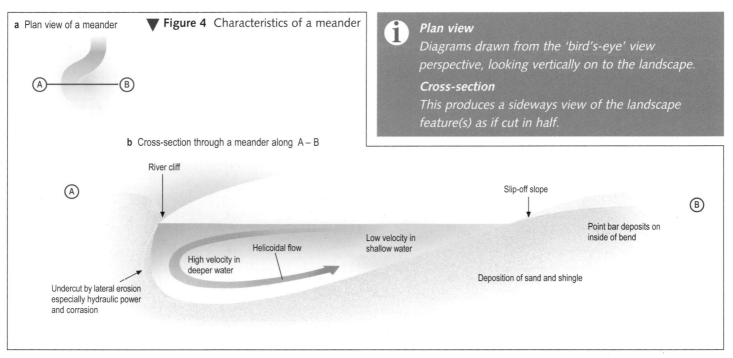

a Plan view of a meander   ▼ **Figure 4** Characteristics of a meander

ⓘ **Plan view**
Diagrams drawn from the 'bird's-eye' view perspective, looking vertically on to the landscape.

Cross-section
This produces a sideways view of the landscape feature(s) as if cut in half.

b Cross-section through a meander along A – B

River cliff

Slip-off slope

High velocity in deeper water

Helicoidal flow

Low velocity in shallow water

Point bar deposits on inside of bend

Undercut by lateral erosion especially hydraulic power and corrasion

Deposition of sand and shingle

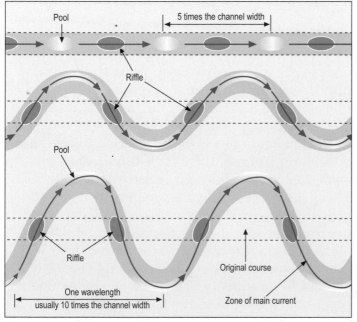

Pool

5 times the channel width

Riffle

Pool

Riffle

Original course

One wavelength usually 10 times the channel width

Zone of main current

▲ **Figure 5** Sequence of pools and riffles in a meander

Meanders are linked with the development of pools and riffles in a channel bed. The riffles are areas of deposition of coarse material that create areas of shallow water. The pools are areas of deeper water between the riffles. The pools and riffles develop in sections along a river channel creating differences in the gradient of the channel. The coarser pebbles create a steeper gradient than in the eroded pools. The pools and riffles are usually equally spaced in both natural and artificial channels. The water increases its velocity as it passes over the riffled surface while it flows more sluggishly out of the deeper pools. The riffles are not static but pebbles and gravel are added to them from upstream at about the same rate as material is lost downstream. The sequence of pools and riffles develops until the average spacing is between 5 and 7 channel widths and the entire channel is meandering (Figure 5).

Meander migration

Meanders change their location over time hence the term 'migrate'. The meanders move in two directions:

- sideways because of lateral erosion. This broadens the floodplain and erodes away the ends of interlocking spurs.

- downstream due to the pattern of erosion in relation to the location of the *thalweg* (the zone of fastest velocity in the channel flow). The greatest erosion is downstream of the midpoint in the meander bend because the flow of the strongest current does not perfectly match the meander shape (Figure 1).

▼ **Figure 1** Meander features and development

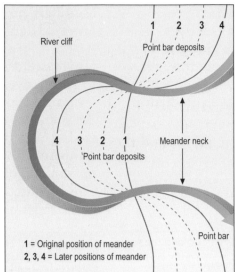

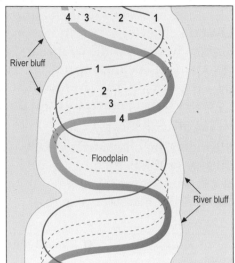

Over time a meander widens and the neck narrows. This is due to erosion on the outside bend of the meander forming a river cliff.

The meanders migrate downstream and the river cliffs 'join up' to form a line of river bluffs. The point bar deposits, which are added to by silt deposited during flooding, build up the thickness of floodplain.

▼ **Figure 2** Formation of an ox-bow lake

key
- Erosion
- Deposition

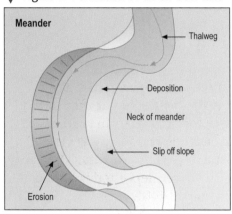

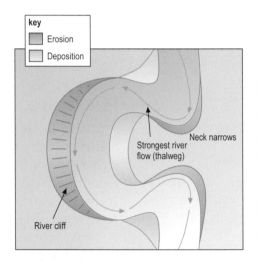

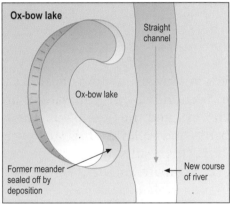

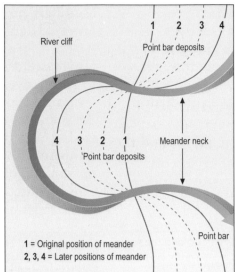

▲ **Figure 3** Meanders and meander scars on the River Mississippi in the USA. Where might the next ox-bow lake form?

Ox-bow lakes

As the meander moves downstream, it is possible for one side of the meander to 'catch up' with the river channel downstream (Figure 2). Eventually the river may break through the neck of the meander causing a major river diversion. The river abandons the original meander channel in favour of the shorter, steeper 'new' route. The formation of the cut-off is normally accomplished at times of high energy of the river, such as at peak discharge during bankfull or flood conditions. Reduced velocity at the entrance to the former meander, especially as floodwaters subside, results in deposition which seals off the meander to leave an ox-bow lake. The water in the ox-bow lake becomes calm resulting in deposition of any sediment and over time the water in the lake may disappear through infiltration and evaporation to leave a meander scar (Figure 3).

Depositional landforms

Levées

Levées are high banks of silt (Figure 4) close to the river channel. They are formed by repeated river flooding, which is most common in the lower course of a river where there is a floodplain. Rivers with well-developed levées generally carry a large load of sand and silt, indicating active erosion in the upper course, and they flood repeatedly.

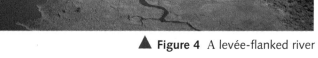

▼ **Figure 5** The formation of levées

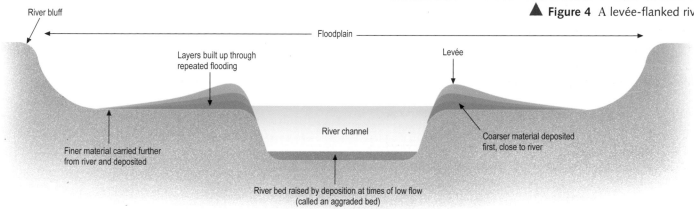

▲ **Figure 4** A levée-flanked river

River bluff

Floodplain

Layers built up through repeated flooding

Levée

River channel

Finer material carried further from river and deposited

Coarser material deposited first, close to river

River bed raised by deposition at times of low flow (called an aggraded bed)

When a river overflows its banks there is an increase in friction between the water that leaves the river channel and the floodplain. The water on the river banks and valley floor is shallower and the velocity falls. This results in deposition of the load. The coarsest material is deposited first building up natural embankments along the channel called levées. In times of low flow such as during a dry season the river may also deposit sand and silt aggrading (building up) the river bed. This raises the river and in some cases may lead to the river level being above the level of the floodplain.

The levées along the banks of the Mississippi are very high; some have been artificially heightened and strengthened to act as flood defences. The river bed has also been raised by deposition or aggradation of material so that the river now flows above the level of its floodplain. This is disastrous when flooding occurs or a levée collapses because the water can no longer naturally drain back into the river. Large stretches of the Mississippi are dredged to increase the capacity of the river channel and to reduce the level of the river.

Floodplains

A floodplain is the most common depositional feature of a river. It is the relatively flat area of land either side of the river forming the valley floor. Floodplains are most well developed in the lower course of a river as the river nears the sea. They are composed of alluvium – river deposited material – and form some of the most fertile soils for agriculture to be found in the world.

The width of a floodplain is determined by meander migration and lateral erosion, while the depth of alluvium on the floodplain is a result of flooding. As meanders migrate downstream, eroding laterally, the valley floor is widened. Point bar deposits and meander scars are incorporated into the floodplain. They are stabilized by vegetation as the meanders migrate and abandon their former courses. Coarser sands and gravel are incorporated into the floodplain in this way.

When the river floods as the water overflows the channel the velocity falls and deposition takes place, contributing, in particular, finer sands and clays to the alluvium on the floodplain. Rivers which flood their lower courses frequently and carry a large load tend to build up great thicknesses of alluvium on the floodplain, such as along the Ganges valley in Bangladesh.

Deltas

Deltas are areas of land at the mouth of a river jutting out into the sea. They are flat areas of land crossed by many stream channels called distributaries. The distributaries are often flanked by levées. The levées are joined together by spits and bars sealing off shallow areas of water forming lagoons. The lagoons are gradually infilled by silt and sand to form marshes and eventually dry land colonized by vegetation. The fertile Deltas of the Ganges and Nile are intensively used for settlement and farming. Deltas are formed by river deposition under special conditions:

- The river must be carrying a large load. The Mississippi carries about 450 million tonnes of sediment into its delta distributaries every year.
- The material must be deposited faster than it is removed by the action of tides, waves and currents.
- Most deltas occur in calm seas with a gently sloping sea bed. Most are tideless or almost tideless.
- The river meets the sea which acts as a break slowing the velocity and encouraging deposition.
- The salt in the seawater on meeting the river water generates an electrical charge that causes particles to coagulate or stick together so increasing their weight and encouraging deposition. This process is called flocculation.
- The river floods frequently in its lower course depositing alluvium in the delta, building up levées and creating new distributaries.

▲ **Figure 1** The Mississippi delta: a bird's foot delta

The deposition does not take place in a haphazard way. Three distinct layers can be recognized in the formation of deltas (Figure 2):

1 The finest materials travel the furthest before being deposited and form the bottomset beds.
2 Covering these beds is a layer of slightly coarser materials deposited to form a slope and called the foreset beds.
3 The upper horizontal layer formed of the coarsest materials is called the topset beds.

Deltas may be classified according to their shape and the extent to which the seaward edge is smoothed. There are two main types:

1 A bird's foot delta, in which fingers of deposited material extend out into the sea along the line of distributaries, such as the Mississippi delta in the Gulf of Mexico (Figure 1).
2 An arcuate delta, typically triangular in shape with a smooth coastline, such as the Nile delta in Egypt (Figure 3).

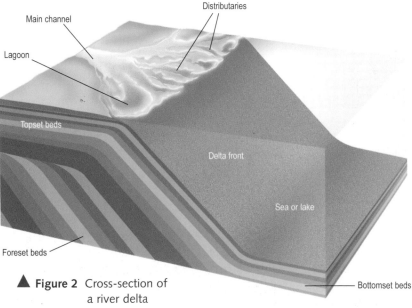

▲ **Figure 2** Cross-section of a river delta

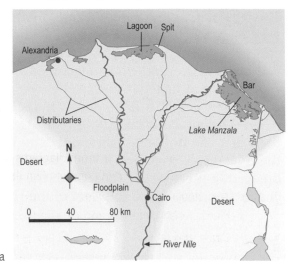

▶ **Figure 3** The Nile delta: an arcuate delta

Alluvial fans

Alluvial fans are fan-shaped landforms similar to deltas but deposited on land. They are often seen:
- where a stream comes from a steep mountain course and enters a flatter plain with a low gradient, e.g. at Spitzbergen, Norway (Figure 4)
- in glacial, temperate or semi-arid environments where there are rapidly changing stream discharges, e.g. in the glaciated valley of the Rhône in Switzerland. Here streams have highly variable discharges between winter and summer and are often braided
- where the stream flows across the fan it often splits into a series of distributaries. The channels become wider and shallower reducing velocity and encouraging deposition. The fans are cone shaped and become broader and shallower away from the apex. The gradient also decreases due to the variation in size of material deposited. Coarser gravel is deposited first, close to the apex; finer sands and gravel are transported further to the edges of the fan.

Braided streams

A braided stream (Figure 5), has islands or eyots of deposited material within the channel. The overall channel is relatively straight although the eyots and smaller channels may rapidly and frequently change their position. Braiding tends to occur in streams where the load contains a high proportion of coarser sands and gravels.

Braiding is a characteristic of streams and rivers with very variable discharges common in semi-arid environments, or glacier-fed streams. In semi-arid environments, torrential downpours lead to considerable overland flow creating streams with high velocities and large loads. Rapid evaporation and infiltration following the storm rapidly reduces the volume and velocity resulting in the deposition of the load. Streams and rivers fed by glaciers have high discharges when there is rapid melting of the ice during the day in summer but low discharges at night and in winter.

At times of high discharge the streams are capable of transporting a large load. However when the velocity falls the stream's competence and capacity are reduced. The large load is deposited forming the eyots and causing the stream to divide into a series of smaller channels.

▼ **Figure 4** An alluvial fan above Tempelfjord, Spitzbergen

▼ **Figure 5** Plan view of a braided stream

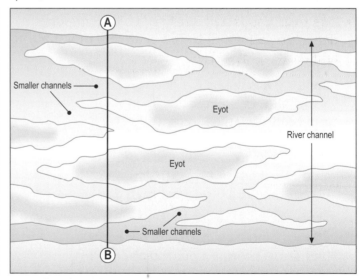

Questions

1. Suggest why there are deltas at the mouths of some rivers, such as the Nile and Mississippi, but no large deltas at the mouths of British rivers?
2. With the aid of one or more diagrams outline the characteristics of a delta and explain its formation.
3. a. For alluvial fans and braided streams, describe their characteristic features and explain their formation.
4. Draw and label a cross-section along the line A-B on Figure 5.

Characteristics of braided streams
- Small islands or eyots of deposited material are found within the channel
- A network of intertwining channels converge and diverge around the eyots
- Braiding is a characteristic of streams with variable discharge
- At times of high discharge, braided streams carry a large load of quite coarse material

Channel landforms

Case Study

along the Mississippi River

The Mississippi River has one of the world's largest drainage basins and it drains 40 percent of all surface runoff in the USA. The Mississippi also carries large quantities of sediment – over 500 million tonnes of material a year, mostly as silt in suspension. Figure 1 compares the Mississippi with some of the world's other large rivers.

South of its confluence with the River Ohio the river meanders across a floodplain in wide loops. The meanders are particularly impressive between Memphis and Baton Rouge, a small section of which is shown in figure 2. The channel has also shifted location on many occasions forming abandoned channels, meander scars and ox-bow lakes such as Eagle Lake and Yazoo Lake, north of Vicksburg, Mississippi. The Mississippi River has created, through lateral erosion and deposition, a floodplain ranging between 50 and 200km wide. The flooding has deposited deep layers of fertile alluvial soil on the floodplain and built up large levées, the natural high banks of silt on the bank of the river. There are over 3500km of levées along the banks of the Mississippi River, some reaching 10m high and 96m wide.

The very large quantities of silt carried by the river forms a delta at the river mouth. The silt is deposited faster than tides and currents can remove it in the relatively sheltered Gulf of Mexico. The bird's foot delta is a series of marshes, lagoons and mud banks crossed by two main levée flanked distributaries.

The value of the floodplain for agriculture, industry and settlement has presented America with one of the greatest challenges – to control flooding along the Mississippi.

River	Length (km)	Drainage area (000s km2)	Discharge at mouth (cumecs)
Nile	6,484	2,881	1,584
Amazon	6,516	7,180	180,000
Mississippi/ Missouri	6,019	3,221	17,545
Yangtze	5,800	1,970	35,000
Congo (Zaire)	4,700	3,822	42,000

▲ **Figure 1** Some characteristics of the world's longest rivers

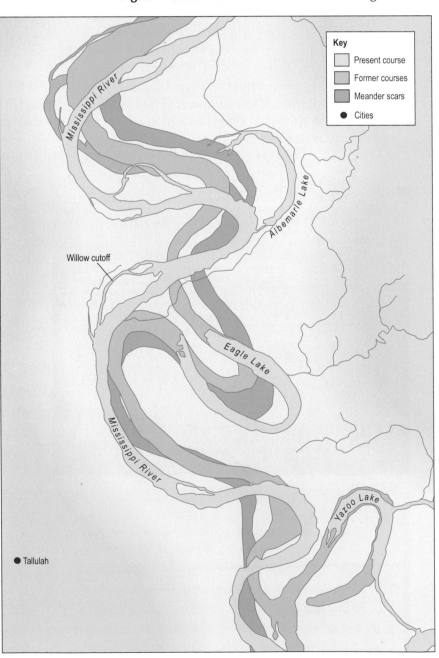

▲ **Figure 2** The Mississippi River just north of Vicksburg.

Channel landforms along the River Tees

Case Study

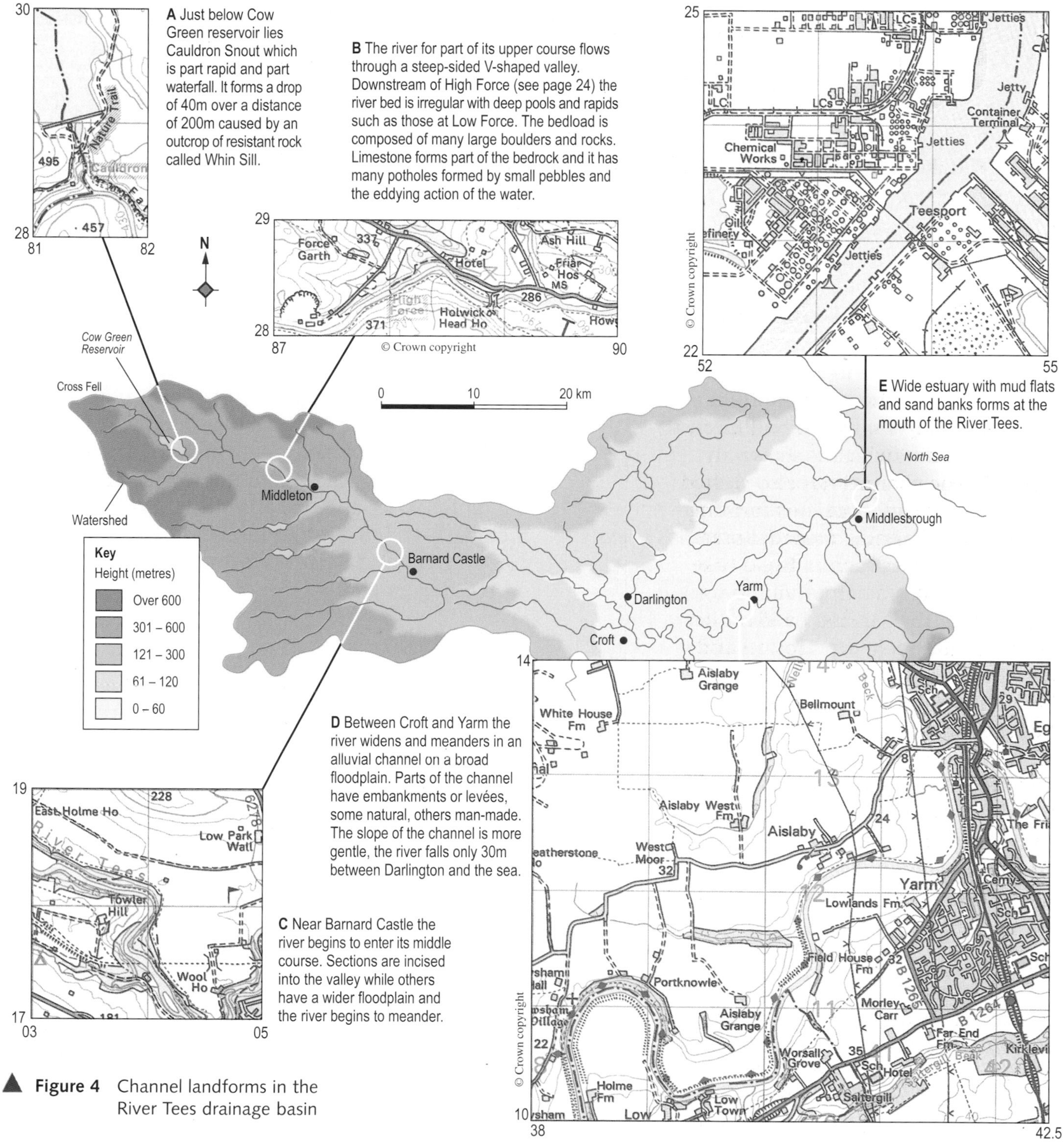
A Just below Cow Green reservoir lies Cauldron Snout which is part rapid and part waterfall. It forms a drop of 40m over a distance of 200m caused by an outcrop of resistant rock called Whin Sill.
B The river for part of its upper course flows through a steep-sided V-shaped valley. Downstream of High Force (see page 24) the river bed is irregular with deep pools and rapids such as those at Low Force. The bedload is composed of many large boulders and rocks. Limestone forms part of the bedrock and it has many potholes formed by small pebbles and the eddying action of the water.
C Near Barnard Castle the river begins to enter its middle course. Sections are incised into the valley while others have a wider floodplain and the river begins to meander.
D Between Croft and Yarm the river widens and meanders in an alluvial channel on a broad floodplain. Parts of the channel have embankments or levées, some natural, others man-made. The slope of the channel is more gentle, the river falls only 30m between Darlington and the sea.
E Wide estuary with mud flats and sand banks forms at the mouth of the River Tees.
Key
Height (metres)
Over 600
301 – 600
121 – 300
61 – 120
0 – 60
Cow Green Reservoir
Cross Fell
Watershed
Middleton
Barnard Castle
Darlington
Croft
Yarm
Middlesbrough
North Sea
N
0 10 20 km
© Crown copyright
Force Garth
Ash Hill
Hotel
High Force
Holwick Head Ho
Chemical Works
Jetties
Container Terminal
Teesport
East Holme Ho
Low Park Wall
River Tees
Towler Hill
Wool Ho
Aislaby Grange
White House Fm
Bellmount
Aislaby West Fm
Aislaby
West Moor
Portknowle
Lowlands Fm
Field House Fm
Morley Carr
Far End Fm
Worsall Grove
Holme Fm
Low Town
Saltergill
Hotel

▲ **Figure 4** Channel landforms in the River Tees drainage basin

Questions

Investigation

Study a local river.

a On a base map of the river, annotate the channel features along its length.

b Write an explanatory account of the channel features.

c Evaluate the importance of extreme events, such as flooding in the formation of the landforms.

Flooding as a hazard

- The physical causes of flooding
- The human causes of flooding
- Flooding as a hazard

The physical causes of flooding

Flooding occurs when the capacity of a river channel is exceeded and water overflows the riverbanks onto the surrounding land. Overland flow may have already taken place. This occurs when the amount of water available exceeds the infiltration capacity. Overland flow generally results from:

- intense precipitation as a result of a convectional thunderstorm when the rainfall intensity is greater than the infiltration capacity. This is most common in semi-arid regions where huge convection storms produce intense downpours. In temperate areas such as the British Isles rainfall is generally much less intense.
- a prolonged period of rainfall resulting in saturation of the soil and overland flow. The infiltration rate also depends upon the rock and soil types. Clay soils are much more prone to overland flow due to their smaller pore spaces. Soils that are already saturated also have a reduced infiltration capacity hence the increased risk of flooding during a prolonged period of rainfall.
- a sudden increase in temperature resulting in rapid snowmelt, often made worse by frozen ground restricting infiltration.

The case studies to follow on the Severn Valley and Bangladesh (pages 34–8) illustrate the physical causes of flooding.

The human causes of flooding

Sometimes human activities may increase the risk of flooding or make the flooding worse. Occasional disasters such as a dam burst can produce catastrophic flooding. The dam burst at an iron ore mine near Seville in Southern Spain in 1999 released highly toxic water that threatened the Donana National Park, caused flooding in the local area and polluted underground water supplies. Land management techniques such as drainage systems, digging ditches, ploughing up and down a slope may also increase the risk of flooding as well as building bridges and embankments. However urbanization and deforestation are the two most common human activities to increase the possibility of flooding an area.

Urbanization

Building new towns or increasing the size of urban areas makes more of the land surface impermeable. It increases the amount of runoff by:

- removing topsoil for construction and compacting the ground with earth-moving machinery
- building roads which increase the impermeable surface area
- building drains and sewers that introduce a rapid means of transport of the water to river channels. This reduces the lag time
- straightening river channels and lining them with concrete to enable building plans to proceed. This leads to faster delivery of water downstream of the urban area increasing the risk of flooding in those areas.

Urbanization alters the shape of the storm hydrograph reducing the lag time and increasing the peak discharge (Figure 1). This happens because there is less water reaching the channel by throughflow and baseflow and more by overland flow. This may present problems for local authorities and water companies who need to respond to these changes in order to prevent flooding in the river basin.

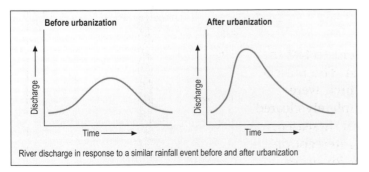

▲ **Figure 1** Before and after urbanization

Canon's Brook basin in Harlow, UK

Case Study

This river basin was affected by the building of Harlow New Town in 1951. Figure 2 shows how the land uses in the river basin changed. The surface area covered by impermeable surfaces grew from 0 per cent to 16.6 per cent and the runoff increased by 59.4mm, an increase of about 30 per cent. However, research showed that the urbanization produced markedly higher flows during the summer but had very little impact on previously recorded flows in the winter. In the winter soils would have been more saturated and there would have been rapid runoff similar to the conditions created by urbanization.

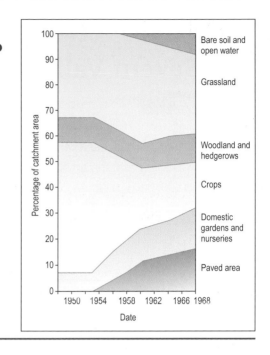

▶ **Figure 2** The land use of Canon's Brook catchment, 1950-68

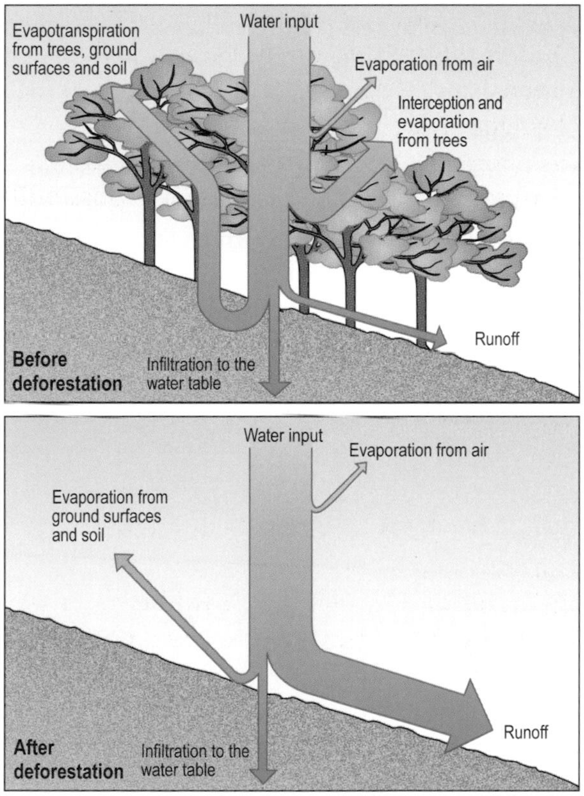

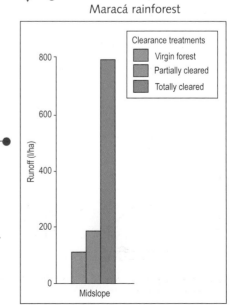

◀ **Figure 3** The hydrological cycle before and after deforestation

Deforestation

The removal of trees (Figure 3) reduces interception and evapotranspiration resulting in increased runoff and soil erosion. The eroded material finds its way into water courses where it aggrades the river bed. This reduces the channel capacity increasing the likelihood of flooding. Deforestation in the Himalayas, the upper reaches of the River Ganges, may be increasing the frequency and intensity of flooding in Bangladesh. In the Amazon Basin and in many other areas of tropical rainforest there is also great concern that deforestation is causing greater extremes of river flow.

The Maracá rainforest in Brazil

Case Study

The Royal Geographical Society carried out an experiment to test the effects of deforestation in the Maracá rainforest in Brazil. The project involved the study of areas of virgin rainforest; areas which were partially cleared of trees and areas which had been completely cleared. Figure 4 shows that the run off increased as tree removal increased. The removal of the trees and other vegetation reduced interception and evapotranspiration creating a large surplus of water for runoff.

▼ **Figure 4** Runoff levels in the Maracá rainforest

Flooding as a hazard in the MEDW

The Severn Valley floods,

Case Study

UK, 1998

▼ Figure 1 Flood alert on the Rivers Severn and Wye

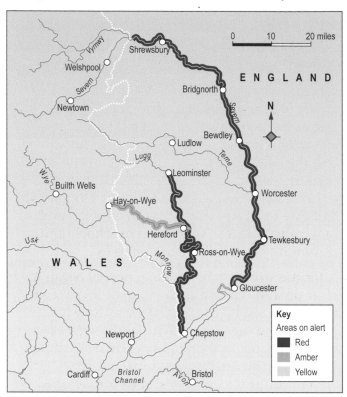

In late October and early November 1998, heavy rains caused chronic flooding in large areas of South Wales, Herefordshire, Gloucestershire, Devon, Cornwall and Northern Ireland. Many areas received the wettest October since records began with more rainfall than in October 1987 when a 'hurricane' brought heavy rains and strong winds to the British Isles. The Shadow Countryside Minister in 1998, Tim Yeo, said that the flooding had been increased by housing developments on greenfield sites.

The River Severn experienced two main flood peaks as rains continued over ten days. The towns upriver were worst affected. The flood peak lessened downstream as the river widens. The first flood peak was 4.4m above the normal winter level at Shrewsbury. The peak moved down river affecting Worcester, Upton on Severn, Tewkesbury and Gloucester. At its peak the River Severn was 4.8m above normal flow level – a 50-year record. The river had a flow of about ten times what would be expected at the time of year.

▲ Figure 2 Shrewsbury lies surrounded by the swollen river Severn. Only a private toll bridge is still open to traffic

▶ **Figure 3** Walking the planks – decking laid along a flooded street in Shrewsbury keeps pedestrians dry

Local people complained that there had been little warning of the likelihood of the floods. The Environment Agency, however, claimed to have published in the media twenty red warnings and a general warning for Wales as well as evacuating people from homes where there were no flood-defence systems. At the height of the floods 46 red warnings were published (Figure 1).

Many people had to be rescued after becoming stranded or trapped in floodwaters including 28 elderly residents of a nursing home. The floods caused the death of at least five people including two canoeists, a farmer who had gone in his tractor to move cattle to higher ground, and a man and a woman who fell into swollen rivers.

Thousands of acres of farmland were under water in South Wales where 400 people had to be evacuated from their homes. Roads and railways had to be closed because of flooding or fallen trees. Several sporting fixtures also had to be abandoned. Houses were flooded up to over a metre deep. As the waters receded it was not just the damage from water which needed to be repaired but also the damage caused by thick deposits of mud and sand carried by the floodwaters.

The River Severn rose high enough to cut off the centre of Shrewsbury (Figures 2 and 3) leaving only one access point across the Kingsland Bridge, a privately owned toll bridge. Tolls were suspended and the council agreed to discuss compensation with the owners of the bridge. Hereford was also under water after the River Wye broke its banks and rose to a record 6m above its normal level. Emergency shelters were set up in schools and community centres for flood refugees.

After the worst of the flooding people began to clear up amidst warnings of contracting Weil's disease caused by coming into contact with untreated sewage. The Environment Agency warned people to thoroughly clear away silt left behind by the floodwaters because it might contain untreated sewage and to contact their GPs if they became ill.

Insurance experts estimated that it would cost between £100 and £400 million to repair the damage caused by the extreme weather conditions and that those living near rivers could face large increases in insurance premiums.

Questions

Causes of the floods in the Severn valley

1   Describe the physical causes of the floods

2   Describe and explain how human activities may have contributed to the flooding.

Effects of these floods

3   Classify the impacts of the flooding into those affecting people, the environment and economy.

The response to these floods

4   Suggest what role each of the following would have had in the short and/or long term in responding to the flooding:

    emergency services
    Environment Agency
    local government/council
    national government
    insurance companies.

Flooding as a hazard in the LEDW
Flooding in Bangladesh,

Case Study

1998

Bangladesh is a country in south-east Asia that suffers annual flooding. The floodwaters bring with them alluvial sediment which makes the delta and floodplains very fertile but frequently the flooding is severe causing loss of life and bringing misery and suffering to the population.

The physical causes of the floods

Bangladesh is prone to flooding because:

- most of the country is the huge floodplain and delta of the rivers Ganges and Brahmaputra. 70 per cent is less than 1m above sea level
- rivers, lakes and swamps cover 10 per cent of the land area
- tropical cyclones bring heavy rain and storm waves cause coastal floods
- snowmelt from the glaciers in the Himalayas in late spring and summer increases discharges
- there are heavy monsoon rains especially over the Himalayas, the uplands in Assam and the Central Indian Plateau.

Of these, the heavy monsoon rains are the main physical cause of the flooding. In some years including 1998 the rains were exceptionally heavy causing river levels to rise and severe floods to occur (Figure 1).

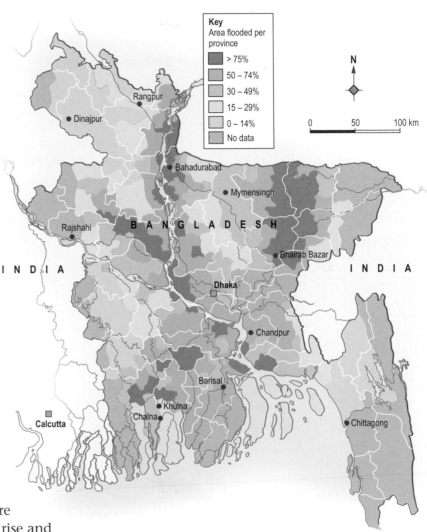

▼ **Figure 1** Flooding in Bangladesh (map adapted from radar-satellite image), 10 September 1998

Key
Area flooded per province

- > 75%
- 50 – 74%
- 30 – 49%
- 15 – 29%
- 0 – 14%
- No data

The human causes of the floods

Some people report that the frequency and severity of the flooding has increased in recent years and blame human activities especially deforestation in Nepal and Tibet, the building of dams in India and the impact of global warming. However, opinions are divided and there are many scientists who claim that there is little evidence that human activities do contribute to the floods.

▼ **Figure 2** Deforestation: the impact of flooding

Removal of forest → Increased overland flow increases river discharge adding to floodwater in summer → Increased input of sediment from bare slopes → Larger load reaches the floodplain and delta more quickly → Channels silted raising channel beds and increasing risk of serious flooding

Deforestation

The Ganges and Brahmaputra rivers have their headwaters in Nepal and Tibet where in recent years the rapidly increasing populations have caused the removal of vast areas of forest to provide fuel, timber and grazing land. In Nepal, 50 per cent of the forest cover that existed in the 1950s has been cut down. The forests play a major role in the hydrology of the upland drainage basins absorbing water from the ground, binding the soil particles and reducing the impact of rain droplets on the ground surface. Overall, the forest cover slows the journey of the water to the river channels reducing the flood risk. The removal of the forest cover has reduced interception and increased landslides, soil erosion and overland flow (Figure 2). The silt and soil is deposited in the river channels causing the raising of the river beds and reducing the capacity of the rivers. It has been estimated that soil is being lost 400 times faster in deforested areas and is raising the river bed of the Brahmaputra by 5cm per year.

Dam building

The building of the Farraka Dam in India in 1971 is blamed for the raising of the river bed of the Hooghly River, a tributary of the Ganges. During the dry season the dam reduces the discharge of the river encouraging sedimentation on the river bed and increasing the risk of flooding.

Global warming

Some people attach considerable blame to global warming and a rise in sea level. The Bangladesh floods in 1998 were notable for their long duration of 56 days. This was blamed by some on the higher sea levels which meant that the surface water on the floodplain took longer to infiltrate. The same people also attribute the especially high rainfall in the Himalayas in 1998 to the increased global temperature.

Urbanization

In Bangladesh, recent development schemes involving the construction of networks of roads and embankments have probably added obstacles to the free drainage of water from the land.

The impact of the flooding in 1998

- Figure 1 shows a map based on a radar-satellite image of the flooding in 1998. Over 57 per cent of the land area was flooded.

- Over 1000 people were killed and millions made homeless.

- In Assam in the north-east more than one million people lost their homes and in the Nalbari district 240 villages were submerged.

- Large amounts of farmland and many properties were washed away.

- An embankment protecting Sandwip, a large coastal island, was breached by a high tide marooning 1,200 families.

- Acute shortages of drinking water and dry food.

- Respiratory infections affected large numbers of people along with outbreaks of diarrhoea and other diseases.

- Short- and long-term risk of serious food shortages with millions of hectares of agricultural land under water.

- As the waters receded brown fields of rotting crops, villages buried in sand and silt and wrecked roads and bridges were left behind. Overall the floods of 1998 cost the country almost $1 billion.

▼ **Figure 3** Flooding in Bangladesh

Case Study | continued

The short-term response to the floods:

By the Bangladesh government
- Distributed money and 400 tonnes of rice
- Provided relief supplies of fresh water, water purification tablets and sanitation services
- Appealed for national unity and calm in the wake of the disaster and the general strike which took place in response to the flooding and accusations that the government failed to get basic goods to the people affected.

By the governments of other countries
Many governments around the world gave aid to Bangladesh during the flood disaster. Some of the donors included:

- The UK with steel bridge materials and 100,000 million tonnes of wheat
- Canada with 12,500 million tonnes of wheat and money for medicines, water tablets, house repair, sanitation and for rehabilitation of farming and fishing
- Egypt with money for medicines
- Saudi Arabia sent two cargo planes with food, medicines, blankets and tents

By The Disaster Forum (a network of aid agencies)
- Provided boats to rescue people and move them and their belongings to higher land
- Supplied medicines to treat and prevent the spread of diseases
- Médecins Sans Frontières used six mobile teams in boats to travel around in one district where the population was literally living in the water
- Supplied clean drinking water by digging and repairing wells
- Monitored the health situation and set up a medical treatment centre
- Distributed fodder for livestock
- Distributed food, plastic sheeting and water purification tablets
- Planned a rehabilitation programme to repair and construct housing and sanitation.

The particular problems in Bangladesh illustrate that floods may not only be the product of extreme physical events such as heavy rain but may have an element of human activity as the cause. The impact of the floods in Bangladesh in 1998 was devastating and the disaster needed help from foreign governments and from aid agencies. This short-term emergency action is described above. However, serious flooding is a common occurrence in Bangladesh and long-term plans have been suggested in order to reduce the severity of the flooding (see pages 42–3). The flooding problem cannot be solved within Bangladesh itself and strategies to control future flooding will need an international approach to tackle issues such as deforestation, dam building and global warming.

Questions

1 a Describe the physical and human causes of the floods in Bangladesh in 1998.
   b Explain the impact of the flooding on the people and landscape of Bangladesh.
   c Using examples, explain the aims of the short-term responses to the flood disaster of 1998.

Investigation

2 Using the Internet or other sources of information investigate another example of serious flooding, such as the Mississippi in 1993.

a Investigate the causes of the flooding and evaluate the extent to which they were a result of physical or human causes.
b Describe and explain the impact of flooding.
c Evaluate the effectiveness of the response to the floods by the local people, local and national governments and any aid agencies involved.

3 What are the similarities and differences in the causes, effects and responses to flooding in the MEDW and the LEDW?

River basin management

- The reasons for river basin management
- Political, environmental and socio-economic issues
- The links between river management and sustainable development

The reasons for river basin management

River basins are managed for two main reasons: water supply and flood prevention. A continuous and clean water supply is needed for domestic, industrial and agricultural uses and sometimes for navigation and the generation of hydroelectric power. The Colorado River case study on page 40-1 is an example of a multipurpose river basin management scheme.

In some river basins the threat of flooding of property and land leads to strategies to prevent or reduce the likelihood of flooding. The scheme for Bangladesh on pages 42-3 is designed to reduce the threat of floods.

In recent years, especially in the developed world, river basin management has taken account of the need for sustainable development of the finite supply of water resources. Water resources need to be managed in a way that will preserve the quality and quantity of water for the future and the natural environment.

Responses and strategies

Up until the late twentieth century strategies of river basin management were often very localized and piecemeal. Individuals, communities and countries would go ahead with plans to solve water problems with no consideration of the impact on other people. For example, the USA has extensively managed the Colorado River drainage basin with little regard for the impact in neighbouring Mexico (see page 40–1). Strategies of river basin management need to have an international perspective where the drainage basin crosses international frontiers. In such situations political factors are important as in the example of Bangladesh where Nepal is partly blamed for the alleged increase in frequency and severity of flooding.

Cost-benefit analysis

River basin mangement schemes inevitably generate both advantages and disadvantages. Developers and financiers weigh up these costs (disadvantages) and benefits (advantages) to decide whether the scheme should go ahead. Such analysis goes beyond the costs in purely financial terms, it also takes into consideration the impacts on the local environment and ecosystems, on local people and on local and national governments. Concern over the environment and the need for sustainable development means that the environmental concerns can outweigh the benefits to a local population.

Strategy	Purpose	Benefits (advantages)	Costs (disadvantages)
Land use regulations	Zonation of floodplain so that land uses such as grazing, that are least likely to be damaged by a floodplain are closest to the river channel	Low cost Promotes most suitable use of land. Quick to implement Effective for long periods	Some losses still likely, e.g. of livestock. Difficult to move settlement and communications
Dams and reservoirs	To reduce flood losses and protect existing land uses. To promote multipurpose use, e.g. for navigation, HEP and recreation	Reduces flooding and costs. Promotes multipurpose use	High costs of construction and maintenance. May take many years to complete. Environmental disadvantages. Sedimentation over time. Displacement of villages by flooding of land
Levées	To increase channel capacity	Reduces flooding by holding more water in the channel	Expensive to strengthen and heighten. Catastrophic flooding if they are breached
Dredging	Increases channel capacity	More water can be contained	Costly, needs to be repeated – only a temporary measure. Affects local ecosystem
Straightening of river channels	Allows faster transfer of water downstream	Reduces flooding in area of strengthening	May increase flooding downstream
Flood insurance	Promotes awareness and attaches costs to individuals if flooding occurs	Spreads costs of flood losses	Often still a heavy reliance on public money to cover flood costs
Warning system	Warn owners of flood dangers Allows advance evacuation or use of sandbags	Less flood damage, property loss and deaths	Of little use if people ignore warnings. A response to problem – does not solve it. Requires good communication network

▲ Figure 1 River basin management strategies

River basin management:

Case Study

the Colorado River, California

The Colorado River (Figure 1) is the most managed river of its size in the world and its water is shared between seventeen million people in Mexico and seven American states. The aridity of the regions supplied by the river make water from the Colorado vital to the economy and well-being of the local populations.

Before large-scale management strategies there were large fluctuations in the discharge of the Colorado River. Snowmelt in spring and summer often caused extensive flooding from April to June and summer thunderstorms caused further variations in the discharge. The floodwater deposited fertile sediments on the floodplains and helped to recharge groundwater supplies. Flood control was one of the main reasons for the first dam proposal in the 1920s. The first dam to be built was the Hoover Dam built on the Colorado and completed in 1935. Since then a further eighteen dams have been built in the river basin and they are all multipurpose schemes to exploit the potential of the resource. The river is used extensively for irrigation, electricity generation, recreation, flood control and domestic and industrial uses.

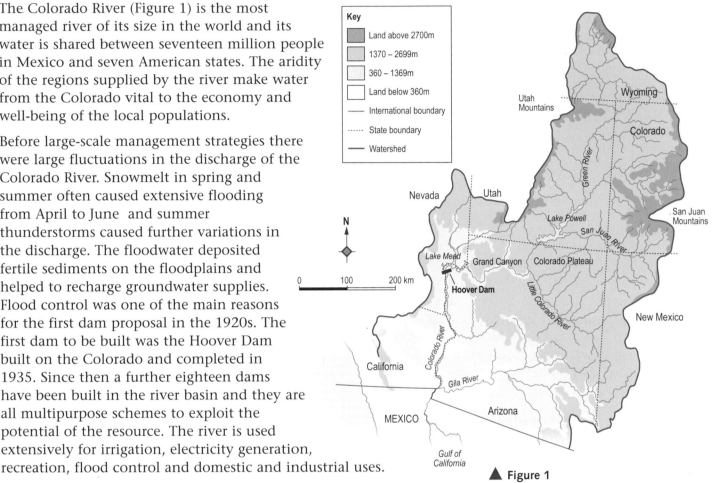

▲ **Figure 1**
The Colorado River

Demand for water continues to grow especially from the agricultural Central Valley of California and from the growing 'Sansan' megalopolis. However, the Colorado River enters the Gulf of Mexico as a mere trickle, almost the entire discharge being used before it reaches its mouth. The demand for water is so great that each state through which the river flows has a water quota called an entitlement. In the lower basin of the Colorado, California is entitled to 58.7 per cent of the water, Arizona to 37.3 per cent and Nevada to 4 per cent. A swift addition sees that this adds up to 100 percent, a source of great tension between California and Mexico. One of the major uses of the river water is for irrigation. The process of irrigation increases the salinity of the water making it undrinkable in the lower stretches. Mexico has been forced to spend $200 million building a desalinization plant in order to be able to use the water.

▼ **Figure 2**
The impact of sedimentation on Lake Mead

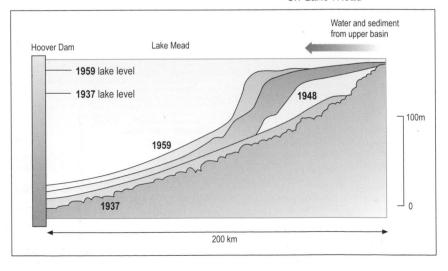

The US Bureau of Reclamation is responsible for controlling the flow of the Colorado and ensuring that flood control is effective. Every year complex calculations take place to establish how much snowmelt will take place and how much space needs to be created in the reservoirs to store the excess water. If insufficient space is created then flooding is likely to occur, but if too much water is released and the reservoirs are not refilled then there is the threat of water shortages later in the year. The release of large quantities of water from the dams leads to considerable erosion of the river channel downstream. The water carries with it very little sediment as this is deposited in Lake Mead, the reservoir created by the Hoover dam (Figure 2). As a result the river has surplus energy for erosion and transportation. Estimates suggest that the Colorado River transports 140 million tonnes of sediment through the Grand Canyon every year. In the past this sediment helped to erode the Grand Canyon and build up the delta at the river mouth with fertile alluvium. Today the equilibrium of the system has been upset.

Advantages

- Growth of tourism now worth ten times more than profits from power generation
- Development of new tourist areas such as Lake Havasu City where old London Bridge was re-erected
- Successful growth of agribusiness based on irrigation producing crops and animals worth over $500 billion a year
- Hydro electric power generating $21 million of electricity supply
- Water supply has encouraged urbanization and population growth

Disadvantages

- Problems of salinity in irrigated areas such as Gila valley caused by evaporation of water from the land surface leaving behind salts
- The high salinity of the water entering Mexico, up to 3 000 parts per million making it unsuitable for drinking and irrigation
- The unfair distribution of water between USA and Mexico
- High costs of water supplies caused by high construction and maintenance costs of dams, reservoirs and aqueducts
- Sedimentation in reservoirs behind dams reducing their lifetime and contributing to more erosion of channels downstream
- Fish, such as squawfish, adapted to turbulent and sediment-laden waters of Colorado prior to damming replaced by clear water species like trout
- Trampling and littering by tourists camping along valley
- Evaporation of water from the reservoirs increasing salinity
- Loss of fertile alluvium once deposited on floodplains
- Retreat of delta starved of deposited material

▲ **Figure 3** The advantages and disadvantages of the Colorado Management Schemes

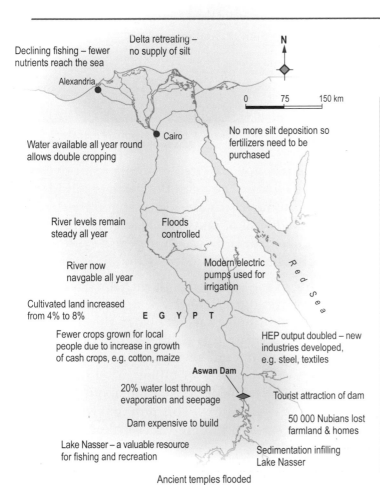

◄ **Figure 4** The advantages and disadvantages of the building of the Aswan High Dam, completed in 1964

Questions

1   Using an atlas:
 a   locate the Colorado basin including its tributaries
 b   identify the seven USA states and Mexico through which the River Colorado flows
 c   investigate the climate details for Arizona
 d   describe the density and distribution of population in the drainage basin
 e   summarize the problems and issues facing those responsible for water management in the area.

2   Explain the costs and benefits of the River Colorado Management Strategies. Who are the winners and losers and why?

Extended prose

3   Study Figure 4. Discuss the costs and benefits of the Aswan High Dam and Lake Nasser to the economy, the environment and the people of Egypt.

River basin management:
Case Study
Bangladesh

Political, environmental and socio-economic issues

In 1959 a water development authority was set up in the then East Pakistan (East Pakistan became Bangladesh in 1971) in response to serious floods in the 1950s. A national Master Plan was prepared which emphasized 'hard' engineering schemes such as embankments, dredging, river diversion, meander cut-offs and by-pass channels. One example is the Meghna-Dhonagoda irrigation project (Figure 1) built between 1964 and 1970 south east of Dhaka. About US$50 million were spent on erecting high embankments to enclose an area of 207km^2 criss-crossed by irrigation channels. In 1980 extra embankments were needed to be built about 3km away from the originals to stop floodwaters penetrating the area.

In July 1987 at the G7 Summit meeting in Paris, major aid donors agreed that the World Bank should co-ordinate efforts by the international community to reduce the impact of flooding in Bangladesh. The World Bank prepared an Action Plan for Flood Control. The plan involved the completion of 3500km of embankments to include compartments for floodwater storage and the facility for controlled flooding to take place. Agriculture would benefit from the supply of water and fertile silt. However, there are many opponents to the scheme who quote the evidence from similar strategies tried along the Mississippi where raised levées and embankments are thought to have made the flooding worse especially when embankments were breached. Such strategies have also increased the need for dredging of the river, the high costs making it inappropriate in Bangladesh, one of the poorest countries in the world. The scheme would also cut off large areas of wetlands valuable for water supply and fishing, a major source of protein in Bangladesh.

Flood control in Bangladesh

Three other flood control measures since 1987 have been suggested:

1 Stream storage by building seven huge dams at an estimated cost of $30–40 billion and taking 40 years to complete. The dams would hold back 10 per cent of the peak flood flow entering Bangladesh.

2 Twelve to fifteen floodplain retention basins to

▲ **Figure 1** Flood prevention – the Dhaka embankment

absorb excess flow diverted from the main rivers and released after the main floodwaters subside. However, some basins already exist and they are often already full of rainwater before the onset of the floods. River diversion may also cause extra silting and dredging costs would be high.

3 Lowering of the water table in the Himalayas by tens of metres during the dry season to create underground storage capacity when the monsoon rains fall. It is estimated that 500 wells pumped at a rate of 1500m^3 per hour for 240 days would extract 21 billion m^3 of water for irrigation leaving space to hold about 10 per cent of the Ganges flow. This proposal would require the co-operation of the Nepalese government.

The relative costs and benefits of the suggested

schemes have led some commentators to suggest that no 'hard' engineering works should take place and no costly flood prevention schemes. In their place they advocate better flood forecasting and warning schemes, improved flood shelters and emergency services to help the victims of flooding. Such schemes would be much cheaper than the building of extensive embankments (Figure 2) or huge dams. They would also use more appropriate technology, in keeping with the knowledge, skills and finances of the communities. They are also less likely to damage or interfere with the many delicate ecosystems in and around the floodplain and delta and would therefore contribute to sustainable development. In addition such schemes avoid political difficulties with neighbouring countries.

In the twenty-first century the approach being adopted includes both 'hard' and 'soft' approaches. Hard engineering structures such as embankments are built to protect densely populated and intensively farmed areas. Low lying, less densely populated areas are used for floodwater storage – a soft approach which also allows natural floodplain processes to occur and benefits soil fertility, fish production and local ecosystems.

Political issues

Bangladesh lies on the delta and lower reaches of the Ganges River. The country has little control over the river that flows through Nepal and India for most of its length. This lack of control and Bangladesh's vulnerability has caused major disagreements between India, Nepal and Bangladesh.

The evidence for deforestation in Nepal and its contribution to the flooding in Bangladesh is not conclusive. Some scientists partly blame the deforestation for the greater flooding, while others point to the large areas of forest cover still intact and the replanting which is taking place. It is also clear that the worst floods have occurred

with exceptionally heavy monsoon rains occurring in all of the drainage basins at the same time.

The Farakka dam on the River Ganges in India has caused considerable controversy. In 1988 the Bangladesh government blamed the Indian government for allowing the flood gates on the Farakka dam to be opened at the height of the monsoon flow. This caused a further flood surge to hit Bangladesh and worsened the already severe floods. The Indian government claimed they had to open the gates to prevent flooding in Calcutta.

In Bangladesh there are also water shortages in the dry season and river water is essential to irrigate crops. However, since 1982 India has extracted more and more water from the River Ganges and increased the storage in the Farakka Dam for use in the dry season. This leaves Bangladesh short of water at critical times of the year – another source of friction between the two countries.

▲ **Figure 2** The building of large embankments on part of the Meghna Irrigation Project

---

Questions

1 Complete a table like the one below to analyse the costs and benefits of the various flood prevention schemes proposed for Bangladesh.

Name and details of scheme	Advantages (benefits)	Disadvantages (costs)

2 Explain why Bangladesh needs international co-operation to plan and implement any scheme to alleviate the flooding problem.

3 Suggest some solutions to the political difficulties currently being faced by those countries through which the River Ganges flows.

River basin management:

Case Study

the UK

In the UK there are two main issues for river basin managers:

- The inequality in supply and demand – the north and west of the UK are the most sparsely populated areas with the least demand for water supplies, but they are also the areas with the highest annual precipitation. In contrast, the south and east are densely populated with almost 50 per cent of the population living south and east of the Severn-Wash line. Demand for water is high but annual precipitation totals are among the lowest in the UK.

- The threat of river flooding – some river basins are prone to flooding which may cause loss of life and considerable damage.

The inequality in supply and demand

In the south and east of England groundwater sources of water are used to their capacity and extraction from surface rivers is at a maximum. Increased demand for water would require additional water supplies to be provided. But how?

The Environment Agency strategy includes three main components.

1. Reservoirs in the north and west to be enlarged and upgraded.

2. Water transfers to take surplus water from the north and west to the south and east.

3. More measures to control demand and encourage the efficient use of water such as education, metering and pricing.

These strategies are to be implemented according to the three principles shown in Figure 3.

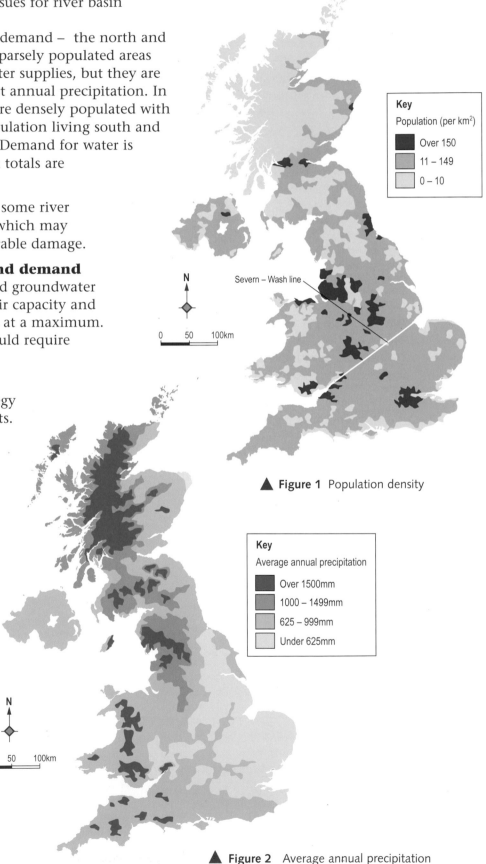

Key

Population (per km²)

- Over 150
- 11 – 149
- 0 – 10

Severn – Wash line

0   50   100km

▲ **Figure 1** Population density

Key

Average annual precipitation

- Over 1500mm
- 1000 – 1499mm
- 625 – 999mm
- Under 625mm

0   50   100km

▲ **Figure 2** Average annual precipitation

The Severn – Thames water transfer scheme

The basic scheme involves the transfer of water from the lower River Severn near Deerhurst to the upper River Thames at Buscot in Wiltshire (Figure 4). The water would move downstream and enter existing reservoirs in the London area. Some water storage would be needed near Deerhurst to allow sediment to settle. Old gravel pits near London could be used for extra storage. The scheme would provide up to 146 million litres a day and capital costs would be £5.7 million (NRA 1994). Two further proposals have been made:

1 Enlarging the Craig Goch reservoir and cutting a tunnel northwards to Llanidloes to transfer the water into the River Severn. Cost £105 million.
2 Cutting a tunnel to Nannerth and transferring water downstream to Ross on Wye where a further tunnel could transfer the water to Deerhurst. Cost £72 million.

However there are potential problems:

Environmental issues

- Mixing 'foreign' water with the Thames water could affect water quality and ecosystems
- Effects on salmon migration along the Severn and Wye rivers
- Pipeline routes affecting conservation and archaeological sites
- Dam enlargement at Craig Goch would affect the Eleynydd Site of Special Scientific Interest (SSSI).

Socio-economic and political issues

- Impact on the economy in the Severn and Wye valleys if recreation and fishing adversely affected
- Costs of the schemes
- Political difficulties of transferring 'Welsh' water to England especially with the recent changes that strengthen devolution.
- Arguments about one part of a country having to suffer environmental damage to provide water outside of the area.

Principle 1: Sustainable development
There should be no long-term environmental deterioration due to water resource development and water use
Principle 2: Precautionary principle
Where significant environmental damage may occur, but knowledge is incomplete, decisions should err on the side of caution
Principle 3: Demand management
Management measure to control waste and consumption, e.g. water meters, should be employed

▲ **Figure 3** Three principles of the Environment Agency's strategy for water provision

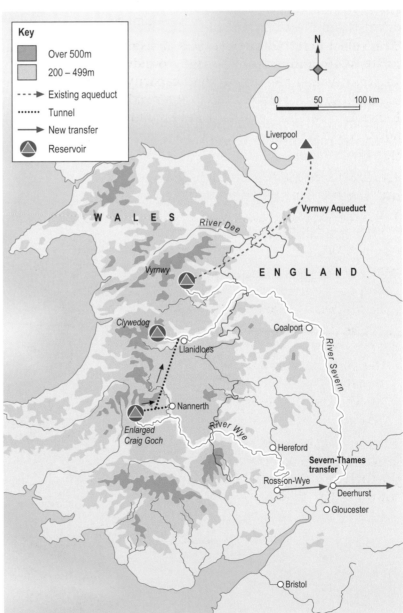

▲ **Figure 4** River Severn to River Thames water transfer

River basin management:
Case Study

the River Tees, NE England

The links between river management and sustainable development

The source of the River Tees is the slopes of Cross Fell, the highest summit in the Pennines at 893m. The area receives over 2000mm of rainfall each year and infiltration is low on the impermeable rock surfaces and saturated peat. Rainfall reaches the river very quickly, often in a matter of minutes so lag times are small and peak discharges often high. The Tees has the characteristics of a 'flashy' river regime and is prone to flooding, especially after the thaw of winter snowfall. The flood threat is made worse by the steepness of the river channel. Water enters the channel quickly and transfer downstream is also fast creating the 'Tees wave' or 'Tees roll' when the water can rise as much as a metre in 15 minutes.

There is a long history of serious flooding along the River Tees especially in the lower course that is also densely populated and the site for many industries including iron and steel making and the massive ICI chemical works. There is a huge demand for water for domestic, industrial and agricultural uses. In addition the pollution from industries and people along the Tees estuary devastated the river wiping out the salmon and trout populations and causing a massive deterioration in water quality. Up until the late twentieth century sustainable development was not a priority and developments were allowed to take place with little concern for the impact on the local environment. Hence serious air, land and water pollution all occurred.

Management strategies (Figure 2) along the River Tees have attempted to:
- reduce the impact of floods
- supply a growing water demand
- reduce water pollution and improve water quality
- increase the recreational use of water.

▼ **Figure 1** Aerial view of Yarm

▼ **Figure 2**   The River Tees drainage basin

In the Upper Tees basin:

- Cow Green reservoir was completed in 1970. The reservoir holds 40 million cubic metres of water and is held back by a huge concrete and earth dam, 21m high. The reservoir regulates the river flow by storing excess water and releasing water in times of low flow to cope with the amounts abstracted in the lower reaches. The reservoir also helps to control the peak flows in the river reducing the threat of flooding
- Grassholme and Selset reservoirs on the River Lune, and the Hury and Baldershead reservoirs on the River Balder, both tributaries of the River Tees

- New development actively discouraged in low-lying areas to reduce the flood risk
- A tunnel connecting Kielder water via the River Tyne to the River Tees is used to add water to the River Tees at times of low flow

The building of reservoirs has advantages for flood prevention and provision of water supply. However, they can be environmentally damaging flooding large areas of land and altering the local climate and ecology of an area.

The Yarm flood defence system

Flooding in Yarm can be traced back to 1575 and over the years there has been extreme damage to the town. A defence scheme has been implemented to cope with the 100-year flood coupled with a high tide and to enhance the riverside environment. Final decisions were taken only after extensive consultation with local interest groups including councils, local people and environmental organizations. The defence system cost £2.1 million and includes:

- reinforced concrete walls clad with stone around the boundary of Yarm
- flood gates to allow access by people and vehicles
- landscaped earth embankment to protect Yarm School
- gabions to reduce erosion along embankments
- pipes to redirect the flow of Skyterring Beck rather than a surface channel
- street lighting, flower beds, street furniture, fishing platforms to enhance environment and amenity value costing £600,000.

In the Lower Tees:

- Improved flood warning systems
- New developments discouraged on unprotected and low lying areas
- River, sea and tidal defences and operation of sluice gates monitored
- The Tees Barrage operated to minimize the risk from both river and tidal flooding. The barrage, opened in 1995 has improved water quality and the amenity value along the 17km of the lower Tees. Salmon have now returned to the River Tees
- Improved navigation through dredging
- Meanders cut. The Mandale Loop was cut through in 1810 shortening the river by 4km and improving navigation

- New sewerage treatment plants and strict laws on dumping and discharges implemented
- Floodplain zoning allows the river to flood naturally and reduces the need for artificial flood protection schemes. The Tees barrage has been designed not to damage the delicate estuarine ecology of the Tees and salmon leaps have been included to allow the migration of the fish upstream. Legislation and new water treatment works have contributed to cleaning up the river and improving the freshwater and marine ecology. Teesmouth and Seal Sands in particular are world renowned sites for seals and migratory birds. Recent management of the area is ensuring the area retains this status and that sustainable development is achieved

Questions

1 a Describe and explain the various methods of river basin management along the River Tees.

b Produce a cost-benefit analysis for the management strategies

c To what extent do the management strategies fulfil the requirements for sustainable development?

Investigation

2 Select a local river and investigate from a variety of sources the river management strategies used. Draw up a table to show a cost-benefit analysis and analyse the effectiveness of the strategies.

Extended prose

3 With reference to one or more examples, describe how and why strategies of river basin management are different between LEDCs and MEDCs.

4 What are the socio-economic, environmental and political factors that need to be considered in projects of river basin management? Illustrate your ideas with reference to case studies.

Chapter 1 Questions

1 a Study the photograph of a river on the slopes of the Andes in southern Chile.

i	Describe the channel features shown which suggest river deposition.	(3 marks)
ii	Why is this river likely to have large variations in discharge between winter and summer?	(2 marks)
iii	Explain how variations in discharge can lead to deposition in the river channel.	(3 marks)

b Explain the formation of channel landforms of deposition which are most likely to develop
at or near the mouth of a river. (7 marks)

Total: 15 marks

2 a Explain why flooding is a severe hazard for people living in some river basins. (10 marks)

b Why are large river management schemes usually undertaken for a variety of reasons
rather than just one? Illustrate your answer by reference to an example or examples. (10 marks)

Total: 20 marks

A note on timing
You are expected to answer question 1 in about 15 minutes. You are expected to answer
question 2 in about 40 minutes, spending an equal length of time on both parts.

Chapter **2** Climatic hazards and change

Antarctica – beauty between the blizzards in this cold desert

Costs and benefits of weather and climate – Tropical Monsoon and Cool Temperate Western Maritime

Climatic hazards

Climatic change at the micro scale

Climatic change at other scales

Costs and benefits of weather and climate

- General atmospheric processes which affect climates
- The Tropical Monsoon climate
- The Cool Temperate Western Maritime climate
- Opportunities and constraints for human activities

General atmospheric processes which affect climates

Solar energy

The Earth's weather systems are driven by energy from the sun. The light rays (short wave radiation) from the sun which penetrate through the atmosphere are absorbed on contact with the Earth's surface. As the Earth's surface absorbs energy, its temperature rises and this heat is radiated into the atmosphere as long wave radiation. The amount of heat energy created varies with latitude and seasons.

Near the Equator the sun shines at a high angle in the sky throughout the year. The greater the angle of the sun, the more concentrated the radiation intensity is per unit area as it strikes the Earth's surface (Figure 1). The short and direct approach of the light rays towards the surface means less loss through scattering and reflection as the rays pass through gases and dust in the atmosphere. More and stronger light energy reaching the surface leads to high rates of insolation. Together with a consistent twelve hours of daylight throughout the year, temperatures in places near the Equator are uniformly hot – around 27°C in every month.

In temperate latitudes the sun is at a lower angle in the sky. Less energy is received per unit area of the surface than in the tropics. Also the longer approach of the sun's rays to the surface means that the percentage of energy lost due to absorption and reflection is higher. Seasonal variations in the amount of insolation are more marked. Summer and winter seasons develop. In summer daylight is longer than twelve hours which gives more hours of incoming solar radiation. This, combined with the sun's higher angle in the sky, can lead to temperatures as high as those in the tropics on

cloudless days. However in winter, daylight everywhere in temperate latitudes is less than twelve hours. The sun's low angle means limited heating power for under half the day. Annual temperature ranges are high, especially in continental locations away from the winter warming influences of the seas and oceans.

So that the Equator and tropics do not become progressively hotter or the Poles and high latitudes progressively colder, a re-distribution of heat energy must constantly take place. Some is transported in the ocean currents. One example is the Gulf Stream feeding warm waters into the North Atlantic Drift, which has a major influence upon the weather and climate of the British Isles and neighbouring areas of western and northern Europe. The rest (over half) is transferred by winds both in the upper atmosphere and at or near the surface.

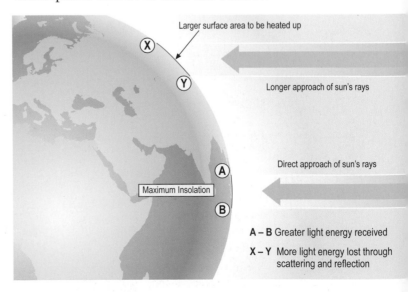

▲ **Figure 1** How the amount of insolation varies with latitude

▼ **Figure 2** A sky full of cumulus clouds –
always an indication of rising air

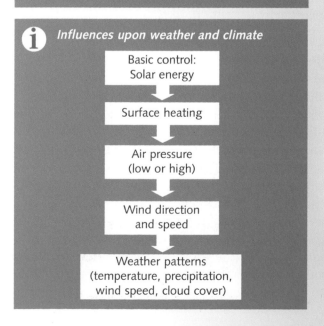

ⓘ Jet streams
*These are transfers of air in the upper
atmosphere, on average above 10,000m
(the height at which jet planes fly). As
they move from Equator to Poles, their
general direction of flow is from west to
east because of deflection caused by the
Earth's rotation. This is why the flying
time for a plane from the UK to the USA
is longer than on the return journey.*

ⓘ Influences upon weather and climate

```
Basic control:
Solar energy
   ↓
Surface heating
   ↓
Air pressure
(low or high)
   ↓
Wind direction
and speed
   ↓
Weather patterns
(temperature, precipitation,
wind speed, cloud cover)
```

Surface heating, pressure and winds

Variations in surface heating cause differences in air pressure. Hot air is lighter and less dense than cold air and has a tendency to rise vertically through the atmosphere. This is known as convection. Cumulus clouds show this process in operation (Figure 2). An area of low pressure forms at the surface in those places where the air is vigorously rising to high levels in the atmosphere, often up to 10,000m or higher. The concentrated heating of the Earth's surface over the Equator is the heat source for the global system of convection and the basis for the world pattern of pressure and winds. Rising hot air at the Equator creates the Equatorial Low pressure belt. Equatorial hot air is transferred towards the poles in high level winds, known as jet streams. The air sinks in polar regions to form the Polar Highs. Air must be transferred by surface winds to feed the rising air at the Equator. Winds would be expected to blow from north to south in the northern hemisphere and from south to north in the southern hemisphere, but they are affected by the Earth's rotation from west to east which deflects them so that they blow from an easterly direction (Figure 3).

▼ **Figure 3** A simplified summary of the global pattern of heat and air transfers

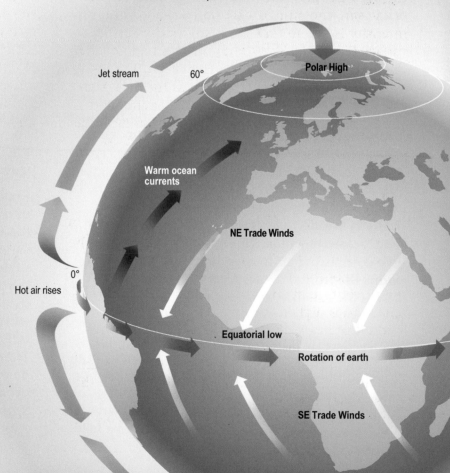

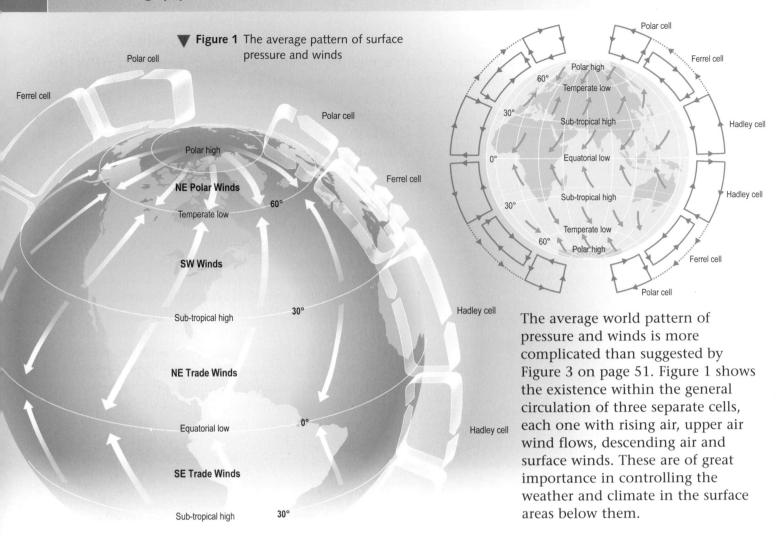

▼ **Figure 1** The average pattern of surface pressure and winds

The average world pattern of pressure and winds is more complicated than suggested by Figure 3 on page 51. Figure 1 shows the existence within the general circulation of three separate cells, each one with rising air, upper air wind flows, descending air and surface winds. These are of great importance in controlling the weather and climate in the surface areas below them.

The effects of high and low pressure on climate

In the two zones of rising air where low pressure forms – at the Equator and in temperate latitudes between 50° and 60° north and south of the Equator – considerable precipitation occurs. When air rises, it cools; moisture condenses and produces clouds. Continued rising, cooling and condensing increases the sizes of water droplets and ice crystals in the cloud until they are released as precipitation. The British Isles lie in a Temperate Low pressure belt where warm tropical air, transported by south-westerly winds, meets cold polar air, transported by north-easterly winds. The resulting collision of the two contrasting air masses along the polar front forms the frontal depressions which are driven across the Atlantic towards the British Isles during all seasons of the year.

In the two zones of descending air where high pressure forms – around 30° north and south of the Equator and near to the poles – little precipitation falls. The molecules of air are heated up as they are forced down through the thicker air of the lower atmosphere. With warming, moisture can be held more comfortably in the air, which makes precipitation less likely. The force of the descending air prevents the uplift of air currents from the surface, even in those areas where surface temperatures are high. Below the sub-tropical high pressure belt are the world's hot deserts and below the Polar Highs are cold deserts such as Antarctica (page 49).

Cool Temperate Western Maritime climate is the official name for the type of climate experienced in the British Isles. What characterizes its weather is variety, but apart from having higher temperatures in summer when the sun shines overhead in the northern hemisphere, weather patterns are similar throughout the year. This is because its location is within the temperate zone which remains under the influence of low pressure and westerly winds all year. The low pressure and westerly wind pattern remains dominant despite the apparent migration of the overhead sun into the southern hemisphere between September and March, which drags the pressure and wind belts a few degrees further south behind it.

Seasonal climates

Other types of climate have patterns of weather which are highly seasonal. One example is the Tropical Monsoon, which affects India, in which there is a great difference between wet and dry seasons in summer and winter respectively. The apparent migration of the overhead sun between hemispheres causes differences in pressure. This reverses wind directions and changes air flows from offshore to onshore with enormous consequences for the amount of precipitation. Figure 2 is a highly simplified summary of the world distribution of pressure and winds in June when the sun is overhead at the Tropic of Cancer and India has the wet monsoon.

ℹ The difference between weather and climate
Weather is made up of the day-to-day variations in temperature, precipitation, wind and cloud. Climate is the long-term average of these different weather conditions. The average is taken over at least a 30-year period so that the effects of fluctuations in weather , which always occur, are evened out.

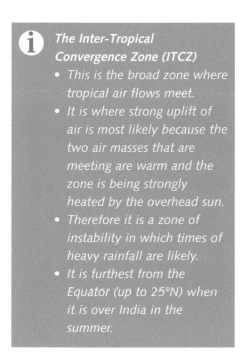

ℹ The Inter-Tropical Convergence Zone (ITCZ)
- *This is the broad zone where tropical air flows meet.*
- *It is where strong uplift of air is most likely because the two air masses that are meeting are warm and the zone is being strongly heated by the overhead sun.*
- *Therefore it is a zone of instability in which times of heavy rainfall are likely.*
- *It is furthest from the Equator (up to 25°N) when it is over India in the summer.*

▼ **Figure 2** A simplified summary of the world pattern of pressure and winds in June

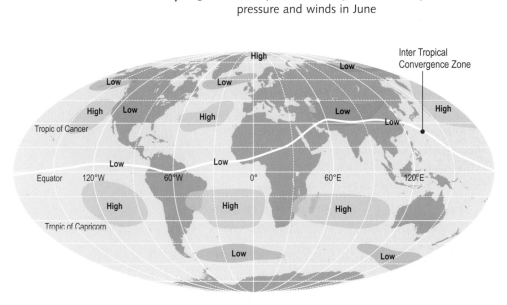

▼ **Figure 3** World distributions of Tropical Monsoon and Cool Temperate Western Maritime types of climate

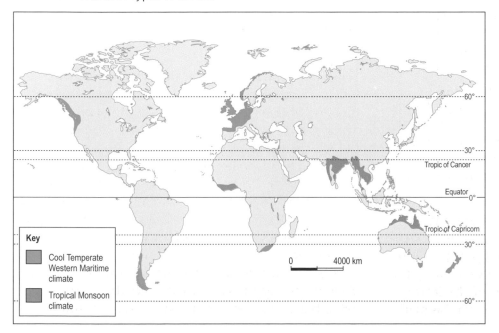

Key
- Cool Temperate Western Maritime climate
- Tropical Monsoon climate

0   4000 km

Questions

1 Why are places in the tropics hotter than those in temperate latitudes?

2 a Describe the world pattern of pressure in June from Figure 2.

 b In what ways is the June pattern different from the average pattern of pressure in Figure 1?

 c Explain the world pattern of pressure in June.

3 Outline the differences in pressure and winds between latitudes 50–60° and 20–30° north of the Equator.

The Tropical Monsoon climate

The term 'monsoon' is derived from an Arabic word meaning 'season'. It is applied to large-scale reversals of wind directions in different seasons. Although these strong reversals occur in many different places in the tropics (such as in China and neighbouring areas of eastern Asia, northern Australia and coastal regions of West Africa, which also have monsoon type climates) they are best developed and their effects are most noticeable in the Indian subcontinent. It is the Indian monsoon which will form the basis for examining the characteristics, causes and effects of a tropical monsoon type of climate which follows. However, even within India there are wide variations between regions in the length of the wet season, the date it begins and the amount of rain that falls.

Characteristics

Although the greatest contrast is between the wet season (which stretches in most places from the end of May to the end of September) and the drought experienced during the rest of the year, it is possible to recognize three seasons by taking temperature into account as well.

- **March to May – the very hot dry season**
  Temperatures rise to their highest levels of the year before the arrival of the rains (see Figure 1). The heat is almost unbearable particularly on the interior plains of the north.

- **June to September – the hot, wet season**
  Over much of India at least 80 per cent of the annual precipitation total falls during these four summer months. Rarely is the rainfall continuous; rather there is a pattern of pulses of very heavy rain inter-spaced by drier periods. Temperatures drop by a few degrees to give people some release from the great heat, but the high humidity still makes it feel uncomfortable.

- **October to February – the warm or hot, dry season**
  Once the wet monsoon season ends, rain falls only occasionally. The generally clear skies allow pleasantly warm temperatures by day but nights can be cool in the mid-winter months.

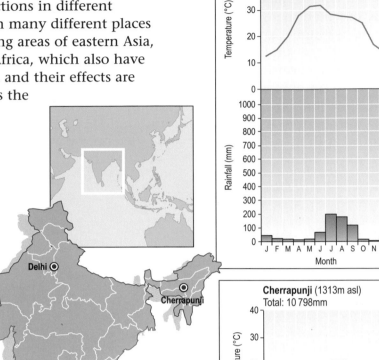

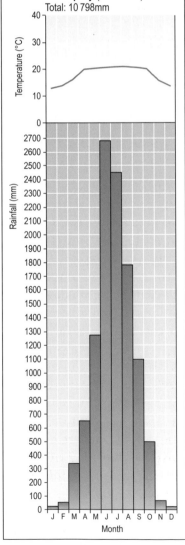

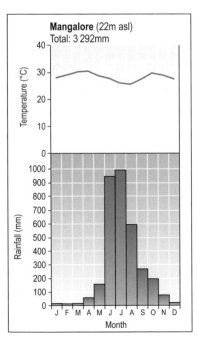

▲ **Figure 1** Climatic graphs for three weather stations in India with a tropical monsoon climate. Variations in temperatures and precipitation reflect location and altitude

▼ **Figure 2** The wet monsoon in India in mid-summer

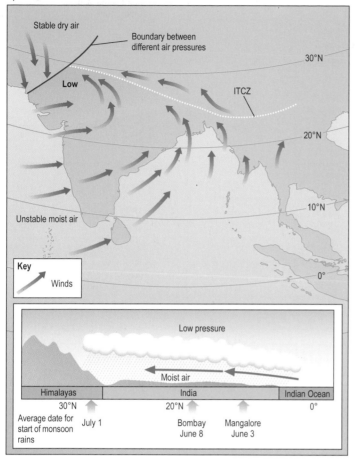

▼ **Figure 3** The dry monsoon in India in mid-winter

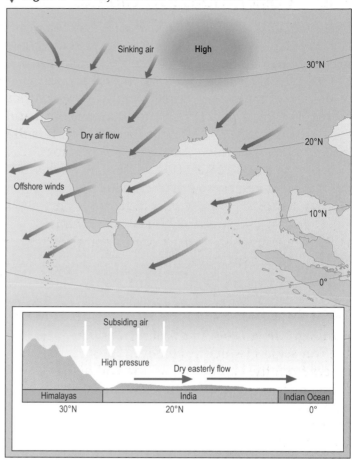

Causes

In mid summer in the northern hemisphere, the changing pattern of surface heating from the sun, which is now overhead north of the Equator, displaces the Equatorial Low and the Inter-Tropical Convergence Zone (ITCZ) northwards. Over northern India a thermal low forms in response to intense surface heating, magnified by the effects of the great size of the Asian landmass. When these two areas of low pressure (Equatorial and thermal) merge into one, air is sucked in from the south west to replace the air that is rising and approaches most of India from the south and south east (Figure 2). This air is moist after having crossed large expanses of ocean. Disturbances in the ITCZ, some of which are caused by variations in air flows within the jet streams, lead to downpours. The downpours are exceptionally heavy where the unstable maritime tropical air meets high relief. Cherrapunji is one of the wettest places on earth, and has unimaginable amounts of rainfall, even for residents of the Lake District and North Wales! The north west of India is much drier than the north east. The wet monsoon winds reach there last and there is more chance of the sub-tropical high pressure with its sinking air, centred over Arabia, spreading its influence eastwards.

From mid-September onwards the subsiding air over northern India is able to re-establish itself after the Equatorial Low and ITCZ have retreated southwards. The Equatorial Low moves south of the Equator which allows the usual world pattern of North East Trade Winds feeding into the Equatorial Low to resume. These are an offshore air flow and give dry weather over most of India. Exceptionally high pressure establishes itself over central Asia in mid-winter due to the coldness of the world's largest landmass so that the outward flow of air from Asia is very pronounced.

ⓘ *Cherrapunji, India*
One of the 'wettest places in the world'
Mean annual rainfall: 10 798mm (Sty Head, the Lake District: 3 250mm)
Wettest month June: 2 695mm
Wettest ever year: 1861 – 22 625mm (a world record – 905 inches or over 75 feet of rain!)

The Cool Temperate Western Maritime climate

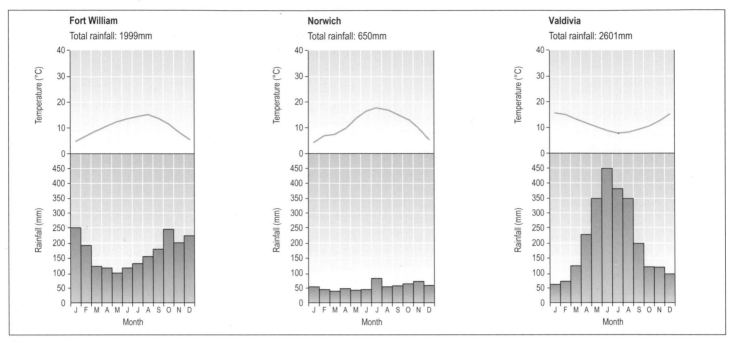

Fort William
Total rainfall: 1999mm

Norwich
Total rainfall: 650mm

Valdivia
Total rainfall: 2601mm

▲ **Figure 1** Climatic graphs for two UK weather stations and for Valdivia, one of the wettest places in southern Chile

Areas with this type of climate are located approximately 40° to 60° north and south of the Equator, although the tapering of the continents in the southern hemisphere means that they extend through a narrower range of latitude there. The extent of these areas inland is largely controlled by relief, which blocks the maritime influences from reaching the middle and eastern sides of the land masses. The extent is widest in Europe where lowlands allow the westerly winds to spread their influence further inland and, in any case, maritime influence on temperatures is particularly strong here because of the great relative warmth of the North Atlantic Drift. In contrast, in both Canada and Chile the presence of the Rockies and Andes mountain ranges restricts the extent of this type of climate to narrow coastal strips.

▼ **Figure 2** It can be very wet in southern Chile

Characteristics

The weather is changeable without marked seasonal differences. Cloud and precipitation are frequent so that long periods of drought and sun, day after day, such as those experienced in the summers of 1995 and 1996 in the UK, represent truly exceptional events. Although regular, only rarely does the rain fall with the intensity that is considered normal in the tropics. Equally, extremes of temperature, either very hot or very cold, are also rare. Summers are usually described as warm and the mean temperature for the warmest month typically lies between 12° and 20°C depending upon latitude and location. Winters are cool or mild, but not cold. Although on some days in winter temperatures may never rise above freezing point, the maritime effect means that the average temperature of the coldest month is typically a few degrees above freezing point. As a result, the annual range of temperature is low and described as equable (i.e. reasonably equal temperatures between seasons). Regular strong winds are a feature of the weather notably in west coast locations.

Causes

High annual and regular monthly precipitation occur because of these areas' locations within the belt which is dominated by low pressure for all the year. The reason for low pressure formation in temperate latitudes is different from that in the tropics. The polar and tropical air masses, which are transporting air from the zones of high pressure to the north and south respectively, have different characteristics. They meet but do not mix. The warm tropical air, being less dense, is forced above the cold polar air along the polar front. Circulations of low pressure develop at points where the air is rising most vigorously and where this coincides with waves in the polar front and active jet streams above. The typical frontal depression with its leading warm front and trailing cold front is created. A line of these forms over the Pacific and Atlantic Oceans and they are driven by the prevailing westerly wind circulation from west to east towards and over land areas.

These frontal depressions gain plenty of moisture from their long sea journeys, most of which falls as precipitation at the two points where the warm air is being uplifted most forcibly. One point is above the warm front which creates a sheet of stratus cloud from which a period of rain and drizzle, lasting for several hours, can be expected in places ahead of the warm front. The second is above the cold front, where the more vigorous uplift of warm air leads to the formation of cumulus clouds. Along an active cold front, precipitation, although shorter, is likely to be heavier and it may be accompanied by thunder and lightning. As frontal depressions move eastwards and develop, the faster moving cold front may catch up and join up with the warm front to create an occluded front along which the considerable uplift of air leads to pulses of heavy rain.

▼ **Figure 3** Formation and development of a frontal depression

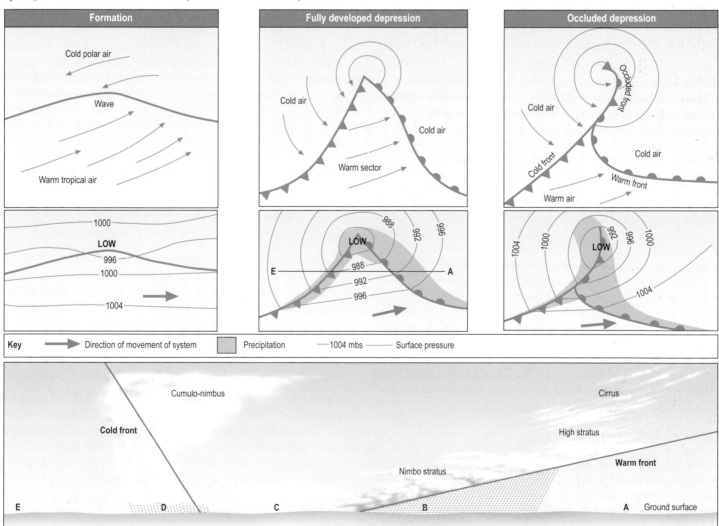

▲ **Figure 4** Cross-section of a frontal depression

The chances of precipitation do not end with the passage of the cold front. A polar air mass follows, either Polar Maritime with an air flow from the north west or Arctic if the air flow is from the north. The cold air is warmed up by its passage south over warmer sea surfaces which encourages the air to rise, leading to the formation of cumulus clouds. These are shower clouds, from which unpleasant mixes of rain, hail and snow may fall, sometimes accompanied by thunder and lightning and driving winds. Coasts and uplands in the west and north of the British Isles are the areas affected most.

Maritime influences exert an enormous control over temperatures. All places with this type of climate have warmer winters than would be expected for their latitudes. The winter sun is at a low angle in the sky and in mid-winter there is daylight for only one third of the day. If only latitude and insolation are taken into account, day-time temperatures below freezing point would be common in mid-winter.

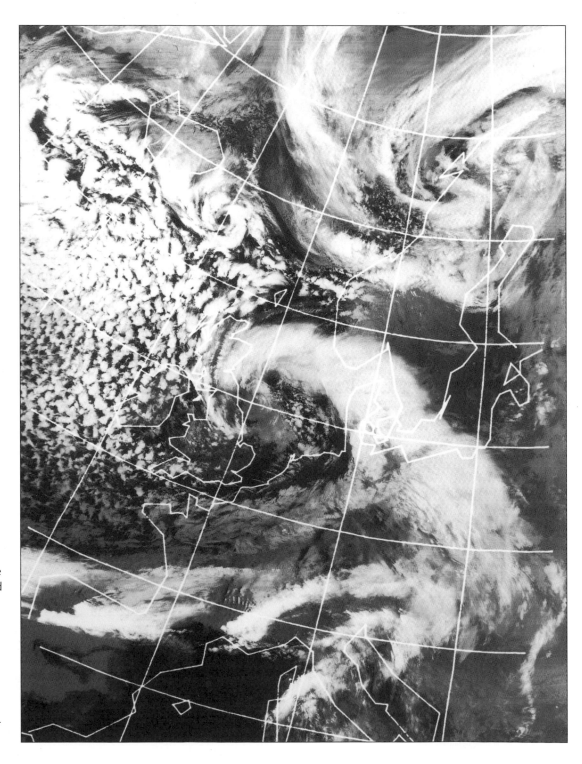

Figure 1 ▶

Satellite image of a frontal depression. The centre of the depression can be recognized by the swirl of cloud over eastern Scotland. The line of continuous cloud from this centre marks the line of the front. The white dots in the rear of the depression to the west of the British Isles are shower clouds formed by surface warming of the polar air mass.

However, the seas and oceans are great stores of heat. In water the energy is distributed through its mass and it cools more slowly; also as water cools at the surface it becomes more dense than that below it and sinks, only to be replaced at the surface by warmer water from below. The westerly winds have had long sea journeys and transfer some of the ocean warmth to adjacent land areas in both hemispheres. In the northern hemisphere the warming effect is increased by the presence of warm ocean currents, the North Pacific and North Atlantic Drifts, over which the westerly winds pass before making landfall. The world's greatest positive temperature anomalies occur in these areas – up to 12°C warmer for its latitude off British Columbia in Canada and an enormous 20°C warmer off Norway in north-west Europe.

Summers are cooler than expected for the latitude. Although there are long hours of daylight and also incoming solar radiation in mid-summer, there are many days with cloud. Reflection and absorption by the clouds reduces the percentage of sunlight which reaches the surface and is available for conversion into heat energy. Over the oceans, rises in surface temperature are slower as more water mixing takes place than on land; land surfaces are also darker anyway thereby absorbing more light.

Causes of the British Isles climate

As for the day-to-day variations which are characteristic of this type of climate in the British Isles, there are several causes.

- The passage of a typical frontal depression involves several changes in temperature, cloud cover and precipitation.

- Not all frontal depressions bring the same weather. Some are shallow with weak fronts marked by a line cloud without rain. Others are deep with strong winds up to hurricane force accompanied by heavy and prolonged periods of rain. Some pass through quickly, while others are blocked 24–48 hours giving one or two days of continuous rain to places below the fronts.

- These depressions lie in the 'battle ground' between tropical and polar air masses and between maritime and continental air. The five air masses which affect the British Isles and bring varied patterns of weather are shown in Figure 2.

- Occasional interludes of anticyclonic (high pressure) weather are drier. Also there are many variations in anticyclonic weather such as between day and night and between winter and summer.

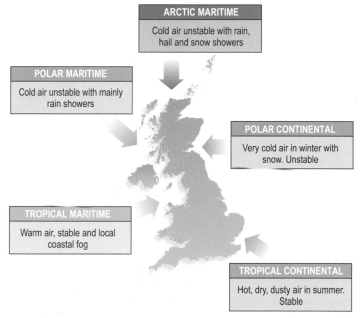

▲ **Figure 2** The five air masses affecting the British Isles

---

Questions

1 a From an atlas, outline the differences in location between Fort William and Norwich.
  b Compare their climates.
  c Give reasons for the climatic differences between them.

2 **Statement 1:** 'Seasonal contrasts are great in areas with a tropical monsoon climate'.

   Statement 2: 'Day-to-day variations are more noticeable than seasonal contrasts in the Cool Temperate Western Maritime climate'.

  a Explain each statement in turn.
  b To what extent is each one valid?

Investigation

3 a Why is anticyclonic weather in the British Isles usually dry?
  b Explain the following characteristics of anticyclonic weather in winter: radiation fog; frost; cold weather by day.
  c Why do summer heatwaves sometimes occur?

Opportunities and constraints for human activities

Tropical monsoon climate

In the tropics temperatures are always sufficiently high for cultivation. So water availability from rainfall is the only climatic control for what can be grown and when. The wet monsoon breaks at almost the same time each year after eight months of little rain. Agricultural practices are geared to its expected time of arrival and average amount of summer rain.

The crop most associated with Asia and the monsoon is padi rice. Rice is a water-loving crop and the concentrated and heavy monsoon rains meet the requirement for flooded fields. On the flat, alluvial floodplains of the big Asian rivers, such as the Ganges, where flooding is common, every piece of land is intensively cultivated. This has created a patchwork of small fields. Rice farming supports the world's highest rural densities of population, for example in the Ganges valley and delta in India and Bangladesh.

▲ **Figure 1** Cultivation of padi rice, which requires fields of standing water for growth

The annual cycle of rice farming	
May	Just before the wet monsoon arrives, the nursery beds are prepared.
June	With the first monsoon rains, the rice seeds are sown in nurseries while the mud is levelled off in the main padi fields.
July	The rice is transplanted into the flooded padi fields where it grows rapidly to keep its head above water levels, topped up by the periodic monsoon downpours.
November/ December	Rice is harvested from fields which have been drained dry after the monsoon rains have stopped.

Tea bushes thrive on the 'bucketfuls of water' (literally) that the monsoon winds deposit on mountain slopes in Assam and around Darjeeling in north-east India – names forever associated with types of tea. Where the annual rainfall is lower in north-west India, wheat replaces rice as the staple cereal crop.

▲ **Figure 2** Part of Asia's rice-bowl where no flat land is wasted

Although a great provider for India's farmers, monsoon rains are highly variable from year to year. Out of the 100 years between 1899 and 1999, more than 15 of them were major drought years in which the rainfall total was at least 25 per cent lower than average. These droughts occur when the summer monsoon breaks late and when the number and length of the break periods without rain increase. Great hardship ensues for farmers and their families, who can only manage to eke out an existence in the wet years. Crop yields are reduced and in extreme cases the crops fail altogether. Perversely there are also years in which the monsoon rains are excessively heavy so crops are washed away and fields, farms and villages are cut off. Worst of all is when a cyclone hits India. Tropical cyclones are apt to develop over the Bay of Bengal in October and November during the retreat of the monsoon. One hit Orissa state in late October 1999.

INDIA IN THE EYE OF 'BIBLICAL' CYCLONE

A 'SUPERCYCLONE' of 'biblical' proportions has hit India's east coast, destroying the homes of more than 1.5 million people. Villages up to 15km inland of the Bengal Sea yesterday remained under water, and power and roads to much of the state of Orissa remained cut. At least 200 fishermen have been reported missing and more than 4,000 people are feared dead after being caught in winds reported to have reached 260 k/p/h.

Continuing storms meant that Indian air force helicopters were yesterday unable to deliver food and fuel to the affected areas. Troops and medical teams trying to clear roads to the region have been unable to reach those needing help. As well as cutting off power, the storm has cut water supplies and almost all communications. The cyclone struck around noon on Friday and is now heading further inland and slowly weakening. The state government of Orissa has sent an emergency request to Delhi asking for massive relief.

The Observer, 31 October 1999

▲ Figure 3

▲ **Figure 4** The leading edge of the cyclone beginning to wreak havoc along the eastern coast of India. Its eye is clearly visible out in the Bay of Bengal.

Cool Temperate Western Maritime climates

People living in the UK and western Europe are relatively sheltered from extreme events such as cyclones. Also there is no equivalent to the blistering heat of India during May before the monsoon breaks which makes any kind of human exertion difficult and uncomfortable. The general absence of extreme winter cold allows construction work and outdoor activities to carry on throughout the winter with nothing more than short interruptions.

Effects on farming

The people most closely affected by weather and climate are farmers. Many of the regional variations in types of farming have a climatic origin, even if at the local level the decisions of farmers and local physical variations in relief, soils and drainage are of more importance. Pastoral farming is more dominant in the wet west than in the drier east of the British Isles. Arable farming dominates in the east wherever extensive lowlands exist such as in East Anglia and the Vale of York. In the cooler north, sheep become much more important than cattle and a more restricted range of crops can be grown, reduced largely to a choice between barley, potatoes and turnips in north-east Scotland where the growing season is short. Farmers in East Anglia have a much wider choice of both cereal and root crops, including wheat and sugar beet. Warmer southern summers give higher yields and therefore greater profitability.

Other activities

Some other activities relate closely to climate. Dams for water supply are mainly located in the wet west where there are also uplands. Water is 'exported' from Wales to the urban and industrial lowland in the Midlands and Merseyside.

The distribution of seaside holiday resorts around the coasts of the UK is far from even. The greatest concentration is along the south coast (including Bournemouth, see page 217) which receives the highest summer temperatures (above 17°C in July) and longest hours of sunshine. The south coast also has the advantage of mild winters and early springs. A complementary function of coastal resorts is residential housing, particularly for retirement.

The highly variable day-to-day weather conditions create problems for organizers of events and for commercial activities which are heavily dependent on the weather. Summer sporting events, notably cricket Test Matches and the Wimbledon tennis tournament, are obvious cases in point.

▼ Figure 1   Summary of some of the effects of climate on land uses in the British Isles

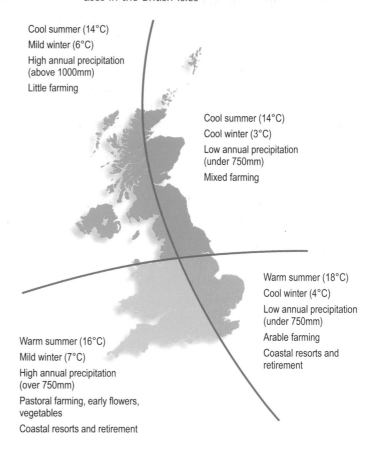

Cool summer (14°C)
Mild winter (6°C)
High annual precipitation (above 1000mm)
Little farming

Cool summer (14°C)
Cool winter (3°C)
Low annual precipitation (under 750mm)
Mixed farming

Warm summer (18°C)
Cool winter (4°C)
Low annual precipitation (under 750mm)
Arable farming
Coastal resorts and retirement

Warm summer (16°C)
Mild winter (7°C)
High annual precipitation (over 750mm)
Pastoral farming, early flowers, vegetables
Coastal resorts and retirement

▼ Figure 2   Rural Shropshire from the Long Mynd on the western side of the UK

Dates have to be fixed well in advance and there are both economic losses and personal disappointments if they coincide with periods of wet summer weather. Seaside resorts are more heavily dependent on day visitors than they used to be. Therefore the summer's weather on weekends and during school holidays often determines whether the season is good or bad for the shopkeepers and fairground operators. When the UK enjoyed two hotter and sunnier summers in 1995 and 1996 than normal, bookings for UK holidays increased and brought a temporary halt to the rise in numbers going to Mediterranean resorts where summer sun can be almost guaranteed. However, that did not help the holiday companies and the airlines. The return of unpredictable summer weather since, in other words normal British summers, has meant that there is surplus summer accommodation in most resorts.

Businesses which have operations that are weather sensitive buy in weather forecasts from the Meteorological Office or private companies. Obvious examples are those connected with transport since the efficient operation of ships, planes, trains and motor vehicles is affected by many different aspects of the weather. Also someone working for your local council has to decide, for example, about the likelihood of ground frost and ice in the winter and whether or not to call out the road gritters.

The accuracy and reliability of weather forecasts has greatly improved. Supermarkets home in on changes in weather. They change or move their stock around according to weather predictions. If hot weather is forecast the space for all kinds of drinks, ice cream and salad produce is increased.

▲ **Figure 3** Haweswater in the Lake District at the end of August 1995

 Reminders of occasional extreme weather events in the UK
Lynmouth flood in Devon in August 1952
* *Over 250mm rain fell in the day, including an intense downpour lasting seven hours*
* *34 killed and nearly 100 buildings destroyed*
* *The River Lyn rose quickly and pushed rocks and giant boulders ahead of it*
* *Trees, telegraph poles and cars were carried away*
* *Fast-moving debris acted as a battering ram demolishing houses and bridges.*

The 'Hurricane' of October 1987
* *There was a rapid fall in pressure in a depression approaching the Channel coast*
* *There was a zone of violent winds (80–120kph) along a warm front*
* *These raced across south-eastern England during the night*
* *They created mayhem particularly through uprooting thousands of trees*
* *All forms of communication were paralysed*
* *Few people were killed only because it was night time.*

The drought of summmer 1995
* *Anticyclonic systems blocked the free passage of Atlantic depressions and their fronts over most of the UK*
* *It was the driest summer since records began in 1727*
* *Average temperatures in August were almost 4°C hotter than normal as the clockwise flow of air around the high pressure centred over the UK drew in hot air from the continent*
* *Rainfall was only 20% of the average as the sinking air of the anticyclone snuffed out any chance of strong convection*
* *Supplies of water dwindled and demand increased in the hot sunny weather.*

Questions

1 a Explain the variations in climate within the British Isles labelled on Figure 1.

   b Where and in what ways does the climate of the UK restrict economic activity?

2 Why is forecasting the weather a commercial activity for the Meteorological Office and some other companies in the UK?

3 Is forecasting the weather easier in London or Delhi? Outline and explain your opinions on this.

Climatic hazards

- Types, characteristics and causes
- The impact of strong winds, drought and heavy rainfall

Types, characteristics and causes

Climatic hazards are severe variations from average climatic conditions which cause problems for the people living in the areas affected. The weather conditions themselves are short term. Drought cannot be considered a climatic hazard for people living in deserts. Rather it is a climatic problem: people don't live in deserts without overcoming the problem first, for example by irrigation. However, drought is a hazard for people living in areas where rain is expected for part or all of the year and then fails to arrive.

Extreme weather conditions occur widely. Blizzards and extreme cold are virtually restricted to polar and cold temperate latitudes, but others, such as strong winds and heavy rain, can happen in most places,

even though they occur more frequently and with greater intensity in the tropics. The impact of drought as a hazard must always be great in the tropics because rates of evaporation are high – 500mm of rain per year allow less crop growth in India than in the UK. The strongest winds and heaviest downpours are associated with tropical revolving storms which are formed by great surface heating over hot tropical oceans.

One way to classify climatic hazards is to use the main causes of problems for people. This gives a three-fold classification:

1 Strong winds
2 Heavy precipitation
3 Drought.

▼ **Figure 1** Formation of hurricanes and cyclones

The sequence of events in a hurricane or cyclone:

- hot seawater (27°C or more) heats the air above
- warm, moist air starts to rise and rises high
- a deep centre of low pressure is created and air is sucked in to replace the rising air
- winds increase to speeds of 150–200kph in a circle which may be 600km across
- torrential rain falls from the towering cumulo-nimbus clouds around the centre
- the 'eye' is a small area of calm where air is sucked down in the centre, surrounded by raging storms and howling wind
- as the storm crosses over land it loses power as its low pressure centre is 'filled in'.

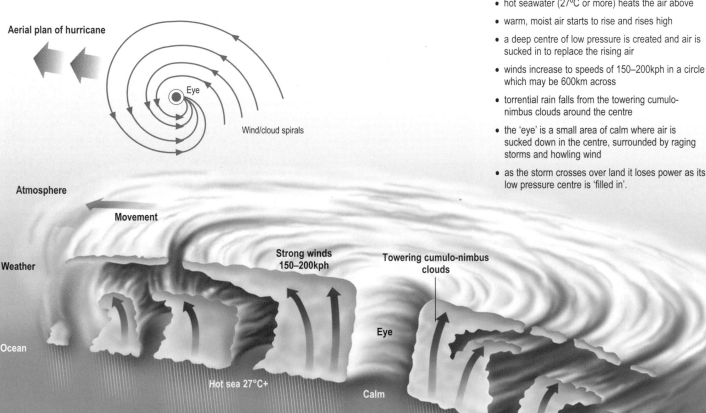

Aerial plan of hurricane

Eye

Wind/cloud spirals

Atmosphere

Movement

Weather

Strong winds 150–200kph

Towering cumulo-nimbus clouds

Eye

Ocean

Hot sea 27°C+

Calm

500 km

1 Strong winds

These are caused by steep pressure gradients – great differences in pressure over short distances. There are regular strong winds associated with the Temperate Low pressure belt. As the pressure falls, air is drawn into the centre of the depression to replace that which is rising. Occasional very rapid falls in pressure lead to wind speeds rarely experienced in temperate latitudes. The UK's October 1987 'hurricane' (page 63) and France's Christmas storms in 1999 (page 68) were exceptions. The oceans of the southern hemisphere, where there are few land masses to interrupt the westerly winds, were feared by sailors, who gave these latitudes names which speak for themselves – the 'Roaring Forties', 'Furious Fifties' and 'Screaming Sixties'.

Less regular, but more severe are the winds associated with tropical revolving storms. Although called hurricanes in the Caribbean and cyclones in the Indian and Pacific Oceans, the reasons for their formation are the same (Figure 1). As these weather systems move they feed off the warm tropical seas, until the point where they begin to cross over land and they lose power as their low pressure centre is gradually 'filled in'.

Tornadoes ('twisters' in American) are much smaller systems and form over hot land surfaces, but they can be very violent and extremely destructive. A trigger is needed to cause a sudden up-current of air. The junction of air masses along a front is a perfect example. Once the vigorous uplift begins, air spirals upwards, sucks in more air, spins faster and faster, and writhes its way over the land at 50kph or more. All the time it is sucking in air it is sucking in debris which includes objects as big as cars – and yes, 'pigs can fly' in a tornado.

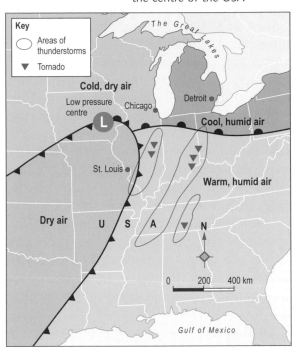

▼ **Figure 2a** Tornadoes: A perfect set up in the centre of the USA

Key
○ Areas of thunderstorms
▼ Tornado

The Great Lakes
Cold, dry air
Low pressure centre
Chicago
Detroit
Cool, humid air
St. Louis
Warm, humid air
Dry air   U S A   N
Gulf of Mexico
0   200   400 km

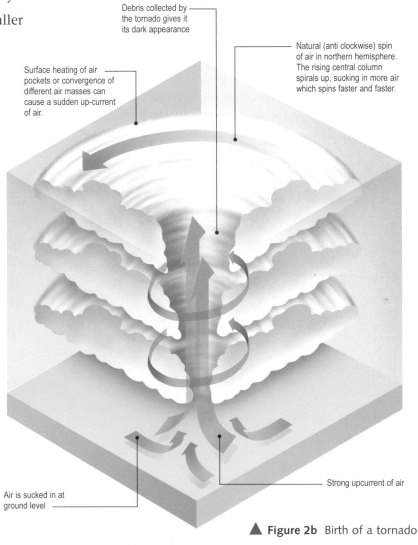

Debris collected by the tornado gives it its dark appearance

Surface heating of air pockets or convergence of different air masses can cause a sudden up-current of air.

Natural (anti clockwise) spin of air in northern hemisphere. The rising central column spirals up, sucking in more air which spins faster and faster.

Air is sucked in at ground level

Strong upcurrent of air

▲ **Figure 2b** Birth of a tornado

◀ **Figure 2c** What a tornado looks like

2 Heavy precipitation

This falls from cumulo-nimbus clouds, which are formed by air rising to high levels in the atmosphere. The most likely cause of this is intense convection from hot surfaces. In temperate latitudes, hot surfaces only exist in summer in inland locations whereas in the tropics they exist in most places all year. Although heavy precipitation does not fall as frequently in temperate areas, from time to time cumulus clouds form in deep and active depressions, particularly along their cold fronts (which is what led to the Lynmouth flood in 1952, page 63). In the tropics the most intense convectional activity occurs along the ITCZ in the Equatorial Low pressure belt, but this is part of the regular annual pattern of weather. Heavy rainfall creates a hazard when tropical revolving storms such as hurricanes and cyclones strike an area.

3 Drought

Periods of unexpectedly dry weather, often for a few months but sometimes for one, two or more consecutive years, are caused by changes in the pattern of pressure and winds. They are always most likely to occur on the edges of the world's major dry areas, the hot deserts. In the wet season, these are the last places to be reached by rain-bearing winds. No matter how weak, the wet monsoon always reaches places in southern and central India; the rainfall may be less than they were expecting and

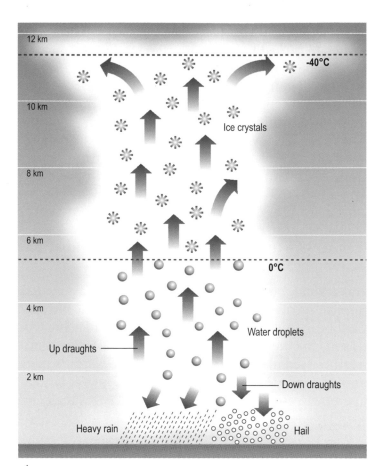

▲ **Figure 1** Inside a cumulo-nimbus cloud

hoping for, but they are not regular sufferers from drought. This is more commonly the fate for people living in north-west India – the last to be reached by rain-bearing monsoon winds (Figure 2, page 55).

▼ **Figure 2** Areas most likely to be affected by climatic hazards

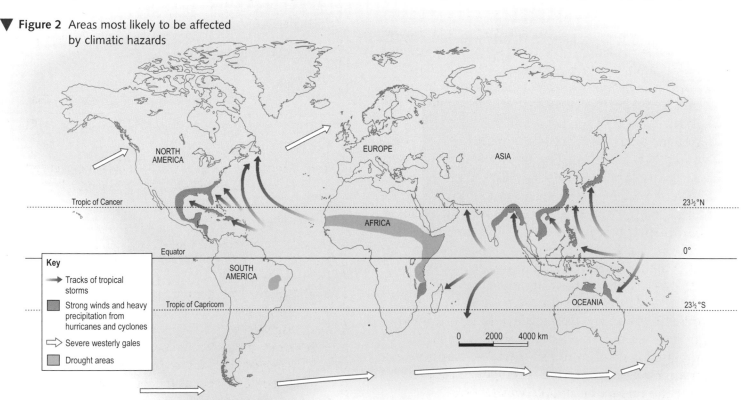

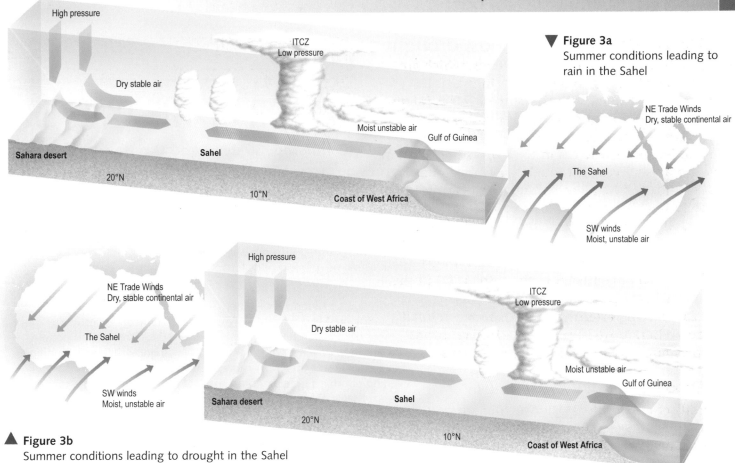

Figure 3a
Summer conditions leading to rain in the Sahel

▲ **Figure 3b**
Summer conditions leading to drought in the Sahel

Africa is a relatively dry continent and has many areas where rainfall is notoriously unreliable. The name of one region has become synonymous with drought – the Sahel which stretches north of the Equator across the continent from the 'Horn of Africa' in the east to the west coast (Figure 3). When the ITCZ migrates northwards in summer, it brings hot, moist, unstable air with it. Disturbances along the front lead to the formation of towering cumulo-nimbus clouds and heavy rain in coastal regions. The amount of rain reduces with distance inland as the influence of descending air from the high pressure over the Sahara becomes a more dominant factor in determining weather conditions. Eventually the dry continental tropical air wins. In many years in the 1970s and 1980s the rains either failed completely or produced only a fraction of the total expected over wide areas. Strong subsidence in the sub-tropical high pressure belt allowed the north-east Trade Winds to carry dry continental air further south, pushing back to the coast the moist south-westerlies and snuffing out convection currents which might have led to rain. In other words, the usual wind directions in mid-summer were reversed and dry, stable continental air dominated instead of moist, unstable maritime air. Year after year of drier than average conditions meant the impact on people was severe.

▼ **Figure 4** Percentage variations of annual rainfall totals in the Sahel (from the mean for 1951–80)

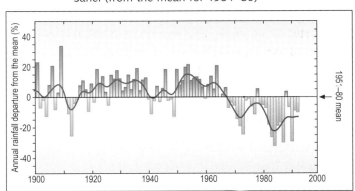

Questions

1 a Explain the atmospheric processes responsible for
   i strong winds, ii heavy precipitation and
   iii drought.
  b For each one,
   i name a place affected
   ii explain when and why it is likely to be affected.
2 a What are the strengths and weaknesses of the classification of climatic hazards used on page 64?
  b Would a classification based on tropical and temperate climates, or another classification, be better? Give reasons for your answer.

The impact of strong winds, drought and heavy rainfall

The strength of climatic hazards is potentially greater in the tropics. Tropical revolving storms and tornadoes require strong surface heating for their formation and development. Instead of experiencing a tornado, areas in temperate latitudes are more likely to experience a whirlwind – which has the same formation and the same principle but less intensity, because there is not the heat to feed its growth and movement.

The majority of countries in the tropics are LEDCs. When hazards strike, the loss of life is often greater than that expected in an MEDC. There is less chance of advanced preparation, of warnings about its arrival, of immediate help and of long-term aid after it has happened. In absolute terms the total value placed on the damage caused may be lower in an LEDC (simply because property and possessions in MEDCs have higher money values attached to them). However, in relative terms the human devastation may be much greater because people are more likely to lose everything they possess without having any recourse to insurance to cover losses.

Preparation for climatic hazards is easier for some types than for others, even in the wealthy USA. For instance, hurricanes which strike the USA now usually lead to little direct loss of life. Hurricanes are major systems which can be tracked by satellites. They remain unpredictable and can suddenly change course or intensify, but the danger from them can be assessed and warnings given to board up property and to evacuate people inland. Tornadoes, however, are small and less predictable. They can leave a trail of total destruction 150m wide with everything else to the sides unaffected. The percentage chance of occurrence can be estimated, tornado warnings can be issued, and preferred corridors of movement are known, but what and who will be affected, and where, are at the whim of each individual tornado as it 'twists' across the hot land.

THE TERROR OF THE TWISTER

Hundreds missing, 36 dead and thousands of homes destroyed in America's 'tornado alley'

The fiercest tornadoes to hit the United States for more than a decade left a huge trail of death, devastation and damage across the central plains states of Oklahoma and Kansas yesterday. Thousands of homes were turned into piles of shattered wood and glass. In some areas whole neighbourhoods looked as though they had been hit by bombs.

Hundreds of residents evacuated their houses after warnings were broadcast on Monday night. This made it difficult to estimate the number of casualties. 'We've got pages and pages of missing people,' said the state governor of Oklahoma. 'We've got whole communities that simply aren't there any more.' The tornadoes struck in the early evening churning up everything that lay in their paths. One tornado was said to have stayed on the ground for more than four hours; these storms rarely last for more than half an hour at full force.

▲ Figure 1a   *The Guardian, 5 May 1999*

▲ Figure 1b An Oklahoma suburban neighbourhood reduced to scrap

 Europe's 'Gale of the century' – *Christmas 1999*
- *Wind speeds up to 200kph*
- *Over 50 killed in France and neighbouring countries*
- *The cities strewn with debris – roofing, fallen trees and crushed cars*
- *More than 10 000 trees uprooted at Versailles*
- *Some places in France without electricity for two weeks.*

Heavy rain

Case Study   in Mozambique, Africa

Climate is at its most cruel when both drought and flood can afflict the same area in different years. In 1995, Mozambique suffered in the great drought which lingered over southern Africa. So widespread were crop failures that many people fled into Zimbabwe and neighbouring countries. TV correspondents filed reports while standing on the sandy bed of the Limpopo river channel, without a trickle of water in sight. In 2000, there were several weeks of torrential rains at the beginning of the year, followed by cyclones hitting the coast and bringing still more heavy rain. Figure 2 shows the enormous extent of the floods in Mozambique in March 2000 after two months of rain. Reports in early March of the flood's impact made grim reading:

- 1 million of the country's 19 million people displaced

- 100 000 trapped by rising waters on roof tops, on shrinking islands and in trees

- malaria running at four times normal levels

- the most productive farming areas all under water.

▲ **Figure 3** Desperate scenes near Xai-Xai, Mozambique

▼ **Figure 2** Flooded areas in Mozambique, Africa

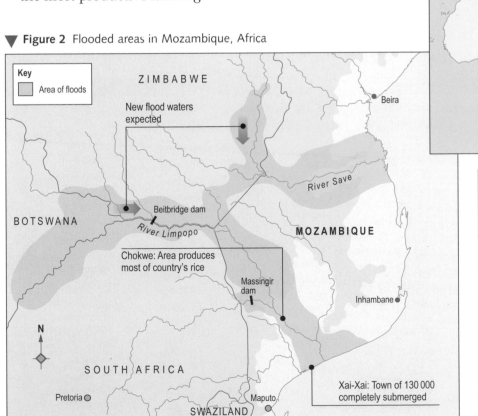

Questions

1 'People in MEDCs do not escape climatic hazards, but people in LEDCs suffer more'. Comment on this statement.

Investigation

2 a Explain the physical causes of drought in the Sahel.

b Outline the human and physical impacts of drought in the region.

The cyclone

Case Study   in Orissa, India, 1999

▲ **Figure 1** The scene of devastation caused by the cyclone that hit the east Indian state of Orissa for 36 hours in October 1999

▼ **Figure 2**

If the UK Met. Office detected the hurricane five days before it reached landfall, one can reasonably ask why so many people died. The Met. Office is recognized as one of the most accurate weather forecasters to the Miami weather office, and few, if any, people die in North America. The problem is one of both communication and infrastructure. The Indian authorities were alerted to the dangers but failed to adequately inform the local population. Partly this is because Orissa has low rates of literacy and few people have access to TVs and radios; partly it is because the state is so vast that it is hard to reach everyone. However, many observers believe that the Indian authorities could have done a great deal more. It is well known that Orissa is prone to hurricanes and yet there has been little by way of education or construction to mitigate the damage.

The Guardian, 23 November 1999

▼ **Figure 3**

What is already evident is the unpreparedness of both the state and central governments for the disaster. What is unpardonable is that it is not something which could have caught the authorities by surprise, like an earthquake... However, it may not be fair to blame the authorities alone because the local people often show a curious reluctance to move to safer places inland. At a time when transistors are found in the remotest of villages, surely they cannot claim to have been caught unawares. Since the cyclones are a regular feature in the region, the local people must be aware of what lies in store if they do not take precautionary measures.

Editorial in the *Hindustan Times*, New Delhi, 2 November 1999

With wind speeds up to 300 kph and tidal waves over 10m, buildings and other structures common in rural India can hardly be expected to remain intact. But the enormous loss of lives is a direct result of the constraining socio-economic circumstances in India. For the marginal farmer, no amount of early warnings of impending destruction are enough to make him abandon his only source of livelihood ... Even if he so desired, he is not likely to find suitable means of transport to put himself and his family out of harm's way ... Once again the cyclone and its aftermath reveal the critical role of information. Access to telecommunications should no longer be considered a luxury but a necessity.

Editorial in *The Times of India*, New Delhi, 2 November 1999

▲ **Figure 4**

India's traumatized cyclone victims cling together in a devastated land

Only sleeping pills can keep the nightmares at bay. Without them, 26-year-old Sheikh Tahajuddin wakes screaming and sweating – from terrifying dreams about the tidal wave that destroyed his village, Muslimpalli, and snatched away everyone he loved. Just 82 people – from a community of more than 200 – were left in Tahajuddin's village by the fierce cyclone and 7m high tidal wave that hit India's eastern state of Orissa. They live in a handful of polythene tents.

Their future, however, is uncertain. The survivors of Muslimpalli have no seeds to plant, no tools to farm with, and the soil has been contaminated by salt. The goats they once sold for meat are gone. Their existing food stocks – from the government and various relief agencies – will last just a few more days. The trauma of this tiny hamlet is mirrored in thousands of other villages across Orissa's once prosperous coastal rice belt. Nearly two months after the disaster, up to 15 million people are living precariously, waiting, as government officials and relief agencies struggle to help them.

The task is monumental. The cyclone's winds, travelling at up to 270km an hour, damaged $1.3bn (£808 million) of public and private property including roads, irrigation works, power lines, schools, thousands of homes and the annual rice crop. Nearly 500,000 draught animals died and 90 million trees – mostly privately owned coconut, cashew and betel nut trees that farmers tended for extra income – were uprooted. Officially, 9 887 people perished, though local non-governmental organizations insist that the actual toll was up to three times that figure.

Relief efforts got off to a rocky start but now state officials are racing to provide subsidized seeds, restore power lines, repair irrigation works and make tractors available so that at least some farmers can plant a vegetable crop next month. But the region's many landless labourers are not likely to find work until the next monsoon season. That means an estimated 5 million people will depend upon some type of food aid or food-for-work for at least another seven months. Even if they are fed, many are so deeply shocked by their losses that they can hardly contemplate how to restart their lives.

▲ **Figure 5**

Adapted from *The Financial Times*, 24 December 1999

Questions

1 Make a list of the key facts about the Orissa cyclone using the headings: date and place; physical features of the cyclone; effects upon people.

2 a Identify
   i the immediate (short term) effects and
   ii the longer term effects upon people living in the region.
  b Comment on the differences in nature and severity between them.

3 a Explain the physical and human reasons why so many people died.
  b Will fewer people die in the next major cyclone in India? Explain your views on this.

Climatic change
at the micro scale

- Modifications of climate by urban areas
- Atmospheric pollution in urban areas

Modifications of climate by urban areas

City growth so totally transforms the natural landscape, and the area covered by many cities is so large that it is not surprising that cities make some of their own weather. Read the newspaper report opposite about Atlanta, USA.

The urban heat island described in Atlanta is the most obvious manifestation that a city can modify the weather and climate of the area in which it lies, but there are other differences between it and the rural area around it (Figure 1).

▶ **Figure 1**

Adapted from *The Guardian*, 23 February 2000

Sweltering Atlanta shows summer in cities will get even hotter

Around Atlanta woodlands had been cut down and farmlands covered by urban land at a rate of 20ha a day for 20 years. The growth has created a sprawling city with roof top temperatures that sometimes reached 70°C; an island of heat so powerful that it generated its own thunderstorms even in what should have been the cool of the night.

What is true for Atlanta is true for cities in both the developing and developed worlds. We are finding that in this dome of elevated temperatures, caused by pavements, buildings and asphalt that soak up the sun during the day and re-radiate it at night, we have differences between the city and surrounding areas of 3, 6 and even 7°C.

In 1997 Nasa flew an aircraft over downtown Atlanta and found the daytime air temperature was barely 27°C, while the ground surface temperature was almost 49°C (120°F). At night from 2–4am, the air temperature was 10–13°C, but the city's surface was still 24°C.

Researchers noted that over a nine day summer period, there were five days when Atlanta's own heat triggered thunderstorms.

▼ **Figure 2** Summary of the average overall effects of the urban area on climatic conditions

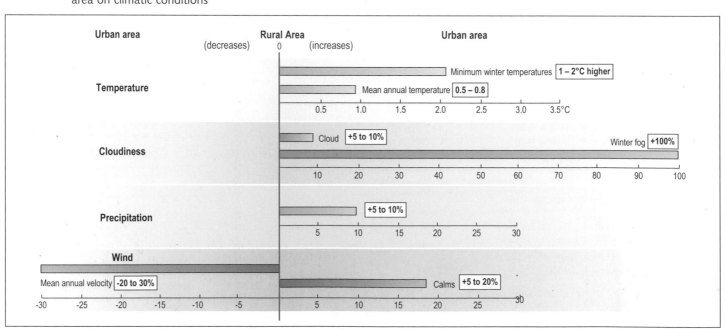

Several factors combine to cause these urban heat islands:

- **Heat produced by people**
Heat escapes from houses, shops and offices. Cars and other vehicles circulate in streets and emit heat. Factories and power stations release heat into the atmosphere by emissions from chimneys and into streams by expelling cooling water. Lighting systems provide local heat.

- **Heat radiated by buildings and urban surfaces**
Building materials have higher thermal capacities than the vegetation and soil surfaces they replace. Bricks, concrete, roofing and road materials absorb solar energy by day, act like a massive storage radiator and release the heat during the night. If you walk past a wall on an evening after a sunny day, it is sometimes possible to feel the heat being re-radiated from it. It has been calculated that tower blocks of flats can absorb six times as much heat as rural surfaces.

- **Less heat loss by evaporation and transpiration**
Wind speeds are lower and there are fewer open spaces covered by vegetation, which means that less energy is used up in releasing water back into the atmosphere.

- **Less heat loss as a result of air pollution**
The greater concentration of pollutants acts like a blanket over the city at night reducing outgoing radiation; there is still a net heat balance even though incoming radiation during the day is reduced by pollution.

▼ **Figure 3** London's heat island

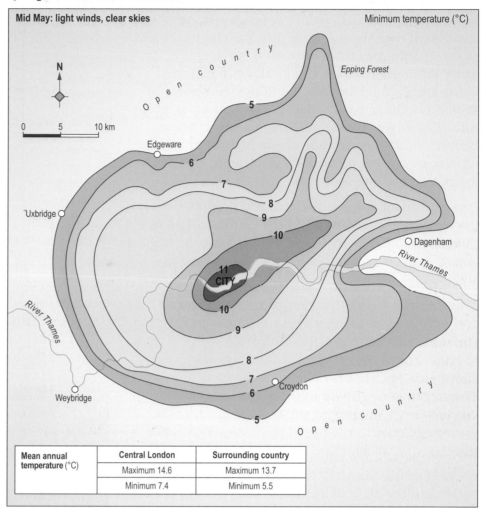

Mean annual temperature (°C)	Central London	Surrounding country
	Maximum 14.6	Maximum 13.7
	Minimum 7.4	Minimum 5.5

London

London's heat island was mapped by Chandler (Figure 2) in the early 1960s. This was based upon readings in an evening in mid-May during anticyclonic weather when winds were light and skies were clear. These were ideal conditions for creating large variations between central London, outer suburbs and rural areas beyond. Note that the heat island is not a perfect circular shape. The presence of cool air in the Thames valley and estuary affects its shape as does the extension northwards of housing areas west of Epping Forest and the Lea valley.

Questions

1 a Define the term 'urban heat island'.
  b Describe the main features of London's heat island in mid-May shown in Figure 2.
  c Identify one location where there was a sharp change in temperature and suggest reasons for it.
  d Give reasons for the general pattern shown.

2 a How much greater was the intensity of London's heat island shown for mid-May compared with the average in the surrounding country?
  b Why was it greater?

Urban climatic features

In general, urban areas reduce wind speeds. Air movement near the surface is disturbed by the height of the buildings so that the main wind flow is in the lower atmosphere above city level. At street level, many areas are sheltered by buildings. However, sometimes the opposite effect is experienced as air is funnelled down streets and along narrow channels between buildings creating locally high wind speeds, capable of causing particularly unpleasant conditions for pedestrians and shoppers.

Large urban areas increase cloud and precipitation. Condensation is favoured in urban air because it is polluted by small particles, which act as nuclei around which droplets of water can condense and grow.

Tall buildings disturb air flows and encourage uplift. This uplift as well as currents of rising air caused by convection from the city's very hot non-natural surfaces can lead to precipitation from thunderstorms (as in Atlanta). Summer thunderstorms appear to be more frequent in north London than elsewhere in the region; rising air currents from the heated surfaces are given extra encouragement to rise by ridges of higher ground.

Poor visibility, haze and smog are more likely because of the 'cocktail' of air pollutants that are present in the air above cities (Figure 1). People have affected the composition of the Earth's atmosphere everywhere, but the greatest changes in air quality are in urban areas.

Particulates are particles in the air added by smoke; they are mainly carbon and hydrocarbons from the incomplete combustion of fossil fuels, although they also include some added compounds such as lead. Their main effect is to reduce incoming solar radiation, which in turn contributes to the formation of low level ozone and smog.

Physical conditions affecting local climate

Some physical conditions favour large variations in local climate and strong urban effects. Anticyclonic (high pressure) weather with calms, clear skies and stagnant air is one. If strong winds blow, the air is stirred up. This mixing creates uniform temperatures over wide areas by not allowing the additional heat radiated to remain and build up within the urban area. The winds also blow away the pollutants and disperse the smog. Another factor is relief. Valleys or flat areas surrounded by higher slopes are more sheltered from general weather influences so more likely to create their own weather. Local conditions

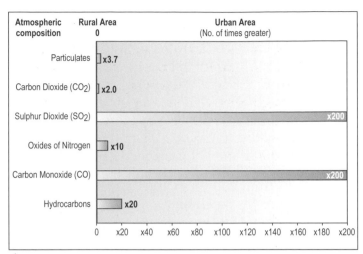

▲ **Figure 1** The greater presence of pollutants in urban areas

can operate and exaggerate the climatic differences. Human factors such as city size and height of buildings should also to be taken into account. Heat island intensity is so great in North American cities such as Atlanta because of the concentration and height of downtown (CBD) skyscrapers.

▲ **Figure 2** The canyon-like streets of North American cities increase the local urban effects on climate so that the urban heat island is more pronounced than in most European cities.

Atmospheric pollution in urban areas

In urban areas traffic is a major source of particulates, unburnt hydrocarbons and gases (Figure 3). They have many adverse effects upon people's health, which is made worse at times when ground ozone levels are high and smog forms. Ozone is a poisonous form of oxygen which plays a vital role for humans and all other forms of life in the upper atmosphere by blocking dangerous ultraviolet radiation. In the lower atmosphere it causes irritation of the bronchial passages, lungs and eyes in humans and damages trees and cereal crops. Precise weather conditions are needed for its formation – light winds, strong sunlight and high temperatures. These are only present from time to time in summer in the UK when anticyclonic conditions replace the more frequent depression weather. However, they are present for half the year during the hot, dry summers in some of the world's top smog spots such as Los Angeles, Athens and Santiago in Chile, all of which are located in regions with a Mediterranean type of climate.

▼ Figure 3 Traffic, pollution and their effects on people

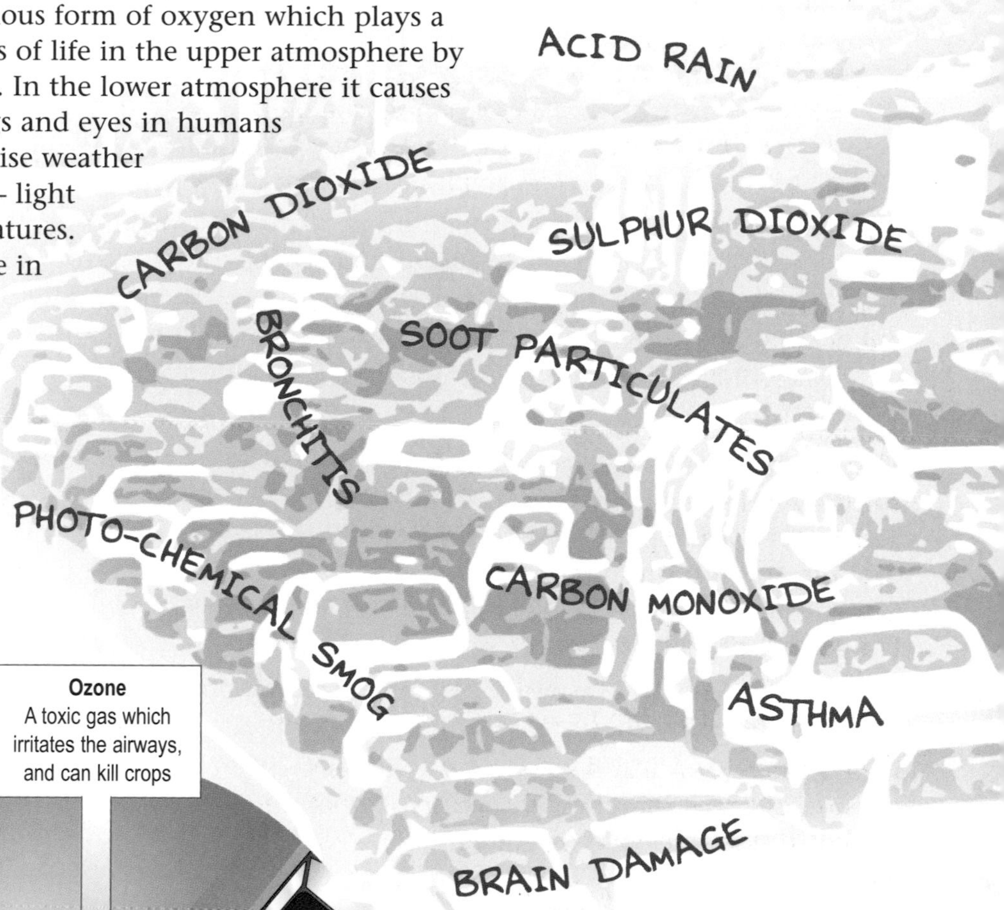

ACID RAIN

CARBON DIOXIDE

SULPHUR DIOXIDE

BRONCHITIS

SOOT PARTICULATES

PHOTO-CHEMICAL SMOG

CARBON MONOXIDE

ASTHMA

BRAIN DAMAGE

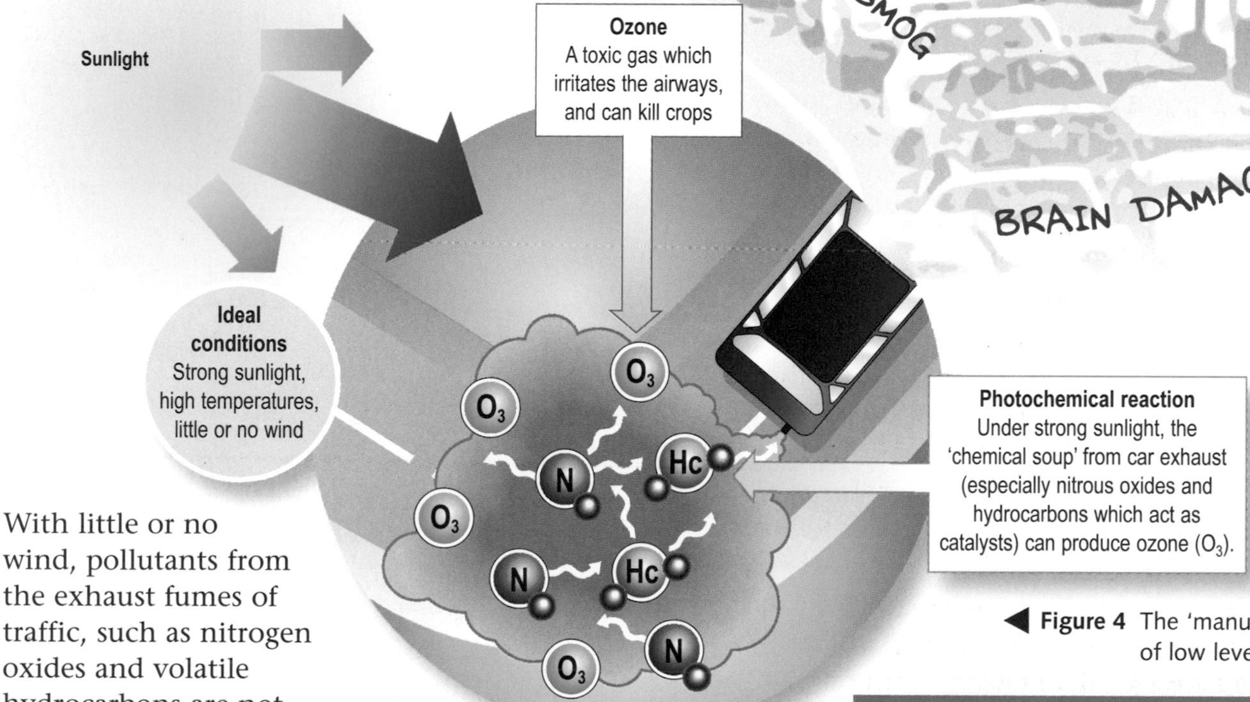

Sunlight

Ozone
A toxic gas which irritates the airways, and can kill crops

Ideal conditions
Strong sunlight, high temperatures, little or no wind

O_3 O_3 O_3 N Hc N Hc O_3 N

Photochemical reaction
Under strong sunlight, the 'chemical soup' from car exhaust (especially nitrous oxides and hydrocarbons which act as catalysts) can produce ozone (O_3).

◄ Figure 4 The 'manufacture' of low level ozone

With little or no wind, pollutants from the exhaust fumes of traffic, such as nitrogen oxides and volatile hydrocarbons are not dispersed. Under strong sunlight a photochemical process occurs which produces high levels of ozone. The result is that a haze hangs over the urban areas accompanied by a smell. Urban ozone levels have been growing steadily since measurements began and peak at times when for example the summer weather in the UK is at its best. Although catalytic converters in cars help to reduce the hazard, concentrations of low level ozone in Europe are increasing at between one and two per cent per year.

ℹ **Catalytic converters**
- They remove many nitrogen oxides, carbon monoxide and unburnt hydrocarbons
- They increase emissions of carbon dioxide by about 10 per cent
- They work most efficiently when engines are hot
- In 1993 they were made compulsory on all new cars in the UK.

Air pollution

Case Study

in London

Before the Clean Air Act of 1956, particulates and hydrocarbons contributed greatly to smog. Fog occurs naturally under anticyclonic conditions in winter in the UK. On evenings when heat escapes from the surface through clear skies, the moist air in contact with the surface is cooled. This leads to condensation around small dust particles in the atmosphere, which is sufficient to reduce visibility to less than one kilometre. Air pollution, when coal was the universal fuel in factories and homes in the UK, converted the fog into smog. It does this by increasing the size and density of the nuclei for condensation (reducing visibility) and by lessening incoming daytime solar radiation by up to a half (reducing solar heating to clear the fog).

Smogs in winter still occur in London and other British cities when meteorological conditions are suitable, i.e. when a lid of cold air, called an inversion, forms over a city and traps the pollution near the ground. It can be a killer for those with respiratory diseases or influenza, but the spread of smokeless zones have made it less common and less vicious than it used to be.

High ozone levels in summer is an increasing problem, obviously not helped by the amount of traffic in London and its slow movement. During hot sunny weather in the summer of 1994 dangerously high ozone levels were reached in London. The public were warned and people suffering from chest diseases and asthma were advised not to take vigorous exercise and to stay indoors.

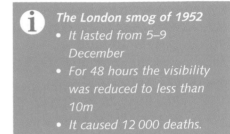

The London smog of 1952
- It lasted from 5–9 December
- For 48 hours the visibility was reduced to less than 10m
- It caused 12 000 deaths.

▼ **Figure 1** Ground level ozone in city centres, July 1994

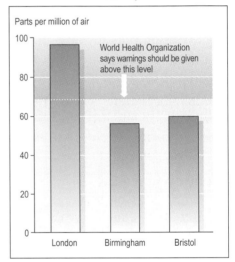

Parts per million of air

World Health Organization says warnings should be given above this level

London   Birmingham   Bristol

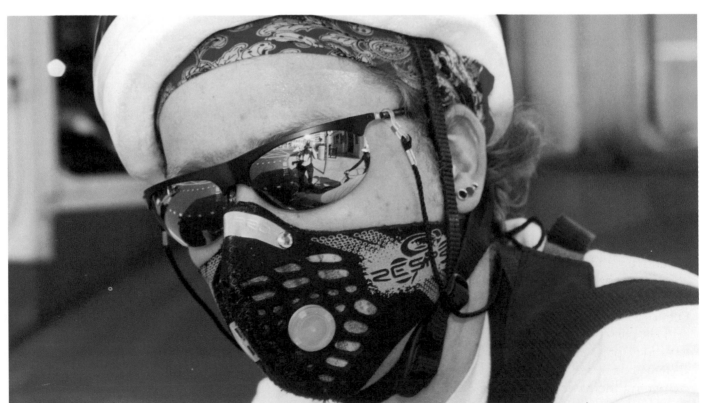

▲ **Figure 2** Street wise ... taking precautions in London against high ozone levels

> ℹ️ **Asthma in the UK**
> Low level ozone and oxides of nitrogen irritate the lungs and are very harmful for people with breathing problems such as asthma.
> - Over 3 million people suffer from it and this is increasing
> - Over 7 million working days are lost each year and increasing
> - Over £1 billion is the estimated cost to industry, commerce, the NHS and government in sickness benefits and increasing
> - Over 14 per cent of all children are affected and increasing.

High ozone levels are not a permanent problem in London because the winter sun is too weak to make it form. Anticyclones dominate the weather for only short periods and frontal depressions regularly drop rain or bring strong winds which remove pollutants and clean or clear the air. It is a serious problem at certain times which is why ground ozone levels are monitored and reported in newspapers and on television and radio.

Controls on emissions from factories and homes have led to great improvements in London's air quality, but reducing emissions from traffic in London is a more difficult task. It is just a part of a broader national problem – increasing numbers of cars on the road (Figure 3), for which national solutions are proving equally difficult to find. The national road building programme was curtailed and in each budget a green tax has been added to fuel prices; there are also hints of improved public transport. In London there are suggestions for blocking off areas in the centre to private motorists, charging tolls for those entering central London with vehicles and improving the underground with funds gained from its partial privatization. There is continued comment about rail operators improving rail services and reducing over-crowding on their peak hour trains. Evidence from cities such as Manchester shows that attractive public transport can drag some commuters away from their cars. In its first year the Metrolink tram service (opened 1992) and its fleet of twenty four trams carried more than nine million passengers, nearly twice the number expected (page 211). However, surveys have shown that some commuters, even after swingeing increases in costs of motoring, would be loath to desert their cars.

▼ **Figure 3** Cars on the road in the UK

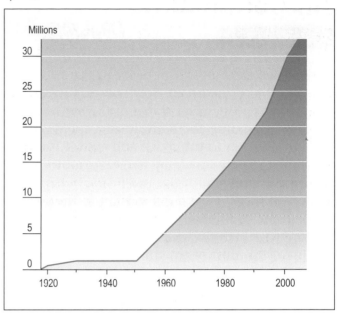

Questions

1 a In what ways and why does air quality in cities differ from that in surrounding rural areas?
  b Why are some urban areas more badly affected by poor air quality than others? Give examples.
  c Outline some of the effects of poor air quality on people.

2 a Explain the physical and human causes of high ground ozone levels and photochemical smog.
  b Why are their occurrences in urban areas increasing?
  c What leads to their reduction and clearance?

3 Make a table of key facts for the London case study using the following headings.
  a **i** Types of smog and changes over time.
     ii Causes.
  b Effects on people.
  c **i** Responses and strategies.
     ii Overall success of these.

Investigation

4 a What elements of air quality are recorded at monitoring stations in the nearest large urban area?
  b Outline how the last two years' results have changed seasonally.
  c When and why were air quality levels
     i particularly good and **ii** very poor.

Poor air quality

Case Study

in Los Angeles

Los Angeles grew in a basin between the mountains and the ocean. From Beverly Hills and Hollywood on the lower slopes of the Santa Monica mountains, the built-up area sprawls more than 80km to the south and east. It is a city of suburbs loosely linked by freeways (motorways) or as one commentator has put it – 'suburbs in search of a city'. It has a dry version of the Mediterranean climate – little rainfall is expected in more than half the year and high pressure is dominant for most of the time. A low-lying basin, many days of low wind speeds, hot sunshine, descending air, low rainfall and low level temperature inversions – there could not be a better collection of natural conditions for the formation of smog. On about half the days in the year a temperature inversion exists which is low enough to trap the pollution and cause photochemical smog, a brownish yellow haze, painful to eyes and nose and harmful to general health. As a city, Los Angeles is a special case. It grew on the assumption the 'automobile is king'. In what other city could you buy a postcard of freeways with a header 'Dig those crazy freeways'? Traffic in the LA metropolitan area went up by another third between 1990 and 2000 and estimates are for it to increase by 50 per cent in the next ten years. Its new public rapid transport system is too little, too late. The consequences are visible each day in the smog and congested freeways that are now as famous as LA traditional landmarks such as Hollywood.

California's Smog City

Los Angeles may be in imminent danger of surrendering its title as the smoggiest city in the USA. With two weeks to go to the official end of the ozone smog season, only one alert has been issued in the region urging people to stay indoors and avoid exercise at midday when the 'fug' is at its worst. At this stage last year seven of these so called stage 1 episodes had been recorded. There were 14 in the whole of 1995 and 23 in the year before.

Air quality in the Los Angeles basin – home to 14 million – has been improving steadily for years under the impact of regulations governing everything from the use of motor mowers, furniture polish and vehicle emissions. This year the arrival of cooler, moister weather associated with the El Niño climatic phenomenon has played a role in damping smog formation, as it did on its last appearance in 1982 and 1983.

But much of the credit for recent improvements has been given to the mandatory state-wide introduction of cleaner burning gasoline (CBG) introduced in March 1996. This single measure, said by the California Environmental Protection Agency to reduce ozone-forming emissions from road vehicles by 15 per cent, had the same effect as removing 3.5 million cars from the road. The Agency said that this fuel was the most important advance since the arrival of the catalytic converter in 1975, when smog records were started.

However, the traffic authorities in Southern California acknowledge that the automobile will continue to be king so that the main focus of the transport is not taking cars off the road, but to make road transport safer and more efficient. Both state and federal hopes for the twenty-first century are being pinned on ITS – Intelligent Transport Systems. This is the collective name given to a vast range of technologies and transport management ideas including traffic control systems that adjust to traffic flows, roadside variable message signs and in-car technologies such as global positioning systems (GPS) navigation.

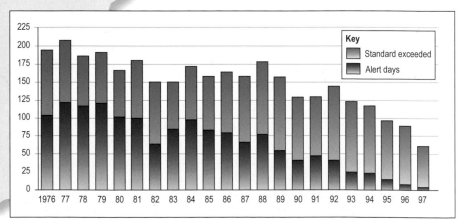

Adapted from *The Financial Times*, 19 September 1997

▲ **Figure 1** Number of days ozone levels in the LA Basin exceeded federal health standards levels

Strategies to improve air quality

in Mexico City

THE GREENING OF MEXICO CITY

Narciso Gomez Vasquez was driving his usual route from downtown Mexico City to the industrial suburbs in the north when something caught his eye: an offer for free financing to convert the city bus he owns from gasoline to natural gas. He estimates he saves $15 a day in fuel since he became one of 50 bus drivers and 200 police cars now filling up at the world's largest natural gas service station just north of the Mexican capital. By 2003, Ecomex aims to triple the number of stations in and around the city, home to one quarter of Mexico's 100 million inhabitants.

Mexico has large reserves of natural gas, which will bring long term economic benefits. However, the move to gas will have an immediate impact on Mexico City's stifling pollution. Vehicle emissions are responsible for 75 per cent of the city's soup-like atmosphere and contribute to more than half of the dangerously high ozone levels, which surpass air quality norms for most of the year. To combat the problem, cars without catalytic converters – some 60 per cent of those on the road – are prohibited from circulating one day of the week. The goal is to convert vehicles in intensive use first

such as buses, taxis and delivery trucks. Ecomex thinks it is only a matter of time before private car owners switch to natural gas as well.

Questions

With the aid of examples,

a outline the strategies for improving air quality in cities.

b evaluate how successful they have been.

Adapted from *The Financial Times*, 13 April 1999

▲ Figure 2

▼ **Figure 3** The goal is to convert up to 300 000 taxis, buses and delivery trucks to natural gas in the next five years.

Climatic change at other scales

- El Niño Southern Oscillation (ENSO) and its impacts
- Global warming and its predicted impacts

El Niño Southern Oscillation and its impacts

La Niña and El Niño

In the southern hemisphere vast areas are covered by oceans and by the Pacific Ocean in particular. Temperature differences within the tropical waters of the Pacific (instead of between land and sea) are more significant here and these differences are between the west and east (instead of north and south).

Of particular importance is what happens off the coast of Peru in South America. Normally the Peru (or Humboldt) ocean current, supplied by water from the Antarctic Drift, transports its cold waters along the desert coasts of northern Chile and Peru. In most years persistent and strong south-east winds push the surface waters westwards to form the Southern Equatorial Current. This gives space for the up-welling of cold water to the ocean surface next to the coast of Peru, thereby keeping the surface water off Peru some 5°C cooler than waters in the western Pacific

Ocean around Indonesia. This normal situation is known as 'La Niña', which means girl. It is named on account of the current's richness in nitrates and nutrients which encourage the growth of plankton which supports copious fish and bird life higher up the food chain.

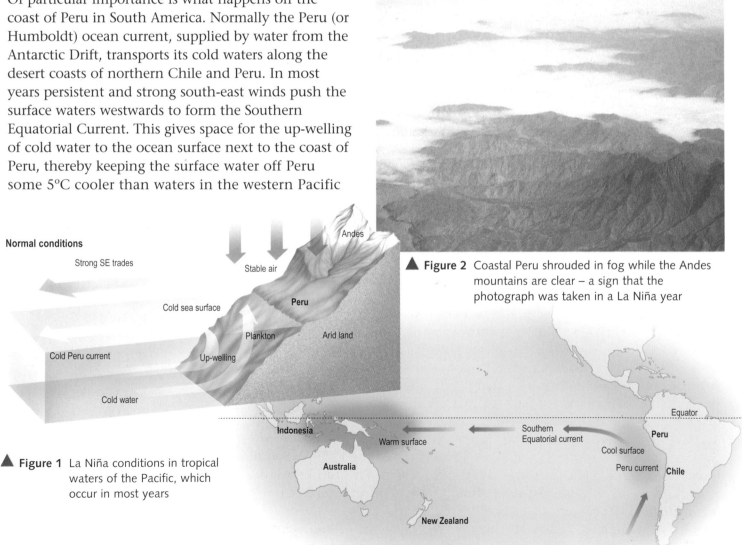

▲ **Figure 2** Coastal Peru shrouded in fog while the Andes mountains are clear – a sign that the photograph was taken in a La Niña year

Normal conditions

Strong SE trades

Stable air

Andes

Cold sea surface

Peru

Plankton

Arid land

Cold Peru current

Up-welling

Cold water

Equator

Indonesia

Warm surface

Southern Equatorial current

Peru

Cool surface

Australia

Peru current

Chile

New Zealand

▲ **Figure 1** La Niña conditions in tropical waters of the Pacific, which occur in most years

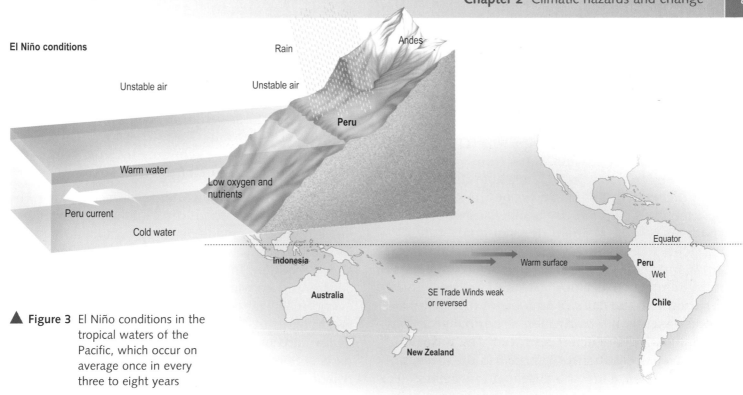

El Niño conditions

▲ **Figure 3** El Niño conditions in the tropical waters of the Pacific, which occur on average once in every three to eight years

The cold Peru current has a major effect upon the climate of adjacent coasts. The hot desert climate extends to within 10° of the Equator, much closer than anywhere else in the world. The cold waters encourage subsidence of air and stable conditions. They act like a western guard for the desert, cooling any onshore winds so that moisture condenses into low level fog instead of rain (Figure 2). This current is important to the economy of Peru. The plankton-rich waters teem with swarms of fish, especially anchoveta. Over a hundred years ago, there was the guano boom. Guano deposits (bird droppings from the great flocks of sea birds which breed on the offshore islands) were exported for fertilizer. In the 1960s the fish meal boom began as the oil-rich anchoveta were processed for export for animal feed. Despite over-fishing, fish meal remains an important export earner (about 15 per cent of total earnings) as well as a big employer in coastal towns.

In occasional years, warm waters appear off the coast of Peru. When the south-east Trade Winds are weaker, waters from the pool of hot water in the western Pacific near Indonesia are allowed to drift east towards South America which reverses the usual flow pattern of surface currents. When this happens, warm waters usually begin to appear off the coast of Peru around Christmas time, which is why Peruvian fishermen called this event 'El Niño', meaning the Christ child. It happens every three to eight years. Scientists believe that it is a periodic temperature correction which reduces the pool of very hot water which has gradually built up in the western Pacific. It is this correction which is termed the El Niño Southern Oscillation (ENSO) and produces the El Niño event. This has knock-on effects on global weather patterns, though mainly in the southern hemisphere and adjacent tropical areas. Although El Niño happens regularly, its strength varies. The last two major events of the twentieth century were in 1982–3 and 1997–8. It also occurred in a milder form on three other occasions between these dates.

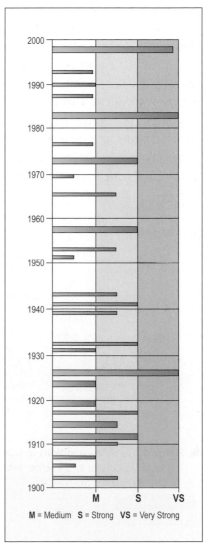

M = Medium S = Strong VS = Very Strong

▲ **Figure 4** The record of El Niño events

The impacts of El Niño (ENSO)

The first places to be affected by El Niño are Peru and its neighbours. Peruvians have had to learn to live with its regular visits, which inevitably have great climatic and economic effects. Arid coastal regions and slopes of the Andes, which in the typical year rarely see rain, suffer from torrential downpours as warm, humid, unstable air moves in from the western Pacific. Snows on the Andean peaks melt. What were dry boulder-strewn river channels become raging torrents of mud, stones and loose debris which sweep away bridges, destroy crops and wash away whole villages (Figure 2). Mass movements such as landslides and mudflows also contribute to the damage and loss of life. Irrigation works, essential for cultivation in normal years and carefully maintained, are destroyed. The warm ocean waters destroy the inshore fish life, because their currents are low in oxygen and nutrients. Many fish move offshore into colder waters which are out of range for fishermen with only small boats. The effects of the 1997–8 El Niño event on Peru and its people included:

- up to 350 dead
- up to 250 000 driven from their homes by the effects of heavy rain
- the shrinking of the economy by 5 per cent because of the failure of the fish harvest.

The 1982–3 event had worldwide effects (Figure 1). It led to droughts, floods, fires and storms, which killed thousands, made many more homeless and caused damage to crops and livelihoods estimated at $13.6 billion. In late 1997 the eastern Pacific off South America warmed up faster and earlier than ever before. The 1997–8 event was held responsible for droughts in Africa, Asia and Australia, and for heavy rains in Ecuador, Peru, Bolivia and other parts of South America. It was considered partly responsible for the forest fires that burnt out of control in Indonesia.

▼ **Figure 1** El Niño's impact on the world in 1982–3

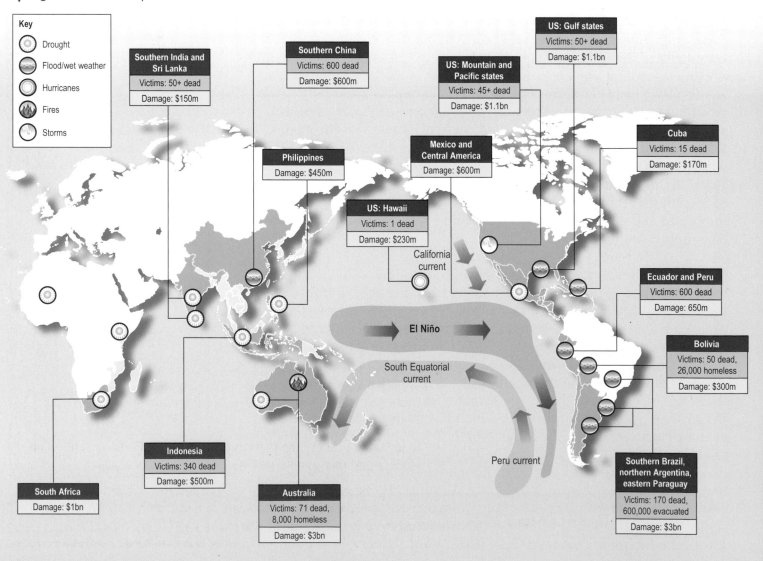

Key
- Drought
- Flood/wet weather
- Hurricanes
- Fires
- Storms

Southern India and Sri Lanka
Victims: 50+ dead
Damage: $150m

Southern China
Victims: 600 dead
Damage: $600m

US: Mountain and Pacific states
Victims: 45+ dead
Damage: $1.1bn

US: Gulf states
Victims: 50+ dead
Damage: $1.1bn

Philippines
Damage: $450m

Mexico and Central America
Damage: $600m

Cuba
Victims: 15 dead
Damage: $170m

US: Hawaii
Victims: 1 dead
Damage: $230m

California current

El Niño

South Equatorial current

Ecuador and Peru
Victims: 600 dead
Damage: 650m

Bolivia
Victims: 50 dead, 26,000 homeless
Damage: $300m

Peru current

South Africa
Damage: $1bn

Indonesia
Victims: 340 dead
Damage: $500m

Australia
Victims: 71 dead, 8,000 homeless
Damage: $3bn

Southern Brazil, northern Argentina, eastern Paraguay
Victims: 170 dead, 600,000 evacuated
Damage: $3bn

However, some areas benefited. A hotter Pacific meant a slightly cooler Atlantic so that fewer hurricanes struck the Caribbean and coasts of the USA. Cooler, moister weather arrived in southern California and the rain helped to clear the smog from Los Angeles (page 78). In Chile rains came and ended a severe drought in the centre of the country, filling reservoirs for water supply and HEP.

▼ **Figure 3** Some of the effects of El Niño in 1997–8

Indonesia
Suffered its worst drought for half a century. Fires burnt uncontrolled, aggravated by slash and burn and clearances by plantation and logging companies. Spread a haze over five neighbouring countries. In a normal year the monsoon rains would have arrived earlier to put out the fires.

Jamaica
Affected by the worst drought for 40 years which led to higher food prices and water rationing

Argentina
Heavy rains delayed the planting of wheat.

Venezuela
Yields of most crops reduced by flooding.

Tanzania
Almost nationwide crop failure caused by drought. Three million faced extreme food shortages.

China
Hit by the worst drought for 20 years.

Papua New Guinea
About 30 000 people starving because of drought.

Ethiopia
Drought threatened the food supplies of 4–5 million people.

▼ **Figure 2** The Peruvian village of San Bartolome destroyed in the El Niño event of 1982–3

▼ **Figure 4** Regions with precipitation anomalies related to ENSO (El Niño) in 1997–8

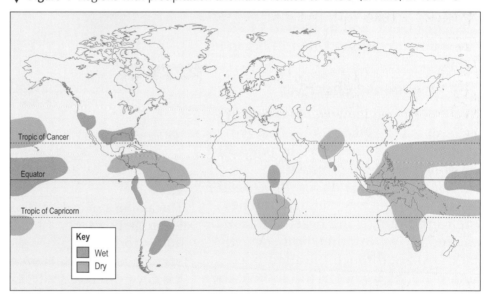

Tropic of Cancer

Equator

Tropic of Capricorn

Key
▢ Wet
▢ Dry

Questions

1 a Outline and explain the characteristics of a 'La Niña' year in the Pacific Ocean and Peru.
   b In what ways and why is an 'El Niño' year different?
   c i Look up what is meant by the term oscillation.
      ii What oscillates in the Pacific so that the full label for El Niño is ENSO?

2 Using Figure 3, show the impacts of the 1997–8 El Niño event on an outline world map (similar to Figure 1).

3 a Describe the pattern of precipitation anomalies in Figure 4.
   b To what extent did the impacts upon precipitation in 1997–8 match those experienced in earlier events (Figure 1)?

Global warming and its predicted impacts

Links between El Niño and global warming

El Niño (ENSO) is the most significant known natural cause of variations in climate to affect many areas of the world at the same time. These ENSO events have been recorded as far back as the 1520s and they have recurred every three to eight years ever since without much notice until the event in 1997/8 hit the news headlines around the globe. Then, with typical media over-reaction, the blame for any bad weather event anywhere in the world was heaped upon El Niño. Much of the media comment linked it to global warming. However scientists have not discovered a direct causal link, except that it is calculated that a warmer Pacific Ocean boosted the Earth's average surface air temperature in 1997 to 14.43°C and in 1998 to 14.58°C, the warmest years since records began in 1860.

The greenhouse effect

Much of the media would also have you believe that the greenhouse effect is something new and caused by pollution for which people are entirely responsible. The greenhouse effect works in the following way. Sunlight reaches the Earth's surface and heats it. To stop the surface over-heating, heat energy is radiated back through the atmosphere into space. Molecules in the air hold the outgoing radiation for a while thereby warming the Earth's surface. The best known of these molecules is carbon dioxide. These molecules act in a similar manner to the glass in a greenhouse which is where the name greenhouse effect comes from. This has been happening throughout the Earth's existence. Without its atmosphere for protection, the Earth would be 33°C colder – frozen and lifeless. The big issue is this – are humans adding enough carbon dioxide to the atmosphere to change it and the climate in significant ways?

The evidence

In among all the speculation, there are two facts:

Fact 1

We are living in a time when the average world temperature is increasing. Figure 1 shows that global warming exists at the present time. The average world temperature for the 30-year period from 1961 to 1990 was 14.0°C, but it has been higher than this every year in the 1990s. When comparing records over 140 years we can be reasonably certain that we are comparing like with like, because climatologists take great care to ensure their records are accurate and consistent.

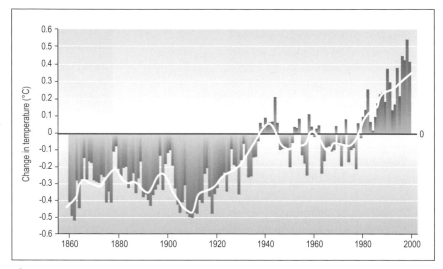

▲ **Figure 1** The annual average temperature of the world 1860–1999 (the 30-year average for 1961–90 is shown as 0)

Fact 2

The amount of carbon dioxide in the atmosphere has increased. Figure 2 shows total cumulative carbon emissions. Over six billion tonnes of carbon dioxide is being added each year by burning fossil fuels. From measurements of air bubbles trapped in the Greenland ice sheet, it has been calculated that before the Industrial Revolution, there were 270 parts per million by volume (ppmv) of CO_2 in the atmosphere which had risen to 360ppmv by 2000.

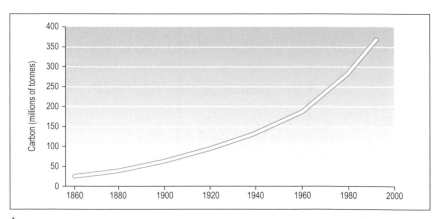

▲ **Figure 2** Total cumulative carbon emissions in the atmosphere

If these two facts are directly related, responsibility for causing global warming by carbon emissions is not equally shared throughout the world. Since 1800 the industrialized world – Europe, North America and the former USSR – have been responsible for more than 80 per cent of carbon dioxide emissions (Figure 3). The current responsibility of MEDCs is highlighted even more strongly when carbon emissions are related to total population (Figure 4). Whilst enormous compared with LEDCs, output in Europe and Japan appears quite moderate when compared to that of North America. The USA alone emits nearly a quarter of all greenhouse gases yet contains only 4 per cent of total world population. Its output is equal to that of all LEDCs in which about 80 per cent of the world's population are housed. There are other greenhouse gases, but these receive less attention because their concentrations are smaller.

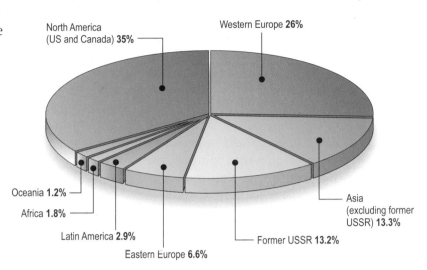

▼ **Figure 3** Responsibility for carbon dioxide emissions since 1800

Greenhouse gases	Sources	Length of time it stays in the atmosphere
Carbon dioxide	Burning fossil fuels, deforestation	Up to 200 years
Methane	Deforestation, decomposition of waste, rice and cattle production	12 years
CFCs	Refrigeration, air conditioning and aerosol sprays	Up to 1000 years or more
Nitrous oxide	Chemical fertilizers	120 years

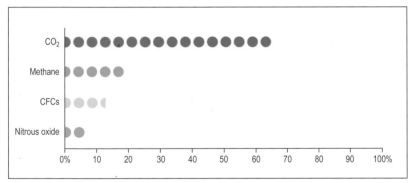

▲ **Figure 5** Relative importance of gases contributing to the greenhouse effect

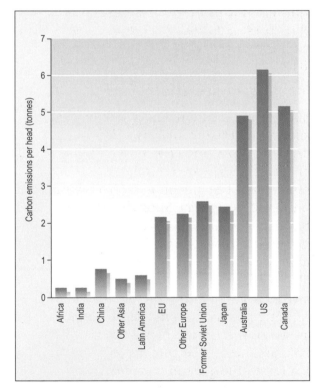

▼ **Figure 4** Carbon emissions per head (1999) for countries and areas

Questions

1　Outline the evidence that global warming is already happening.

2 a　What is the natural greenhouse effect of the atmosphere?

b　Explain the relative importance of the different greenhouse gases.

c　Outline how and why the responsibility for emitting these gases is not equally shared between the countries of the world.

Impacts of global warming

Global warming has already had some impacts that can be measured. Winters in the late 1990s in the UK have been milder with lower snowfall than previously. The Arctic ice cap is thinning by 10cm a year and it has shrunk by some 40 per cent over the past few decades. Mountain glaciers have been retreating at a rapid rate in every continent. Sea levels are already 18cm higher than a hundred years ago. Global warming is blamed for severe weather events such as heavy rains, strong winds and drought. With how much validity? That is more a matter of opinion. The most realistic expectation, if present trends continue, is an increase in average world temperature of up to 2°C during the twenty-first century.

▲ **Figure 1** Fact: glaciers in the Beagle Channel used to extend down to sea level but few of them do today.

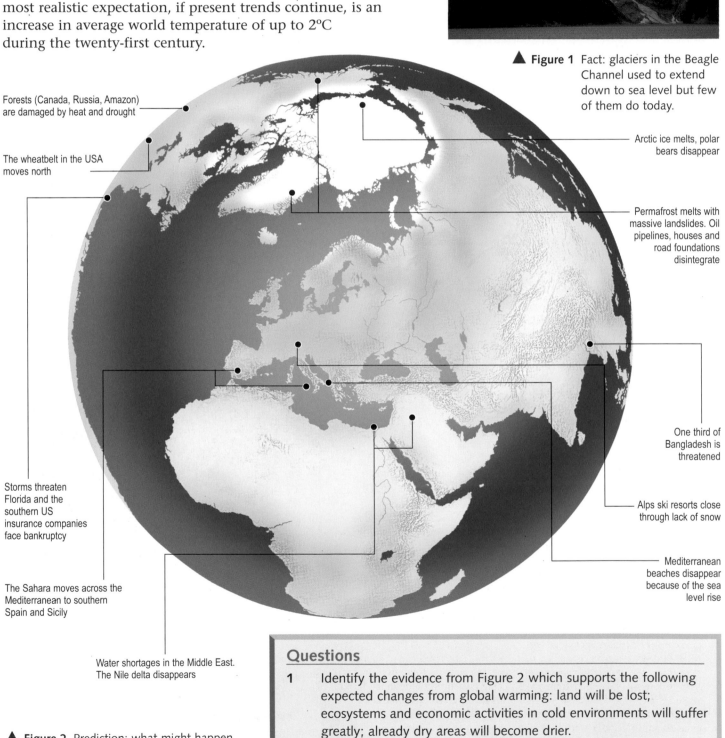

Forests (Canada, Russia, Amazon) are damaged by heat and drought

The wheatbelt in the USA moves north

Arctic ice melts, polar bears disappear

Permafrost melts with massive landslides. Oil pipelines, houses and road foundations disintegrate

One third of Bangladesh is threatened

Alps ski resorts close through lack of snow

Mediterranean beaches disappear because of the sea level rise

Storms threaten Florida and the southern US insurance companies face bankruptcy

The Sahara moves across the Mediterranean to southern Spain and Sicily

Water shortages in the Middle East. The Nile delta disappears

▲ **Figure 2** Prediction: what might happen in the northern hemisphere by 2050 if present trends continue

Questions

1   Identify the evidence from Figure 2 which supports the following expected changes from global warming: land will be lost; ecosystems and economic activities in cold environments will suffer greatly; already dry areas will become drier.

2   What serious economic consequences could result?

Predicted impacts of global warming in the UK

Case Study

Key
■ Areas of UK less than 5m above sea level

Edinburgh
Carlisle
Liverpool
King's Lynn
Bristol
London

London
Southend-on-Sea
Gillingham
Maidstone
Margate
Chichester
Southampton
Brighton
Hastings
Eastbourne
Portsmouth

N

0 20 40 km

▲ **Figure 3** Areas most at risk from flooding by rising sea levels:
- salt marshes and wetlands destroyed
- present coastal sea defences overwhelmed
- sand dune coastlines eroded.

▲ **Figure 4**
A practice closing of part of the Thames Barrier. It is expected to continue to offer flood protection to London until after 2050. It is a high-tech solution which takes into account rising global sea levels and local subsidence. Elsewhere sea defences are barely adequate to protect against present, never mind future, conditions.

South to get 'Bordeaux climate by 2050'

Global warming will widen the UK's climatic gap between the wet north and the dry south, a government review body warned. The north and west of the country will become even wetter with more flooding. The south and east will become drier with frequent droughts. The climate of the London area will be similar to that of the Bordeaux region today. Wine growing will be a more widespread type of farming.

Likely beneficiaries include tourism and recreation, forestry with a predicted increase in timber yields and some farming in upland areas. There is a longer list of losers. Farmers in most of England will suffer from soil erosion and reduced crop yields through drought. The insurance industry is vulnerable; the cost of weather-related claims has been rising rapidly since the mid-1980s. Drought-related subsidence, storms and flooding will all lead to many more claims over the next few decades. All may be affected by health problems if, for example, insect-borne diseases become established.

The review predicts an increase in the average UK temperature from 9°C to 10.6°C by 2050. At the same time global sea levels will rise by 35cm, causing problems in low lying regions.

Greenpeace was hostile to the review: 'The climate is changing but policies aren't. The government is doing pathetically little in the face of this massive ecological threat'.

Adapted from *The Financial Times*, 3 July 1996
▲ **Figure 5**

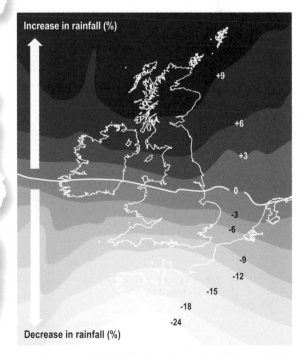

Increase in rainfall (%)

+9
+6
+3
0
-3
-6
-9
-12
-15
-18
-24

Decrease in rainfall (%)

▲ **Figure 6** Predicted changes in precipitation in the UK by the 2050s

Political responses to global warming

At the Earth Summit in Rio in 1992 the world's nations attempted to tackle a range of environmental problems, which included the issue of climatic change. Although 150 nations signed treaties aimed at reducing the greenhouse effect, these were non-binding. Governments were too concerned with short-term economic costs of action. For example, despite President Clinton's 1993 commitment to reduce US emissions to 1990 levels by 2000, emissions in the USA increased by over 3 per cent a year in both 1995 and 1996. Curbs on emissions in the USA, such as increased fuel efficiency measures for cars or higher energy taxes, were considered to be too unpopular politically.

The Kyoto conference in late 1997 was more tightly focused on climate change. The Kyoto Protocol, which despite months of preliminary discussions was still a compromise agreement, laid down mandatory reductions in carbon dioxide emissions of 5.2 per cent by 2010 compared with 1990 levels. It was signed by 84 nations, including the USA. Significantly it was not ratified by the US Senate. These mandatory limits on emissions (from cars, power plants and other major users of fossil fuels) only applied to MEDCs. LEDCs, including some rapidly industrializing countries with considerable coal reserves of their own such as China and India, were excluded. The USA hopes to achieve most of its target for cutting carbon dioxide through emissions trading, thereby allowing it to carry on with the same or increased emissions by buying up carbon credits saved by other countries.

Environmentalists argue that the level of reduction agreed in Kyoto is nothing like enough; some have suggested that the target needed to be 60 per cent, applied worldwide, to have any major impact. The 43-strong Alliance of Small Island States is so worried that it called a special session at the United Nations in September 1999 demanding greater efforts to combat climate change and rising seas. Some of these tropical islands with palm-fringed sandy beaches look like paradise, but the coral atolls of which many are made in whole or in part are only a metre or two above current sea levels and could literally be washed away (Figure 1).

▼ **Figure 1** Island nations under threat

	Population	Surface area (km²)
Palau	19,000	459
Nauru	11,000	21
Seychelles	76,000	455
Tonga	98,000	747
Niue	2,000	260
Cook Islands	19,000	236
Tuvalu	11,000	26
Marshall Islands	60,000	181

▶ **Figure 2**
Penang, Malaysia. Tropical paradise, but for how much longer?
The sand bags were put there as a precaution against El Niño in 1997–8

UK leads world in carbon dioxide cut

Britain will exceed its target for reducing carbon dioxide emission by such a large amount that it will have as much as £100 million worth of carbon credits to sell to the United States or any other country that will buy to meet its legally binding target. The fact that the UK will comfortably exceed its United Nations legally binding target of 12.5 per cent by 2010 is mainly because of the mass switch to electricity generation by natural gas, a far less polluting means of generating electricity than coal.

The UK is expected to take a lead in renewed international negotiations due in the Hague in November where it is hoped Europe would ratify the Kyoto Protocol and allow international carbon trading to begin. Estimates vary about how much a tonne of carbon will be worth in international trade, but it could be as much as £15. Britain will have up to 8 million tonnes to sell.

Among the initiatives announced yesterday were revised energy efficiency targets in homes. The government has finalized the climate change levy on industry.

For the future 'We must move into renewable energies, fuel cells to drive cars, and other technologies that cause no carbon pollution,' the government's environment minister said.

▲ **Figure 3** A wind farm in Wales

Adapted from *The Guardian*, 10 March 2000

A considered view is that it makes no sense to over-react to the possible consequences of global warming, nor does it make any sense to ignore them. The temperature of the Earth has always fluctuated. It was only 10 000 years ago that the Earth emerged from the Ice Age caused by a fall of 4–5°C in world temperatures. A rise of 1°C will just bring the UK back to temperature levels in the warm period between AD1000 and 1300. However, there is no doubt that some areas are seriously at risk from rising sea levels caused both by thermal expansion of the water and by ice melting. There are other impacts which are as yet uncertain. There is the need to do something. A mixed policy that stresses energy conservation, cleaner emissions and the increased use of alternative energy sources would appear to be a prudent approach to some, if not to all. However, there is still the possibility that something other than greenhouse gas emissions has greater responsibility for the current global warming, such as sun spots, whose influence on weather and climate is not as yet fully understood.

Questions

1 The USA holds the key to taking measures to prevent global warming. Outline and explain your views on this.

Investigation

2 a Outline the various methods of energy conservation and for making emissions cleaner.
 b Identify and comment upon the potential usefulness of four different alternative energy sources.

Investigation

3 a Outline the main features of an LEDC's (e.g. Bangladesh) physical geography which make it vulnerable to rises in sea level.
 b Outline the nature and effects of current natural hazards. Why might their effects worsen?
 c Outline the LEDC's present major land uses and economic activities and suggest how they may be affected in the future.

Chapter 2 Questions

1 a Figure 1 shows how the effects of hurricanes upon the USA have changed with time.

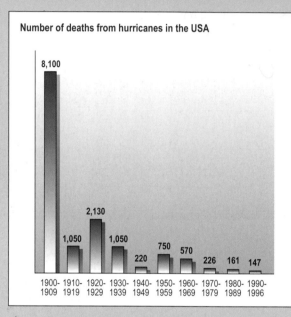

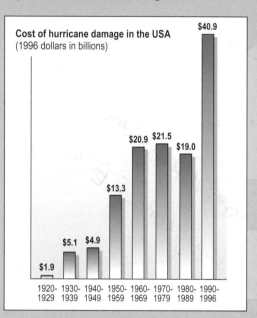

▲ Figure 1

    i   Describe the main changes shown.   (2 marks)

    ii Suggest why these changes have happened.   (3 marks)

    iii Would you expect the same changes to have happened in an LEDC?
Explain your answer.   (3 marks)

  b Explain the origins of tropical revolving storms such as hurricanes.   (7 marks)

Total: 15 marks

2 a Make a comparative study of precipitation between the Tropical Monsoon and
Cool Temperate Western Maritime types of climate.   (10 marks)

  b Why do variations from the average in precipitation cause problems for people in
both MEDCs and LEDCs?   (10 marks)

Total: 20 marks

A note on timing
You are expected to answer question 1 in about 15 minutes. You are expected to
answer question 2 in about 40 minutes, spending an equal length of time on both parts.

Chapter 3 Energy and life

Wintersdale Dene in County Durham, an ancient deciduous woodland with a carpet of wild garlic

Characteristics of ecosystems

Succession and climatic climax vegetation

Human modification of ecosystems

Soils

The impact of human activity on soils

Characteristics of ecosystems

- Ecosystems and biomes
- Characteristics of ecosystems
- Processes in an ecosysytem: energy flows, food chains and trophic levels
- Nutrient cycling
- Productivity in natural and agricultural systems

Ecosystems and biomes

Ecosystems

Deciduous woodlands, tropical rainforests and deserts are all examples of ecosystems. Ecosystems tend to be named by the most easily recognizable feature, the vegetation. However, as shown in Figure 1, the concept of an ecosystem is more than just the trees and other plants that can be seen.

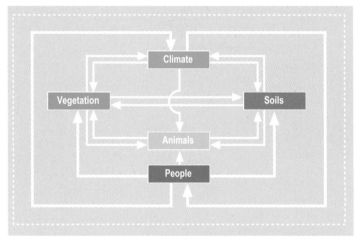

▲ **Figure 2** Freshwater ecosystem along the River Brora, North East Scotland, with managed vegetation in the background

◀ **Figure 1** The components of an ecosystem

An ecosystem is a natural unit with biotic and abiotic components that interact with each other. Biotic components are the living organisms – the animals, micro-organisms, trees and other plants found in an ecosystem. The abiotic components are the inorganic or physical and chemical elements of the ecosystem. These include the soil, climate, relief, geology and drainage. The interactions of the biotic and abiotic parts produce a stable system that is in equilibrium. This means that the plants and animals interact with one another and with the non-living elements in the system, but the ecosystem remains in balance with little change, unless there is a change to one of the elements.

In an ecosystem the flow of energy and the cycling of nutrients through the ecosystem maintain the balance or equilibrium. The equilibrium may be upset for a variety of reasons, such as climate change, human activity and plant and animal diseases.

Studying ecosystems is a useful way to look at the combination of plants, animals (including human activity), soil and atmosphere together. Ecosystems can be studied at a variety of scales, for example, from a single oak tree or a pond through to large-scale ecosystems such as the tropical rainforest, tundra or deciduous woodland.

A small-scale ecosystem:
Case Study

a hedgerow

▼ **Figure 3** A small-scale ecosystem – a hedgerow

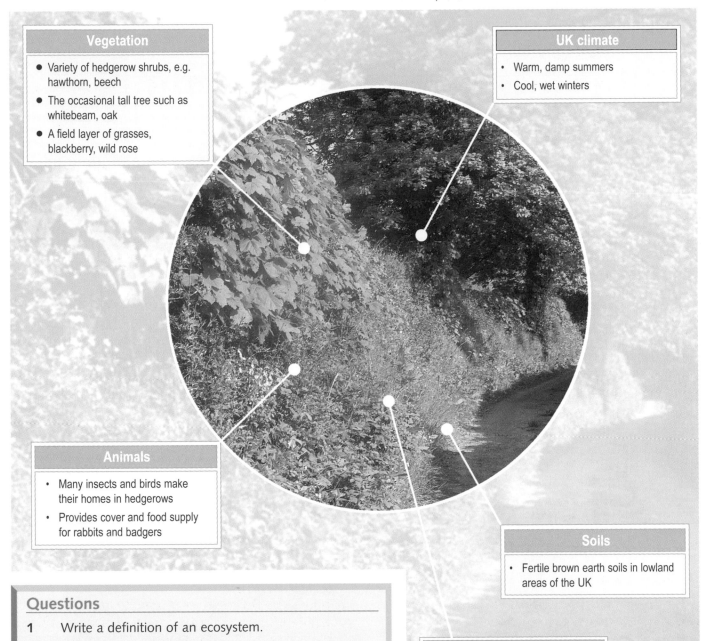

Vegetation

- Variety of hedgerow shrubs, e.g. hawthorn, beech
- The occasional tall tree such as whitebeam, oak
- A field layer of grasses, blackberry, wild rose

UK climate

- Warm, damp summers
- Cool, wet winters

Animals

- Many insects and birds make their homes in hedgerows
- Provides cover and food supply for rabbits and badgers

Soils

- Fertile brown earth soils in lowland areas of the UK

People

- Farmers may trim the hedges each year to encourage bushy growth and for appearance
- Local people collect blackberries, elderberries, rosehips
- Large sections of hedgerows have been removed to allow large-scale mechanization of farms

Questions

1. Write a definition of an ecosystem.

2. What is the difference between the abiotic and biotic components of an ecosystem?

3. For the hedgerow in Figure 3 or another small-scale ecosystem you have studied:
   a. produce a more detailed version of Figure 1 to summarize its main features
   b. list the biotic and abiotic components of the ecosystem
   c. explain how you think the ecosystem is in equilibrium
   d. suggest ways in which the equilibrium may be upset.

Biomes

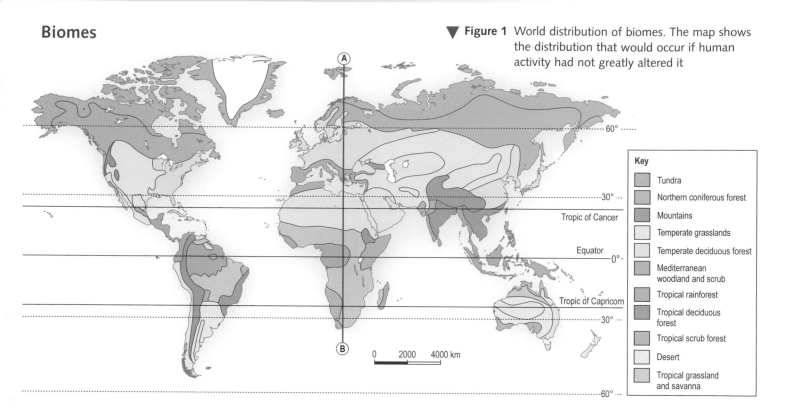

▼ **Figure 1** World distribution of biomes. The map shows the distribution that would occur if human activity had not greatly altered it

Key
- Tundra
- Northern coniferous forest
- Mountains
- Temperate grasslands
- Temperate deciduous forest
- Mediterranean woodland and scrub
- Tropical rainforest
- Tropical deciduous forest
- Tropical scrub forest
- Desert
- Tropical grassland and savanna

The term biome is used to describe the very large-scale or global ecosystems. A map of world biomes tends to be a map of world vegetation zones (Figure 1). These major global ecosystems are closely linked to the global distribution of climate and soils (Figures 2 and 3). Climate has a strong influence on soil type and similar climatic areas tend to have similar soils. These major soil types are called zonal soils. In turn there is also a close link between the climate and the vegetation type. The climate tends to be the controlling factor in the location and distribution of types of vegetation. In areas with a hot, wet equatorial climate the dominant vegetation is tropical rainforest. In countries such as Britain, the west coast maritime climate is associated with deciduous woodland. The dominant vegetation in an area is called the climatic climax vegetation.

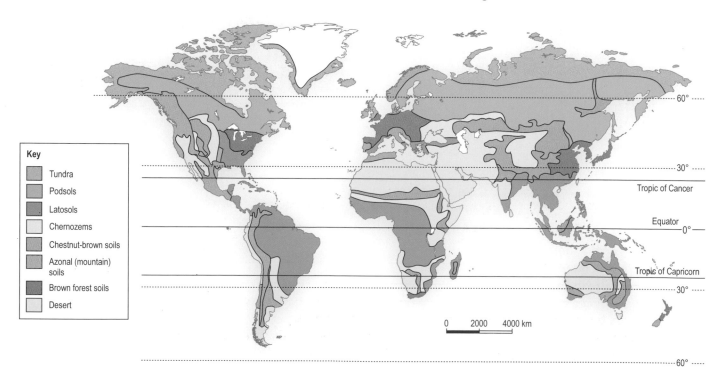

Key
- Tundra
- Podsols
- Latosols
- Chernozems
- Chestnut-brown soils
- Azonal (mountain) soils
- Brown forest soils
- Desert

▲ **Figure 2** World distribution of the main zonal soils

▼ **Figure 3** World distribution of climatic zones

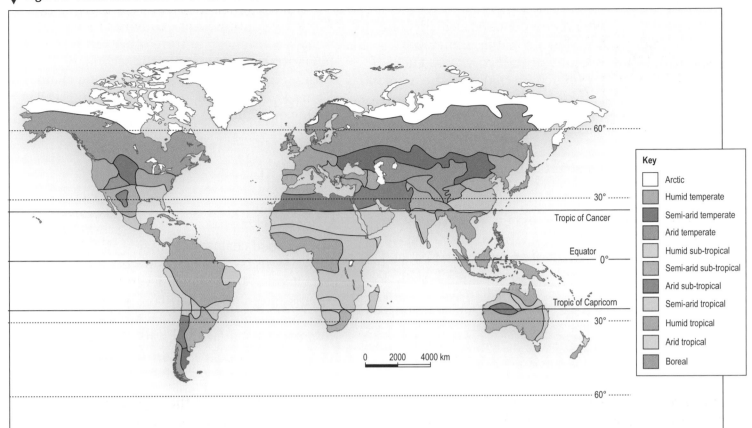

Figure 4 shows how climate, soils and vegetation interact. Climate affects soils mainly though its influence on precipitation and rates of evapotranspiration. The climate also influences the flora (plant life) and fauna (animal life) as different plants and animals can tolerate different temperature ranges and amounts of precipitation. Soils influence the vegetation as different plants can tolerate different levels of soil moisture and acidity. In turn, the amount of dead organic matter from the vegetation has an impact on soil types.

▼ **Figure 4** The relationship between climate, soils and vegetation

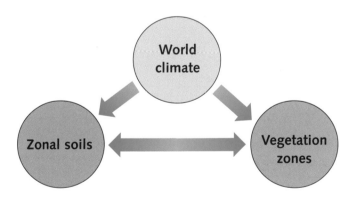

Questions

1   Using Figures 1, 2 and 3 complete a table like the one below. Follow transect A-B on Figure 1.

Biome	Climate	Vegetation types	Soil type	Locations

2 a Describe the world distribution of soils, vegetation and climate.
  b To what extent is there a link between the world distribution of soils, vegetation and climate?
3   What is the difference between an ecosystem and a biome?

Characteristics of ecosystems

In an ecosystem there are two organic elements: the biomass and the dead organic matter, sometimes referred to as the structure of the ecosystem. The organic elements are interconnected with the inorganic elements by two main processes:
- a flow of energy   • a cycling of nutrients.

Biomass

Biomass is the total amount of living matter present at any moment in an ecosystem. It includes organic matter found above ground, e.g. stems, leaves and animals, as well as that found below ground e.g. roots, micro-organisms and burrowing animals. Biomass is usually measured as the dry weight of organic matter per unit area, for example in tonnes per hectare or kilograms per square metre. The largest biomass is found in the tropical rainforest where the huge trees contribute to a biomass of 4 500 grammes/m². One of the smallest is found in tundra areas where the mosses, lichens, grasses and small shrubs generate a biomass of only 60 grammes/m².

Dead organic matter

Dead organic matter includes:
- the litter layer - the dead twigs, leaves and branches not yet decayed, found on the surface of the soil
- soil humus – the decayed organic matter incorporated into the soil.

In some ecosystems, e.g. tundra, grassland, the dead organic matter is greater than the biomass in both volume and weight.

Processes in an ecosystem: energy flows, food chains and trophic levels

The main source of energy for all ecosystems is from the Sun. Green plants absorb solar radiation during photosynthesis. Only green plants can photosynthesize and use the Sun's energy in this way so they are called primary producers.

The energy produced is used by plants:
- for growth when the weight of the plant increases and more energy is stored in the plant
- for plant processes, for example transporting chemicals, root uptake of water and nutrients.

When animals eat plants they take in the energy stored in the plant structure. These animals are called herbivores or primary consumers and they use the energy:
- to perform life processes e.g. breathing, movement, internal transport, generate heat etc.
- to synthesize materials to keep healthy and to grow.

Secondary consumers or carnivores may eat these primary consumers. In turn, other carnivores or tertiary consumers may eat the secondary consumers. This process is called a food chain (Figure 1). Each level in the food chain is called a trophic or feeding level.

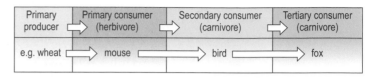

Primary producer	Primary consumer (herbivore)	Secondary consumer (carnivore)	Tertiary consumer (carnivore)
e.g. wheat	mouse	bird	fox

▲ **Figure 1** A food chain

Very few food chains have more than four or five trophic levels because of the loss of energy, mostly in the form of heat, at each level (Figure 2). For example, green plants only convert some of the Sun's energy into plant tissues. Most is reflected from the plant surface and some is used by the plant for life processes. When herbivores eat green plants energy is also lost in performing life processes such as in movement, generating heat and digestion. About 90 per cent of energy is lost at each level, mostly in the form of heat, leaving only 10 per cent available for growth. Therefore, there is an efficiency of about 10 per cent across each link in a food chain. This energy loss at each stage in a food chain means that any producer or consumer may only support a small number of organisms above it in the chain. Food chains are very simple representations of ecosystems and often not very realistic. A better representation is the food web which shows the more complex picture. However, it is even better to use pyramids (information box) that group the producers and consumers into trophic levels.

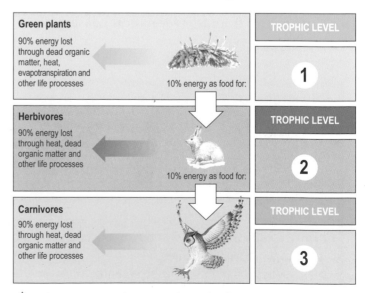

▲ **Figure 2** Energy loss at each trophic level

Pyramids

1 Pyramids of number

The area of the rectangle is proportional to the numbers of plants and animals at each tropic level. Using this method, most food webs are pyramid shaped with the largest rectangle at the base. However, there are some exceptions e.g. the numbers of caterpillars on a cabbage.

2 Pyramids of biomass

These pyramids use the weight of organic matter per unit area, rather than the number of plants or animals. They always produce a pyramid shape because one trophic level can only support a smaller biomass above it because of the energy loss across each trophic level.

Pyramids of number

fox	—— T3 Carnivores
rabbit	—— T2 Herbivores
grass	T1 Green plants

birds	T = Trophic level
caterpillars	
	— cabbage

Pyramids of biomass

50 kg	—— young human
1000 kg	— beef cattle
8000 kg	animal fodder

Nutrient cycling

In all ecosystems plants and animals need nutrients such as calcium, phosphorous and nitrogen to survive. These nutrients or chemical elements are circulated within the ecosystem, often summarized as a nutrient cycling model (Figure 3).

▼ **Figure 3** A model of nutrient cycling

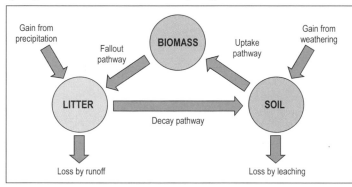

NB The model represents the storage and flows of NUTRIENTS in the ecosystem not the size of the biomass, soil and litter.

The model has three circles that represent the amounts of nutrients stored in an ecosystem.

1 The biomass – living plants and animals.
2 The soil – dead organic matter or humus in the soil.
3 The litter – dead organic matter lying on the soil surface.

Between each store the series of arrows indicates the flows of nutrients.

- The uptake or growth pathway between the soil and biomass store indicates the uptake of elements such as nitrogen, potassium and phosphorus from the soil.
- The fallout pathway represents the death of plants and animals and the addition of nutrients to the litter store.
- The decay pathway between the litter and the soil represents the decomposition of the litter to humus and the return of nutrients to the soil.

The nutrient cycling in an ecosystem is an open system and the nutrient storage may change over time.

- Chemical elements may be added to the soil by the weathering of rocks.
- The litter may receive additional nutrients brought by precipitation, lightning or wind-blown leaves.
- Animals may move between ecosystems transferring nutrients.
- Nutrients may be lost from the ecosystem as a result of overland flow or leaching.

Positive human impacts

People may add nutrients to the cycle through organic fertilizers (dung, manure), inorganic fertilizers (manufactured compounds of potassium, nitrogen, phosphorus etc.) and planting of trees and other plants.

Negative human impacts

In general, human activity has a negative effect resulting in a loss of nutrients from an ecosystem.

- Deforestation removes trees and vegetation in an area and may result in soil erosion.
- Farming practices can lead to overcultivation and overgrazing.
- Shortages of wood may lead to the use of crop stalks and manure for fuel that could otherwise replace nutrients on farmland.
- Irrigation may sometimes lead to greater leaching of nutrients from soils.
- Harvesting removes nutrients from the ecosystem.

Questions

1 Define the terms **i** biomass and **ii** dead organic matter.

2 Explain why green plants are called primary producers.

3 With the aid of a diagram, explain why there are rarely more than four or five trophic levels in a food chain.

4 With the aid of diagrams, explain why pyramids are a better representation of ecosystems than food chains or food webs.

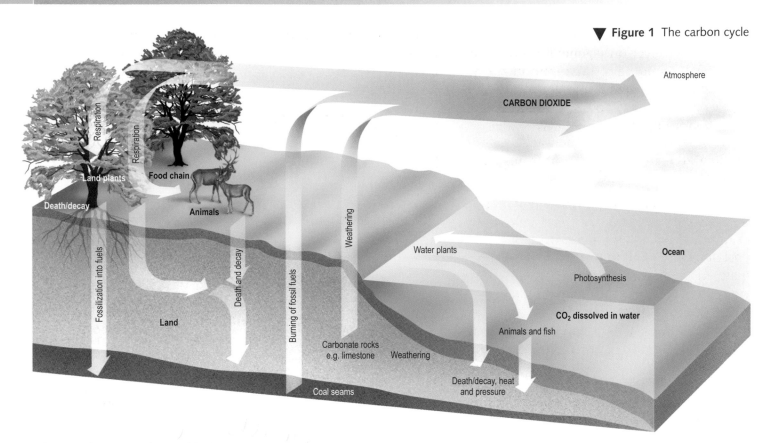

The carbon cycle

One chemical element circulated within an ecosystem is carbon (Figure 1). Carbon is mixed with oxygen to form carbon dioxide. Green plants take in carbon dioxide from the atmosphere through their leaves. The process of photosynthesis converts the carbon dioxide into carbohydrates such as glucose The plant uses the carbohydrates for life processes and for growth. Glucose, for example, may be built up into larger molecules such as starch and stored. Some may be used to make cellulose for plant cell walls. The carbon may then become a static part of the ecosystem uninvolved in any further cycling for a long time. Eventually the plant may be eaten or it may die and the carbohydrates can be broken down and returned to the cycle. Plants that are eaten pass through the digestive system of the animal. Some of the carbohydrate is used to provide energy by respiration or it may be stored as fat. Respiration returns some carbon dioxide to the atmosphere. Carbohydrate not absorbed from the digestive system is egested as waste and returned to the ecosystem where it is decomposed. The decomposers, such as bacteria and fungi, use the carbohydrates as an energy source, the respiration once again leading to the return of carbon dioxide or methane (CH_4) to the atmosphere. Eventually the herbivore may die or be eaten by a carnivore.

Some living organisms are not decomposed but may be fossilized. These sources of carbon, e.g. coal and oil, are used as a fuel by people. The burning of the fossil fuels to provide energy releases carbon dioxide back into the atmosphere.

Productivity in natural and agricultural systems

Productivity is the rate at which energy is absorbed or fixed by green plants. There is a distinction made between gross primary production and net primary production.

- Gross primary production (GPP) is the total amount of energy that is absorbed and used for life processes and for growth.
- Net primary production (NPP) is the element that is used for growth only.

Net primary productivity is, therefore, the growth rate of vegetation measured by the increase in the biomass over a year. It is normally measured in dry weight of tissue per unit area per year, e.g. tonnes per hectare per year or kilograms per square metre per year.

Plant productivity is affected by:
- light
- temperature
- carbon dioxide
- nutrient availability
- water

Productivity is greatest where all of these are in abundant supply, such as in tropical rainforests, and lowest where they are lacking, such as in tundra and desert areas.

The oceans cover about 70 per cent of the Earth's surface yet only generate about one-third of the total net primary productivity. The land surface generates two-thirds of the Earth's productivity. The world's forests are particularly important. The forests contribute 46 per cent of the total productivity, about 27 per cent from the tropical rainforests alone.

The overall impact of human activity has been to reduce productivity. Pastureland, for example, has only about one-third of the productivity of forested land and cropland may reduce productivity by as much as 75 per cent. The average net primary productivity of cultivated land is 700 grammes/m²/year compared with 2200 grammes/m²/year in the tropical rainforests (Figure 2). Rice has a net primary productivity of 600 grammes/m²/year for one crop. Where double or treble cropping takes place then productivity approaches that of the forests in temperate latitudes. However, it remains less than the productivity of the natural tropical forests that it replaces.

Despite the low contribution of about 8 per cent to total productivity, cultivated land produces about 70 per cent of all food for human consumption. Grazing land generates about 19 per cent of all productivity and produces about 15 per cent of human food. The forests contribute 47 per cent to productivity. They are an important timber supply, but at a maximum they only provide about 10 per cent of human food supplies.

Human activity can also try to increase net primary productivity by:
- selection and breeding of high yielding varieties of animals and crops
- increased inputs of labour, machinery, fertilizers, pesticides etc.
- intensive farming techniques such as double or treble cropping and irrigation
- shorter food chains – the most efficient trophic level is the second i.e. that of the herbivore or, in human terms, the vegetarian. Many more people can be fed from a hectare of wheat or rice than on the animals grazed on the same area of land.

▼ **Figure 2** Net primary productivity in land and fresh-water ecosystems

Ecosystems	Mean net primary productivity (grammes/m²/yr)	Annual total primary net productivity (10^9 tonnes)
Tropical rainforest	2200	47.4
Deciduous forest	1200	7.0
Tropical grassland	900	12.0
Temperate grassland	600	7.2
Coniferous forest	800	7.8
Tundra and alpine	140	1.3
Desert	90	1.3

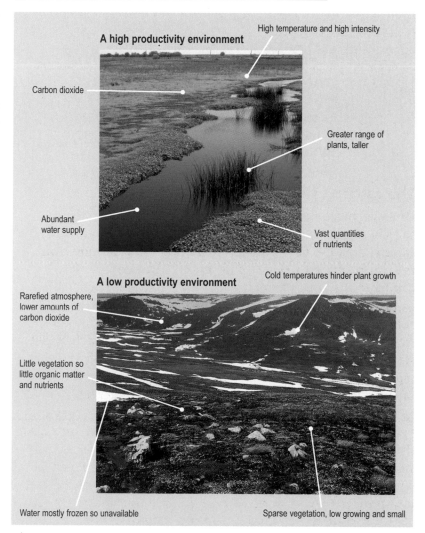

A high productivity environment
High temperature and high intensity
Carbon dioxide
Greater range of plants, taller
Abundant water supply
Vast quantities of nutrients

A low productivity environment
Cold temperatures hinder plant growth
Rarefied atmosphere, lower amounts of carbon dioxide
Little vegetation so little organic matter and nutrients
Water mostly frozen so unavailable
Sparse vegetation, low growing and small

▲ **Figure 3** High and low productivity ecosystems

Questions

1   Explain the role of each of the following in the carbon cycle:
    i land plants, and **ii** atmospheric carbon dioxide.

2   Using Figure 2 suggest which is the most productive ecosystem and why?

3 **a** Why does the cultivation of land usually reduce mean NPP?
  b What are the disadvantages of reducing global NPP?

A low productivity ecosystem:

the Arctic tundra

Location

Arctic tundra is found in high latitudes and Arctic/Alpine regions; a wide zone to the north of the boreal forests.

Climate

Winters are severe, often with long periods of very cold conditions (Figure 1). Temperatures are low with an annual average of about 0°C, with six months of temperatures below freezing. Precipitation is mostly in the form of snow, totals are low and irregular, often below 250mm. The land is often subject to permafrost (permanently frozen ground) although there may be some surface thaw in summer. The growing season is very short, often less than 50 days. There are strong winds throughout the year. Although there is plenty of water in the environment much of it is unavailable to plants because it is frozen or temperatures are too cold for uptake by roots. This is called physiological drought.

Soils

Soils may be frozen throughout the year with waterlogged surface layers in summer. There are large areas of bare rock (rock deserts) or areas with very poor soil development. These thin, rock strewn soils are called lithosols. They tend to be low in organic matter. In more favourable areas for soil development podsols (see page 124) are formed. These soils tend to be waterlogged or gleyed.

Vegetation structure and types

- Sparse and scattered with no trees except towards the southern limit (Figure 2).
- Poor species richness, i.e. low biodiversity with typically less than 100 species of plant.
- Most plants are mosses, lichens, grasses, sedges, dwarf shrubs or annual flowering plants.
- Often only one layer of vegetation.
- There is a zonation of the vegetation from north to south in Arctic areas. Towards the northern limit of plant growth, mosses and lichens are dominant in scattered communities. Moving southwards, conditions become slightly less severe and sedges and grasses also grow eventually giving way to shrubby heathland. Towards the southern limit of the tundra small trees such as birch and willow become scattered across the grasslands and heathlands.

Adaptations of the vegetation

- Frost and wind-resistant species, no tall plants.
- Seeds and buds lie dormant in the soil ready to germinate as soon as the thaw occurs.
- Low, creeping growth form to protect against strong winds.
- Shallow roots to cope with permafrost and solifluction.
- Special relationships between some species for survival e.g. mycorrhiza, a fungus, lives on the roots of heather. The fungus helps seedlings to establish by decomposing organic and mineral matter and passing them to the plant in a dissolved state. In return the fungus has its 'home' on the heather. In this way the heather can survive in the nitrogen deficient soils.
- Plants are adapted to conserve moisture e.g. by having thin leaves, thick cuticles, hairy leaves and protected stomata (pores in the leaves) in rolled leaves.

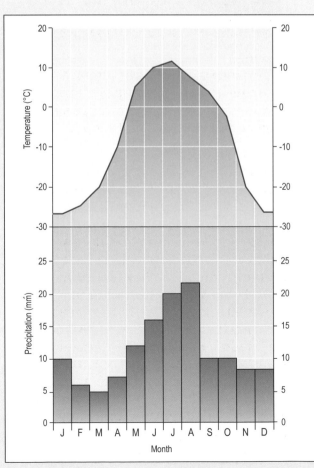

▲ **Figure 1** Climate graph for Fort Yukon

▲ **Figure 2** A tundra landscape

Nutrient cycling

Nutrient levels are low and the cycling of nutrients slow due to the cold climate (Figure 3). There is little storage and circulation of nutrients and low rates of other inputs and losses. The amount of nutrients stored in the biomass is small due to the limited amount and small size of the vegetation. The vegetation grows only slowly and is mostly evergreen so little litter reaches the soil on an annual basis. Decomposition of the litter is slow. The activity of decomposers is restricted by the intense cold for most of the year. Hence the soils contain only limited quantities of organic matter. The limited chemical and physical decomposition of the rocks restrict inputs of nutrients from weathering. The low overall precipitation limits inputs of nutrients from snow or rain and also limits the amount of overland flow or runoff, which may remove nutrients from the litter. The presence of permafrost inhibits leaching of materials.

Productivity

Net primary productivity 140 grammes/m²/year
World total = 1.1×10^9 tonnes per year

Fauna

Insects, migratory birds in summer, lemmings, hares, foxes, wolves, owls, reindeer, caribou etc. Many large animals migrate to follow the food supply.

Human impact

The traditional way of life of the Inuit and Lapps caused little disturbance to the environment. Their lifestyles, involving hunting and fishing, were compatible with the biome. The Lapps particularly would migrate with the large animal herds hunting for food, as they needed it. Their lifestyle was sustainable within the ecosystem. More recently human activity has caused more disturbances with oil exploration, mining and the building of roads and pipelines. Damage to the ecosystem is inevitable due to its fragility caused by its slow growth, the ease with which it can be damaged or destroyed and the slow recovery rates.

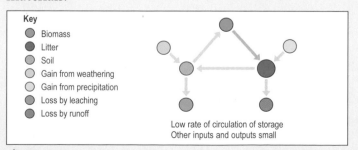

Key
- Biomass
- Litter
- Soil
- Gain from weathering
- Gain from precipitation
- Loss by leaching
- Loss by runoff

Low rate of circulation of storage
Other inputs and outputs small

▲ **Figure 3** Nutrient cycling

A high productivity ecosystem:

Case Study

the tropical rainforest

Location
The tropical rainforests of the world are located mainly between 10° north and south of the Equator (Figure 1 on page 94). The areas include:
- parts of South and Central America including the Amazon basin
- parts of West Africa including Congo
- parts of Indo-Malaysia and the north coast of Australia.

Climate
Figure 1 shows a climate graph for Manaus in the Amazon Basin. Tropical rainforests grow in the humid tropics where annual rainfall totals are often in excess of 2000mm and in some areas may total over 3000mm per year. The rainfall is evenly distributed throughout the year although in some areas there may be a short dry season lasting one or two months. Temperatures in the rainforests are uniformly high with a mean monthly temperature of 27°C and an annual range of only 4° from 24°–28°C. Humidity is often over 80 per cent. The climate gives greenhouse conditions ideal for the rapid growth of vegetation.

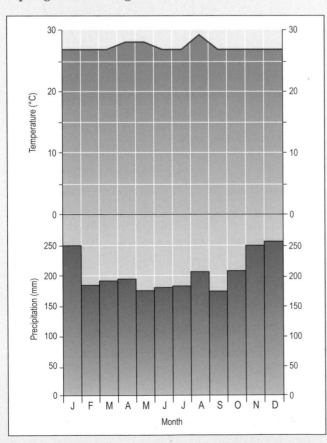

▲ **Figure 1** Climate graph for Manaus in the Amazon Basin

Soils
Many people believe that because there is dense vegetation in tropical rainforests the soils are fertile. However, the soils are infertile latosols which are rich in iron, giving the strong red colouring. They are a product of intense weathering and leaching and high acidity. The latosols often have little organic matter due to rapid decomposition and uptake by the vegetation.

Vegetation structure and types
The forest is stratified and five layers can often be recognized (Figure 2).
- Epiphytes such as lianas (creepers) may stretch from the forest floor to the canopy using other trees for support.
- There is great diversity with often over 200 different species in one hectare.
- Species include teak, mahogany and rosewood.
- Parasitic and saprophytic plants, which feed on the dead organic matter, are found in the shaded lower layers and on the forest floor.

Adaptations of the vegetation
- Trees have slender trunks and thin, smooth bark to allow maximum water loss and because there is no need for protection against frost.
- Trees are tall, 30-50 metres high, to reach the sunlight for maximum photosynthesis.
- Trees often have buttress roots to give support and to allow massive uptake of water and nutrients for the tree to survive.
- Cauliflory is common where the flowers and fruits appear on the tree trunks.
- Leaves are grown and cast off continually, reflecting the all year round growing season and giving the rainforest an evergreen appearance.
- Leaves are often leathery and have a simple shape, with drip tips. This helps the leaves to shed water, encourages transpiration and prevents the development of disease and parasites in the tropical conditions.
- Often there is very little development of the shrub and ground layers due to a lack of light except in clearings or by riverbanks.
- Vegetation grows rapidly due to the hot, wet climate.

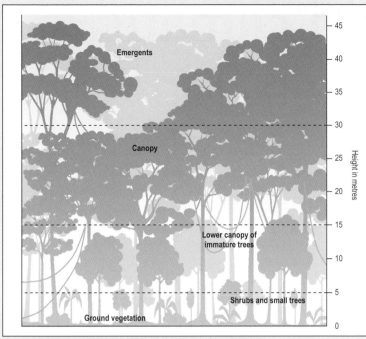

▲ **Figure 2** Structure of the tropical rainforest

Nutrient cycling

The nutrient cycling model (Figure 3) has a huge store of nutrients in the biomass reflecting the massive trees and the complex layering of the vegetation. The litter store is relatively small due to the rapid decomposition of any dead organic matter reaching the forest floor in the hot, wet conditions. The soil store is small too due to the very rapid uptake of the nutrients by the vegetation. Hence the cycling of the relatively small nutrient stock in the rainforest is rapid, almost leak-free and continuous due to the lack of any seasonal variation in the climate. At any one time, the majority of the nutrients are held in the vegetation. Losses by leaching and runoff can be significant in the very wet climate.

Productivity

Net primary productivity = 2200 grammes/m^2/year – the highest of any natural ecosystem.

Fauna

There are about 30 different species per hectare including insects, apes, monkeys, snakes and rodents.

Human impacts

The traditional inhabitants of the rainforests, e.g. the tribes of Indians in the Amazon, were well adapted to life in the rainforest – hunting, gathering, fishing and practising shifting cultivation. Their way of life was in harmony with the environment and sustainable as long as numbers were small and density of population remained low. However, in recent years population growth and the development of the rainforest for roads, mining, agriculture and settlement has seen large areas deforested with negative impacts upon the ecosystem. The deforestation removes the majority of the nutrients from the rainforest leaving behind relatively infertile latosols exposed to heavy rain, which causes leaching and soil erosion.

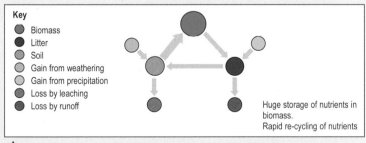

▲ **Figure 3** Nutrient cycling diagram: tropical rainforest

Questions

1   On a world outline map, mark and label the distribution of tundra and tropical rainforest environments.

2   Does your map represent the present distribution of these two vegetation types? Explain your answer.

3   Explain how the vegetation types are adapted to the environment (climate and soils).

4   Describe and explain the nutrient cycling diagrams for each biome.

5   Explain the differences in biomass and productivity of the two biomes.

Investigation

6   Using a variety of other resources – ICT, texts, magazines etc. – produce a similar case study for a different biome e.g. deciduous forest, boreal forest, hot desert.

Succession and climatic climax vegetation

- Arresting factors
- Plant succession:
  - primary succession
  - secondary succession

In an area the vegetation will alter and adapt to changes taking place within the environment. The change in the vegetation is called plant succession. Eventually a stage is reached when no further changes take place. The vegetation is then in equilibrium with its environment and this is the climatic climax vegetation. The climax vegetation will then be maintained until a further climate, soil or other change takes place in the ecosystem.

In the climax vegetation, the dominants are the tallest plants able to grow in the environment. In tropical rainforests these are the emergents which grow up to 50 metres high, while in tundra areas the dominants may be the lichens and mosses only a few centimetres above the ground level. At the global scale this gives rise to specific vegetation zones because the climate has a strong control over the dominant plants in an area. These dominant plants can be recognized such as oak in deciduous woodland and lichens in the tundra. The situation, however, can be more complex due to the many small-scale variations in climate, relief, soils and drainage in an area.

In general, Britain's climate would suggest that deciduous woodland should be the climatic climax vegetation. While this is true for large areas it is a broad generalization. In the Highlands of Scotland (Figure 1) for example, the relief and altitude mean steep slopes, a colder, damper climate and thin, acid soils. As altitude increases deciduous woodland gives way to coniferous woodland and on the summits of the mountains, tundra vegetation is the natural vegetation. Similarly in the Brecklands (Figure 2), a lowland area in south-east England, conifers and heathland are the sub-climax vegetation due to the sandy, infertile soils.

Arresting factors

Sometimes the plant succession is interrupted and the climatic climax vegetation is not achieved. This is a result of arresting factors such as:

- events in the natural environment, e.g. volcanic eruptions, mudflows, hurricanes, fires caused by lightning

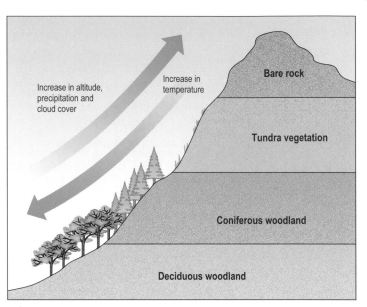

▲ **Figure 1** The zonation of vegetation in the Scottish Highlands

Increase in altitude, precipitation and cloud cover

Increase in temperature

Bare rock

Tundra vegetation

Coniferous woodland

Deciduous woodland

▲ **Figure 2** The sandy Brecklands in south-east England

- human activities, e.g. burning, clearing and grazing of land, diversion of water supplies, dam building, urban and transport developments
- local variations in relief, soils and drainage, e.g. lakes, sand dunes, mountains.

These arresting factors may all prevent the climatic climax vegetation being established and other vegetation may be dominant for long periods. This is called sub-climax vegetation. If the sub climax is a consequence of human activity the term plagioclimax community is often used.

Plant succession

Plant communities that are in succession but not at the climax vegetation stage are called seral communities or seral stages and the whole succession is called a sere. There are two main types of sere:

- priseres or primary succession on new inorganic surfaces where there has been no pre-existing soil formation or vegetation
- subseres or secondary succession on sites where there has been some previous soil formation and vegetation but the climax vegetation or a succession has been interrupted by arresting factors.

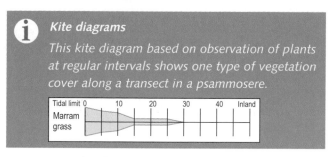

ⓘ Kite diagrams

This kite diagram based on observation of plants at regular intervals shows one type of vegetation cover along a transect in a psammosere.

▼ **Figure 3** Classification of seres

Priseres	Xerosere (dry environment)	Lithosere (bare rock)
		Psammosere (sand dunes)
	Hydrosere (wet environments)	Hydrosere (fresh water)
		Halosere (salt water)

Primary succession

Case Study

Primary succession begins on a bare inorganic surface where there has been no pre-existing vegetation or soil formation. Examples of primary succession are rare in the world, as most land surfaces have had time for soil and vegetation to develop. Primary successions will take place on:

- bare rock surfaces exposed by quarrying
- material left behind after landslides and mudflows
- new land created by lava flows from volcanic eruptions, e.g. Krakatoa, a volcanic island that erupted in 1883.

The first organisms to colonize the bare rock are the pioneers, usually mosses and lichens that do not need any soil to survive. The lichens and mosses gradually break down the rock into particles of sand, silt and clay. Parts of the mosses and lichens die adding dead organic matter or humus to the minerals to form a soil. The soils gradually become richer and deeper as the humus content increases. Eventually grasses and herbs germinate and grow as wind, water, birds or animals transport seeds in. The grasses and herbs become dominant shading out the mosses and lichens. Over time the grasses and herbs are replaced by seedlings and shrubs until eventually young trees dominate. The faster-growing species appear first, later replaced by the slower-growing dominants to create the climax vegetation of the area.

A lithosere: Krakatoa, a volcanic island

Krakatoa was an uninhabited volcanic island located near the Equator with a hot, wet equatorial climate. In 1883 the volcano erupted leaving four small islands and presenting scientists with a unique opportunity to study the regeneration of plant life on the islands. Figure 4 gives a time line for the plant succession on what remained of Krakatoa after the 1883 eruption.

Since Krakatoa lies only 40km from the mainland of Java, seeds dispersed by the wind and by birds could reach it reasonably quickly. These formed the majority of the plant species present in the first fifty years following the eruption. The equatorial climate with hot temperatures and high rainfall also provided ideal conditions for rapid plant growth and for rapid weathering of the volcanic ash and lava to form soils rich in plant nutrients. However, the number and variety of species remain less than in an old established rainforest where typically there are between 40 and 100 species within one hectare. It may be thousands of years before the great biodiversity of the climatic climax rainforests is recovered.

▼ **Figure 4** Time line succession on Krakatoa

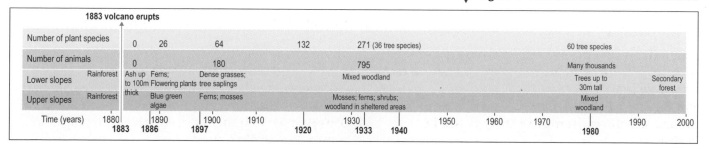

Case Study – Primary succession

A hydrosere: Loch A'Mhuilin (Isle of Arran in Scotland)

This small lake on the Isle of Arran lies behind a ridge of material deposited towards the end of the last Ice Age. The lake exhibits the characteristic features of a hydrosere, the succession from a fresh water surface with small pioneer plant species to a sub-climax vegetation of alder and willow. The climax vegetation of oak and beech woodland has not been achieved due to the impact of human activities clearing grazing land as well as grazing by red deer and rabbits. The succession occurs in six seral stages that are identified by the growth of different plant species (Figure 1).

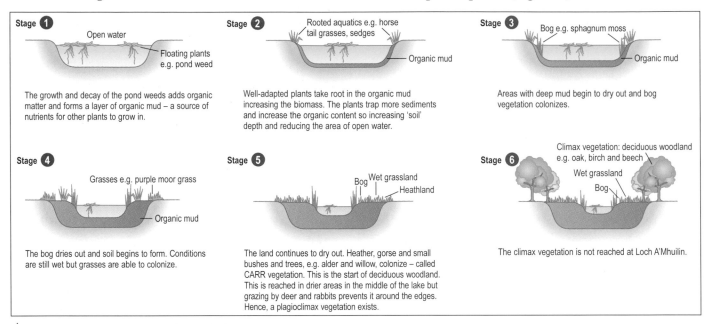

Stage 1 Open water. Floating plants e.g. pond weed
The growth and decay of the pond weeds adds organic matter and forms a layer of organic mud – a source of nutrients for other plants to grow in.

Stage 2 Rooted aquatics e.g. horse tail grasses, sedges. Organic mud
Well-adapted plants take root in the organic mud increasing the biomass. The plants trap more sediments and increase the organic content so increasing 'soil' depth and reducing the area of open water.

Stage 3 Bog e.g. sphagnum moss. Organic mud
Areas with deep mud begin to dry out and bog vegetation colonizes.

Stage 4 Grasses e.g. purple moor grass. Organic mud
The bog dries out and soil begins to form. Conditions are still wet but grasses are able to colonize.

Stage 5 Bog, Wet grassland, Heathland
The land continues to dry out. Heather, gorse and small bushes and trees, e.g. alder and willow, colonize – called CARR vegetation. This is the start of deciduous woodland. This is reached in drier areas in the middle of the lake but grazing by deer and rabbits prevents it around the edges. Hence, a plagioclimax vegetation exists.

Stage 6 Climax vegetation: deciduous woodland e.g. oak, birch and beech. Wet grassland, Bog
The climax vegetation is not reached at Loch A'Mhuilin.

▲ **Figure 1** Seral stages at Loch A'Mhuilin

A psammosere: sand dunes in Northumberland

Figure 2 shows a transect across sand dunes on the Northumberland coast. The pioneer species are found on the seaward side on the embryo dunes. The fore dunes and yellow dunes that form the main ridge are largely colonized by marram grass which is highly adapted to the relatively dry, salty and exposed conditions. Marram grass has leaves that can fold to reduce evapotranspiration and long roots to reach underground water sources. The plants can also send out new shoots as fast as old ones are buried. Behind the main dune ridge are the older, grey dunes often lower in height and sheltered by the main dune ridge. Soils on the grey dunes are deeper, richer in organic matter and therefore able to hold more moisture. The species variety increases with small flowering plants and the occasional shrub able to colonize. In the low-lying land between the dunes some areas have marshy slacks forming hydroseres where species such as sedges, reeds and willows dominate. On the landward side of the dunes small trees, e.g. birch and alder, colonize while further inland the climatic climax of oak and ash dominate.

▼ **Figure 2** Transect across the sand dunes at Druridge Bay, Northumberland

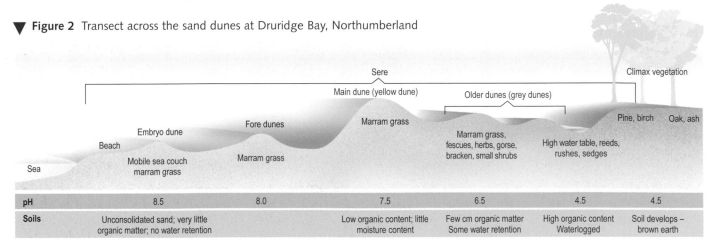

Sere

Main dune (yellow dune)   Older dunes (grey dunes)   Climax vegetation

Fore dunes   Marram grass   Pine, birch   Oak, ash

Embryo dune   Marram grass, fescues, herbs, gorse, bracken, small shrubs   High water table, reeds, rushes, sedges

Beach

Sea   Mobile sea couch marram grass   Marram grass

pH	8.5	8.0	7.5	6.5	4.5	4.5
Soils	Unconsolidated sand; very little organic matter; no water retention		Low organic content; little moisture content	Few cm organic matter Some water retention	High organic content Waterlogged	Soil develops – brown earth

Secondary succession

In large areas of the world the vegetation was once in equilibrium with its environment, that is it was the climax vegetation. However, various arresting factors, either natural, such as fires, or as a result of human activity, such as agriculture, have modified or destroyed the pre-existing vegetation. If the arresting factor is relaxed or removed then succession towards the climax vegetation can begin again. This is called a secondary succession or subsere and the vegetation passes through a series of well-defined stages just as in primary succession.

A plagiosere results from the direct or indirect effects of human activity. There are few parts of the world where human activity has not had an impact on the vegetation. Human activity tends to have a retrogressive impact producing communities that are less complex and reducing biodiversity, e.g. when forested lands are replaced with grassland for grazing. The overall impact is for successions to be arrested or deflected such that the climax vegetation is not achieved. However, should the human influence be relaxed then succession can commence and a plagiosere results.

Secondary successions begin on ground where there has been some soil formation and a pre-existing vegetation has been modified or destroyed. Secondary succession is a very common process in many parts of the world today.

Secondary succession
in Florida

Succession from a plagioclimax community in North Florida

At the University of Florida, USA, research into succession has been taking place for many years. The climax vegetation of the area is hardwood trees although part of the study area had been used as farmland. Farming is an arresting factor and the climax vegetation had been removed and replaced with a plagioclimax community. The arresting factor was then relaxed by the farmland being abandoned.

The land was tilled (Figure 3) and after a month it became green with weeds. After five years blackberries and dog fennel dominated the vegetation (Figure 4) while after fifteen years loblolly pines were beginning to dominate. These trees are fast growing although once the canopy develops, any pine seedlings have too little sun to develop and it is the shade-tolerant seedlings of the slower growing hardwoods that become dominant. After 40 years the hardwood trees, especially sweetgum, are growing below the canopy of the tall loblolly pines (Figure 5). If the succession is not interrupted the site will eventually support hardwoods and the loblolly pines will only occur where they are able to colonize openings left by the collapse of large trees through wind or lightning.

▲ **Figure 3** The plot is tilled

▲ **Figure 4** Blackberries and dog fennel dominate

▲ **Figure 5** Underlayer of fast-growing hardwoods (loblolly pines)

Human modification
of ecosystems

- Human intervention and modification
- Deforestation
- The impact of deforestation

Human intervention and modification

The impact of human activities on deciduous woodland in Britain

In Britain the climate may be described as a cool temperate type with relatively mild winters, cool summers and an evenly distributed rainfall. The climatic climax vegetation for this climate type is deciduous forest.

In large areas of Britain oak trees would dominate the forest, although local variations in geology, soils and climate cause other species to dominate. For example, the calcareous soils of chalk and limestone areas are dominated by ash and beech forest. Figure 1 shows the theoretical distribution of climax vegetation in Britain.

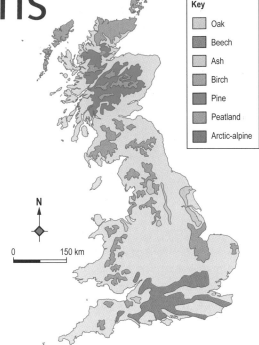

Key
- Oak
- Beech
- Ash
- Birch
- Pine
- Peatland
- Arctic-alpine

▲ **Figure 1** The theoretical distribution of climatic climax communities in Britain

Most of Britain is covered in plagioclimax vegetation today. In total only 9 per cent of Britain is wooded and this includes plantations of coniferous trees as well as the ancient deciduous woodlands. The ancient deciduous woodlands cover only a very small part of England (Figure 2). This is due to a number of arresting factors, mostly connected with human activities, which have halted succession to the climatic climax vegetation. These human activities include:

- land for urban uses such as residential, commercial and transport, e.g. the building of the Newbury by-pass removed ancient woodland for its construction
- fields for cultivation and grazing
- timber to use in the construction industry, e.g. much of the woodland in the valleys of the Tyne, Wear and Tees was used for the early ship-building industries
- in early times fuelwood and the burning of woodland to drive out game for hunting
- introduction of exotic species, i.e. species of trees that are not native to Britain, e.g. sycamore
- acid rain and other types of pollution
- recreational uses
- lack of suitable management.

Since 1930, 7 per cent of English ancient woodland has been lost. Figure 3 shows the main causes of the forest removal.

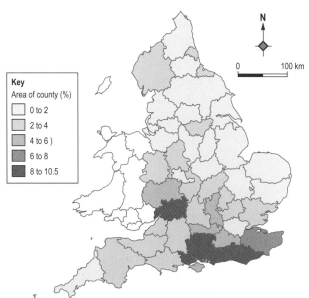

Key
Area of county (%)
- 0 to 2
- 2 to 4
- 4 to 6)
- 6 to 8
- 8 to 10.5

▲ **Figure 2** Areas of ancient woodland in England as a percentage of the land area in each county

Reason for loss	Area in hectares
Agriculture	20 304
Urban development	6 498
Mineral extraction	1 965
Total	**28 767**

▲ **Figure 3** The main causes of forest removal in England since 1930

Acid rain in north-west Europe

Over recent years many forests in north-west Europe, especially the coniferous forests, have experienced high rates of 'die-back' where the needles or leaves discolour and turn yellow. In some areas trees have died. In addition, many freshwater lakes and rivers have shown signs of increased acidification. Many ecologists have blamed acid rain for these problems.

Acid rain is precipitation that has been polluted by emissions of sulphur dioxide and/or oxides of nitrogen in the atmosphere. In the atmosphere these gases react with water vapour to form sulphuric acid and nitric acid. The acids fall to Earth in the form of snow or rain or as dry depositions of sulphuric or nitrogen salts. Rainwater usually has a pH of 5.6, which is slightly acid, but a pH of 2.1 has been recorded at Pitlochry in Scotland. The main sources of the pollutants are the burning of fossil fuels – coal, oil and gas. Since the Second World War, the emissions of sulphur dioxide and oxides of nitrogen have greatly increased because of:

- growing industrialization
- increased use of electricity – more coal, oil and gas-fired power stations
- higher car ownership
- major volcanic eruptions, e.g. in 1991 Mount Pinatubo released 31 million tonnes of sulphur into the atmosphere.

Acid rain has had severe consequences in some areas, with adverse effects on freshwater ecosystems, damage to vegetation, corrosive effects on buildings and increased leaching of minerals from soils.

In Britain the problem is in the upland areas of Scotland, the Lake District and Wales where precipitation totals are higher. A study in mid-Wales showed a dramatic decline of the population and distribution of the dipper. The dipper is a small bird that inhabits streams feeding off caddis fly larvae and mayfly nymphs. These insects are very sensitive to water quality and cannot survive acid conditions. In 25 years, the acidity of the river has increased from pH6.5 to pH4.5. Acid rain and conifer afforestation are thought to be the main causes. During this time the numbers of dippers has severely decreased (Figure 4).

Acid rain is an international problem. Norway, for example, contributes very little acid rain but 92 per cent of sulphur deposition in the country comes from other countries, mostly from Britain. Figure 5 shows the amount of damage caused to forests in Europe. Over 50 per cent of trees in some forests in Germany have shown some signs of damage. Various international conferences have been held, e.g. in Oslo in 1994, and international agreements made to limit emissions of the harmful gases. Germany has agreed to reduce sulphur emissions by 83 per cent and has spent £250 million stabilizing damaged forest areas by adding lime to soils, lakes and rivers.

Country	Forest expanse (km²)	Extent of damage (km²)	Percentage damaged	Sulphur (000s tonnes per year)
Finland	194 000	67 900	35.0	162
Norway	83 330	4 100	4.9	50
Sweden	265 000	10 600	4.0	116
Netherlands	3 090	1 548	50.1	141
Belgium	6 160	1 100	18.0	244
Luxembourg	820	423	51.6	6
France	150 750	2 796	1.8	923
Switzerland	12 000	4 320	36.0	31
Austria	375 400	9 600	2.4	75
Italy	63 630	3 180	5.0	1252
Poland	86 770	22 730	26.2	2270
Germany	102 230	41 740	40.8	3522
Czech and Slovak Republics	46 000	12 500	26.1	1450
Hungary	16 700	1 837	11.0	710

▲ Figure 5 Acid rain damage to forests in Europe

Questions

1 a What is acid rain and how is it formed?

 b Explain the impact of acid rain on forests and drainage.

 c On an outline map of Europe construct a choropleth map to show the percentage of forest damaged in the European countries shown in Figure 5. Describe and explain this pattern.

 d Explain why acid rain is an international problem.

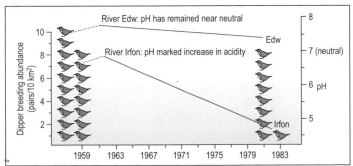

▲ Figure 4 Changes in the pH and number of dippers in the rivers Irfon and Edw in Wales

Pollution of aquatic ecosystems in the UK

Water pollution is the introduction of damaging substances that would be harmful to organisms living in the water or to other users. After the Industrial Revolution water pollution increased in the UK as a result of new agricultural practices, the growth of urban populations and advances in industrial technology. In the UK the main sources of water pollution are from:

- silt and sewage flowing down river
- toxic chemicals and industrial wastes being discharged into river systems
- nitrates and phosphates from agricultural fertilizers
- acid rain.

Some pollutants, such as heavy metals or high levels of acidity, are immediately toxic to aquatic plant and animal life. However, others lead to the slow death of plants and animals within the ecosystem through a process called eutrophication. Eutrophication occurs when concentrations of nitrogen and phosphorous are too high and blue-green algae and phytoplankton multiply to produce algal blooms. The algae spread like a blanket over the surface of the water, especially when the weather is warm. The growth of the algae decreases the oxygen available in the water, which eventually affects the whole food chain.

Today, water quality is an important global issue and in the UK there are many European Union directives and national government guidelines about acceptable standards of water quality especially if it is to be used for drinking water. Companies and individuals can be heavily fined for causing water pollution (Figure 1). There are also various International Agreements to control dumping of industrial discharges. For example, in 1990 it was agreed to reduce discharges of 38 poisonous substances into the North Sea by 50 per cent by 1995.

The government's pollution watchdog has published a list of the dirtiest companies in England and Wales. The first ever 'Hall of Shame' names multinational chemical company, ICI, at number one, followed by three waste companies and one of the privatised water firms.

The Environment Agency wants the list to draw attention to what it says are inadequate fines being handed down by the courts. It says these are often too low to deter big companies from working to avoid such problems in the future. 'Tough action by the Environment Agency in the field needs to be matched by tougher penalties,' said its chief executive, Ed Gallagher. 'The average fine for a prosecution last year was £2786. Clearly this is not sending out a strong enough message to deter large businesses that have the potential to seriously damage the environment.'

During 1988, the Agency took out a total of 744 prosecutions resulting in total fines of just over £2m. ICI paid almost a fifth of that figure, more than the next four biggest payers put together.

ICI rejected the list as 'yesterday's news'. 'It relates to already well-publicized events at three of our plants in 1997 where action to prevent recurrence has already been taken,' said the company.

BBC Online

▲ **Figure 1** Factories releasing chemicals into water

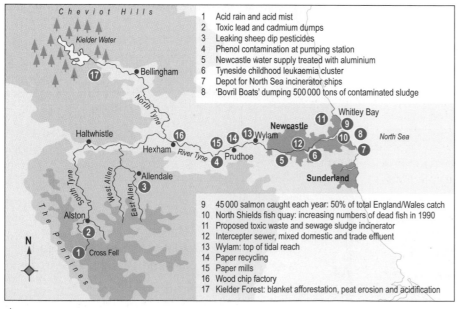

▲ **Figure 2** The River Tyne: ecological problems in 1990

1 Acid rain and acid mist
2 Toxic lead and cadmium dumps
3 Leaking sheep dip pesticides
4 Phenol contamination at pumping station
5 Newcastle water supply treated with aluminium
6 Tyneside childhood leukaemia cluster
7 Depot for North Sea incinerator ships
8 'Bovril Boats' dumping 500 000 tons of contaminated sludge
9 45 000 salmon caught each year: 50% of total England/Wales catch
10 North Shields fish quay: increasing numbers of dead fish in 1990
11 Proposed toxic waste and sewage sludge incinerator
12 Intercepter sewer, mixed domestic and trade effluent
13 Wylam: top of tidal reach
14 Paper recycling
15 Paper mills
16 Wood chip factory
17 Kielder Forest: blanket afforestation, peat erosion and acidification

Many rivers and coastal areas in the UK have seen a dramatic improvement in water quality in recent years although water pollution is still an issue. In 1994, sewage was responsible for 30 per cent of major pollution incidents, industry 25 per cent and agriculture 15 per cent. Figure 2 shows some of the ecological problems facing the River Tyne in 1990. Since that time the Northumbrian River Authority has spent a lot of money improving the river and its water quality so that by the year 2000 salmon had returned to spawn in the river – an indication of improved water quality. The articles on the following page show some recent incidents of water pollution in the UK.

▼ Figure 3

TAPS TURNED OFF IN THE WORCESTER AREA

In April 1994 about 100 000 people in the Worcester area of the Severn valley were unable to use their tap water. A factory at Wem, upstream of the affected area, had discharged a chemical into the water making it unfit for human consumption.

▼ Figure 4

Acid water in old mine shafts threatens river life

Acid water from old mine shafts threatens to enter watercourses along the Wear valley in north-east England. The acid water would pollute domestic water supplies and kill the living organisms including fish. British Coal is currently maintaining some pumps in the old mine shafts at a cost of several million pounds a year to prevent contamination of water supplies. However, once privatized it is unclear as to who will be responsible

The Guardian, 15 April 1994

▼ Figure 5

FISH POISONING LINKED TO FACTORY

The Environment Agency has traced pollution that killed thousands of fish in the River Wey in Hampshire to a factory near Alton. It said it is planning to take legal action against the company for allowing ammonia to poison the river. Chemists have been analysing samples and tankers are being used to flush out the contaminated water. A three-mile stretch of the river was contaminated. A member of the public who noticed foam and a strong smell called the Agency. The fish population of the river in the area was completely devastated with brown trout, chubb, roach and perch floating on the surface. The Ministry of Agriculture, Food and Fisheries has advised farmers not to use water from the river but South East Water says there is no risk to the public drinking supply.

BBC Online, 29 March 1999

▼ Figure 6

Water polluters face new laws

New laws to prevent companies from polluting rivers are coming into force on Monday. Firms in danger of polluting water can now be ordered to take preventative action before contamination occurs – and may be prosecuted if they do not do enough. Under the new laws, the Environment Agency may serve a Works notice where there is a significant risk of pollution. The notice will clearly outline what a company needs to do and a deadline for the work to be completed.

Until now the Environment Agency only had limited pollution prevention powers, focused on businesses who have the go-ahead to discharge waste into rivers. The construction industry, in particular, escaped censure although it accounted for 625 reported pollution incidents per day across England and Wales in 1998.

BBC Online, 29 April 1999

Questions

1 Using examples, explain the main causes of water pollution in the UK?

2 Produce a pie chart to show the main causes of major pollution incidents in the UK.

3 a Using Figure 2, describe the sources of water pollution:
   i upstream of Wylam on the River Tyne in 1990
   ii downstream of Wylam in 1990.

4 Suggest ways in which the pollution has been reduced to allow the return of salmon to the River Tyne by 2000.

Deforestation

There has been dramatic deforestation across the world as a whole (Figure 1). It is estimated that 35–40 per cent of the original forest has been removed by felling, grazing or burning. The vegetation that has replaced the forested areas is often smaller in size and less species rich, and so overall there has been a reduction in the Earth's biomass and net primary productivity.

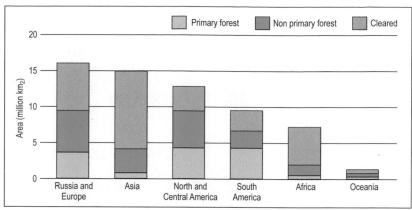

▲ **Figure 1**   Many of the Earth's natural forests have been cleared or degraded

Until the beginning of the twentieth century the greatest impact of deforestation had been in temperate latitudes, the Mediterranean and monsoon Asia. Rates of deforestation today are much greater in the northern boreal (coniferous) forests and, particularly, in the tropical rainforests.

The main causes of deforestation are:
- extraction of the timber as a resource for industry and export as in Sweden, Brazil and Indonesia
- creation of new land for residential, industrial and transport uses such as the Trans-Amazonia Highway in Brazil
- extension of agricultural land to feed and house a growing population, e.g. the Transmigration programme in Indonesia and the Jengka Triangle project in Malaysia
- mining of minerals, e.g. the Carajas project in the Amazon Basin
- creation of dams for the generation of HEP e.g. the Itaipu project on the border between Brazil and Paraguay
- attempts to reduce third world debt by encouraging inward investment by multinationals and TNCs, e.g. the hamburger ranches, coffee and rubber plantations in many countries with tropical rainforest.

The causes of deforestation: Indonesia

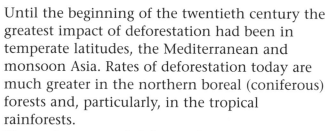

Indonesia is the largest archipelago in the world with over 3000 islands including Borneo, Java and Sumatra (Figure 2). The islands lie on or close to the Equator. The climate is equatorial – hot and wet – and the typical vegetation is tropical rainforest giving Indonesia the name of the 'Amazon of south-east Asia'. Indonesia has 10 per cent of the world's tropical rainforest but rapid deforestation is a major issue for the country (Figure 3).

The causes of deforestation are the subject of some debate in Indonesia. For some the main causes are the role of the government, its development projects and the commercial logging companies. Others see the very high densities of population and the expansion of slash and burn farming in order to increase food supply as the main cause of the deforestation. In recent years the World Bank and others have altered their views and the balance has swung towards the role of government and the logging companies as being the main cause. Figure 4 shows the main causes of the deforestation.

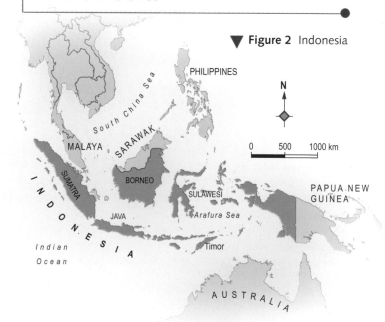

▼ **Figure 2** Indonesia

▼ **Figure 3** Estimated rates of deforestation in Indonesia

1970s	300 000 hectares per year
1980s	600 000 hectares per year
1990s	1 million hectares per year

Figure 4 The causes of deforestation in Indonesia

Socio-economic

- Unemployment – there is rapid population growth and high unemployment. The logging industry employs 700 000 people directly.

- Economic development – in 1994 wood and wood products produced about $5.5 billion in export earnings. About 70 per cent of the world's hardwoods are exported from Indonesia earning it the nickname 'the plywood king'. The money is valuable to help develop the country economically, to provide for the fast growing population and to pay off large debts.

- The logging itself removes the trees, but the heavy machinery damages others that are not commercially useful but which are used by locals for food supply and medicines.

- The local people farm using slash and burn techniques. The growing population has seen an expansion of the plots of land being cleared for farming.

- Road building sponsored by the government to support the logging companies has destroyed large areas of rainforest.

Political

- The government's Transmigration policy has destroyed about 900 000ha of rainforest. The scheme clears the forest to make way for settlements and farmland in order to house people prepared to migrate away from the overcrowded cities, especially Jakarta.

- The government is eager to pay off international debts and the logging industry brings in a high revenue.

- Until 1998, the military government provided concessions to timber companies which are often run by powerful people who may also have political influence.

- The government rarely enforces selective logging regulations.

- No replanting policies have been in place to replace the deforested areas.

- There is limited control or no desire to stop illegal logging.

Figure 5 Satellite image of smoke from forest fires in Indonesia

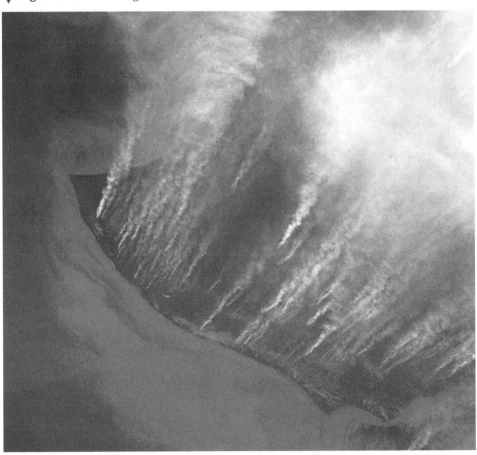

ⓘ *Slash and burn farming is a subsistence form of farming common in the tropics and well adapted to areas with a low population density in rainforest environments. The local people select a plot of land to clear. They chop down and burn the existing vegetation protecting any trees of any value to them. The soils are relatively infertile so the ash from the burning fertilizes the soil. For a few years the people are able to grow and harvest crops to feed themselves. Ultimately the land becomes infertile and they are forced to move on and clear a new plot of land.*

The impact of deforestation

Deforestation is very much a global issue. It brings both advantages and disadvantages to the countries that have areas of rainforest and to those who depend upon the rainforest products. Some people are very much opposed to the development of the rainforests because of the negative impact on the ecosystem and the indigenous people (Figure 1). Others, and particularly the governments and logging companies, support the development of the rainforests. They see the advantages of:

- increased employment and incomes
- more land for settlement and farming to feed and house a growing population
- reducing debts through increased export earnings
- the opportunity to go along a road of development to improve the quality of life for the country's inhabitants
- a source of food, timber and drugs for the MEDW
- a scenic resource for tourism.

Some would say that the attitude of some people in the western world is hypocritical because countries like Britain did much the same to their own forests in the name of progress, albeit some time ago. The countries of the MEDW have an important role to play. Many of these developed countries fuel the deforestation by their demands for rainforest products e.g. rubber, drugs and hardwood timber. The MEDW use tropical products to make 20 per cent of all drugs. Cheap meat supplies in the MEDW are achieved by using cheap animal feeds such as cassava grown on farmland created out of rainforest. The USA obtains meat supplies from huge 'hamburger' ranches set up in the rainforests of Mexico, Panama and Costa Rica.

In many countries it is also difficult to accurately measure the impact of the deforestation. Precise figures for forest clearance are not available and some would say that the problem is much over-stated.

There are good arguments both for and against deforestation of tropical rainforests. The negative impact on the ecosystem and indigenous people is clear but it is difficult to persuade those making a profit from the tropical rainforests – including many companies in the MEDW and those who would bear the economic, social and political costs of protection – to change the pattern of exploitation. Is the pressure for conservation, so often heard today, as great as the pressure for exploitation? Is there a middle road to take?

In several countries there are moves towards managing the rainforests for a sustainable future. Strategies include:

- conservation of areas in national parks with core areas, where no disturbance is allowed, and other zones that allow tourism and native settlements as in Malaysia
- sustainable management of the forest by replanting strategies
- developing rural village communities for local populations to reduce pressure on the forest
- developing green tourism and eco-tourism
- 'debt for nature' where foreign debts are written off in return for conservation of specific areas
- charging higher prices for timber and products and increasing recycling
- sustainable management of fuelwood supplies or providing adequate alternatives.

Physical
Impact on the water cycle
    Bare soil increases overland flow
    Reduced interception of moisture
    Increased flood risk in rivers and streams
    Reduced transpiration may reduce rainfall
    Increased sediment load in rivers

Impact on soils
    Increased soil erosion through overland flow
    Gulleying
    Increased risk of landslides and mudflows
    Increased leaching causing loss of soil nutrients
    Reduced soil fertility
    Formation of impermeable duricrusts on soil surface

Impact on climate
    Greater reflection of Sun's rays from lighter soil surface (increased albedo)
    Tree burning increases carbon dioxide levels in the air contributing to global warming
    Increased daily (diurnal) range of temperature
    Rainfall decrease
    Reduced production of oxygen

Impact on plants and animals
    Primary forest destroyed, replaced by anything from bare ground to a less species-rich secondary forest
    Reduced biodiversity
    Threatened extinction of some species
    Reduced net primary productivity

Socio-economic and cultural
    Loss of traditional way of life for indigenous people
    Loss of land
    No immunity against new diseases introduced
    Killing of local people who try to defend their land
    Migrants moved into rainforests often have a very low standard of living

▲ **Figure 1** The possible negative impact of deforestation in the rainforests

The effects of deforestation in Indonesia

Case Study

Loss of rainforest and the associated fauna and flora in Indonesia is particularly significant because the country has the largest number of mammal species in the world, over 20 000 plant species and 17 per cent of the world's birds. Several species of fauna and flora are facing extinction and continued deforestation is likely to lead to reduced biodiversity, reduced biomass and lower rates of net primary productivity.

There are conflicts between indigenous people such as the Moi people and the logging companies, e.g. the Intimpura Timber Company. The logging company threatens the way of life of the Moi people. The government granted a logging licence to the company in 1990 for 339 000 hectares of land. The traditional landowners were not informed and representations by the Moi to the local government,

the army, the company and forestry service have had no effect. None of them will recognize any form of land rights by the Moi people. As a result of their protests the Moi have been labelled 'security disturbers'- an official term used to silence any form of indigenous protest.

Pollution of air, land and water are consequences of the deforestation. Increased soil erosion causes the silting of rivers and streams and oil spills from machinery pollute the soils and water. As Figure 2 shows, serious air pollution in Malaysia was a major problem from the forest fires in Indonesia in 1997. The fires were a product of deliberate fires lit by loggers and farmers using slash and burn to clear land. The situation was made worse by a drought in the country at the same time.

▼ **Figure 2** Extracts from newspaper reports about the air pollution in Malaysia in 1997

Indonesian brush fires spread smoke to Malaysia and Singapore

Since the first of September, out of control forest and bush fires in Borneo and Indonesia have blanketed the neighbouring countries of Singapore and Malaysia with thick smoke.

Not only is the smoke itself dangerous to people's health, but the industrial and automobile pollutants trapped below the smoke also pose a serious threat.

Experts are recommending people wear special masks; surgical masks would not be enough. In addition, Singapore has told its elderly and ill residents to stay indoors.

Up to 20 million people in Indonesia have been affected with throat and respiratory inflammations and diarrhoea.

18 September 1997

The thick smoky haze covering Malaysia has gone from bad to worse, forcing the government to declare a state of emergency. In some of the hardest-hit areas, private and public offices and schools have been closed. Some airline flights have also been cancelled due to poor visibility. The smog emergency in Kuala Lumpur has sent thousands of Malaysian residents to the hospital – over 2700 adults and 3800 children were treated for infections, over 1000 for asthma-related illnesses and about 500 for eye problems.

19 September 1997

The Indonesian Environment Minister called for the evacuation of 45 000 people from the town of Rengat in Sumatra where the visibility is down to zero. Local factories have been ordered to stop operations and traffic is restricted.

But, despite the poor air conditions a golf tournament in Kuala Lumpur went ahead as scheduled. 'Generally the players have taken it very well' said the tournament director. Players have been told that masks are available if they feel the need. Most golfers however declined the offer.

Malaysia is sending 1200 fire-fighters to Indonesia to help fight the brush and forest fires that now blanket three countries with thick smoke. In addition, a team of French experts is on the way and Japan is sending equipment to assist the efforts.

In the meantime 5000 people a day are heading to hospitals with breathing problems. In some areas the Air Pollution Index (API) is above 800. Any API above 500 is dangerous to people's health.

23 September 1997

Air pollution worsened in Kuala Lumpur as monsoon winds changed direction to the south-east. The winds are expected to change back to the north-east tomorrow but officials have warned that the haze will remain until the monsoon period in November. The government has endorsed a plan to spray water using sprinklers mounted on tops of buildings above seven storeys high to reduce dust in the air.

7 October 1997

Extended writing

Evaluate the impact of deforestation in Indonesia.
(Remember, impact includes both disadvantages and advantages.)

Soils

- Definition of soil
- Soil formation
- The characteristics of soils
- The characteristics of brown earths and podsols

Definition of soil

Soil is the uppermost layer of the Earth's crust composed of weathered material or regolith to which has been added humus (decomposed dead organic matter). Soils therefore are made up of mineral particles from the regolith, organic matter from the humus and also air and water.

A soil profile (Figure 1) is used to identify and describe different soil types. It shows a vertical column of soil usually separated into a series of horizontal layers called horizons. Each horizon is distinct in its colour, moisture content, texture and organic matter content. The horizons are called A, B and C. A is the uppermost topsoil, where most material is added or removed from the soil. B is the subsoil, a zone where material mainly accumulates. Horizon C is the parent material, usually the weathered mantle or regolith.

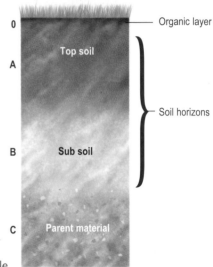

▶ **Figure 1** A soil profile

Soil formation

The process of soil formation is called pedogenesis and it is a product of three main processes:
- the weathering or breakdown of minerals
- the incorporation of decomposed organic matter (humus)
- the movement of water through the soil.

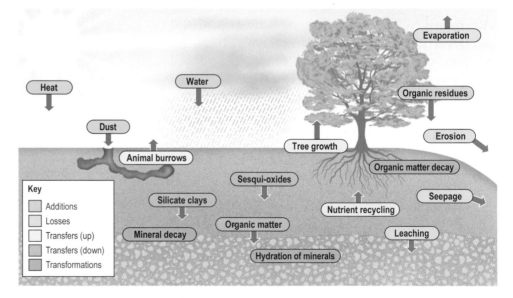

▶ **Figure 2** Soil system diagram

The weathering of soil minerals

Weathering is a natural process of the breakdown of rocks *in situ*. It is responsible for producing 100 000 tonnes/km² per year of mineral particles in Britain alone. The mineral particles in a soil are important in determining the structure, texture and acidity of a soil. There are three main types of weathering shown in the information box.

The relative importance of the weathering processes changes across the globe. The hot, wet climates in areas close to the Equator favour chemical weathering. However, its importance decreases with increasing distance from the Equator and physical weathering tends to dominate in higher latitudes where climates are colder and drier. Overall, chemical weathering is the most active, mostly by the reaction of acidified rainwater, although in any environment it is possible to have all three types of weathering operating.

Organic matter in soils

The organic matter in soils includes dead animal and plant remains and waste products of living organisms. The majority of the organic matter is supplied to the soil surface as litter, e.g. leaf-fall in autumn in Britain. The litter is then decomposed and mixed with the minerals in the upper layer of soil (the A horizon) by earthworms, insects, bacteria and fungi. The organic matter eventually decomposes to form humus, a black or dark-brown jelly-like material in which the plant tissues are no longer recognizable. During decomposition plant nutrients such as carbon dioxide, water, chemical salts and nitrogen are released.

Humus is essential for plant life because it holds water and oxygen, releases chemical salts during decay and helps bind the soil into aggregates improving the texture.

Mull humus is usually associated with lowland areas of deciduous woodland or grassland in Britain where brown earth soils dominate. The humus is dark brown or black, well decomposed, rich in nutrients and only slightly acid with a pH of 5.5–6.5. The humus is usually well mixed with the mineral matter in the A horizon

Mor humus is common in areas of moorland and below coniferous forests in Britain. These environments are characterized by high rainfall, cold temperatures and acid parent rocks. The humus tends to be black, poorly decomposed and acid with a pH of 3.5–4.5. The humus contains few nutrients and is often not incorporated into the A horizon but forms a thick layer of peat over the mineral particles below.

The movement of water through the soil

The movement of water through the soil forms a part of the hydrological cycle (see pages 7–9 in Chapter 1). Once infiltrated into the soil, water may be evaporated or taken up by plants and transpired. Any remaining water may move through the soil laterally as throughflow or percolate vertically towards the ground water (Figure 3). This is largely governed by the soil water budget, the relationship between precipitation and evapotranspiration.

If precipitation is greater than evapotranspiration there is a positive soil water budget and the net water flow is downwards through the soil. This is typical in the upland areas of Britain where there is high precipitation and relatively low temperatures.

In areas such as the hot deserts there is a negative soil water budget. Potential evapotranspiration exceeds the precipitation total and the net water movement is upwards through the soil.

The movement of water in soils also involves the movement of a variety of other materials. Chemical salts or bases, clay, iron, aluminium, silicon and organic matter may all be moved around by water within the soil.

Water movement and the translocation (movement) of materials in soils are a major component of soil formation. The movement causes some soil horizons to become eluviated, i.e. to lose materials, while others are illuviated, i.e. gain materials. The processes of eluviation and illuviation produce the different layers or horizons in soils and give them their unique characteristics that determine the different soil types.

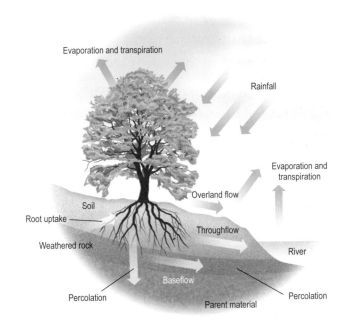

▲ **Figure 3** Water movement through the soil

Questions

1 Using Figure 2, complete a table to show the inputs, outputs, transformations and flows within the soil system.

2 a Write your own definition of a soil.
  b Examine briefly the roles of weathering, organic matter and water movement in soil formation.

The downward movement of water in soils: leaching

Leaching is the downward movement of water through the soil carrying with it soluble bases such as calcium, magnesium and potassium. The amount of water movement and its acidity determines the degree of leaching that takes place. Acidity encourages the removal of calcium and other soluble bases from the soil in a process called cation exchange (Figure 1).

Cation exchange

Cations are positively charged ions such as hydrogen and calcium. Rainwater is usually slightly acid having dissolved carbon dioxide out of the atmosphere to create a weak solution of carbonic acid. The acidified rainwater contains cations in the form of hydrogen ions (H^+ ions). The H^+ ions replace the Ca^{2+}, K^+ etc. on the clay particles, hence the term cation exchange. This creates a solution of soluble calcium hydrogen carbonate that is leached from the soil. The clay particles now have many more hydrogen ions. The accumulation of hydrogen ions increases the acidity of the soil.

Podsolization is a more severe form of leaching that creates podsol soils (see page 124). They are formed as a result of the intense downward movement of iron and aluminium whereas leaching only removes the soluble bases.

Acid rainwater
(Weak carbonic acid)

$2H_2CO_3$

Cation exchange

Ca^{2+} H^+

K^+

Mg^{2+} Clay micelle

Acidification of clay

$H^+ H^+$ H^+

K^+

Mg^{2+} Clay micelle

Leaching of calcium

$Ca(HCO_3)_2$

Calcium leached from soil as calcium bicarbonate

▲ **Figure 1** Cation exchange

Restricted water flow

Under normal circumstances the pores or spaces between soil particles are partly filled with water and partly filled with air (oxygen). However when waterlogging occurs the pores are filled with water and there is no oxygen present. This results in gleying when red ferric iron is reduced to grey ferrous iron. This produces grey gleyed soils perhaps with some red or orange mottling where pockets of air have re-oxidized the iron compounds. The organic material builds up and remains on the soil surface as a thick mor humus or peat.

Upward movement of water in soils

A negative soil water budget occurs when rates of evapotranspiration are higher than precipitation. The result is the upward movement of water and materials through a soil profile. The process is common in the arid regions of the world where it may lead to salinization but also in regions with a protracted dry season such as the temperate grasslands where chernozem soils (Figure 2) are formed.

Salinization

In regions with a hot, dry climate any water from rainfall or groundwater sources close to the soil surface moves upwards through the soil by capillary action. On nearing the surface the water is evaporated leaving behind high concentrations of salts, e.g. calcium, sodium and magnesium. In extreme cases a crust of salt may form on the soil surface making the land useless for plant growth causing desertification.

In many parts of the world with arid climates irrigation has been the answer. However irrigation has accelerated salinization and today about 10 per cent of the world's irrigated land is damaged. Along the banks of the River Colorado in south-west USA the river water is extensively used for irrigation. In the great summer heat, the upward movement and evaporation of water forms crusts of salt on the land surface. In some areas plant growth is impossible due to the high salt concentrations. Farmers also return the irrigation water back to the River Colorado, further increasing the salt concentration of the river. In Mexico the water is too salty to use for irrigation and a $200 million desalinization plant has been built to remove the salt.

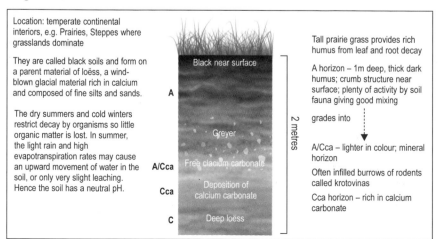

Location: temperate continental interiors, e.g. Prairies, Steppes where grasslands dominate

They are called black soils and form on a parent material of loëss, a wind-blown glacial material rich in calcium and composed of fine silts and sands.

The dry summers and cold winters restrict decay by organisms so little organic matter is lost. In summer, the light rain and high evapotranspiration rates may cause an upward movement of water in the soil, or only very slight leaching. Hence the soil has a neutral pH.

Black near surface

A

Greyer

Free calcium carbonate

A/Cca

Deposition of calcium carbonate

Cca

Deep loëss

C

2 metres

Tall prairie grass provides rich humus from leaf and root decay

A horizon – 1m deep, thick dark humus; crumb structure near surface; plenty of activity by soil fauna giving good mixing

grades into

A/Cca – lighter in colour; mineral horizon

Often infilled burrows of rodents called krotovinas

Cca horizon – rich in calcium carbonate

◀ **Figure 2** Chernozem soils

Summary

Soils are formed as a result of:

• weathering of parent material producing the inorganic element of the soil
• the incorporation of organic matter
• the movement of water in a soil profile.

These three elements combine together to produce different soil types in various parts of the world.

The process of soil formation is affected by:

Climate

The climate is a dominating factor in soil formation. The climate controls the balance between precipitation and evapotranspiration and has a strong influence upon the vegetation that can grow in an area. The nature and degree of weathering is also influenced by climate. As the maps on page 94 show, the distribution of zonal soils closely matches the distribution of world climate types. For example, regions with arid climates have only sparse vegetation. Soils are generally low in organic matter and the lack of humus produces soils with inferior texture, structure and fertility.

Vegetation

The vegetation controls the amount and type of organic matter that is produced and influences the supply and movement of water. In some parts of the UK, planting of coniferous plantations to replace deciduous woodlands has taken place. Deciduous woodlands are associated with relatively fertile brown earth soils and these have been changed into less fertile podsols as a result of the afforestation. The conifers place few demands on the soil for nutrients and there is less nutrient cycling. Leaching removes the bases increasing the soil acidity and reducing its fertility. The litter of pine needles also take much longer to decompose and produce a mor humus that contributes to the acidity and the formation of podsols.

Topography

The shape of the land has an impact on soil formation through its influence on drainage and processes of weathering and mass movement. Soils drain well on slopes, although drainage may be excessive on steep slopes leading to leaching and even soil erosion. On valley floors and upland plateaus soils may become waterlogged and gleyed.

Time

Soils may take thousands of years to form. In Britain the soils are mostly less than 10 000 years old and many are still forming on the deposits left behind at the end of the Ice Age. In regions of tropical rainforest the soils are much deeper. The soil formation processes have not been interrupted by any Ice Ages, the climate encourages rapid chemical weathering of parent material and the dense rainforest provides large quantities of organic material.

Parent material

The parent material of a soil is the rock or alluvium or boulder clay etc. on which the soil is formed. It provides the inorganic or mineral element of soils and has a strong impact on a soil's texture, structure and acidity. Igneous rocks such as granite are acid and resistant to weathering. The minerals weather only slowly to produce thin, acid soils that are infertile and only support a limited range of well-adapted plants. By contrast, soils developed on loëss, wind-blown glacial material, are fertile and rich in calcium. The loess is unconsolidated fine-grained material that weathers easily.

Fauna

Earthworms, bacteria and other soil fauna have a key role to play in the decomposition and incorporation of organic matter into soils. Neutral or slightly acid soils have high concentrations of soil fauna. Such soils are usually well aerated and humus is well mixed into the upper horizons of the soil. The soil fauna cannot tolerate highly acid conditions and soils in this category often have a thick mor humus where little decay and mixing has taken place.

Human activity

The impact of people on soils can be both positive and negative. Positive influences include using organic manure or dung that increase the organic matter content and improve structure, texture and water retention. However, most human impact is negative and includes compaction of soils by trampling or heavy machinery, irrigation, overgrazing, overcultivation and deforestation. The impact of people on soils is looked at more closely in the final section of this chapter.

The factors that affect soil formation and the processes of soil formation produce a range of soil types each with their own distinctive texture, structure, acidity and water content. These soil characteristics will be considered next.

Soil formation in a valley:

Case Study

the Isle of Arran in Scotland

The Isle of Arran was covered by glaciers during the last Ice Age. Since the Ice Age ended about 10 000 years ago soils have formed on the material deposited by the glaciers as they retreated. The weathering of the glacial deposits may have taken about 100 years but the horizons take thousands of years to be formed. The process of primary succession occurred as the soils became progressively deeper and richer in organic matter.

On the Isle of Arran the climax vegetation cover would be deciduous forest and the typical soil, brown earth. However, in the last 5 000 years human activities have caused extensive deforestation. Trees were removed for fuel, building materials and for agriculture. The loss of trees and the high rainfall increased leaching causing podsolization and the formation of podsols especially in the upland areas where the parent materials are acid. The brown earths still survive in the lowland areas where rainfall is lower and the conditions are warmer and more sheltered. In the waterlogged areas of Arran there are extensive areas of peat that have been cut for fuel for many centuries.

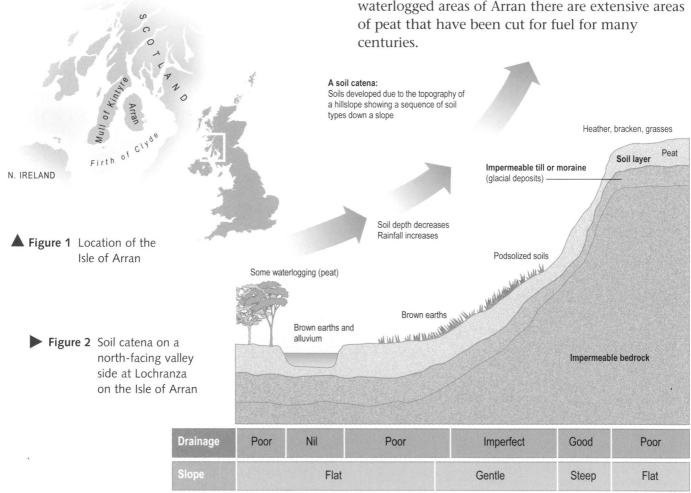

▲ **Figure 1** Location of the Isle of Arran

▶ **Figure 2** Soil catena on a north-facing valley side at Lochranza on the Isle of Arran

A soil catena:
Soils developed due to the topography of a hillslope showing a sequence of soil types down a slope

Heather, bracken, grasses

Peat

Soil layer

Impermeable till or moraine (glacial deposits)

Soil depth decreases
Rainfall increases

Podsolized soils

Some waterlogging (peat)

Brown earths

Brown earths and alluvium

Impermeable bedrock

Drainage	Poor	Nil	Poor	Imperfect	Good	Poor
Slope	Flat			Gentle	Steep	Flat

Questions

1. What has been the role of each of the following in the formation of soils on the Isle of Arran:
   i water movement in the soil
   ii organic matter
   iii weathering to produce inorganic matter?

2. Explain how the soil forming factors outlined on page 116 have had an impact on soil formation on the Isle of Arran.

3. Describe and explain the soil catena shown in Figure 2.

The characteristics of soils

Texture

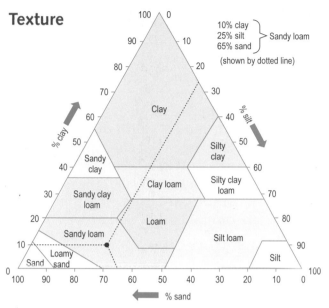

▲ **Figure 3** Soil textural triangle

Texture is the proportion of sand, silt and clay-sized particles in a soil. The texture is usually shown on a textural triangle as shown in Figure 3.

Soil texture is important because it affects plant growth. The texture affects the size and spacing of soil pores (the spaces between soil particles) and hence directly affects the moisture content and aeration of soils. In clay soils, for example, there are many very small micropores that retain water, exclude air and give the soil strong cohesive properties. As a result clay soils are often waterlogged and do not drain easily. In contrast sandy soils have large macropores that hold air but not water. They are free draining and often dry soils. A loam soil is the ideal situation. It has a balanced texture with a mixture of pore sizes.

Soil texture also affects the amount of nutrients in a soil. Sandy soils with large pores often lack nutrients and require large applications of fertilizer for successful crop growth. Organic matter is rapidly decomposed in the oxygen rich pores but it is easily washed away by the free drainage. Clay soils adsorb nutrients very well but the frequent waterlogging and lack of oxygen may cause peat to develop. Loams are the ideal soils as they hold the nutrients.

Structure

Soil structure is the way the soil particles group together to form 'peds' or aggregates (Figure 4). The ideal soil structure is a crumb structure with a particle size between 3 and 6 mm. This structure gives a good balance of air, water and nutrients in the soil.

Size class	Type of structure	Description of aggregates	Appearance of aggregates (peds)
1–6mm	Crumb	Small, fairly porous spheres; not joined to other aggregates	
1–10mm	Platy	Like plates; often overlapping hindering water passing through	
5–75mm	Blocky	Like blocks; easily fit closely together; often break into smaller blocks	

▲ **Figure 4** Types of soil structure

Acidity

The acidity of a soil is determined by the concentration of hydrogen (H^+) ions. Soils that contain large quantities of hydrogen ions are the most acidic soils.

The acidity of a soil can be increased by:
- leaching and cation exchange (see page 118)
- rainwater, a weak solution of carbonic acid
- organic acids released during decomposition.

The consequences of high levels of acidity are:
- increased removal of calcium and other bases from the soil
- iron and aluminium become very soluble and even toxic to fauna and flora
- clay minerals disintegrate releasing more iron and aluminium
- organic matter becomes soluble and is washed out of the soil.

The ideal situation is a soil that is neutral or only slightly acid, i.e. a pH of 5.5-6.5. This would ensure a good soil structure and the presence and availability of plant nutrients.

Horizon development

Most soils contain horizontal layers or horizons that are distinctive in their colour, moisture content, texture and organic matter content. The origin of these horizons is very closely linked with the movement of water in soils. The water movement causes eluviation and illuvuiation. It is the movement and redeposition of clay, iron or organic material that helps to distinguish soil horizons. In some soils, e.g. podsols, water movement is a major feature and the horizons are well developed and distinctive. In other soils, e.g. the brown earths, leaching is very slight so distinctive horizons are not visible although a gradual zonation through the A, B and C horizons may be identified.

The characteristics of brown earths and podsols

Brown earths

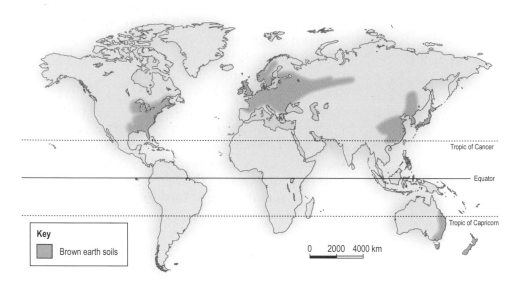

Figure 1 Global distribution of brown earth soils

Global distribution

Figure 1 shows the global distribution for brown earth soils which are closely associated with deciduous forests. The brown earths are mostly located between 30° and 55° north of the Equator. The largest expanse covers a large part of Western Europe including England and Wales, the east coast of the USA, parts of western and central Europe and eastern Asia.

Distribution in Britain

The brown earths group of soils covers about 45 per cent of the land area in England and Wales (Figure 2). They are common in the lowland areas (below 300 metres) on permeable, non-acid parent material. The most common vegetation types are deciduous woodland and grassland. The soils are fertile so large areas of deciduous woodland have been cleared over the centuries to form some of the best crop growing and grazing land in Britain.

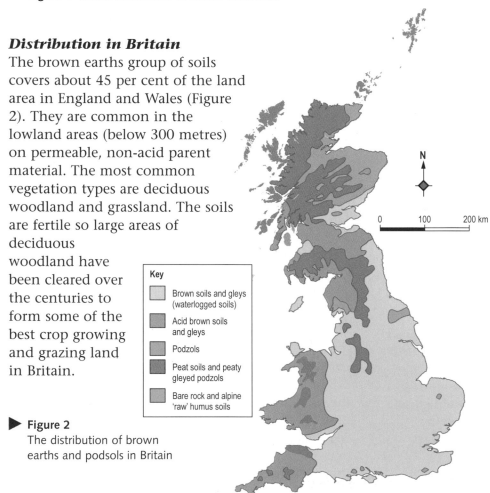

Key
- Brown soils and gleys (waterlogged soils)
- Acid brown soils and gleys
- Podzols
- Peat soils and peaty gleyed podzols
- Bare rock and alpine 'raw' humus soils

Figure 2
The distribution of brown earths and podsols in Britain

Climate

The brown earths are located in regions with a humid temperate climate (Figure 3) typical of Britain with few extremes of temperature or rainfall. Rainfall totals are low to moderate, below 800mm per year, and temperatures range from 4°C in the winter months to 17°C during the summer.

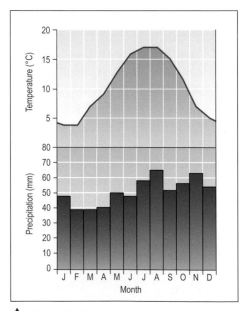

Figure 3 Climate graph for London, UK

Vegetation

The natural vegetation in areas with brown earth soils is deciduous woodland (Figure 4). The trees lose their leaves in winter adding valuable organic matter to the soil.

▼ **Figure 4** Autumn woodland at Allen Banks, Northumberland

Soil characteristics

Brown earths (Figure 5) are well-drained fertile soils with a pH of between 5.0 and 6.5. Figure 5 shows a typical soil profile for a brown earth. The reddish-brown A horizon is often over 30cm in depth. It is biologically active with many soil organisms mixing the mull humus with the mineral particles. Figure 5 shows the boundaries between the horizons as a dotted line. This indicates that there is rarely a precise boundary but that the horizons tend to merge into one another. This is particularly true between the A and B horizons where mixing by soil fauna is still active. The lack of distinctive horizons also reflects the limited leaching in the soils. Only the more soluble bases are moved down through the profile. The B horizon is mostly composed of mineral matter derived from the parent material shown by horizon C. The parent material is generally permeable and non-acid, e.g. loam.

▶ **Figure 5** Soil profile of a brown earth

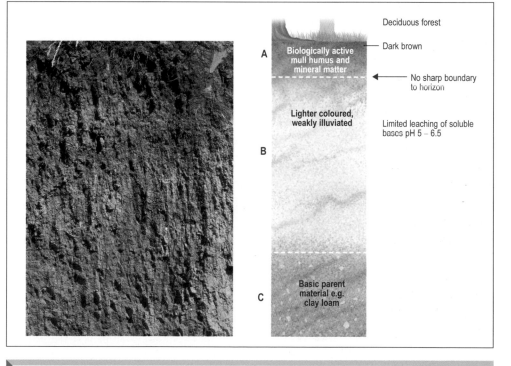

Human impact

Brown soils are fertile and make excellent agricultural soils. Large areas of deciduous woodland have been cleared over the centuries in Britain to make room for crop growing and grazing. Good yields are possible without the installation of drainage and a minimum of fertilizer use. In some areas the soils are being degraded by:

- the impact of acid rain largely through industrial pollution
- soil erosion as a result of intensive farming practices e.g. monoculture and hedge removal
- afforestation with coniferous plantations
- urbanization leading to the total loss of the soil to the ecosystem.

Questions

1 Using Figure 2, describe and explain the distribution of brown earth soils.

2 Describe the soil profile shown in Figure 5.

3 Explain the role of climate and vegetation in the formation of brown earths.

4 What are the main processes responsible for the formation of the soil?

5 Discuss the impact of human activities on brown earth soils in Britain.

Podsols

Global distribution

Podsols are associated with the boreal forests – the northern coniferous forests that stretch across northern Canada, Europe and Asia (Figure 1). The zone generally lies between 55° and 80° north of the Equator. There are very few areas with podsols in the southern hemisphere due to the absence of any large landmasses at this latitude.

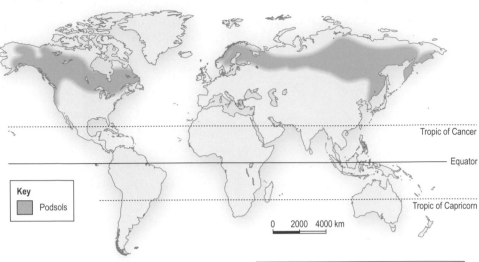

▼ **Figure 1** Global distribution of podsols

Key
Podsols

0   2000   4000 km

Distribution in Britain

Podsols are associated with the wetter and cooler areas of Britain. They are the characteristic soils towards the west of the country, in Scotland and in the upland moorland environments, see Figure 2 on page 122. They are generally associated with impermeable, acid parent materials, e.g. quartzite or sandstone, although some lowland areas with sandy parent materials, e.g. the Brecklands, also have podsol soils.

Climate

The climate is typically cool and wet in areas with podsols in Britain although they are a feature of much colder climates in the northern parts of Canada, Europe (Figure 2) and Asia. Areas with podsols in Britain have temperatures that range between 4° and 15°C with rainfall totals in excess of 1000mm. The growing season may be below six months of the year. Rates of evapotranspiration are low but precipitation totals are high giving considerable surplus moisture for leaching and podsolization to take place.

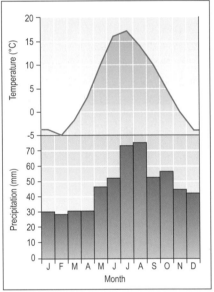

▶ **Figure 2** Climate graph for Uppsala in Sweden

▲ **Figure 3** Coniferous forest

Vegetation

Podsols are typically found below 'acid' vegetation, e.g. coniferous forests (Figure 3), heathland, heather moorland and tundra vegetation. These vegetation types produce only small quantities of acid litter that releases humic acids into the soil and contributes to the formation of a mor humus.

Soil characteristics and formation

Figure 4 shows the typical soil profile for a podsol. At the surface there is a thick peaty mor humus because the cold, wet, acid conditions hinder the work of decomposers. Below the peaty layers there is an Ea horizon. Still part of the A horizon the E stands for eluviation. This zone has been strongly eluviated leaving a bleached or grey horizon. The soluble bases along with iron, humus, clay and organic matter are washed out of the Ea horizon. The B horizon, in contrast, is strongly illuviated. The percolating water redeposits the iron, humus and clay etc. from the Ea horizon. The soils are acid with a typical pH of between 3.5 and 4.2. The boundaries between the horizons are sharp, as indicated by the solid lines on Figure 4, reflecting the strong eluviation and illuviation and the very limited faunal activity.

Formation of podsols

The process of podsolization is responsible for the soil formation. It is a more severe form of leaching in which iron and aluminium, clay and humus as well as the soluble bases are eluviated.

Podsols are formed where there is surplus moisture for the leaching process. Levels of acidity are also high enough to increase the solubility of iron and aluminium and to reduce the activity of decomposers. Intense leaching removes the soluble bases by the process of cation exchange. The lichens and acid peat that collect at the surface release organic acids, e.g. fulvic acid, as they decompose. These acids are chelating agents. They attack clay particles and cause the release of iron and aluminium in the soil to form chelates. Chelates are very soluble and easily washed down the soil profile in a process called cheluviation. Hence the iron and aluminium is eluviated from the upper horizons and illuviated lower down. Lower horizons are often less acid so the iron and aluminium become insoluble and are re-deposited. Sometimes the deposition of the iron leads to the formation of a hardpan where the iron is deposited in an impermeable layer lower down in the soil. This may lead to the waterlogging of the surface layers of soil.

In the process of podsolization insoluble particles such as clay and organic matter may also be moved in suspension through the soil profile. This process is called mechanical downwash.

Human impact

Podsols are of limited agricultural value due to their lack of fertility. They have few bases essential for plant life . Cultivation is only possible through:

- the repeated addition of large quantities of fertilizers
- drainage and deep ploughing to break up any hardpans and to mix the A and B horizons
- frequent liming to neutralize the acidity.

In general, podsol environments are used for sheep grazing and forestry in coniferous plantations. In Britain they form some of the most scenic landscapes in the country; they are also home to deer, rabbits, red grouse and a variety of other species. This makes these environments popular areas for tourism and recreation. Current issues affecting environments with podsol soils are pollution mainly by acid rain, afforestation and management of visitors due to the growth in tourism.

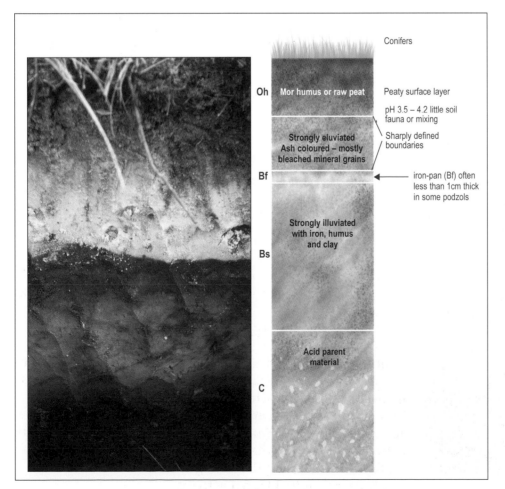

		Conifers
Oh	Mor humus or raw peat	Peaty surface layer
		pH 3.5 – 4.2 little soil fauna or mixing
	Strongly eluviated Ash coloured – mostly bleached mineral grains	Sharply defined boundaries
Bf		iron-pan (Bf) often less than 1cm thick in some podzols
Bs	Strongly illuviated with iron, humus and clay	
C	Acid parent material	

Figure 4 Soil profile of a podsol

Questions

1. Describe and explain the global distribution of podsols.

2. Describe the soil profile shown in Figure 4.

3. Explain the role of climate and vegetation in the formation of podsols

4. What are the main processes responsible for the formation of the soil?

5. Discuss the impact of human activities on podsols in Britain.

The impact of human activity on soils

- Human activity and soils
- The impact of modern farming
- Soil erosion, salinization and desertification

Human activity and soils

People depend upon soils for a large part of their food supply. It is a vital resource and Figure 1 summarizes the beneficial and detrimental effects people may have on the soil.

Farmers have a primary role in caring for and protecting the soil resource. However, this often conflicts with their aim of providing a food supply for a growing population and with modern farming techniques that are not always beneficial to the soil.

Figure 2 shows the causes and amount of soil degradation in the world since 1945. The greatest degradation occurs as a result of farming activities. By the year 2000 poor farming practices had caused deterioration in soil quality on over 600 million hectares of land, about 40 per cent of the available cropland in the world. Some areas were so severely damaged that the land had to be taken out of production.

▼ **Figure 2** Soil degradation caused by human activity, 1945-90

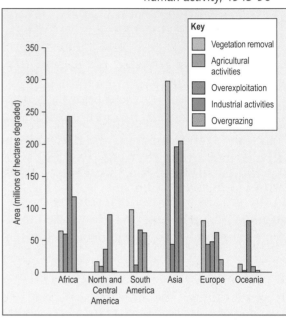

▼ **Figure 1** The impact of people on soils

Positive impacts

- Adding fertilizers especially organic manure and dung. This increases the organic content in the soil, improving soil structure and water retention capacity.
- Drainage improves water movement and reduces waterlogging.
- Terracing on steep hillsides reduces overland flow and soil erosion.
- Contour ploughing creates ridges and furrows around a hillslope which reduces soil erosion by water.
- Organic farming involves a wide number of farming practices designed to maintain and improve soil structure and texture.
- Windbreaks reduce erosion of the soil by the wind.
- The addition of agricultural lime to the soil reduces soil acidity and improves soil structure.
- Well-planned irrigation schemes, with adequate drainage, improve soil quality.
- Ploughing to provide aeration.
- Crop rotations that allow fallowing give the soil time to build up a store of nutrients.

Negative impacts

- Overcultivation by repeatedly growing nutrient-demanding crops in the same location e.g monoculture.
- Overgrazing occurs when the carrying capacity of the land is exceeded i.e. when there are too many animals for the available resources.
- Deforestation depletes the nutrient stores in an ecosystem as well as exposing the soil to erosion by wind or water.
- Urbanization removes vegetation and reduces the overall soil total by covering it with impermeable concrete and tarmac surfaces.
- Building of roads, mining and quarrying activities may cause subsidence of the ground and disruption to soils.
- Overuse of inorganic fertilizers may lead to a reduction in the organic matter in soils and a deterioration in soil structure.
- Hedgerow removal, overgrazing and overcultivation may all lead to accelerated erosion of soils.
- Irrigation without adequate water supplies and drainage causes salinization of soils.
- Compaction by heavy machinery weakens soil structure.
- Monoculture places heavy demands on the nutrients in the soil.
- Desertification may result from overuse of the land for crops, animals and timber.

The impact of modern farming

The twentieth century has seen, both in the LEDW and MEDW, that countries experienced often quite dramatic changes in farming practices. The aim of the changes was, without exception, to increase agricultural production in order to feed the world's growing population. There were two main ways in which agriculture changed:

- intensification of farming by increased use of agrochemicals, higher yielding strains of plants and animals etc.
- extensification of farmland, i.e. extending the area of land that is farmed by, for example, removing hedgerows, new irrigation and drainage schemes etc.

However, while most of the changes generated higher yields they also brought disadvantages and in the long term some have proved unsustainable and the land is now useless for agriculture. An analysis of a selection of modern farming practices follows.

Inorganic fertilizers

Nitrogen fertilizer is one of the most effective ways for a farmer to increase yields. Since 1960, the use of nitrogen fertilizers has increased fivefold although the increase is much slower now. In countries of the MEDW, many farmers over-fertilized their land and the excess, not taken up by plants, readily dissolved and was washed out into surface streams and groundwater supplies. This pollutes the water and presents a threat to the ecosystems and to human health. Babies are particularly sensitive to high nitrate concentrations which prevents the red blood cells operating correctly leading to insufficient oxygen and 'blue-baby syndrome'. Nitrate runoff into watercourses may also cause algal blooms that are toxic to aquatic organisms. The high nitrate levels fuel the growth of the algae. When the algae die and decay the oxygen in the water is rapidly depleted so causing other plants and animals to be starved of an oxygen supply. This process is called eutrophication and can lead to a massive decline in local catches of fish, an important food source. In many developed countries today, including those of the EU, there are guidelines on fertilizer application to reduce these problems. Much research is being undertaken towards making fertilizers more efficient and to find ways to trap agricultural runoff before it reaches water courses.

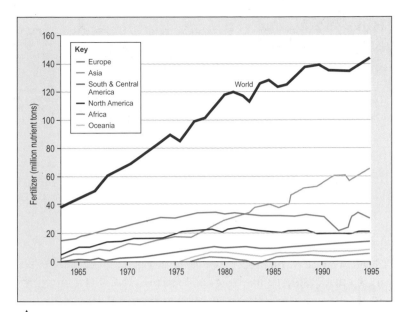

▲ **Figure 3** More fertilizer, more food – but more pollution too

As Figure 3 shows, agriculture has contributed in a major way to the increased supply of nitrogen available to plants but there is a limit to the amount that natural systems can absorb and the surplus is likely to result in:

- eutrophication of lakes and watercourses
- a decline in soil fertility as the nitrogen in the soil forms weak acids and encourages leaching of soil nutrients such as calcium, magnesium and potassium
- reduced biodiversity through the extinction of some grass species not tolerant of high levels of nitrogen. In the Netherlands species-rich heathlands are being converted into species-poor grasslands that can tolerate the nitrogen
- increased nitrous oxide in the atmosphere leading to smog, acid rain and increased global warming
- threats to human health.

▲ **Figure 4** Crop spraying

Heavy machinery

The drive to intensify has seen the development of huge agricultural machinery e.g. tractors, combine harvesters, hedge trimmers and crop sprayers (Figure 1). The huge wheels and weight of the machines damages the soil by compaction of the soil particles. This destroys soil structure often making it impenetrable to moisture, air and plant roots. In severely compacted areas, e.g. at farm gates, the soil may be unable to support any plant life leading to the creation of bare ground that becomes a quagmire when wet and a hard, cracked surface under dry conditions.

▶ **Figure 1** Heavy agricultural machinery

Monoculture

Monoculture is the specialization of farming activities into the growth of a single crop. In some cases monoculture is a product of the natural environment e.g. intensive rice growing areas where few other crops are suited to the particular conditions. However, in many cases and especially in the MEDW, monoculture is a response to the intensification of farming and a drive to increase yields. In East Anglia in Britain the traditional farming was mixed and used crop rotation. The rotation included some leguminous plants such as clover, which fix nitrogen, and animals whose manure contributed organic matter to the soil. Gradually the farms became more intensive and specialized eventually concentrating on a very limited range of crops, e.g. wheat and barley.

However, this intensification and the repeated use of the land for a single crop has the following consequences:
- increased use of artificial fertilizers to maintain soil fertility
- loss of organic matter from soils causing a deterioration in soil structure

▲ **Figure 2** Growth of prairie-like landscape in East Anglia

- crop–specific pests become a problem e.g. potato blight
- hedgerow removal causing the loss of habitats and soil erosion
- compaction of soils through the use of large, heavy machinery
- weed infestation requiring the use of pesticides
- 'prairieization' – creating a uniform and monotonous landscape (Figure 2).

Drainage and irrigation

Overall, irrigating land increases food production. In many countries of the LEDW it has been a central part of the Green Revolution in order to increase food supplies for their growing populations and to produce surplus agricultural products to increase export earnings. The United Nations Food and Agriculture Organization (FAO) has predicted that irrigated land will increase by 0.8 per cent a year expanding from 123 million hectares in 1990 to 146 million hectares in 2010. Despite the advantage of increased yields, irrigation also has its problems:
- spread of disease as carriers, e.g. mosquitoes and guinea worms, expand into the irrigation channels and dams
- using sewage water for irrigation can spread diseases, e.g. cholera outbreaks in Chile in the 1970s and 1980s were linked to eating salad crops irrigated with wastewater
- excessive use of freshwater supplies
- salinization of the land.

Irrigation projects along the Senegal River

Case Study

▲ **Figure 3**   Farmers using irrigation channels in Senegal

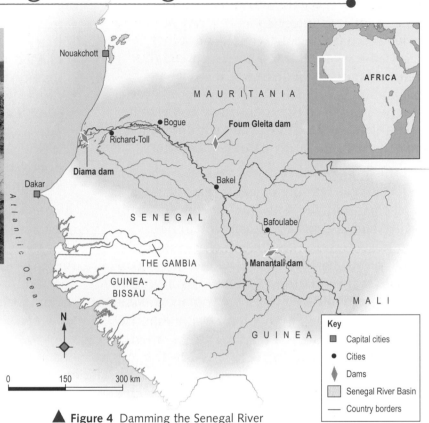

▲ **Figure 4** Damming the Senegal River

As part of a multipurpose scheme on the Senegal River (Figure 4) two new dams were built with the aim of:

- controlling flooding in some parts of the valley
- providing a constant water supply in a drought prone area
- providing water to irrigate 375 000 hectares of land mostly in Senegal and Mauritania (Figure 3).

The dams were completed by 1987 and were filled by 1991. Some of the irrigation projects are now complete and yields of rice and sugar cane have increased although not as rapidly as predicted. However the scheme has also brought disadvantages:

- increased schistosomiasis carried by snails that live along the irrigation channels
- no significant improvement in the diet for the local people; 36 per cent of children still suffer from chronic malnutrition
- reduction in traditional crop growing areas that grew a wide variety of food, replaced with more rice
- relocation of 10 000 people in Mali, some to areas with insufficient farmland and water
- a reduction in livestock production as herders have lost pastureland due to the increase in irrigated areas and the reduction in the annual flood that brought water and fertile silt to the grazing land
- conflicts between pastoralists and farmers and other ethnic groups over land ownership and rights.

ⓘ *Sustainable development is the ability of one generation to hand over to the next at least the same amount of resources it started with. It should be development which helps all people. Sustainable development should:*
- *respect the environment and cultures*
- *use traditional skills and knowledge*
- *give people control over their land and lives*
- *use appropriate technology – machines and equipment that are cheap, easy to use and do not harm the environment*
- *generate income for communities.*

Questions

1 Produce a table of the advantages and disadvantages of modern farming practices.

2 Analyse the impact of the irrigation project along the River Senegal.

3 To what extent does the project fit the concept of sustainable development outlined in the information box?

4 Suggest some alternative, more sustainable projects that could have been used.

Revolution in organic farming

Modern farming practices in the MEDW since the Second World War have led to an intensification of farming in order to increase yields. Many of the practices also have negative consequences:

- increased loss of soil through erosion
- decreased nutritional quality of foods
- exploitation of animals in intensive factory farms
- negative impact on the countryside and wildlife, e.g. through hedge removal and eutrophication
- expansion of genetically modified foodstuffs.

It is in the interests of society as a whole to develop more sustainable farming practices that use fewer farming chemicals, less water, less energy and cause less ecosystem disruption while maintaining agricultural diversity. This drive to more sustainable forms of farming has led to a 'revolution' in organic farming in many countries in the MEDW. In contrast, many countries in the LEDW already practise organic farming due to the absence of high technology and agrochemicals.

In Britain in the early 1970s there was the beginning of a demand from some consumers and farmers for certification of organically-produced foods by the Soil Association (Figure 1). Today about 80 per cent of UK organic food is certified by the Soil Association.

In the UK the numbers of organic farmers remained small until 1995 when the Organic Aid Scheme was launched by the government to help farmers through the difficult and costly conversion to organic farming. Today organic land in Britain is still less than 0.5 per cent compared with about 4 per cent in Germany. Currently the demand for organic foods in the UK is very large and about 70 per cent of organic food is imported from the more developed European and American markets.

In order to achieve the aims set out in Figure 1, organic farming systems:

- minimize the use of synthetic fertilizers, pesticides, feed additives and other chemicals
- maintain soil fertility and structure by crop rotation and crop residues
- control weeds and pests by using biological pest control and crop rotations
- provide good quality organic fodder for animals
- use free-range methods of rearing animals and do not overstock land
- keep processing and packaging to a minimum.

In comparison with organic farming, modern intensive farms produce high yields and, until recently, farmers gained a good standard of living. Perhaps this explains why in the UK, while the demand for organically-grown produce has increased, the numbers of farms converting to organically-grown produce is still small. However, the potential gains to the environment and especially soils through organic farming practices are huge. Figure 2 looks at the relative costs and benefits of organic farming compared with conventional farm practices for soils.

The Soil Association's principal aims of organic agriculture and processing are to:
- produce food of high nutritional quality
- encourage and enhance natural systems
- maintain and increase long-term fertility and conservation of soil
- promote the healthy use, proper care and conservation of water
- use renewable resources as far as possible
- work with materials that can be reused or recycled
- minimize all forms of pollution
- maintain the biodiversity of the agricultural system and its surroundings
- give livestock an acceptable quality of life
- progress towards an entire organic production chain, which is both socially just and ecologically responsible.

▲ **Figure 1** Aims of organic farming

▼ **Figure 2** Costs and benefits of organic farming

	Organic farming	Conventional farming
Soil nutrients/fertility	Replenished by legumes, organic manure, crop rotation practises	Replenished by inorganic fertilizers
Organic matter	Kept high or improved by using organic manure, crop stalks etc.	Often depleted through not adding any organic matter to the soil or by harvesting crop stalks for straw
Soil structure	Minimum use of heavy machinery for spraying, harvesting and ploughing limits compaction. Organic matter preserves drainage	Compaction by frequent use of heavy machinery, lack of organic matter
Soil drainage/water content	Organic matter retains moisture, good structure encourages free drainage	Compaction, lack of organic matter matter reduces water-holding and drainage properties of soil
Soil erosion	Minimized through high organic matter content, good moisture-holding capacity and by land management, e.g. mixed farming, rotations and use of cover crops to give continuous cover	A problem where hedgerow removal has taken place, in soils with low organic matter and in areas of monoculture with land left bare for parts of the year

Soil erosion

Soil erosion is the removal of soil by wind or water. It is a natural process but is often accelerated by human activities. In the four major food-producing countries in the world – the USA, former Soviet Union, China and India – the total losses are estimated to be 13.6 billion tonnes per year.

Human causes of soil erosion

Some farming practices encourage erosion to take place:
- ploughing up and down hillsides leaves furrows that encourage the water to flow downhill
- leaving the land fallow between crops and the removal of vegetation exposes the underlying soil to the direct effects of wind and water.
- deforestation, overgrazing and overcultivation
- ploughing that loosens the surface soil and harms the soil structure
- removal of hedgerows that would normally deflect the wind away from the surface and the roots that would help bind the soil particles together.

Accelerated soil erosion presents problems for those areas affected. The soil becomes infertile and eventually the land may have to be abandoned for any form of farming. The eroded sediments, nutrients and chemicals may cause water quality in local rivers to deteriorate and in severe dust storms air quality is seriously affected. In areas of severe erosion by water, gulleys may be formed.

Figure 3 shows areas in the USA where excessive soil erosion is taking place. In many of these regions projects have been established to attempt to reduce soil erosion. One project is the Great Lakes Basin Programme in which every $1000 spent saves 174 tonnes of soil, 35 kgs of phosphorus and 13 kgs of nitrogen and educates the local people on techniques to reduce erosion. The reduced erosion is also helping to improve water quality in the Great Lakes. Figure 4 gives details of one scheme – the Fish Creek Watershed project.

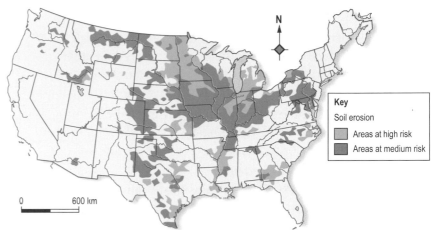

▲ **Figure 3** Soil erosion on cropland, 1997

▲ **Figure 4** The Fish Creek Watershed Project

Fish Creek is 48 km long and drains 352sq km of agricultural land in Ohio and Indiana. The Creek is a wooded valley and one of the top ranked biodiversity sites in the Great Lakes region.

Problems
Excessive soil erosion causing:
- the loss of the most productive upper layer of soil
- sedimentation in local streams
- reduced crop yields
- pollution of local streams by sediments and chemicals
- damaged mussel beds in the lower drainage basin.

Solutions
- land protection and treatment
- restoration of wetlands, for example by building fences to keep out cattle
- reforestation of 77 ha with hardwoods and planting of grass
- conservation ploughing using special machinery
- planting no-till corn that requires less field preparation. Although yields are slightly lower, profits are increased due to reduced ploughing. The increased profit per acre on corn is $15 and on soybeans $8.50
- public consultation and education, e.g. distribution of newsletters

Results
- 13 farmers now use conservation techniques on about 1620 ha of land
- about 31 500 tonnes of soil are being saved annually
- the local people are now educated about endangered mussels and conservation practices.

Salinization

Many arid and semi-arid areas of the world have naturally high levels of salt in the soils. These are areas where evapotranspiration exceeds precipitation. Therefore water movement is generally upwards in the soil and the water carries dissolved salts with it. These salts are deposited in the surface layers of the soil giving high concentrations of salt. Human activities may however increase the salt concentration in a process called salinization. The following are the main causes of increased salinization.

Irrigation

Adding water to the ground raises the level of groundwater in the soil. The water table may become close enough to the surface for capillary action to occur. The water rises through the soils eventually evaporating concentrating any salts in surface soils. In addition there may be direct evaporation of the water from the irrigated land adding to salt concentration. This is a particular problem in rice growing areas where large quantities of water are added over the soil surface.

Vegetation clearance

Removing vegetation allows more rainfall to percolate into the ground causing the groundwater levels to rise and an opportunity for saline water to collect closer to the surface. This has been a particular problem in parts of southern Australia.

The impact of salinization

- River water becomes more saline and may be unfit for human consumption.
- The increase in salts, especially sodium, causes the soil structure to collapse making the soil impermeable.
- The land can no longer support vegetation due to the poor soil structure. Desertification may occur or at best the growth of xerophytic (drought-resistant) and salt-tolerant plant species.
- The bare ground may become subject to wind and water erosion.

Solving salinization problems

1 Removing the salts by adding huge quantities of fresh water and adequate drainage in order to 'flush' the salts out of the soil. This is however expensive and difficult to achieve in some low-lying areas where the water table is close to the surface or where fresh water is in short supply.

2 Planting and harvesting salt-accumulating plants.

3 Conversion of the salts into less harmful substances that are more easily leached from the soils, e.g. by adding gypsum.

4 Controlling the process of salinization by adding less water. This is achieved through:
   - using sprinklers rather than traditional irrigation methods
   - lining canals to reduce seepage
   - using more salt-tolerant plant species.

Salinization:
Case Study   in south west Australia

South-west Australia receives less than 900mm of rainfall per year and there are high rates of evapotranspiration. Between 20–20kg of salt lie below every square metre of land. About 14.6 million hectares of land have been cleared for grazing and cropping in south-west Australia. The reduced vegetation cover has resulted in more rainfall reaching the ground water raising water tables and mobilizing the salt in the soils. Water tables in un-cleared areas are up to 10m lower than in neighbouring wheat producing areas. Figure 1 shows the projections for salinized areas of land in south-west Western Australia. By 2010 some estimates say that 16 per cent of land will be affected by salinization and that it will be the best agricultural lands that are affected. In addition the salinity of local stream networks will be increased making them unsuitable for human use and affecting the stream's ecosystem.

Today some clearing controls have been implemented and small areas are being afforested where moisture levels are high enough.

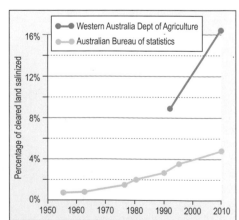

▲ **Figure 1** The growth in the area of salinized land in south-west Western Australia

▲ **Figure 2** Salinized land in South West Australia

Desertification

Desertification is the process whereby land is turned into desert as a result of human activity and/or climatic change (Figure 3). As the previous sections show soil erosion and salinization are just two processes that may result in desertification whereby the land can no longer support any vegetation. There is considerable debate over how permanent the changes may be. Recent research has shown that areas once barren as a result of desertification are now regenerating following the end of drought conditions.

Questions

1. What is soil erosion?

2. Describe the human activities that may lead to increased rates of soil erosion.

3. Summarize the main issues involved with the problems of soil erosion in the Fish Creek area.

4. Explain the advantages and disadvantages of the Fish Creek Watershed project.

Extended writing

5. a Explain the causes of salinization.
   b With reference to examples, describe the impact of, and solutions to, problems caused by salinization and desertification.

▼ **Figure 3** A summary of the causes of desertification

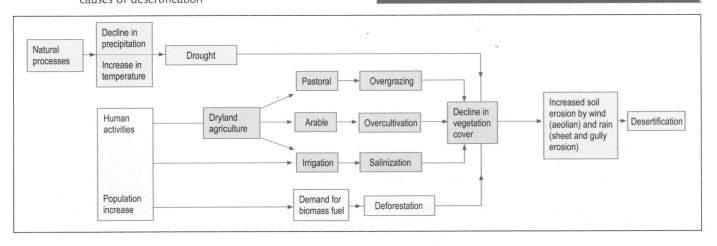

Figure 1 shows the global extent of desertification. Areas most affected are in the arid and semi-arid regions of the world in both the MEDW and LEDW and where rain is unreliable (between 250 and 400mm per year). The characteristics of regions affected by desertification include:

- a decrease in plant and animal species, hence a decrease in biomass
- reduced net primary productivity
- reduced soil organic matter
- increased soil salinity and compaction
- increased erosion and dust storms.

Areas likely to be affected by desertification can be managed and the vegetation returned. Recent satellite photographs have shown that the vegetation is returning to some areas of the Sahel helped by average and above average rainfall in the late 1990s. Figure 2 demonstrates some of the techniques that may be used to manage desertification.

▼ **Figure 1** The global extent of desertification

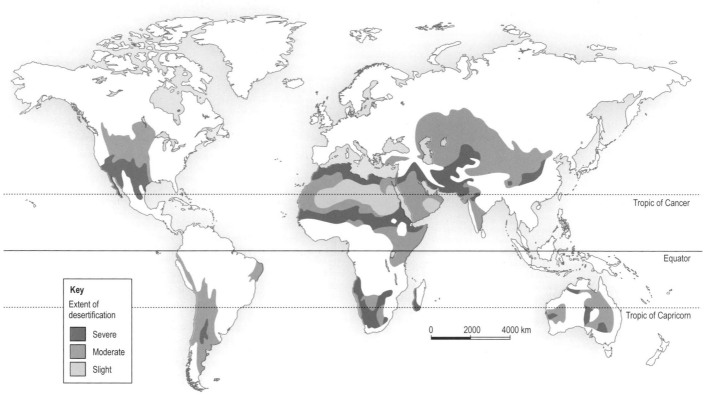

Key
Extent of desertification

- Severe
- Moderate
- Slight

Tropic of Cancer

Equator

Tropic of Capricorn

0   2000   4000 km

▼ **Figure 2** Tackling desertification

Reducing overcultivation by:
- increasing yields with fertilizers and higher yielding/drought-resistant seeds
- using crop rotations
- using irrigation in dry seasons.

Reducing overgrazing by:
- controlled burning of grasslands
- reduced numbers of cattle – higher yielding breeds and improved medical care of animals
- rotating grazing land.

Reducing deforestation by:
- providing alternative fuel supplies, e.g. biogas plants
- sustainable forestry projects and tree planting schemes.

Improve soils by:
- using animal manure and crop stalks as fertilizer
- terracing on steep slopes
- providing windbreaks to reduce erosion
- planting leguminous crops
- reducing salinization.

Changing the socio-economic conditions by:
- reducing birth rates to keep populations within the carrying capacity of the land
- developing local economies with commercial agriculture, alternative employment in craft industries or tourism
- providing loans or grants.

The Sahel
Case Study   in North Africa

One region seriously affected by desertification is the Sahel on the southern fringes of the Sahara desert in North Africa. The Eden Foundation is working on the Tanout region of the Niger (Figure 3) to help reverse the process of desertification. The main agricultural zone lies to the south of Tanout where in recent years the vegetation has decreased leaving the bare soil open to wind erosion. The landscape is brown and bare for most of the year (Figure 4) and the local people report less rainfall.

Most farmers cultivate millet, irrigate winter cash crops, e.g. peanuts, and hunt for deer. However, yields are only one-seventh of those 40 years ago. The reduced yields are a result of desertification caused by farmers slashing and burning their fields to grow crops. The slash and burn techniques have caused the decimation of trees and other perennials that once sheltered the millet and added to soil fertility. The bare ground has been eroded by the wind and sand dunes now encroach on. The dunes were formed from soil eroded within the agricultural zone where the trees have been cut down. About 250 000 hectares of land are being lost each year in the Niger to desertification.

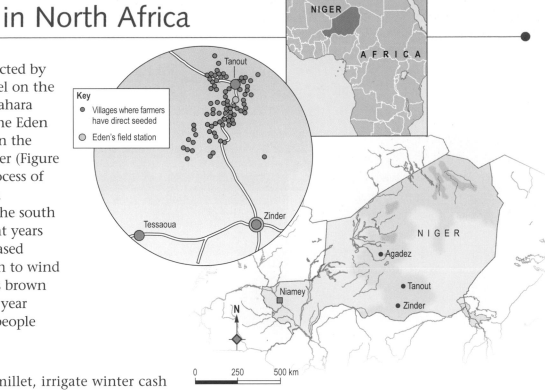

▲ **Figure 3** Location of the Tanout region, Niger

Solutions implemented by the Eden Foundation include:
- research at field stations and advice and demonstrations to farmers
- providing seeds to the farmers
- re-vegetation of perennials that naturally re-seed and regenerate. The perennials stabilize the soil against soil erosion and improve fertility as well as being a potential source of food and timber for fuel and building materials.

▲ **Figure 4** Landscape of North Africa

Chapter **3** Questions

1 a Study Figure 1, which was taken in a clearing in a tropical rainforest.

▶ **Figure 1**

    i Describe and comment upon what is happening.   (4 marks)

    ii Outline the political factors that can lead to deforestation in tropical rainforests.   (4 marks)

  b Explain why tropical rainforests have the highest net primary productivity of any global biome.   (7 marks)

Total: 15 marks

2 a Explain, with examples, why soils develop different characteristics.   (10 marks)

  b Why can both physical and human factors be responsible for arresting the progress of a plant community towards the climatic climax vegetation of the area?   (10 marks)

Total: 20 marks

A note on timing

You are expected to answer question 1 in about 15 minutes. You are expected to answer question 2 in about 40 minutes, spending an equal length of time on both parts.

Chapter 4 Population

Crowds celebrating the
Velvet Revolution in Prague,
Czech Republic

Population distribution and density

Population change

Migration

Population structure

Population distribution
and density

- Distribution and density of population
- Physical and human factors affecting population distribution and density
- Studies of population distributions at different scales

Distribution and density of population

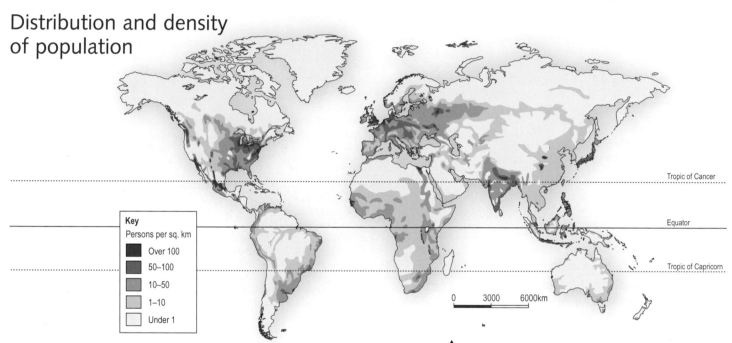

▲ **Figure 1** The distribution of the world's population

The distribution of population is the way people are dispersed or spread across the landscape or where people live whereas the density of population is the number of people who live in an area, usually measured in people per square kilometre. Densely populated means there is a very high density or many people living in an area. The opposite of this is sparsely populated which means there is a very low density or a few people living in an area.

There are over 6000 million people in the world today. The distribution of the world's population is very uneven (Figure 1) with some areas being very densely populated while others are almost totally uninhabited.

Areas in Europe and Asia that have been settled for a long period of time have some of the highest densities of geopulation. Europe and Asia have over 85 per cent of the world's population while the New World, including North America and the three southern continents, has less than 15 per cent of the world's population.

The world's population also varies latitudinally. Less than 10 per cent of the world's population live in the Southern Hemisphere. About 80 per cent of the world's population lives between 20 and 60 degrees north of the Equator. However, this area also contains some of the world's largest deserts and mountain ranges – areas with very sparse populations.

The primary concentrations of population where densities exceed 100 per square kilometre are in south and east Asia, Europe and the north east of North America. These areas include regions with high living standards as in the USA and the UK and the densely populated areas of India and south-east China where living standards are lower.

Secondary concentrations of population where densities are between 25 and 100 per square kilometre are numerous and widespread across the world. They include California in the USA, coastal Brazil, the Nile Valley, West Africa, south-east Australia, France, Turkey and Mexico.

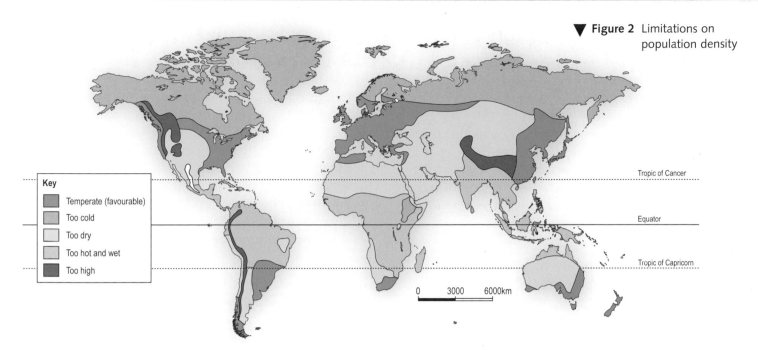

▼ **Figure 2** Limitations on population density

Key
- Temperate (favourable)
- Too cold
- Too dry
- Too hot and wet
- Too high

Tropic of Cancer

Equator

Tropic of Capricorn

0   3000   6000km

Areas with low population densities of between 2 and 25 people per square kilometre include Norway, New Zealand, Canada, North Africa and Patagonia in southern Argentina. Areas with less than 2 people per square kilometre may be considered empty areas. These areas total more than 64 per cent of the world's land area making them far more significant than areas of high density. Between 35 and 40 per cent of this land area is regarded as uninhabitable and includes the high mountainous areas such as the Himalayas, the hot and cold deserts and areas with impenetrable rainforest (Figure 2).

In general, areas with environmental advantages tend to be densely populated and affluent while those with disadvantages tend to be sparsely populated with social and economic deficiencies. There are exceptions to this such as some areas with high densities of population which have very low living standards and low levels of economic development, for example Bangladesh.

The nature of the population distribution can be shown using the Lorenz Curve (Figure 3). The curve shows the amount of regularity in a distribution; the more concave the curve the greater the inequality in the distribution.

The Lorenz Curve

Figure 3a shows the physical spread or distribution of people over an area. The diagonal represents a totally even dispersal, i.e. 10 per cent of the people live on 10 per cent of the land area, 50 per cent live on 50 per cent of the land area, etc. However, in reality this rarely occurs and most population distributions are more akin to the situation represented by the curve where 40 per cent of the population live on 10 per cent of the land area, 80 per cent on 45 per cent of the land area, etc.

Figure 3b shows how the Lorenz Curve may also be used to show the degree of inequality in a society in the distribution of resources such as food, wealth, medical care, political power, etc. In the curve shown 80 per cent of the population hold only 20 per cent of the society's wealth. The 80 per cent may well be considered the underprivileged in the society, the remaining 20 per cent the privileged.

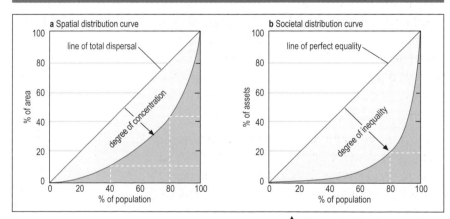

▲ **Figure 3** The Lorenz Curve

Questions

1   Describe the differences between population density and population distribution.

2   Describe the world pattern of population distribution.

Physical and human factors affecting population distribution and density

The world's population is unevenly spread across the land surface but so too are wealth, food, medical care, water supply and other socio-economic and political factors. The explanation for the uneven distribution lies in a mixture of physical and human factors (Figure 1) as well as the historical development of an area. Factors having a positive impact are likely to encourage high population density whereas those having a negative impact are likely to deter population leading to sparsely populated areas.

Initially people chose to live in an area where the environment could support them. The physical reasons such as water supply, fertile soils for crops, wood for fuel, land not liable to flooding were all important. The greater the potential of the environment the more likely the area was to be populated and for densities to increase. Over time people have exercised increasing control over the environment hence the importance of human factors including economic potential – the ability of people to earn a living in an area.

The highest concentrations of population are found in coastal areas with about two-thirds of the world's population living within 500km of the sea. This emphasizes the importance of coastal locations for accessibility, trading and climate. Low altitudes are also important with 56.2 per cent of the world's population living between 0 and 200m above sea level (27.8 per cent land area) and 80 per cent living below 500m above sea level (57.3 per cent of the land area). In the UK 80 per cent of the population lives below 100m above sea level.

High altitudes place a physical limit on human habitation because of low oxygen levels; however in hotter climates higher altitudes may be an advantage because they are cooler. Hence, there are several capital cities at high altitudes, e.g. La Paz (3640m), Quito (2580m) and Mexico City (2355m). Mountainous areas with steep slopes, rugged terrain and exposure to cold, wet and windy climates restrict access, settlement and cultivation. They are usually sparsely populated areas although technology can

▼ **Figure 1** Physical and human factors affecting population distribution and density

Physical factors	Positive impact	Negative impact
Relief	Lowland and gently undulating terrain	Steep, mountainous land
Soils	Fertile, easily worked soils, e.g.loams and alluvium	Infertile soils, acid, leached and stony
Climate	Absence of extremes of rainfall or temperature. Enough rainfall and adequate temperatures for crop growth	Severe climatic conditions – too hot, cold, wet or dry although low temperatures and aridity are the real limiting factors
Vegetation	Vegetation that is easy to clear or valuable land, e.g. grasslands	Dense forest difficult to penetrate and clear
Drainage	Well drained soils for farming,adequate water supply for domestic, industrial and agricultural uses	Marsh and swamp, lack of water supply
Position	Coastal, estuary locations accessible to the outside world and for trade	Interior locations, remote and isolated from the outside world
Resources	Good fish stocks, mineral and energy supplies	Lack of resources, e.g. fish, energy supply and minerals

Human factors	Positive impact	Negative impact
Social	Underpopulation giving a surplus of resources able to be sold for profit	Overpopulation leading to the **carrying capacity** being exceeded and a shortage of resources.
	Traditions and religious beliefs lead to population growth, e.g. amongst Muslim and Catholic communities	Tradition of low birth rates
Economic	Good infrastructure, i.e. roads, rail, electricity, water and other services	Poor infrastructure, e.g. lack of communications and poor services
	Good export trade and wealthy markets	Limited export trade and poor markets
	A varied economic structure with agriculture, industry and services offering a large range of employment opportunities	Limited employment opportunities
	Intensive farming	Extensive farming
Political	Political stability, mature politically	Political instability, newly independent, history of war
Historical	Settled for a long time	Only recently settled

increasingly overcome the problems. Building tunnels and avalanche shelters allow mountain railways and roads to be built, and resistant strains of crops and breeds of animals allow limited farming to take place. However, the economic costs are high and most areas with difficult relief are sparsely populated except where security or economic resources are important. The hill top villages in southern Italy are a product of repeated invasions in the past. Densely populated areas are mostly located in lowland areas, e.g. the North European Plain, the Nile valley and Ganges delta. There are exceptions such as the Amazon Basin where rainforest limits settlement, also Siberia which is a barren, cold wasteland, and the interior of the Prairies in Canada where the remote location has hindered settlement.

In areas of extreme climate indigenous populations exist by having made considerable physiological and social adaptations to the environment. The Inuit, for example, have adapted by having thick layers of subcutaneous fat, special clothing and housing. However, the populations of the area remain sparse. High temperatures do not restrict population but combined with a lack of rainfall few people can survive. The hot deserts cover about 20 per cent of the world's land surface yet support only 0.4 per cent of the world's population. The people tend to live close to oases, aquifers and rivers such as the River Nile.

During the twentieth century valuable minerals were discovered in some parts of the world where the climate restricts human habitation, e.g. oil reserves in Alaska, Libya and the Middle East. In order to exploit the valuable resources settlements are supported by modern technological developments and by external supplies of water, food and clothing.

The type and scale of economic activities have considerable influence on population distribution. About two-thirds of the world's population still rely on agriculture so that unsuitable areas for farming remain sparsely populated. Low-lying areas, especially temperate zones, are more densely populated and areas capable of producing high yields also have very high densities of population, e.g. the Ganges Delta. Different agricultural systems produce different population distributions, for example in shifting cultivation the distribution is dispersed and sparse whereas in areas of intensive market gardening populations are more concentrated. However areas where populations are dependent upon agriculture tend to be fairly evenly distributed overall. Once industrialization and urbanization begin to occur then populations tend to become more concentrated in the developing towns and cities.

Changes in population distributions tend to be a result of:
- technological advances, e.g. the reclaiming and settlement of the polders in the Netherlands or the Industrial Revolution in Britain that fuelled urbanization and the concentration of people into urban areas
- political factors, e.g. the creation of the state of Israel in 1948 led to an influx of Jews; and in 1917, during the Russian Revolution, Russians were forcibly moved eastwards to open up and develop Siberia.

Questions

1 a Construct Lorenz Curves to show the following distributions:.

A	Population (%)	Land area (%)
World	56	28
	80	57
	100	100

B	Population (%)	Altitude
UK	80	Below 100m asl
	100	Below 1000m asl

b Describe and explain the patterns shown by the curves.

2 Explain why the distribution of the world's population is uneven.

3 Select two geographical areas with different densities of population – one low and one high. Describe and explain the different densities in the areas chosen.

Studies of population distributions at different scales
Population distribution and density

Case Study

in the UK (MEDC)

Europe is one of the most densely populated parts of the world. However, within Europe there are wide variations in both distribution and density (Figure 1). The UK is one of the more densely populated countries in Europe with a density of 239 people per square kilometre.

Within any one country there are also variations. Figure 2 shows the density of population in the UK. The densely populated conurbations and south east of England contrast sharply with the sparsely populated uplands largely in the north and west of the UK.

Country	Density (people/sq km)
Belgium	322
Netherlands	388
Luxembourg	146
France	105
Italy	190
Spain	81
Portugal	115
Switzerland	164
Austria	91
Norway	13
Denmark	120
Sweden	19
Finland	15
Germany	216
Ireland	58
UK	239

▲ **Figure 1** Population statistics for selected countries in Europe (2000)

Key (People per km²)
- Over 150
- 11 – 150
- 0 – 10

Cities and towns (population)
- Over 1 000 000
- 500 000 – 1 000 000
- 100 000 – 499 000
- 25 000 – 99 000

N

0   50   100km

▲ **Figure 2** Map showing the population density in the UK

Factors affecting the UK distribution and density of population

Before the Industrial Revolution population in the UK was quite even, although the more fertile agricultural areas such as East Anglia were able to support much higher densities of population than the cold, wet uplands which were sparsely populated. This pattern can still be seen today with low population densities, mostly below 10 people per square kilometre, in the highland areas because of their unsuitability for agriculture and their remoteness. The land is too steep for farm machinery, the soils are often thin and rocky and there are few lines of communication. The economic potential is low, i.e. there are few opportunities for farming and industry. Occupations are mostly confined to extensive hill sheep farming, forestry, tourism, quarrying and water companies.

Population densities are higher, between 10 and 150 people per square kilometre, in the more fertile lowland areas where farming opportunities are greater and villages, market and mining towns

have developed. The highest population densities are found in the urban areas where the greatest employment opportunities exist. In some towns and cities densities may reach over 1000 people per square kilometre and over 80 per cent of the UK population live in the urban areas. Over 50 per cent of the UK population lives in the seven major conurbations.

During the Industrial Revolution in the UK energy sources, especially coal, became the foci for industrial growth and population concentration. Mining towns developed and there was a general movement of people from the countryside to the towns. Industrialization and urbanization resulted in the growth of large cities and conurbations and an increasing concentration of people in urban areas. Six of the seven conurbations in the UK developed as a result of the availability of coal resources. Greater London, the capital city, is the exception.

The North region of England

`Case Study`

The North region is a government administrative region in which four classifications of population density can be recognized (Figure 3).

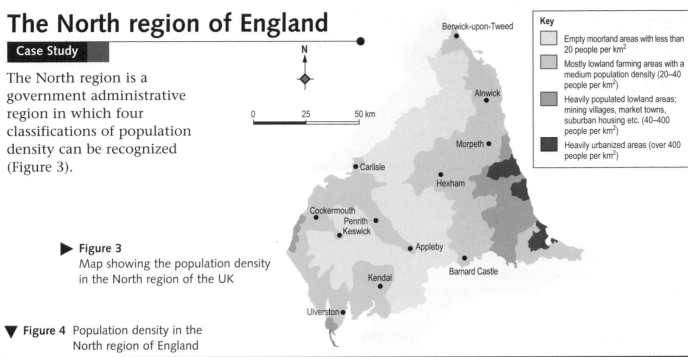

► **Figure 3**
Map showing the population density in the North region of the UK

Key
- Empty moorland areas with less than 20 people per km^2
- Mostly lowland farming areas with a medium population density (20–40 people per km^2)
- Heavily populated lowland areas; mining villages, market towns, suburban housing etc. (40–400 people per km^2)
- Heavily urbanized areas (over 400 people per km^2)

▼ **Figure 4** Population density in the North region of England

	Low density	Medium density	High density	Ultra high density
Distribution	40% land area 2% population	40% land area 30% population	15% land area 35% population	5% land area 33% population
Density (people per sq km)	Less than 20	20–40	40–400	Over 400
Reasons	Moorland, exposed, too high and wet, remote, steep slopes	Lowland, good farmland, some primary industry and services	Traditional mining and industrial towns that declined and are now diversifying and attracting new investment	Urban areas including conurbations
Settlements	Farms, hamlets, villages, market towns	As for low density areas and larger market towns	Villages, towns	Large towns and cities
Examples	Cheviots, Pennines, Cumbria	Tynedale, Northumberland coast, Weardale and Teesdale Valleys	Consett, SE Northumberland, Mid Durham	Tyneside, Wearside, Teesside

In recent years, while the overall population distribution has remained relatively static there have been changes in the population densities in certain areas. The most remote rural areas have continued to lose population as hill sheep farming declines and the younger generations seek higher wages and access to education and services in the urban areas. The conurbations have lost population especially from the inner-city areas as a result of redevelopment schemes and the process of counter-urbanization. As a result the rural areas, especially those adjacent to the large urban areas, have seen an influx of people and a rise in population density.

Questions

1. Using Figure 1 and a blank outline map of Europe construct a choropleth map to show the population density of the selected countries of Europe.

2. Using Figure 4 construct a Lorenz Curve for the population distribution and land area in the North region of England.

3. Describe and explain the population distribution and density in the North of England.

4. Describe the ways in which the distribution and density is changing in the North of England.

Population density

Case Study   in Newcastle-upon-Tyne

Newcastle-upon-Tyne is the main city in the Tyneside conurbation in north-east England. The regional study (p143) showed it to be an area with ultra-high population density. However, there are considerable variations in population density within the city. Some of the lowest densities coincide with the Central Business District (CBD). Here the concentration of shops and offices mean there is a low residential population although the daytime population of commuters and shoppers is huge. The highest densities of population are found in the inner city immediately surrounding the CBD. The zone extends along the river banks and includes large areas of Victorian terraces – high density housing. In addition many of the once middle-class terraces have been sub-divided into flats and one-room bed-sits. These multi-occupancy dwellings add to the high density. Lower densities are found towards the edges of the city where suburban detached and semi-detached housing estates dominate. Much of this housing is occupied by single households and the dwellings use larger areas of land which reduces overall population densities. One or two anomalies exist where parts of the city have been redeveloped. Areas with high-rise flats to the west of the city built in the 1960s and 1970s have population densities as high as those in the inner city. Another anomaly lies to the north of the CBD, the Town Moor (in Moorside Ward), an area of common land with no housing and still preserved from future development.

▼ **Figure 1** Population density in Newcastle-upon-Tyne, 1996

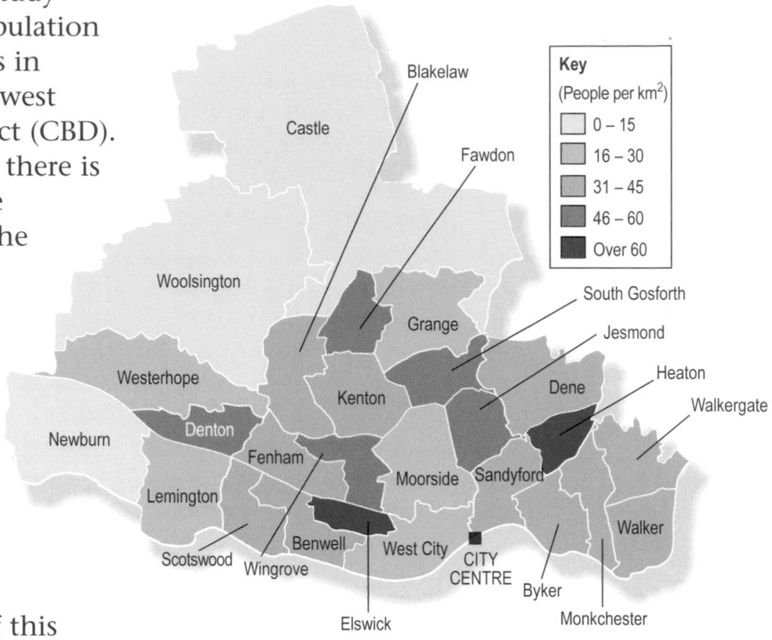

Key
(People per km^2)
- 0 – 15
- 16 – 30
- 31 – 45
- 46 – 60
- Over 60

Questions

1   For Newcastle-upon-Tyne or an urban area of your choice analyse the pattern of population density within the city.

Population distribution and density

Case Study   in Peru

Peru lies on the Pacific coast of South America. The physical environment is varied with coastal deserts in the west, the high mountain ranges of the Andes and the dense tropical forests of the Amazon Basin in the east. The pattern of population distribution and density within the country (Figure 2) reflects these geographical contrasts and history of settlement.

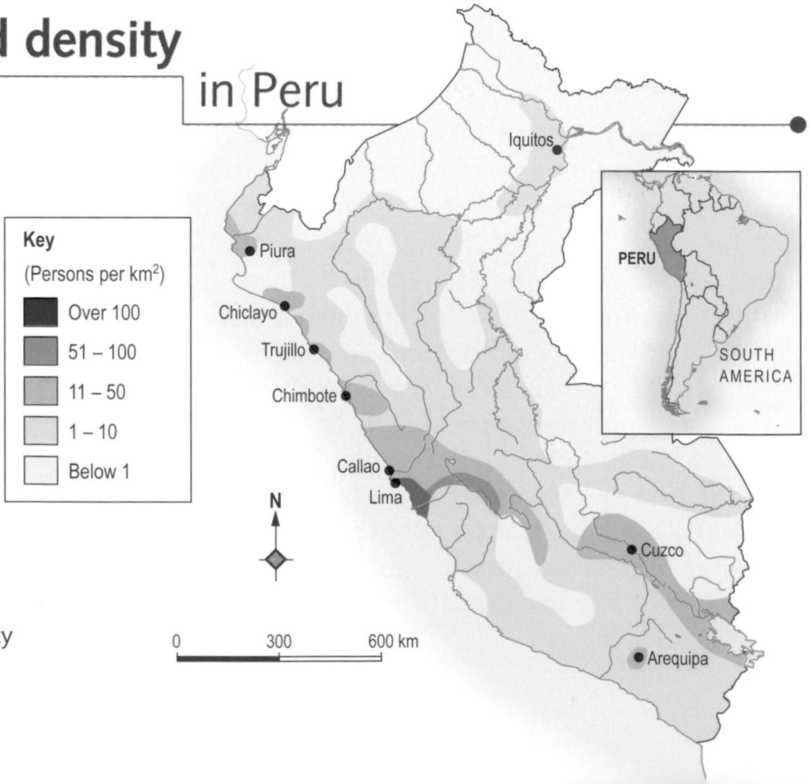

Key
(Persons per km^2)
- Over 100
- 51 – 100
- 11 – 50
- 1 – 10
- Below 1

▶ **Figure 2** Population density in Peru

Peru may be divided into three main regions according to altitude:
- coastal region in the west below 2000m
- central Sierra region over 2000m
- eastern region below 2000m.

The coastal region

In the coastal region there are:
- large areas of unpopulated desert
- pockets of high densities of population where irrigation water is available or where the towns and cities are located.

Densely populated areas are found where glacier-fed streams come from the Sierra mostly in north and central Peru. The south is much drier except near Arequipa, Peru's second largest city, where the land is irrigated using a river originating in the snow-covered peaks and glacial lakes of the Andes Mountains.

During the Spanish conquest towns were established centrally within the irrigated lands. Lima is 10km from the coast within an area of irrigated land either side of the River Rimac. The early settlements have continued to be the major urban centres despite the growth of trade at the coast. Ports and harbours have remained small and in recent years many have declined as Callao, the port for Lima, has dominated the export trade.

The Sierra

This area of volcanic peaks and glaciated mountains supports about 38 per cent of Peru's population and over 80 per cent of the rural population. In the high plateau region there is some limited grazing by sheep, llama and alpaca herders and some mining camps. Cerro de Pasca, a mining town, is the largest settlement. Below 4000m and especially close to Lake Titicaca farming of hardy crops such as potatoes and barley are possible. Population densities reach 230 people per square kilometre on the cultivated land. The major centres of population are found between 2500 and 3500m where there are fewer frosts and the growing season is longer. Maize, wheat and root crops are grown and dairying is important. The largest settlements are found in the valleys where good transport routes link the settlements to Lima, the capital city. The largest

settlement is Cuzco (258,000 population), an ancient Inca capital and now a major tourist resort. Population densities in this area are about 175 per square kilometre – much higher than at the coast.

The eastern region

In this region the Andes Mountains slope downwards to give way to the rainforests of the Amazon Basin. Population densities are low, below 3 people per square kilometre, due to:
- remoteness and isolation
- difficulty of communications
- dense tropical rainforest difficult to penetrate
- the warm humid climate with very heavy rainfall, over 2000mm per year.

The main inhabitants of the area are the indigenous Amazon tribes who live in the forest, alongside the riverbanks or since 1940 along the roadsides. Iquitos is the regional centre with a population of 266,000. It has a limited range of industries and some timber processing for export.

Questions

1 Explain the difficulties posed for people in the three regions of Peru.

2 Explain why the Sierra can support higher densities of population than the eastern region.

3 Explain why the population is concentrated in small nuclei separated by large areas of empty land.

Investigation

4 Select a country of your choice from the LEDW. Using a variety of sources including ICT describe and explain the pattern of population density and distribution.

Extended Writing

5 To what extent is the pattern of population distribution in countries of the LEDW more linked to physical conditions than to economic conditions.

Population change

- Natural population change – birth rates, death rates and migration
- Measures of fertility and mortality
- Rates of natural increase or decrease
- The Demographic Transition Model

Natural population change

On the global scale population change is usually measured by the relationship between the crude birth rate and crude death rate. The world's population has shown constant growth due to birth rates being higher than death rates (Figure 1). In very few countries has the crude birth rate ever been lower than the crude death rate so that the global increase in population has continued (Figure 2). Most recent population projections suggest that world population growth has now peaked and is slowing down. By 2050 estimates suggest world population will be between 7.3 billion and 10.7 billion and the bulk of the births will be in the poorest regions of the world (Figure 3).

On the global scale migration of people has no effect on the total population change. For a country or region however, the population growth rate must also take account of migration. For example, in Australia in 1999 the natural increase was 0.7 per cent but the population growth rate was 1.1 per cent due to immigration.

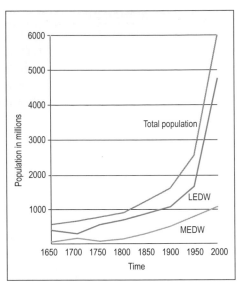

▲ **Figure 1** The growth in world population since 1650

Mother Earth is pleased to announce the birth of its six billionth inhabitant (baby doing fine; mother needs constant attention)

It could have happened a few weeks ago, as some calculations suggested. It could happen in a few weeks' time, as others predict. It could even be happening now, as you are reading this article. Whenever it is – or whenever it was at some point this autumn, for a split second the world's population hits six billion.

What we can say for sure is that in the space of less than 200 years the human species will have been transformed from a few hundred million to eight, nine or ten billion.

Can the planet Earth sustain such an increase without people starving? But while that is perfectly proper concern it is in some ways the easiest to answer, for yes it is theoretically possible to produce the food.

The concern is that since most of the additional food production comes from irrigated land, there will be sufficient water to continue to meet the demand.

The world's population is rising very rapidly and will continue to do so for a while yet. But the total fertility rates – the numbers of babies born to each mother – are plunging. Most of the world bar Africa, is close to, or below, replacement rate and in Africa rates are falling fast too. The reason the population is still rising is because the last baby boom means that there are lots more potential mums, women of child-bearing age. But those mums are having fewer babies.

This change is happening very quickly. Back in the middle 1960s just about every country in the world was above replacement rate. Here in Britain in 1965 the average was 2.9 babies. Now it is just under 1.8. The highest fertility rate among the large developed nations is in the US and there they are just at the 2.0 point. In Germany fertility rates are down to 1.3 babies, while in Italy and Spain it is 1.2. In Japan it is 1.4. Once you get down to those levels and wait

a generation, population starts to fall quite fast.

The really dramatic change in the last few years... is the collapse of fertility rates in developing countries. Africa is the only substantial region in the world where fertility is much above replacement rate. There the average mother has more than five children though the number is projected to fall below two by 2035. Meanwhile population growth in some parts of Africa will sadly be restrained by disease, in particular the scourge of Aids. In China (thanks in part to the one-child policy) population growth is well below replacement rate. In India the fertility rate is under three, though that is still high enough for India to pass China in population in 25 years' time. In Latin America fertility rates are down to 2.5.

Falling fertility in developing countries means that their societies will age just like ours. By about 2050 the median age in the developing countries will be about 40, roughly the same as Germany or Japan now.

▲ **Figure 2** Adapted from *The Independent Review*, 6 October 1999

Measures of fertility and mortality

Fertility

Crude birth rate is the simplest and most frequently used measure of fertility although other measures are possible including the fertility rate. In general, high fertility rates are associated with developing countries and low fertility rates with the developed countries (Figure 1, page 148). However, the generalization does not always hold true due to the variety of factors that affect birth rates.

Factors affecting birth rates

Demographic structure The age–sex composition of a population is important. Areas with large numbers of young adults are expected to have high birth rates as in new towns or areas with a high proportion of immigrants. Areas with a high proportion of elderly people or children or with few females have low birth rates.

Education In general, countries with high levels of education have lower birth rates and smaller family sizes due to:
- knowledge of birth control (Figure 2, page 148)
- greater social awareness of the benefits of smaller families
- higher incomes and a desire for more material possessions.

Religion The Muslim and Catholic religions encourage large families. Traditionally they actively oppose any form of contraception and hence countries dominated by these religions tend to have high birth rates, e.g. Eire, Algeria.

Social customs In the UK today the average age when people get married is now 30 years old. More women are now following their careers for longer and delaying having children. In contrast in Hindu culture it is traditional for girls to marry at about the age of 16 and to give birth to at least 10 children. In other cultures polygamy encourages high birth rates and in others the desire for a male heir results in large families to ensure at least one male survives.

Diet and health High birth rates are often found in societies that suffer both poverty and poor diet. There tends to be a close correlation between high levels of mortality and fertility – the need for people to have large families to ensure that some survive.

Politics Population growth tends to be reversed by wars. The large number of young males fighting in the wars and the many who lose their lives limits population growth.

However, the impact tends to be in one generation only as the traditional baby boom occurs once peacetime returns. In Europe this fertility bulge occurred between 1918 and 1920 and again between 1946 and 1949 following the two world wars.

Governments may also influence birth rates through various population policies, some designed to increase the birth rate but more usually to decrease it. During the 1930s Germany encouraged high birth rates with grants and medals. In the twentieth century China operated a very strict one child only policy to try to control poulation growth.

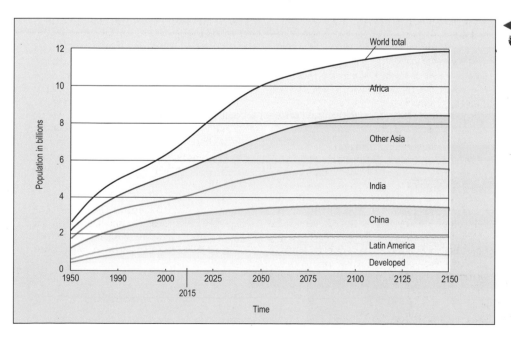

◀ **Figure 3** Population projections by region based on the UN medium forecast

▼ **Figure 1** World distribution of crude birth rates

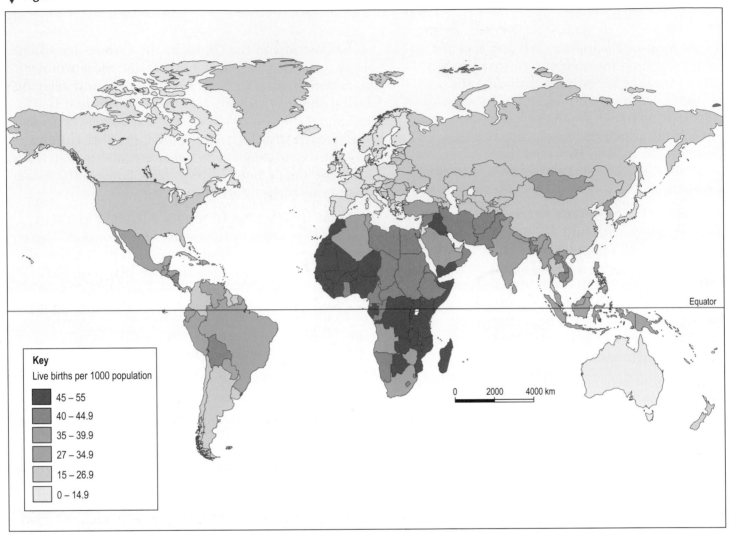

Equator

Key
Live births per 1000 population

- 45 – 55
- 40 – 44.9
- 35 – 39.9
- 27 – 34.9
- 15 – 26.9
- 0 – 14.9

0   2000   4000 km

▼ **Figure 2** The use of contraception

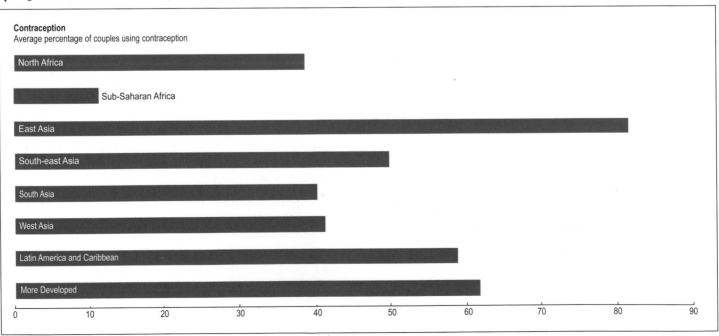

Contraception
Average percentage of couples using contraception

North Africa

Sub-Saharan Africa

East Asia

South-east Asia

South Asia

West Asia

Latin America and Caribbean

More Developed

0   10   20   30   40   50   60   70   80   90

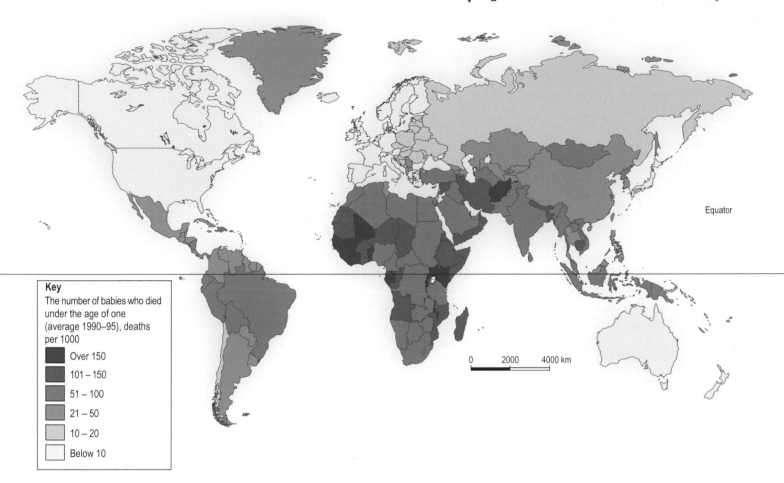

▼ **Figure 3** World distribution of infant mortality rates

Key
The number of babies who died under the age of one (average 1990–95), deaths per 1000

- Over 150
- 101 – 150
- 51 – 100
- 21 – 50
- 10 – 20
- Below 10

Equator

0   2000   4000 km

Mortality

Crude death rate is the most common measure of mortality although infant mortality and life expectancy are two other common measures used. As with fertility, mortality rates tend to decrease with increasing levels of economic development in a country. However there are a variety of factors that affect mortality and some relatively poor countries can have lower levels of mortality than in the UK and other developed countries.

Factors affecting mortality

Demographic structure Countries with ageing populations have higher death rates. This is the case in the UK and death rates are particularly high in some of the popular retirement resorts along the south coast.

Medicine Death rates tend to be lower where there is good access to medical care as measured by the number of people per doctor. This measure often shows up great disparities between the developed and developing countries in the world.

Social class More affluent groups in societies tend to have lower death rates than the poorer sections probably due to the latter's:
- poor housing conditions
- inadequate clothing and diet
- inability to access or afford medical care
- employment in more difficult or dangerous occupations.

Countries with social security and welfare benefits such as the UK tend not to have such marked differences between social class and mortality.

Place of residence Death rates tend to be higher in urban areas than in the countryside probably due to:
- crowded living conditions
- high traffic densities
- atmospheric pollution
- nervous stress.

Population Concern

▼ Figure 1 Population data for selected countries

Country	Population (1999) (millions)	Crude birth rate	Crude death rate	Natural increase (%per yr)	Infant mortality rate	Life expectancy (years)	Urban population (%)	Under 15 years (%)	GNP ($US) (1997)	People per doctor	Fertility rate
UK	59.4	12	10	0.2	5.9	77	89	19	20,870	300	1.7
France	59.1	12	9	0.3	5.0	78	74	19	26,300	333	1.7
Germany	82.0	10	10	-0.1	4.9	77	86	16	28,280	370	1.3
Spain	39.4	9	9	0	5.5	78	64	15	14,490	262	1.2
USA	272.5	15	9	0.6	7.0	77	75	21	29,080	420	2.0
Japan	126.7	10	7	0.2	3.7	81	79	15	38,160	600	1.4
Egypt	66.9	26	6	2.0	52	65	44	39	1200	1300	3.3
Sierra Leone	5.3	47	18	2.9	136	48	37	45	160	12,500	6.3
India	986.6	28	9	1.9	72	60	28	36	370	2439	3.4
Tunisia	9.5	22	7	1.6	35	69	61	35	2110	1852	2.8
Brazil	168	21	6	1.5	41	67	78	32	4790	1000	2.3
Mexico	99.7	27	5	2.2	32	72	74	35	3700	621	3.0
Ghana	19.7	39	10	2.9	66	59	37	46	390	25,000	5.4
Nigeria	113.8	43	13	3.0	73	54	16	45	280	5882	6.2
Mozambique	19.1	41	19	2.2	134	44	46	46	140	33,333	5.6

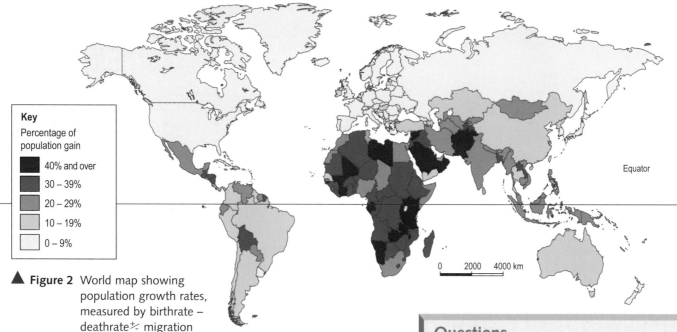

Key Percentage of population gain: 40% and over; 30 – 39%; 20 – 29%; 10 – 19%; 0 – 9%

Equator

0 2000 4000 km

▲ Figure 2 World map showing population growth rates, measured by birthrate – deathrate ± migration

Rates of natural increase or decrease

Populations change over time and there are also spatial differences in population growth. On the global scale Figure 1 on page 146 shows that world population growth rates began slowly but gradually increased until the middle of the twentieth century when very rapid growth occurred. This pattern is not reflected in all countries. In the UK and most countries of the MEDW high population growth occurred before the twentieth century. The population explosion in the twentieth century is explained by the large natural increase in many countries of the LEDW. Countries in Africa and Asia have the highest growth rates while many developed countries have rates approaching zero (Figure 1).

Questions

1 a Using the data in Figure 1 draw scattergraphs to show the relationships between some of the factors, e.g. the relationship between fertility and level of development or the relationship between mortality and the level of development. The level of development can be measured by GNP or people per doctor. Alternatively you could calculate a Spearman's rank Correlation Co-efficient.

b Describe and explain the results of your analysis.
Describe and explain the world pattern of population growth shown in Figure 2.

The Demographic Transition Model and population

The Demographic Transition Model (Figure 3) attempts to show the stages through which a country's population growth will pass.

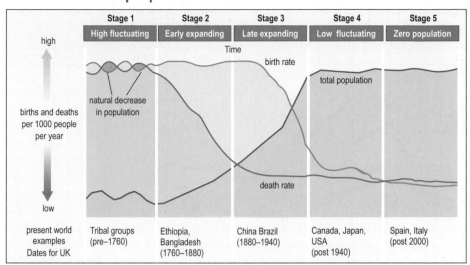

▶ **Figure 3** The Demographic Transition Model

Stage 1   High stationary phase
Both the birth rates and death rates are high, often between 30 and 40 per 1000, although they tend to fluctuate due to the impact of wars, famine, drought and disease. Overall the population remains relatively stable. Today there are no countries in Stage 1 although some remote tribes in tropical rainforest regions with only limited or no contact with more developed countries may have these characteristics.

Stage 2   Early expanding phase
The birth rate remains high but the death rate starts to fall producing high rates of natural increase and hence population growth. In the developed world the birth and death rates were always much closer together than in the developing world so population growth in countries like the UK never reached the rate of growth seen in some third world countries. Sierra Leone is a contemporary example of a Stage 2 country with a birth rate of 47 per 1000 and a death rate of 18 per 1000. The natural increase of 2.9 per cent will cause the population to double (at current rates) in just 24 years from 5.3 million to 10.6 million. The infant mortality rate has decreased but is still high at 136 per 1000 live births and life expectancy is only 48 years. Family size remains large with a fertility rate of over 6 and 45 per cent of the population are under 15 years of age.

The economic and social problems of countries at Stage 2 are enormous. The economies remain largely agricultural producing a few primary products for export. In Sierra Leone 70 per cent of the population is employed in agriculture and it generates 38 per cent of the country's wealth. The annual income is only $140 per person, one of the lowest figures in the world. Sierra Leone is in the poverty trap created by a low mortality rate, largely the product of imported medical aid, and massive population growth that far exceeds the economic development of the country. This is the major difference between the experience of the developed and the developing worlds – population change in the MEDW was a product of economic development. In the LEDW population change has occurred without the economic development to support it.

Stage 3   The late expanding phase
In Stage 3 the pace of population increase begins to slow down as the death rate continues to fall but the birth rate also begins to decrease. Towards the end of Stage 3 the mortality rate levels off and so birth and death rates converge, natural increase declines and population growth slows. Tunisia is a country currently part way through Stage 3 with a birth rate of 22 per 1000 and a death rate of 7 per 1000 giving a natural increase of 1.5 per cent.

The infant mortality rate of 35 and the average life expectancy of 69 years are both much better figures than those for Sierra Leone reflecting a better standard of living and economy. About 56 per cent of the population is urbanized although the economy is much less industrialized than was the case in the UK at the end of Stage 3.

Stage 4 The low stationary phase
Overall this stage has both low birth and death rates giving low natural increase and low overall population growth. During this phase the death rate is largely stable although the birth rate shows more variability with the occasional 'baby booms' often linked to times of particular economic prosperity or as in many European countries the rise in birth rates following the two world wars. Many countries in the MEDW have now reached Stage 4.

Stage 5   Zero population growth and population decline
The first model had just four stages although it is generally accepted that a fifth stage is needed to represent those countries such as Sweden, Germany and Italy whose population is now below replacement level. This means there is a natural decrease in the population as birth rates have fallen below the death rate.

The usefulness of the Demographic Transition Model

The model provides a useful generalization of the expected pattern of population change in many countries. However, not all countries or regions within countries will pass through all of the stages or at the same rates (Figure 4, page 152). The model takes no account of the different rates of change in different parts of the world or the impact of the size of the base population and any effects of migration.

Hence relatively low growth rates in a country such as China produce massive increases in the population total due to the large base population. The model is however useful for making comparisons between countries and for linking population change to changing economic and social conditions. It also has a predictive element in that future changes may be forecast.

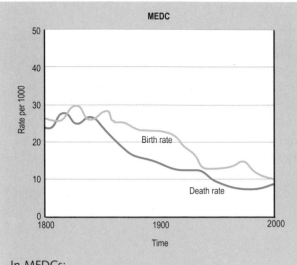

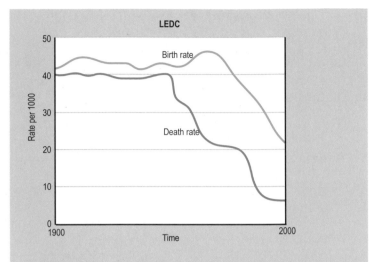

In MEDCs:

- Most have passed through all of the stages
- At Stage 4 by about the 1960s
- Some now moving into Stage 5
- Took about 200 years to move through the stages
- Growth rates rarely exceeded 1 per cent per year
- Economic growth led the transition.

In LEDCs:

- Not yet passed through all stages
- Many entered Stage 2 in mid-twentieth century
- Many still in Stages 2 or 3
- Huge gap between birth and death rates so high population growth
- Population increase exceeds 4 per cent per year in some countries although most about 2 per cent now
- Moving through stages more rapidly
- Driven more by government policies and western medical aid
- Economic development lagging behind.

 **Figure 4** Population transition in LEDCs and MEDCs

The Demographic Transition Model and population change in the UK (MEDC)

Case Study

Prior to 1840 birth and death rates were both relatively high. During most years the birth rate was slightly higher than the death rate so natural increase was slow. In some years, for example during outbreaks of disease, the population would decrease. The high death rates and low life expectancy gave a high proportion of young people. These proportions decreased with increasing age. The high birth rates were a product of the lack of birth control and family planning, the need for large families in the hope that some would survive and to provide labour to work on the land. Most people were farmers and farm labourers at this time. Diseases and the lack of medical knowledge caused the high death rates, especially amongst children. At the time there were few doctors, certainly no National Health

Service and little knowledge of antiseptics. In some years there were food shortages due to periods of drought and diets were restricted to what could be grown on the land. In many areas of the UK there was no piped water supply or sewage disposal so that a clean water supply and good standards of sanitation were absent.

During the nineteenth century the agricultural and industrial revolutions fuelled urbanization. For many people living conditions did not improve and birth and death rates remained high. The high densities of population in urban areas caused disease to spread more rapidly. Atmospheric pollution and dirty and dangerous jobs in factories kept death rates high.

In the middle of the nineteenth century the medical revolution began to take place and laws were passed to improve the health and safety of people in the work place. Improved health care and knowledge about hygiene all helped to reduce infant mortality and to increase life expectancy. The agricultural revolution in the countryside improved the quality and quantity of food available improving people's diets and health. Extensive water and sewage systems began to be installed and gradually death rates began to fall although birth rates remained high. Improved political stability also played its part with fewer deaths in riots and civil war. By 1875 the death rate had been halved to about 15 per 1000.

After 1880 the death rate continued to fall and the birth rate also began to decrease due to:
• improved knowledge of family planning techniques
• a lower infant mortality rate reducing the need to have large families
• increasing urbanization and industrialization.

By 1920 more people were surviving into the older age groups (Figure 1). There is also evidence that the birth rate was falling with fewer in the 0-14 age group. From 1920 onwards the birth and death rates continued to fall. Standards of living had risen and the growth of the consumer society meant there was less desire for large families and a bigger demand for large houses, cars, holidays and other material possessions. In addition the status of women had undergone radical changes. Many

women went on to higher education and their own careers. This meant that many married and had children later.

By the end of the twentieth century birth and death rates were both low with a natural increase of just 0.2 per cent. This suggests that in the future there will be zero population growth or even population decrease as the birth rate falls below replacement level. Large numbers of elderly people are increasingly surviving to much older ages than before. This presents new problems for the country in accommodating and caring for the elderly with the provision of pensions, care homes and geriatric medical services.

UK governments have needed to make few interventions to control population. Overall the welfare state policies have been supportive of families with family allowances and other benefits.

	1840	1880	1920	1940	1980	2000
0 – 14	36	36	26	24	19	19
15 – 29	28	26	28	19	22	20
30 – 44	18	18	21	23	21	22
45 – 59	11	13	15	18	20	20
60 – 74	6	6	8	12	12	12
75+	1	1	2	4	6	7

▲ Figure 1 Britain through the ages (% of population in each age group)

Year	Birth rate (per 1000)	Death rate (per 1000)	Total population (millions)
1700	36	30.5	4.8
1720	35.5	34.0	5.0
1740	38.0	36.0	5.0
1760	36.5	30.0	5.5
1780	38.0	9.0	6.4
1820	36	20.5	12.0
1840	31	20.0	15.5
1860	34	22.9	20.0
1880	33	20.0	26.0
1900	28	17.0	32.5
1920	20	12.5	37.0
1940	14.5	13.0	41.5
1960	17.5	11.5	46.0
1980	14.0	12.0	49.5
2000	12.0	10.0	59.4

▲ Figure 2 Population change in England and Wales 1700–2000

Questions

1 a Using Figure 2 draw on a single graph the birth rate, death rate and population growth for the UK since 1700.
  b On the graph mark and label when each of the four (or five) stages of the Demographic Transition Model occurred in the UK.
  c Write a detailed justification for your choices.
  d Describe and explain the changes shown by the graph.

2 To what extent does the UK's population change over time match the pattern in the Demographic Transition Model?

3 Produce separate lists of economic, social and political factors that have affected UK population growth.

Population change

Case Study | in Japan (MEDC)

Throughout the Middle Ages Japan's birth and death rates were generally high (Figure 1). Japan's population was in Stage 1 and gradually moved towards Stage 2 of the Demographic Transition Model from about 1870. At the time there was a subsistence economy needing a large workforce so birth rates were high. Death rates were also high in the absence of modern medicines and sanitation especially in the rural areas. Natural increase varied between 1 and 1.6 per cent. Diseases such as tuberculosis and dysentry were also common. Infant mortality rates were particularly high, over 100 per 1000 people. From about 1870 more people moved to the towns and cities to work in industry and food shortages were rare. As a result the birth rate increased.

In 1950 Japan's population structure shows the impact of the large losses during the Second World War with a gap in the 30–40 male age group. During the post-war period there was an 'economic miracle' when industrialization proceeded at a very rapid rate. As is typical, the birth rate increased following the war. The rapid population growth caused the government concern enough to legalize abortion. This caused a dramatic drop in the birth rate. By 1979 the country had proceeded to the end of Stage 3 of the Model and both birth and death rates were low. The impact of industrialization was to reduce birth rates as mechanization removed the need for large amounts of labour. People were more affluent and more concerned with material possessions than having large families. Death rates have also fallen reflecting Japan's healthy lifestyle and advanced technology. However, the population is ageing rapidly and, as fewer children are born, the death rate is set to increase.

Japan's progress through the Demographic Transition Model has been very rapid particularly through Stages two and three. There was also a more marked increase in population growth between Stages 1 and 2 than in most countries.

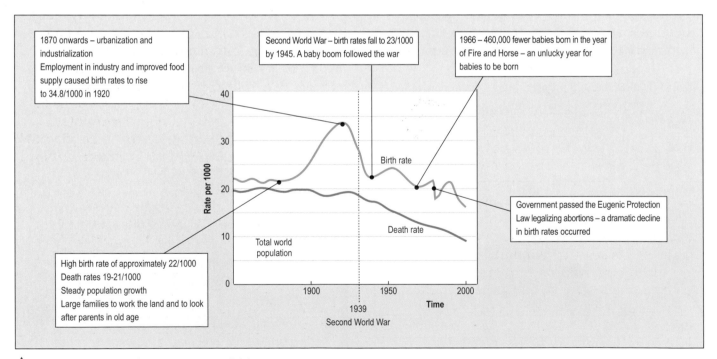

▲ **Figure 1** Demographic Transition Model for Japan

Population change

Case Study in India (LEDC)

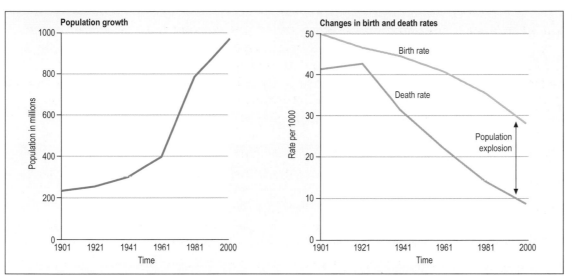

◀ **Figure 2**
Population change in India

Up until 1920 India was in Stage 1 of the Demographic Transition (Figure 2). Birth rates were high due to a lack of knowledge about birth control, the desire to have a large family so children could work in the fields and to counter the impact of high infant mortality rates. In addition male children have long been highly prized for religious reasons, as heirs, and to look after their parents when they are old. Death rates were high due to poor health care and a lack of hygiene. Life expectancy was low and living conditions poor. The death rate was 46 per 1000 in 1921.

After 1920 the death rates declined steeply while the birth rate remained relatively high causing a true population explosion. The movement into Stage 2 was connected with India's development as a British colony which brought improved medicines, health care, water and sanitation services. Child mortality began to fall as well as the death rate as a whole. At the same time industrialization and new agricultural techniques improved the quality and quantity of food produced. The population growth produced a population in which over 50 per cent were below 15 years old. When this section of the population reached child-bearing age population growth continued rapidly.

Since about 1985 India has moved into Stage 3. The death rate is levelling off and the birth rate is high but beginning to decline. As families become smaller the decline in birth rate is likely to become more rapid. However,

the natural increase is still very high largely because of India's large base population. The current population is 987 million and it is continuing to expand through a natural increase of 1.9 per cent. The crude birth rate is 28 per 1000 per year and the crude death rate 9 per 1000 per year. The death rate is quite low in comparison to many European countries. This is not surprising in a country where 36 per cent of the population are below 15 years of age and only 4 per cent are over 65 years old. Today India ranks quite high among the industrialized nations but the population is still largely agricultural with very low incomes. In 1997 the GNP per capita was only $370. In the future the population is likely to continue to grow. Attempts by the government to encourage smaller families are still failing due to the largely rural population with strong social and religious traditions.

Questions

1 a Summarize the main features of the population changes in India and Japan on two tables like the one below:

Stage	1	2	3	4	5
Time period					
Birth rate					
Death rate					
Natural increase					
Population growth (high, medium, low)					
Factors affecting: birth rates					
death rates					

b Compare and contrast the patterns of population change in Japan and India.

Migration

- Types of migration
- Laws and models of migration
- Changes in migratory patterns over time
- International migrations

Types of migration

There are many different types of migration and they can be classified in three ways according to:

1 the cause of the movement, e.g. if it is forced or voluntary
2 the distance moved, e.g. if it is international when national frontiers are crossed or internal within a country
3 the type of area from and to which the migration occurs, e.g. from 'rich' to 'poor'.

1 Cause

Unconscious drifts of population
These were far more common in the past than they are today. They include tribal wanderings and those of gypsies and vagrants.

Forced or compulsory migrations
These occur when there is no personal choice. They are mostly unhappy events that may result from:

- religious or political persecution, e.g. the Jews forced out of Nazi Germany
- wars that create refugees, e.g. the Palestinian Arabs forced out of the newly created Israel after 1948
- forced labour, e.g. the Slave trade
- racial discrimination, e.g. the Ugandan Asians expelled by Idi Amin in the 1970s
- famine causing a lack of food, e.g. the refugees from Mozambique in 2000
- natural disasters, e.g. floods, droughts, earthquakes, hurricanes, volcanoes such as the eruption of Mount Soufriere which forced many people living in Montserrat to leave in the late 1990s
- overpopulation, e.g. the Vietnamese boat people transported out of Hong Kong.

ⓘ *A simple definition of migration is the movement of people. However, there is a concept of 'permanence' in the United Nations' definition: 'A change of residence lasting more than one year'. Therefore, the United Nations' definition would not include seasonal movements of, for example, pastoral nomads or fruit pickers, commuters and tourists. These are best termed circulatory and temporary movements that are usually short term where those involved eventually return to their previous location.*

ⓘ *The slave trade began in the fifteenth century and many Black Africans were forcibly taken to work on the plantations established in the New World by mainly European colonizers. The slave trade was abolished at the beginning of the nineteenth century but by then about 10 million Africans had been transported.*

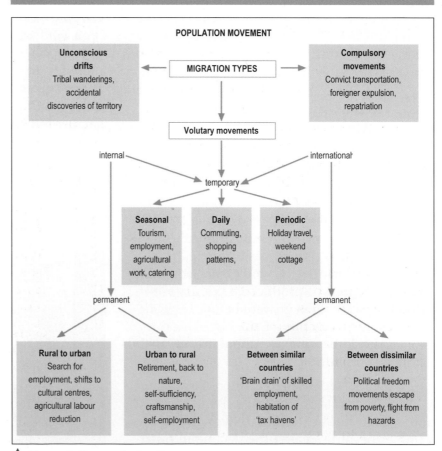

▲ **Figure 1** Types of migration

Most forced migration is international, involving the movement of people across the frontiers of countries. In the twentieth century most forced migrations were a result of large-scale warfare. During the First World War over 6 million people, mostly from the defeated countries, migrated across Europe. The Second World War had an even greater impact displacing about 60 million people. Some people, especially Jews, left Germany to escape the Nazi regime and many others were evacuated during the war. Once the war was over there were huge movements of different ethnic, labour and linguistic groups, for example Poles were deported from Russia and Germany; Slavs migrated to, the then, Czechoslovakia. More recently, civil wars such as those in Rwanda have created large numbers of refugees who have fled to neighbouring countries.

Voluntary migrations

These are migrations where there has been personal choice. Most voluntary migrations are internal, i.e. they take place within a country and many are over relatively short distances. Voluntary migrations are a product of a range of diverse factors that determine human choice. They may be physical, economic, social or political but ambition, knowledge and energy to move are also important.

Today, increased wealth, better communications, greater knowledge and the desire for a higher standard of living mean movements are more frequent and widespread. These are the most prevalent types of migrations today and cover all scales from intra-urban to international. The majority of voluntary migrations are a result of:

- employment, e.g. British doctors to USA, Mexicans to California
- trade and economic expansion, e.g. pioneer movements of Europeans into the Prairies in the nineteenth century
- better climates, e.g. retired Americans to Florida, retired British to Devon, Cornwall and the south coast
- friends, relatives, marriage
- territorial expansion, e.g. the expansion of the Roman Empire, the Bantus incursion into South Africa
- social amenities including education, e.g. West Indians into Britain, rural to urban migration in many cities of the LEDW.

▲ **Figure 2** Refugees from Rwanda in Tanzania

Questions

1 Define migration.

2 Redraw Figure 1 so that it reflects the United Nations' definition of migration.

3 To what extent does Figure 1 show elements of the three possible ways of classifying migrations – by cause, by distance and by type of origin and destination?

4 a On two world outline maps plot the examples from the text of the voluntary and forced migrations. Use arrows to indicate the movements and colour code each one for whether it took place in the nineteenth or twentieth century. Label each arrow.

 b Describe and comment upon the results of the mapping.

2 Distance

Internal migration

A variety of internal movements may take place (Figure 1) including:

- highly local movements, e.g. moving house in the same district
- urban to urban, e.g. in the UK in the 1980s and 90s many people moved from urban areas in northern Britain to the more affluent and growing areas in the south and east
- rural to urban, e.g. from NE Brazil into the large cities such as São Paulo and Rio de Janeiro. This is the most common type of movement in the LEDW today
- urban to rural, e.g. the counter-urbanization movements in many countries of the MEDW today. People move into the rural areas in search of a higher standard of living and more pleasant surroundings
- rural to rural, e.g. the pioneer advances in the USA in the nineteenth century when settlers spread across the Midwest
- inter-regional movements, e.g. migrants to Alaska from other parts of the USA to work in the oil industry.

▼ **Figure 1** Patterns of migration for a large coastal city

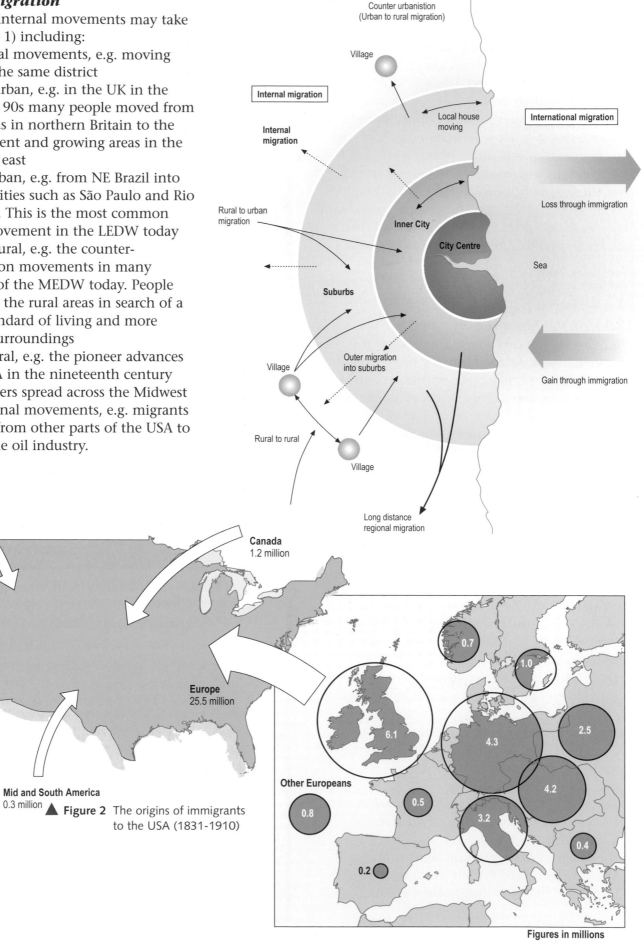

▲ **Figure 2** The origins of immigrants to the USA (1831-1910)

The majority of internal migrations involve short distances, mostly to areas with a familiar cultural background and no language problems. The main constraints to internal migration are:
- economic, e.g. a lack of employment opportunities or suitable housing
- social, e.g. family ties or low incomes making people immobile.

As affluence increases so does mobility and internal migration increases accordingly. In the USA about 20 per cent of the population change their address each year, this falls to 10 per cent in the UK and to only 4 per cent in the LEDW.

International migrations

Migrants may also face the challenge of new climates, cultures, institutions, political systems and languages. In recent centuries international migrations have been mainly voluntary such as the colonization of the USA when between 1800 and 1924 60 million people moved into North America (Figure 2); or the migration of Asians into Central Africa. In recent decades many countries have tightened their immigration policies and many such as the USA are now highly selective about whom they will allow in. As a result the majority of international migrations are now forced.

3 Type of area

These are usually international migrations and may involve movement from poor to rich countries such as the movement of West Indians to Britain in the 1930s; poor to poor countries such as refugees moving from Mozambique into neighbouring African states; rich to rich countries such as the 'brain drain' of UK doctors to Canada and the USA; rich to poor countries such as the movement of charity workers and missionaries to work in countries of the LEDW (see page 166

Laws and models of migration

The push-pull model

This model summarizes the two sets of forces responsible for most migration (Figure 3). Push factors force people away from their current residence while pull factors attract people to a new destination.

▼ **Figure 3** The push-pull model of migration

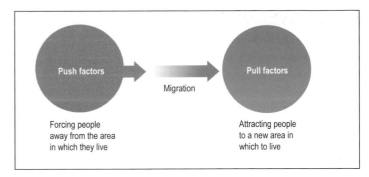

In some cases the push and pull factors are complementary so a person will migrate from an area with poor housing and high unemployment to one where the housing is better and there are more jobs available. In other cases one factor dominates, for example in the cases of natural disaster or political persecution the push factor is dominant and results in forced migration.

▼ **Figure 4** A variety of push and pull factors

	Push	Pull
Physical	Inaccessibility Harsh climates Natural disasters	Attractive scenery Fertile soils Lack of natural hazards
Economic	Unemployment Poverty High rents Heavy taxation	High living standards Good wages Promotion Resource exploitation
Social	Discrimination Lack of housing Bereavement Growth of family	Good welfare services Relatives and friends Marriage Higher education
Political	Civil unrest Persecution Planning decision	Freedom of speech Propaganda Political asylum

Voluntary migrations are the result of a complex range of decisions about the push and pull factors. No two people will necessarily make the same decision given the same set of factors because perceptions and the relative importance of factors will be different. As a result Lee refined the simple push-pull model.

Ravenstein's and Stouffer's Law

The Lee Model

The origin and destination of the migration have both positive and negative attributes (Figure 5). There will be factors in the area where the person lives, and the area where the person would migrate to, that would both encourage the person to stay (positive factors) and encourage the person to move (negative factors). Each person would interpret these factors differently according to age, sex, marital status, socio-economic status and education. There may also be some neutral factors that play no part in the decision-making process. Lee's model also introduces the concept of intervening obstacles that need to be overcome before the migration can take place. These reduce the likelihood of a migration taking place and include:

- in international migration the need to obtain a work permit or visa
- the costs of moving
- anxiety about moving to a new place perhaps with a different culture, religion or language.

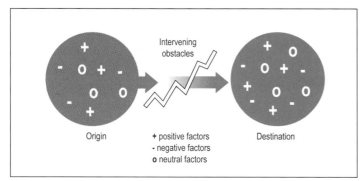

Origin   + positive factors   Destination
         - negative factors
         o neutral factors

▲ **Figure 1** The Lee Model

Ravenstein's laws of migration (1880s)

Ravenstein attempted to generalize about patterns of migration in the late 1800s and early 1900s. He developed a number of laws of migration:

1 'Most migrants travel short distances and with increasing distance the numbers of migrants decrease'.
   This law is based upon the assumptions that the higher travel costs and a lack of knowledge of more distant places acts against large volumes of migration.

2 'Migration occurs in stages and with a wave-like motion.' Based on his observations in the late nineteenth and twentieth centuries that migration occurred in steps with people gradually moving up the settlement hierarchy – from rural areas to villages, to towns, to cities and finally the capital city.

3 'Migration increases in volume as industries and commerce develop and transport improves, and the major direction of movement is from agricultural areas to centres of industry and commerce.'

4 'Most migrants are adult. Families rarely migrate out of their country of birth.'

5 'Women are more migratory than men within their country of birth but men more frequently venture beyond it.'

Laws 4 and 5 refer to the way the process of migration may be age and sex selective. In some countries, especially in the LEDW, young adult males tend to migrate from the countryside to the towns. They have fewer family ties in their place of birth, they have more energy and are attracted by the better employment opportunities and city life. In MEDW countries early retirement has led to increased migration in the age groups over 55. In general the more educated professional people are more migratory than unskilled and manual workers.

Since Ravenstein developed his laws and theories various other researchers have refined them and produced a series of further ideas.

Stouffer's law of intervening opportunities (1960s)

Stouffer argued that the volume of migration was less to do with distance and population totals than the opportunities in each location. There are links with Ravenstein's laws 2, 3 and 4 above. Stouffer's law of intervening opportunities states that the amount of migration over a given distance is directly proportional to the number of opportunities at the place of destination, and inversely proportional to the number of opportunities between the place of departure and the place of destination. The intervening opportunities may persuade a migrant to settle in a place en route rather than proceeding to the originally planned destination.

Changes in migratory patterns over time

Migration in the UK

Case Study

International migrations

Migrants from mainland Europe first inhabited the UK. They were mostly Anglo Saxons who founded villages about 800–1000AD many of which have survived to the present day.

In the nineteenth and early twentieth centuries there was international out-migration to the countries that formed part of the British Empire. The colonies were a source of raw materials and food used to support the Industrial Revolution in the UK. At the time the UK population was rising rapidly so there was surplus labour that could be used to develop and colonize the New World in Africa, North America and Australasia. Wealth from the colonies gave the UK political power and influence in Victorian times. Gradually economic links with the former colonies and Commonwealth countries have declined due to the dominance of the EU in trading.

From the 1950s to early 1970s the UK was a focus of immigration of people especially from the Commonwealth countries such as the West Indies and Indian sub-continent but also from China, Hong Kong and the Ugandan Asians forced to flee from political persecution. The UK economy was growing quickly at the time as part of the post-war recovery and employment was available. Society was also changing more towards a 'consumer society'. There was a great demand for labour in the factories and in the service industries that were still relatively labour intensive. The UK became a more cosmopolitan society which brought with it both advantages (new skills, enhanced cultural diversity and a labour source) and disadvantages (increased racial tension, conflict at times of high unemployment). In-migration to the UK is now strictly controlled, so much so that the movement other than for asylum seekers has largely ceased.

Internal migration in the UK

A general drift from north to south

During the middle and late twentieth century large numbers of workers in the north of the UK moved to the south of the country. Regions such as north-east England had relied on the coalfields, shipyards, iron and steel producers, chemical industries and heavy engineering to provide thousands of jobs. These industries declined making thousands unemployed.

	Northern England Push factors	Southern England Pull factors
Economic	Decline in traditional industries. High unemployment. Closure of services. Limited investment in new markets.	Dynamic growth area. Access to wealthy EU markets. Large home market. Focal point for motorway network, major airports.
Social	Low wages. Limited entertainment and educational opportunities.	Entertainment and education opportunities. Easy contacts with bankers, company directors.
Physical	Decaying physical environment. Remote from markets and economic core in EU. Colder, wetter climate.	Nearness to Europe. Warmer, drier climate. Pleasant environment.
Cultural	History of skilled work. Conservative with a small 'c'.	Dynamic, cosmopolitan area.
Political	Lack of investment. Peripheral from centre of decision making.	Great pulling power of London. Close to centre of government.

The consequences of the drift to the south

	Advantages	Disadvantages
To the north	Relieves unemployment. Less pressure on services. Low house prices.	'Brain' drain of skills. Often age and sex selective. Local spending reduced leading to decline in services and the environment. House prices stagnate.
To the south	Fills job vacancies. Adds to social and cultural variety.	High housing costs and living costs. Overcrowding, and traffic congestion. Overheating of the economy.

▲ **Figure 1** The causes and consequences of the drift to the south

In 2000 one deep mine remains in north-east England at Ellington in Northumberland and it currently relies on a government subsidy to keep it open for the next four years. There is only one steelworks at Redcar and one shipyard. Despite government policies to attract new industries, which included grants and tax concessions, most new industries are lighter manufacturing and service-based industries that could not absorb the thousands of workers made redundant by the closures of the heavy industries. The experience of north-east England was not unique. Clydeside, West Yorkshire, Lancashire and the Midlands all suffered major decline in the traditional industries.

In contrast the modern economic growth at the time was overwhelmingly concentrated in the south and east of England so workers moved there to find employment and a higher standard of living (Figure 1). The 1991 census showed that there was still a general drift of population from north to south. The north of England was still losing population although the greatest losses were from Merseyside. The greatest growth areas were in the counties neighbouring London such as Surrey and Kent although growth extends into East Anglia, Oxfordshire and as far west as Dorset.

Images of the North

▲ **Figure 1** Ellington Colliery, the last underground mine in north east England. Still working in 2000 but for how much longer?

▲ **Figure 2** Still working but reducing the number of workers as a result of rationalisation

Decline in the conurbations

In the latter half of the twentieth century all of the conurbations lost population (Figure 3). People have moved out of the inner cities in particular but also from the suburbs. The movement tended to be selective and included:

- younger families looking for more open space and larger houses
- those with higher incomes able to afford larger houses and the costs of commuting
- those with higher skills looking for work in modern footloose industries and offices.

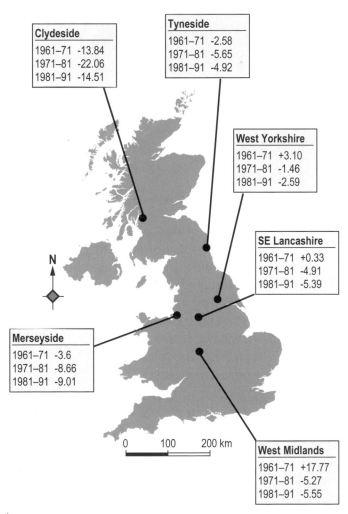

Clydeside
1961–71 -13.84
1971–81 -22.06
1981–91 -14.51

Tyneside
1961–71 -2.58
1971–81 -5.65
1981–91 -4.92

West Yorkshire
1961–71 +3.10
1971–81 -1.46
1981–91 -2.59

SE Lancashire
1961–71 +0.33
1971–81 -4.91
1981–91 -5.39

Merseyside
1961–71 -3.6
1971–81 -8.66
1981–91 -9.01

West Midlands
1961–71 +17.77
1971–81 -5.27
1981–91 -5.55

N

0   100   200 km

▲ **Figure 3** Population change in UK conurbations (per cent change per decade)

People have moved into the rural urban fringe surrounding the cities, often leapfrogging the protected green belt areas established after the Second World War to prevent urban sprawl. Around Greater London the establishment of the green belt encouraged the new town movement. Eight new towns were built within a 20 to 30 mile radius of London and people moved into them in their thousands. More recently people have also moved into the smaller towns and villages surrounding the cities.

There has been a very small movement of the wealthy back into some inner-city areas.

	Advantages	Disadvantages
To the inner cities	Reduces unemployment and the pressure on services. Space for immigrants moving into the area.	Leaves a decaying 'heart', decline of the community and the environment. Local councils receive less money from rates and taxes so little money to invest in area. Creation of ghettoes. Social unrest, high crime rates.
To the fringe	Increased use and demand for services.	Increased house building. Cost of housing and living rise. Increased pollution and traffic congestion. Loss of farmland for housing, offices and industry.

▲ **Figure 4** The consequences of the outward movement of people from the inner cities

Gentrification schemes have produced some very high quality housing and apartment developments especially as part of dockland redevelopment schemes, e.g. in the Canary Wharf area of London and St Peter's Basin in Newcastle-upon-Tyne.

Rural to urban migration

For centuries the rural areas have lost population as people, especially the young, moved towards the economic core areas in search of jobs, education, improved services and higher standards of living. Today, the most remote rural areas continue to lose population partly because of the crisis in farming. The loss of population may be a welcome relief from overpopulation in these areas with low economic potential but the depopulation also has disadvantages:

- dereliction and abandonment of farms and farmland
- loss of village services, e.g. schools, shops and bus services
- growth of second homes forcing house prices to increase beyond the reach of locals
- imbalanced age and sex structures reducing birth rates and leading to an ageing population with its knock-on effects on farming and social activities.

However, rural areas close to the large cities are generally seeing an increase in population as people move there in search of a better quality of life.

Migration in
Case Study north-east England

Figure 1 summarizes the main migratory movements in north-east England. From early times the population became clustered into a core area of economic activity centred upon Tyneside, Wearside and Teesside with smaller sub-cores in areas such as Carlisle, Durham and Darlington. The peripheral areas are still largely areas of out-migration. Here rural to urban migration has dominated to leave sparsely populated areas. Rural to urban migration has caused the towns and cities to expand through suburbanization. People have moved within and between cities and towns. Overall up until the late twentieth century the core regions were growing at the expense of the peripheral areas. In recent decades there has been a reversal of this trend and more and more people are leaving the towns and cities to live in the rural areas especially those adjacent to the towns and cities and commuting has increased. However, the most remote areas in the Pennines and Cumbria are still losing population.

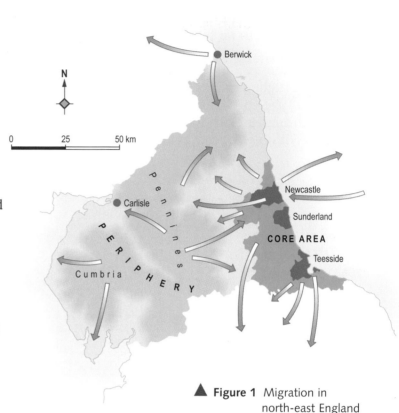

▲ **Figure 1** Migration in north-east England

Internal migration in the north-east

This includes:
- the migration of people from remote rural locations to lowland farming areas, market towns and the large urban areas
- the migration away from declining mining villages and towns particularly in the early and mid-twentieth century. Many miners moved to areas where pits were still operating either within north-east England or to Yorkshire, Lancashire and Kent
- the depopulation of decaying inner-city areas as people move from the nineteenth-century terraces into suburban homes
- the growth of suburbs with people moving from the inner cities or migrating from the countryside
- the growth of smaller towns and villages close to the economic core, e.g. Morpeth and Durham
- the decline of towns and villages in the periphery, e.g. Berwick
- the decline of old heavy industries, such as shipbuilding caused out migration from the towns and cities some to other regions of the country.

Movements of people outside of the region have been greater than movement into the region. There has been a net loss of people of about 0.8 per cent of the population each year. Unskilled and semi-skilled workers in particular have moved to other regions in the UK in search of employment and higher standards of living.

International migrations in the north-east

- Movements of people abroad have continued for a long time with international migrations from the north-east to the New World in the nineteenth and twentieth centuries.
- Immigration of people from abroad today is closely tied in with new inward investment into the region, e.g. Japanese managers and workers at Nissan in Washington and other Japanese owned factories in the north-east. In the past the north-east has received immigrants from China, India, Pakistan, etc. Many have established their own businesses but there are also professional and managerial people such as doctors and lawyers.
- Emigration today is much reduced although there is still something of a brain drain of highly skilled and professional people abroad, e.g. doctors going to Canada and the USA.

Regional migration

Case Study   in Brazil

Figure 2 shows the main patterns of internal migration in Brazil since the middle of the twentieth century. The greatest movements have been out of the North-East region where successive droughts have led to crop failure, famine and poverty. The dominant direction of movement has been to the large urban areas in the South-East region including São Paulo, Rio de Janeiro and Belo Horizonte. The migration has reduced the problems of overpopulation in the North East by relieving some pressure on food supplies, water and fuelwood but the area now has fewer people of working age, especially males due to the age and sex selectivity of the migration. In the cities the migrants provide a cheap labourforce but the huge volume of migrants into the cities has caused great problems, including:

- the growth of vast sprawling shanty towns that lack basic amenities
- a shortage of schools, hospitals and other services
- overpopulation, congestion and pollution
- high levels of disease
- a shortage of jobs and low pay leading to a large informal sector
- social problems of family breakdown, crime and delinquency.

Smaller scale movements into the interior of Brazil reflect the opening up of the rainforest in the North and the establishment of Brasilia as the capital city in the Centre West (Figure 2). The government provided various inducements for people to move into the rainforest such as free housing and land. However, the transmigration has not always been successful due to the difficulties of establishing permanent cultivation on the infertile soils. More long-term migrations are associated with employment in the logging and mining companies.

▼ **Figure 1** Inter-regional population migration

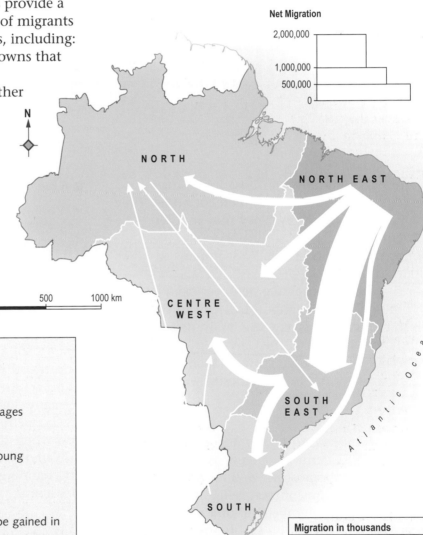

Net Migration

2,000,000	
1,000,000	
500,000	
0	

Migration in thousands	
Region	Net gain or loss
North	+63
North East	-2373
South East	+825
South	+489

▼ **Figure 3** Push and pull factors for migration from the North East to South East regions in Brazil

Push factors for the North East region
- Low unreliable rainfall often less than 750mm
- Periodic droughts and crop failure
- Poverty, starvation and malnutrition
- Limited employment opportunities and low wages
- Few people own their land
- Overpopulation
- High mortality rates especially amongst the young
- Infertile soils, often salty or leached.

Pull factors for the South East region
- Better paid jobs available in factories
- More employment opportunities – work can be gained in the informal sector
- More comfortable housing and better quality of life than in the rural areas
- Access to education and other services, e.g. medical care, entertainment
- More reliable sources of food.

International migrations

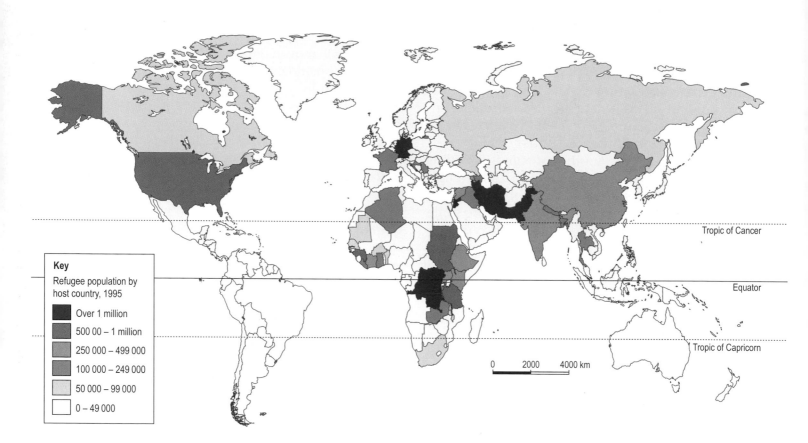

▼ **Figure 1** Refugee population by host country

Key

Refugee population by host country, 1995

- Over 1 million
- 500 00 – 1 million
- 250 000 – 499 000
- 100 000 – 249 000
- 50 000 – 99 000
- 0 – 49 000

International migrations are those involving movement across frontiers between countries. They can be forced or voluntary. They may involve movement from:

- poor to rich countries, e.g. West Indians to Britain in the 1930s
- poor to poor countries, e.g. refugees from Mozambique into neighbouring African states
- rich to rich countries, e.g. the 'brain drain' of UK doctors to Canada and the USA
- rich to poor countries, e.g. the movement of charity workers and missionaries to work in countries of the LEDW.

Refugees

The United Nations High Commission for Refugees (UNHCR) in 1951 defined refugees as people who flee their country because of 'well founded fear of persecution for reasons of race, religion, nationality, political opinion or membership of a particular social group'. The definition still holds true today.

There has been a massive increase in the numbers of refugees in the world (Figure 3). Up until the late 1970s the total number was below 3 million but this had grown to over 30 million by the year 2000.

▼ **Figure 2** Refugees by region (millions)

Africa	6.7	Europe	1.9
Latin America	0.1	Asia	5.0
North America	0.7	Oceania	0.1

The figures include all refugees of concern to the UNHCR including those internally displaced within their own country and some returnees being helped to reintegrate back in their own countries.

Figure 1 shows the distribution of refugees in the host countries in 1995. The countries with the highest numbers of refugees include Iran, Zaire, Pakistan, Germany, Tanzania and the Sudan. The distribution is largely due to their geographical location – adjacent to areas where there is civil war and conflict. The refugee problem is greatest in Africa and Asia (Figure 2) where long standing ethnic or political conflicts are most widespread.

- *One person in every 120 in the world today has been forced to flee his or her home as a result of violence, persecution or war.*
- *22 million people across the world are refugees, returnees or displaced persons.*
- *8 out of 10 refugees are women or children.*
- *Displaced persons have been forced to leave their homes but unlike refugees remain in their country. The war in former Yugoslavia created large numbers of displaced persons.*
- *Returnees are refugees who have returned to their own country. The repatriation may be voluntary or forced as in the case of some of the Vietnamese boat people forced to return from Hong Kong.*

▲ **Figure 3** Growth of world refugee population

Refugees returning to

Case Study

Mozambique

Mozambique, once a Portuguese colony, became independent in 1975. Sixteen years of civil war followed and brought farming to a standstill, destroyed schools and health centres and most other facilities. A third of the 17 million population fled their homes from the violence and torture into the neighbouring countries of Tanzania, South Africa, Malawi, Zambia and Swaziland. The war ended in 1992, a peace treaty was signed and gradually 1.7 million people from other countries and 4 million internally displaced people returned home (Figure 4). The people returned to a country with little or no food or water, no roads, houses or schools. However, many of the families were reunited and seemed able to forget the war and start to rebuild their homes and lives. Two good rainy seasons helped agriculture to be re-established and the government accepted Western aid to help rebuild the infrastructure. The UNHCR also put in place an ambitious project to spend $100 million to buy food, seeds, tools and building materials to construct and repair wells, roads, schools and health centres. An important area of work was also to clear the land mines left behind after the civil war ended. About 50 per cent of the projects set up by the UNHCR

were successful before the commission withdrew.

Mozambique remains one of the poorest countries in the world and since the end of the civil war has faced other equally appalling disasters such as drought and severe flooding in 1997 and 2000 that caused loss of life and major displacement of peoples as well as ruining crops.

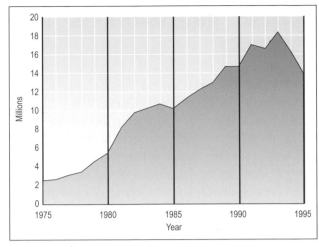

▶ **Figure 4** Refugees returning home to Mozambique by bus

Turkish 'guestworkers' in Germany

Case Study

Following the Second World War Germany was in a state of economic collapse. The country had lost over 4.5 million people in the war and many more, especially the Jewish population, had left the country for fear of persecution. There was nothing short of an economic miracle as Germany used aid from abroad to develop new industries in many cities. However there was a serious shortage of labour that threatened the industrial recovery. This was solved by importing 'guestworkers', especially from Turkey, former Yugoslavia, Italy and Greece. These countries were mostly much less developed than Germany. When the Berlin Wall was built more labourers moved into West Germany from the east. The migration of 'guestworkers' brought both advantages and disadvantages to the host country, the losing country and to the migrant and his family. These are summarized in Figure 2.

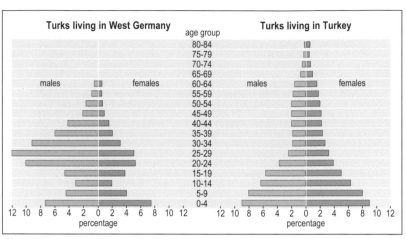

▲ **Figure 1** Population structure of Turks in Germany and Turkey, 1990s

	Advantages	Disadvantages
To Germany	Cheap source of labour to do dangerous jobs such as in asbestos factories; and unskilled work and dirty jobs not wanted by the German people, such as street cleaning;	Cause of racial tension at times of high unemployment in Germany Need to provide housing, services and specialist education to cope with language difficulties low paid work such as catering and farming
To Turkey	Reduces unemployment and pressure on resources Earns foreign exchange	Lose best skilled people needed in home economy Decline of farming and services Reduces birth rate in rural areas
To the migrant	Higher wages, higher standard of living than in Turkey Miss their family	Social problems of integration due to foreign language and customs Newly learned skills of little use Turkish economy
To the migrant's family	Money sent back from migrant raises standard of living Family life may break down	Lose the young males vital to work in the villages

▶ **Figure 2** The impact of 'guestworkers' in Germany

Migrants should learn German, claims minister

Foreigners who move to Germany's largest state, North Rhine-Westphalia, should be given compulsory lessons in German, a minister in the local government has proposed.

Ilse Brusis, a social Democrat, believes a state-run system of German lessons would help immigrants to find jobs.

The comments are the latest contribution to heated debates over immigration and education now raging between the Social Democrats and the right-wing Christian Democrat Union in the run up to a regional election on May 14.

Mrs Brusis, North Rhine-Westphalia's social affairs and labour minister has criticised the CDU for striking an anti-immigrant tone.

She said the state's two million foreigners and future arrivals, should be made to feel truly a part of German society. Learning German would be essential to that process.

'For a successful integration it is necessary that we give immigrants the feeling that they are welcome and that they have opportunities,' she said.

'To improve the opportunities of young immigrants further we have to tackle the topic of learning a language because this is the key condition for a successful school and professional education.'

The minister said Germany should take up ideas pioneered by the Netherlands, where a law was passed two years ago making Dutch lessons and other education courses compulsory for foreigners.

From *The Daily Telegraph*, 27 April 2000

▲ **Figure 3** Article about the migration to Germany

Summary of the consequences of migration

Economic and environmental

Advantages	Disadvantages
Losing area	**Losing area**
• Less strain on land and resources. • Lowers unemployment • May earn money through migrant sending it back to their family with further multiplier effects on the economy.	• Loss of skilled workforce. • Reduced need for people to farm the land
Gaining area	**Gaining area**
• Gains a workforce.	• Costs of housing, food, clothing and other refugees in the LEDW services – a particular problem with and cities with high rates of urban migration.

Social

- There is a redistribution of the population which tends to become more concentrated into core urban areas such as in southern Britain and the south-east coast of Brazil.

- Areas that lose people tend to have declining birth rates and an ageing population.

- Areas gaining population, especially the cities in the developing countries gaining through rural to urban migration, also experience high rates of natural increase.

- Life is still very difficult for many migrants living in poor housing conditions with access only to poorly paid work.

Cultural

- The migration of people especially across international boundaries leads to a spread of cultures including languages and religions and the creation of cosmopolitan societies.

- Cultural intolerance in societies may lead to racial disharmony and prejudice. The fear of racism often leads to immigrant communities living in the same areas, e.g. the Jewish, West Indian and Asian areas in London, the Black ghettos in New York.

Political

- The migration of population connected with the growth of colonial territories exported different cultures, languages, religions and education systems to different parts of the world.

- Political tensions may result from migration as with the Chinese people migrating into Malaysia and the Tamils into Sri Lanka.

Questions

1 Using Figure 1 describe the impact of the migration of guestworkers from Turkey to Germany on the population structure of both countries.

2 a People's attitudes to migration may be positive and negative. Read the press article in Figure 3. Which elements of the article would suggest positive attitudes and which would suggest negative attitudes?

  b Suggest reasons for the different attitudes.

3 For Brazil or another country/region of your choice describe and explain the causes and consequences of internal migration.

4 Discuss and justify the likely attitudes of the migrants and the hosts in each of the following examples of migration.

  a A German industrialist needing 300 factory workers

  b An unemployed German national

  c A British resident in Kent facing increased taxes to pay for the housing and policing of Kosovan refugees

  d The government of Tanzania already struggling to cater for its own population and faced with refugees from Mozambique

  e The USA government with application forms from UK doctors

5 For each of the examples in question 4 consider your own attitudes.

Population structure

- Introduction
- Variations in population structure over time and spatially
- The implications of different structures and changes in structure

Introduction

Population structure is the make-up of the total population in a country or area where people are grouped by age and sex. The graphical technique used to summarize age structure is the population pyramid. The pyramid shape reflects the fact that, in all but exceptional circumstances in any society, there are more young people than middle aged, and more middle-aged people than old. People die at all ages from diseases and accidents; for some this happens within one year of birth (infant mortality). Living is a risky business at any age, but the risks of death from fatal disease or malfunction of vital body organs increase significantly from the age of fifty onwards, hence the tapering off of the age groups towards the top of the graph.

The study of a population structure tells you a great deal about a country. The height and shape of a country's population pyramid gives clues about crude birth rate, life expectancy and likely level of economic development. Figure 1 suggests that the crude birth rate in the UK is low and lower than it has been; age groups over 65 are well represented which suggests high life expectancy. The life expectancy of women is shown to be greater than that of men. Overall such demographic characteristics indicate a country with a high level of economic development.

Dependency

Dependency ratio is directly linked to the age structure of the population. To calculate this, a country's population is split into the economically active age groups, which is usually taken to be those between 15 and 64 years old, and the non-economically active age groups, usually taken to be those under 15 and 65 or older. The dependency ratio is calculated as a percentage using the formula:

$$\frac{\text{number of non-economically active (0–14 + 65 and over)}}{\text{number of economically active (15–64)}} \times 100$$

As populations in MEDCs age, another ratio, the old-age dependency ratio, is being increasingly used as an indicator of the degree of dependence of the elderly upon the income generated by those of working ages. It is calculated by:

$$\frac{\text{number of people 65 and over}}{\text{number of working age (15–64)}} \times 100$$

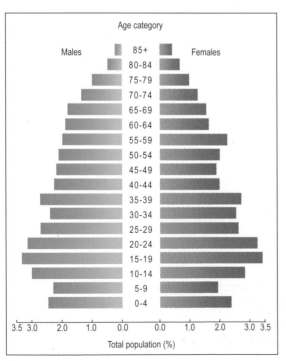

▲ **Figure 1** Example of a population pyramid — the UK in 1991

> ℹ️ *How to construct a population pyramid*
> - *Percentages of the total population or total numbers of people are shown along the horizontal scale. This scale is split so that 0 is in the middle; from the middle the scale increases on both sides, one side for males and one for females.*
> - *Age groups (usually in 5 year intervals such as 0–4 and 5–9) are plotted up the vertical scale. The youngest is placed at the bottom and the oldest at the top.*
> - *Horizontal bars, split in the middle, are drawn to represent the percentages or numbers of males and females within each age group.*

ℹ️ *How to interpret a population pyramid*

1 Start at the bottom.
This shows you what happened in the recent past and suggests what is likely to be happening at the present.

- *Observe bar widths at the base of the pyramid. A wide base for a country suggests high birth rates. A narrow base suggests low birth rates. A base narrowing from the age groups above suggests a declining birth rate.*
- *Add up the percentages in the bars for age groups within the range 0–14 years; this gives you the size of the young dependent population.*

2 Next go to the top.
- *Examine the width of the bars for the post-65 age groups, as well as how high above 75 the top of the pyramid extends (if these age groups are shown).*
- *Observe bar widths at the top and the overall height of the pyramid. A wide top to a high pyramid indicates long average life expectancy in a country.*
- *Add up the percentages in the bars for age groups 65 and above; this gives you the size of the old dependent population.*

3 End by looking in the middle.
- *Check for larger than expected variations between one or more age groups compared with those above and below.*
- *Longer than expected bars for certain age groups suggest a baby boom generation, or in-migration. Shorter than expected bars suggest more deaths from for example disease or war, or alternatively out-migration.*
- *Add up the percentages in the bars for age groups 15–64, which gives you the size of the independent population (those of working age upon whom the young and old depend).*

▼ **Figure 2** The two groups of dependents in any population

Variations in population structure over time and spatially

Variations over time

The population structure of a country changes over time as demographic factors change, notably:
- birth and fertility rates
- infant mortality, death rates and life expectancy
- rates of migration in and out of the country.

These demographic factors are reflected in the shape of the population pyramid which acts as a historical record of population change.

Questions

1 From Figure 1,
  a state the percentages in the economically active age groups and the non-economically active age groups
  b describe the main features of the country's population structure.

2 Population data for one of the world's least economically developed countries is given below.

Age groups	Percentages	
	Male	Female
0–4	11.0	10.9
5–9	8.4	8.4
10–14	6.5	6.6
15–19	5.0	5.1
20–24	3.9	4.0
25–29	3.1	3.2
30–34	2.4	2.4
35–39	2.0	2.0
40–44	1.7	1.7
45–49	1.4	1.3
50–54	1.2	1.2
55–59	1.0	1.0
60–64	0.8	0.8
65–69	0.7	0.7
70–74	0.5	0.4
75+	0.4	0.3

  a Draw its population pyramid.
  b Compare this pyramid with the one shown in Figure 1.
  c Comment on the differences between the two pyramids.

Population structure

Case Study

in the UK

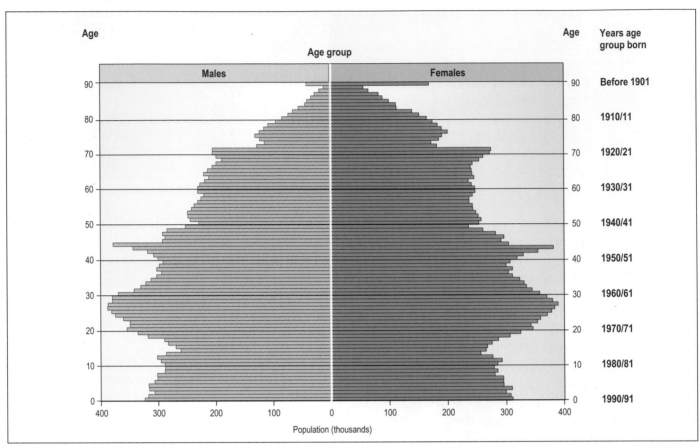

Population (thousands)

▲ **Figure 1** Population pyramid of England and Wales for 1991

A more detailed version of the population pyramid for England and Wales shows a relatively straight pyramidal shape in 1991, but with some bulges and indentations within it, which disrupt the general pattern (Figure 1). These can only be explained satisfactorily by considering the circumstances that existed at the time when the age-groups in question were born. For instance, people in their late twenties in the middle of the pyramid are more numerous than those in their teens, which shows that birth rates were higher in the 1960s than in the 1970s. Rising prosperity in the 'swinging sixties' is used to explain what is sometimes referred to as the 'baby-boomer' decade. Numbers around the age of 45 form another bulge in the pyramid. Again you need to go back to the time when these people were being born for the explanation. This was the 'post-war baby boom'; it was a time of celebration after the end of hostilities and the return home of men from service in the armed forces. Those who were 80 or over in 1991 were born before 1910 when

birth rates and average family sizes were much higher than they are today. Great improvements in medical care and the development of new drugs for treatment of hitherto fatal conditions have aided the survival of many of them.

Population pyramids for the age make-up of the total British population at 40-year intervals are given in Figure 2. There was little change between 1840 and 1880. At that time population structure was dominated by the young; almost two out of every three people were aged under thirty. The numbers and percentages in the low to middle-age groups would have been even higher had it not been for high net rates of out-migration. During the nineteenth century people from the UK (along with those from other European countries) populated the New World and colonies in Africa, Asia and Australasia. Birth rates were high in Victorian times and families with eight to ten children in them were not uncommon.

▼ **Figure 2** Population structure in Britain 1841–1981

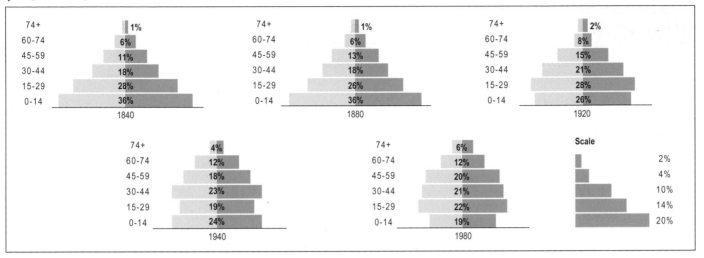

A big change can be noticed between 1880 and 1920 as the percentage of those aged under 15 fell by ten per cent due to a decline in birth rates and lower infant mortality. Fewer deaths in early and middle adult life led to an increase in the number of elderly people. Despite some small scale fluctuations in birth rates, these trends have continued. Life expectancy has shown a consistent increase. The establishment of the NHS, despite all the recent criticisms of the service it provides, made health care available to all. Rising standards of living and new developments in medical technology have also contributed. Life expectancy for those born in the UK in 2000 is over 74 years for a man and over 79 years for a woman.

The net result is that in 2000 the UK has an 'ageing population'. The proportion of the population aged 50 and over increased from about one in six at the start of the twentieth century to close to one in three at the end. There has been a significant increase in what might be described as the very elderly — people living into their eighties and beyond. Projections suggest that these will form over 5 per cent of the population by 2021 when there will be more than three million of them. At the same time the number of people aged under 16 has been falling. It is predicted that, some time between 2011 and 2021, the numbers aged 65 and over will exceed those under 16 for the first time (Figure 3).

▼ **Figure 3** Numbers of dependents in the UK, actual and projected 1971-2021

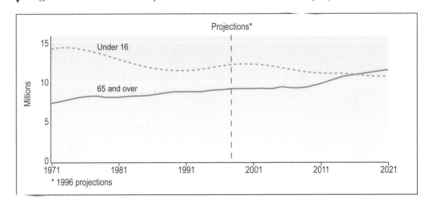

ⓘ The UK's population at the beginning and end of the twentieth century

Population	1901	The population of the UK was 38 million. The annual number of deaths was about the same as today.
	1999	Population increased to over 59 million.
Birth rates	1900	About 1 million babies were born each year around 1900 giving a crude birth rate of about 26 per 1000 people.
	1998	717,000 live births in the UK representing a crude birth rate of 12.2 births per 1000 people.
Infant mortality	1900	About 1 child in 7 did not live to his or her first birthday. The infant mortality rate was therefore about 143 per 1000.
	1998	The infant mortality was 5.6 per 1000.
Migration	1901–11	About 800,000 more people migrated out of the UK than into it.
	1997	60,000 more people migrated into the UK than out of it.

The Demographic Transition Model and population structure

Changes in rates of natural increase over time are shown in the demographic transition model (pages 151–2). As crude birth rates and crude death rates are the two factors used in formulating this model, it is not surprising that different population structures can be recognized for each of five stages in the model. Population pyramids can be drawn which illustrate the demographic features for each stage. Population pyramids can convey sequential changes in population structure which accompany rising levels of economic development over time.

Stage 1

The distinctive features of pyramid **a** in Stage 1 are its low height and uneven distribution of age groups. Birth rates are relatively constant and high, but epidemics, famines, accidents and conflicts lead to fluctuations in death rates. These affect some age groups more than others in an erratic way. This structure is restricted to only a few countries or peoples which are among the world's poorest, e.g. tribes in the Amazon rainforest

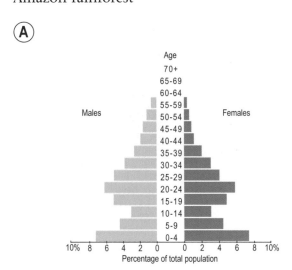

The result is that the young make up the largest percentage and dominate the age structure. In some countries those under 15 contribute over 50 per cent of the total population. Pyramid b is typical of LEDCs at a low level of economic development such as many countries in sub-Saharan Africa.

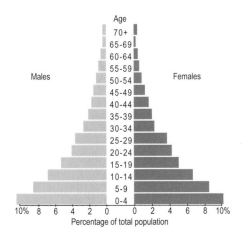

Stage 2

The most characteristic feature of pyramid b in Stage 2 is the width of its base. The spread of modern medical science, improvements in standards of public health, better nutrition and greater access to clean water combine to bring down the death rate quickly. This reduction occurs first in the cities and then spreads, albeit often slowly, to rural areas. However, for traditional and social reasons the birth rate remains high until greater and more widespread socio-economic changes occur.

Stage 2—3

Pyramid **c** straddles the divide between Stages 2 and 3.

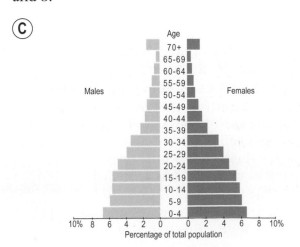

Economic development in a country gradually leads to changes in the structure of employment. Secondary and tertiary activities overtake the primary sector. Increased personal incomes and improved standards of living are slowly translated into social changes which foster a natural desire to reduce family size. This is seen first by the reduction in the width of the base of the pyramid and later by a more regular upright shape to the pyramid overall. By the time Stage 3 is fully reached, as in pyramid **d**, the changes caused by a significant reduction in birth rate have led to one of the pyramid's most marked features — the bulge in age groups among those of working age, born at times when birth rates were higher. Pyramids **c** and **d** are typical of those countries which are undergoing or have undergone real economic growth such as the world's Newly Industrializing Countries.

Stage 4

By the time Stage 4 is reached birth rates and death rates are similar and there is less variation in size between different age groups than for any other stage. This is why pyramid e is tall and almost straight, and there is only a slow drop in length of bars with age. This depicts the mature population structure of many MEDCs. The fertility rate in some of them has fallen below 2.1, the level needed for long-term natural replacement of the population. Once official census data becomes available, from which to construct a pyramid for a country in Stage 5 of the demographic transition model, even further trimming of the width of the base of the pyramid can be expected.

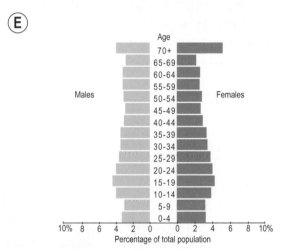

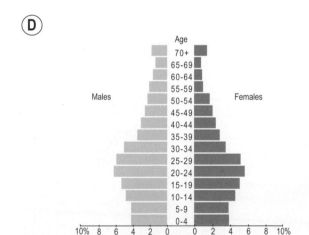

Questions

1 **a** Sketch and label population pyramids to describe how population structures of countries change over time with higher levels of economic development.

   b Explain these changes.

2 Outline all the evidence that you can find which shows that in 2000 the UK has an ageing population.

Spatial variations in population structure

Spatial differences between countries are shown by the variations in population structure at different levels of economic development. Sometimes only a line, rather than the full pyramid, is used to summarize differences in structure between LEDCs and MEDCs. The two extremes are shown in Figure 1.

Within a country, population structures can change from one area to another or, on a still smaller scale, between one part of a large urban area and another. Within LEDCs, big differences in standards of living and quality of life between urban and rural areas are quite normal. Greater poverty in the rural areas of Brazil and India is referred to on pages 184. Figure 2 shows the average disparity in access to three social services within LEDCs. The result is that in rural areas life expectancy is lower and death rates are higher. Ways of life have changed less in rural areas and children are regarded as useful sources of labour in farming and as parental guardians in old age. Combined with low levels of education and limited provision of family planning clinics, these help to provide the explanation for crude birth rates remaining stubbornly high in the countryside while those in urban areas have tumbled. The effects on population structure in rural areas is that under 15s are better represented and over 50s are under-represented compared with the averages for the whole country, producing a pyramid with a wider base and a lower, narrower top than in urban areas.

▼ **Figure 1** Summary lines for national population structures

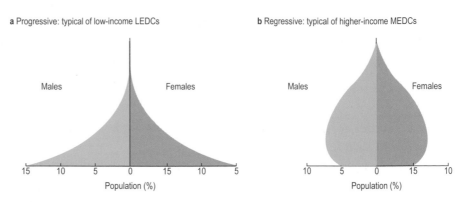

a Progressive: typical of low-income LEDCs

b Regressive: typical of higher-income MEDCs

▼ **Figure 2** Urban–rural disparity in access to social services in LEDCs

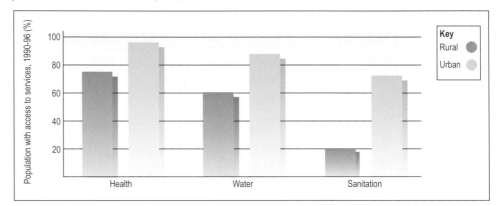

▲ **Figure 3** Children living in a remote jungle region in Ecuador. The usual rule is the more remote the rural location, the higher the birth rate.

The effects of migration

Internal migration also affects population structures and leads to variations within the country. Population pyramids drawn for rural areas that are greatly affected by out-migration of young people of working age have an indented middle section in which the age groups between 15 and 40 are under-represented. Sometimes this is more pronounced for males than females. Particularly in the early stages of migration men are more likely to migrate leaving the wife and family behind in the village until they have become established in the city. However, patterns of migration vary between world regions. For instance, in many South American countries men and women migrate in almost equal numbers whereas in countries in southern and eastern Africa, movements by men seeking work for economic reasons in the cities or mines are dominant. The effects that migration can have upon a city's population pyramid are shown in Figure 4. Dar-es-Salaam is the chief port of Tanzania which makes it the main focal point for migrants from the countryside.

Within big cities in LEDCs spatial variations in population structure exist wherever segregation based upon the socio-economic characteristics of the residents has occurred. In wealthy neighbourhoods family sizes are likely to be lower and life expectancies higher than in the housing areas built by and for the poor. A population pyramid drawn for the inhabitants of San Isidro and Miraflores where the houses of the rich are concentrated in Lima in Peru (page 219) would not be too different from that for an MEDC; perhaps the base would be slightly wider reflecting an average of two or three children in the family. Some shanty towns have matured into urban townships after long settlement and improvements in services. Population structures here are likely to be better balanced across the age groups than in squatter settlements or the more recently established shanty towns. The latter are more likely to be dominated by those of working age and their children; when they recently migrated to seek work in the city the elderly were left in the villages. Anyway life is too much of a struggle for many of them to survive into old age.

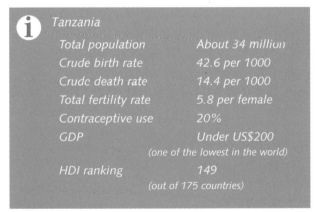

Tanzania

Total population	About 34 million
Crude birth rate	42.6 per 1000
Crude death rate	14.4 per 1000
Total fertility rate	5.8 per female
Contraceptive use	20%
GDP	Under US$200 (one of the lowest in the world)
HDI ranking	149 (out of 175 countries)

▲ **Figure 5** Dar-es-Salaam

▼ **Figure 4** Population pyramids for Tanzania

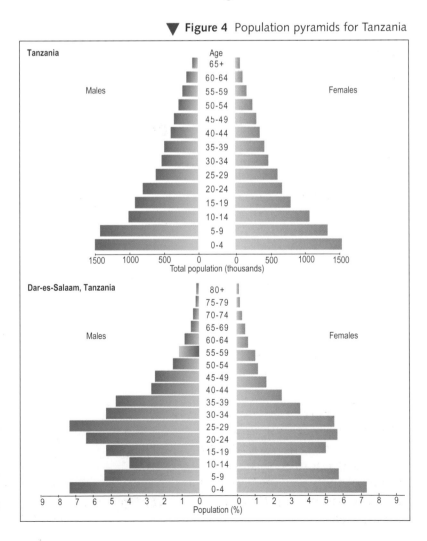

Racial demographic differences within MEDCs

In MEDCs demographic differences between urban and rural areas are less noticeable or non-existent. Differences in birth rates between ethnic or other groups can be more significant as a cause of spatial variations in population structure, particularly between long established groups and recent arrivals. Ethnic/racial groups or migrants of the same nationality almost invariably have an uneven spatial distribution within a country because, for a variety of social and economic reasons, they congregate in certain places. At the local level, groups segregate themselves in cities so that a particular group is overwhelmingly concentrated in only one residential area within the urban area. In American cities these areas are often given labels like 'Little Cuba' in Miami where refugees and migrants from Cuba make up the majority of the population. Spatial variations in population structure result.

A classic example of a multi-racial country leading to differences in population structure between areas is the USA. The US Census Bureau identifies five different groups, between whom are some significant differences in crude birth rates (Figure 1).

People of Hispanic origin (from Mexico and other Spanish-speaking lands in Central and South America and the Caribbean) are the most recent arrivals among the racial groups. They come from mainly Catholic less economically developed countries. Their attitudes towards birth control and family sizes are from their home countries and their own family backgrounds. In-migrants, both legal and illegal, are mainly economic. Differences in wage rates and general standards of living between the USA and neighbouring countries are so wide that the pull of the USA for the 15–35 age groups in Central American and Caribbean countries is almost irresistible. This means that the Hispanic population in the USA is a young population composed of a higher proportion of those in the child-bearing age groups. In those states and metropolitan areas where significant concentrations of Hispanics occur, the population structure is dominated by those of working age and children; age groups over fifty are seriously under represented compared with the American average. Over a quarter of the population of California is Hispanic and this is increasing. The greatest urban concentrations are in Los Angeles (especially Long Beach), Anaheim, Riverside and San Diego, as well as significant proportions in New York, Chicago and Miami.

Distribution of the elderly within MEDCs

Within MEDCs the elderly are also unequally distributed. Figure 2 shows where retired people in the UK are more heavily concentrated. Retirement is the time when some decide to move. They are no longer tied to their place of work. Sometimes cash can be released from selling the house and can be used to buy another that is smaller or located in a cheaper part of the country.

▼ **Figure 1a** Racial demographic differences in the USA
Crude birth rates (per 1000) by race and origin (1995)

All races	14.8
White	14.2
Black	18.2
American Indian	16.6
Asian or Pacific Islander	17.3
Hispanic origin	25.2

Wall Street Journal Almanac 1998

◀ **Figure 1b** Distribution of births by race and origin (%) 1990–2050

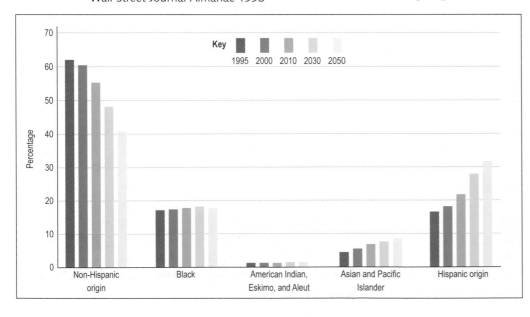

Key: 1995 2000 2010 2030 2050

Coastal areas and scenic regions are particularly attractive to those anticipating more leisure time. Moving south is more attractive than moving north because of the south's warmer climate. Withstanding cold weather is more of a problem for the elderly. This is why counties in the west country such as Devon and Dorset and well sheltered south coast resorts such as Bournemouth, Brighton and Eastbourne show higher than average percentages of people over 65 in their population structure. However many pensioners are too poor to consider moving. In rural areas they often make up high percentages because the younger people have all left to seek work in the cities and in the south. The more remote the region, the higher the proportion of elderly is the general rule.

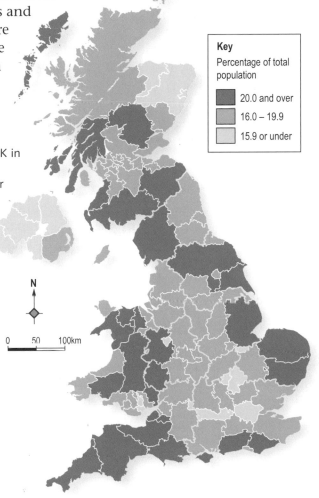

► **Figure 2** Population of retirement age in the UK in 1997. The map shows males aged 65 and over and females aged 60 and over as a combined percentage of the total population in counties.

Key
Percentage of total population

- 20.0 and over
- 16.0 – 19.9
- 15.9 or under

Questions

1 Sketch and label pyramids for each of the following to show variations in population structure within a country:
   a a rural area compared with an urban area in a LEDC
   b a retirement town compared with an expanding new town in a MEDC
   c a high-income white neighbourhood in an American city compared with a low-income Hispanic neighbourhood.

2 **Investigation**
   Using UK Census Data,
   a for the largest city near to where you live,
      i examine the age structure in two contrasting areas
      ii use the socio-economic characteristics and locations of the two areas to explain the differences.
   b i Draw the age-sex pyramid for a south coast retirement town.
      ii In what ways is it different from the pyramid for the whole of the UK?

3 Describe and suggest reasons for the distribution of retired people in the UK shown in Figure 2.

The implications of different structures and changes in structure

Youthful populations in LEDCs

The main problem caused by population structure which faces governments in most LEDCs is their large percentages of young people. The young are expensive in their demands for services notably education and health. Their constantly increasing numbers has left no breathing space for governments and other authorities to catch up with, and begin to satisfy, the demands for schooling. Outside the large cities attendance at secondary school is rare in LEDCs. What is worse is that there is going to be a persistent increase in numbers of young people well into the future, even if the young of today do more to limit the size of their families than their parents did. However, there is a brighter side. The young of today are a country's human resources of tomorrow. The young of working age are the dynamic group in a population whose energies will foster growth, change and economic development should the political administration and business organization in the country provide the favourable conditions for it to happen.

Ageing populations in MEDCs

The main problem caused by population structure which faces the majority of governments in MEDCs is one of ageing populations and their likely economic and social impacts. Welfare provision for the less well-off and less fortunate members of society such as the young, the old, the sick and the unemployed is a widely accepted government responsibility in MEDCs. Welfare costs are going up. Even in the UK which is less generous than many other European countries they take nearly one quarter of the GDP (Figure 1). In turn nearly half of all the benefits paid out by the UK government are for the elderly. The NHS estimates, for example, that 41 per cent of its spending goes on the over 65s.

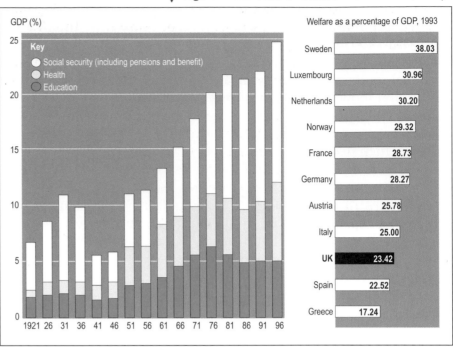

▼ **Figure 1** The costs of welfare in the UK and Europe

Some governments, looking at the predictions being made for numbers of retired and elderly people, are becoming quite alarmed at the prospect of how much pensions and care and health services are going to cost them in the not too distant future. The costs of state pensions and other forms of welfare have to be borne by those of working age through taxation. State pensions generally are paid out on a pay-as-you-go basis. Today's national insurance contributions and taxes pay for today's pensions and welfare benefits; there is not an accumulated fund. Taxes also have to fund education and welfare for all the other age groups.

Many old people do have private pensions; however, the pay out from these depends upon the profits being made by companies which in turn places dependence for income generation upon today's working population. Therefore what is really important in predicting future costs from ageing populations is the size of the old age dependency ratio. How many people of working age will there be to support each person 65 years old and above? In Figure 2 predictions for five MEDCs are given and they do not make good reading for governments, although the UK is shown to be in a better position than the other four.

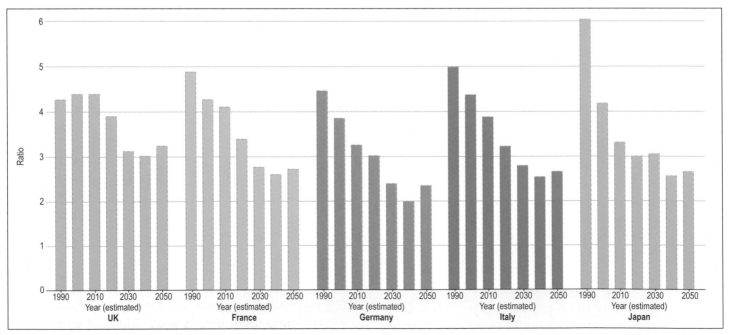

▲ **Figure 2** Predictions for the ratio of the number of people of working age (15–64 years) to support each old person (65 years and above)

Many governments are in a dilemma. Because pensions in the future will be paid for by people working at that time, workers will need to be asked to pay higher taxes. What has been described as 'the pensions time bomb' is looming in Europe because benefit levels were set when both life expectancy and the proportion of elderly people were much lower than today. Current pensioners are understandably unwilling to take a pension package which is inferior to the one they paid their taxes for when working. Also as numbers of pensioners increase, they become a more powerful political lobby. Governments in democracies cannot afford to ignore them when election time comes around. Governments also know that the predictions being made for the size of future old age dependency ratios in MEDCs are unlikely to be wrong. If anything further advances in medical science are likely to make the dependency ratio worse by prolonging life. Birth rates are static or going down. The problem is further aggravated by the trend towards early retirement and ageism in the work place which means that people from progressively younger ages are contributing less in tax.

Some plans and changes are being made. One move already under way is to increase retirement ages (Figure 3). Another is to make it compulsory for a greater proportion of those in work to contribute to private pension schemes. A third is to change, and thereby reduce, the way in which the pension funds are distributed to try to protect the less well off at the expense of the better-off pensioners. This is needed most in countries such as Italy and France, which have exceptionally generous state schemes, but all attempts by governments to make changes so far have met with great and well organized opposition from workers.

▼ **Figure 3** Examples of retirement ages in MEDCs

Country	Pension age Male/Female	Planned changes
Australia	65/60	Female retirement age rising to 65
Canada	65/65	Already changed
Denmark	67/67	Already changed
Germany	65/60	Female retirement age rising to 65
Iceland	70/70	Already changed
Republic of Ireland	65/65	Additional old age pension paid at 66
Italy	60/55	Male retirement age rising to 65, female to 60
Norway	67/67	Already changed
UK	65/60	Female retirement age rising to 65. Proposals to raise retirement age to 70 for both sexes.
USA	65/65	Rising to 67 for both sexes.

There are some beneficial consequences of an ageing population. The leisure sector is boosted by the elderly using facilities mid-week outside the weekend peak and taking holidays during off-peak months outside school holidays. SAGA began as a specialist company providing holidays just for pensioners. Now it targets all of the over 50s, offers worldwide holiday destinations and supplies a whole range of other financial services. How much of the luxury market for round the world and Caribbean cruises would be left without the retired? Some manufacturing companies have been similarly successful in finding niches to tap into the pensioner market for products such as chair lifts and mobile wheel chairs which improve the quality of life of the elderly. A proportion of pensioners are sufficiently wealthy to bear the full costs of health services, private nursing at home or residential care in a home. This has offered many commercial opportunities. Some large properties, formerly of limited commercial value because of size and location, have been converted into profitable residential homes (Figure 4).

▼ **Figure 4** Two Victorian houses in southern Manchester – now a residential home for the elderly.

However, there is no such thing as a 'typical pensioner'. There are social disparities between different groups of elderly people. Some live in rented accommodation, have no savings and must rely entirely upon state pensions. They have a low quality of life even without illnesses. Others are healthy and wealthy. It was for this group that an American airline adopted the advertising slogan 'Fly First Class – or your heirs will'.

Questions

1 Identify and explain the political, social and economic implications of ageing populations.

2 In what ways and why are the population problems of MEDCs and LEDCs different?

Chapter 4 Questions

1 The table below gives recent population data for twelve of the EU countries.

Population (1999 figures per 1000)			
Country	Live births	Deaths	New immigrants
Austria	9.5	9.4	1.1
Belgium	11.1	10.1	1.0
Denmark	12.5	11.1	1.9
France	12.6	9.1	0.8
Germany	9.3	10.3	2.3
Greece	9.9	9.5	1.4
Republic of Ireland	14.3	8.4	5.0
Italy	9.1	9.9	2.3
Netherlands	12.6	8.9	2.7
Spain	9.4	9.4	0.9
Sweden	9.9	10.6	1.4
UK	11.9	10.8	2.9

▲ Figure 1

a   i Name all the countries in the table which had a natural decrease in population in 1999. (2 marks)
    ii Outline the reasons for natural decreases in population in some MEDCs. (4 marks)
    iii Explain why the total population is increasing in all twelve of the EU countries in the table. (2 marks)

b In which stage or stages of the demographic transition model should the EU countries in the table above be placed? Justify your answer. (7 marks)

Total: 15 marks

2 a Describe and explain the economic and social impacts of an ageing population. (10 marks)

b To what extent is it true that younger people (aged under 30) are more likely to *migrate* than are old people (aged 65 and above)? (10 marks)

Total: 20 marks

A note on timing
You are expected to answer question 1 in about 15 minutes. You are expected to answer question 2 in about 40 minutes, spending an equal length of time on both parts.

Chapter 5

Settlement processes and patterns

New York. The tallest skyscrapers in mid-town and downtown Manhattan indicate the areas of greatest commercial activity

Settlement processes

- **urbanization**
- **suburbanization**
- **counter urbanization**
- **re-urbanization**

Settlement structure

Size and spacing of settlements

Settlement processes

- Urbanization
- Suburbanization
- Counter urbanization
- Re-urbanization

Cities are dynamic places. They are places of growth and change. Almost half of the six billion people in the world in 2000 live in urban areas and the proportion is growing (Figure 1). In spite of the social, economic and environmental problems associated with the world's big cities, which receive much publicity, cities are soon going to be the preferred living places for the majority of the world's population. Historically, cities have been the places in which new economic and social developments have occurred. As centres of commerce and manufacturing industry they became and they remain centres of wealth and invention. Living conditions in shanty towns in cities in LEDCs may look appalling to the eyes of people living in MEDCs, but studies show that rural poverty in LEDCs is much worse (Figure 2). Rural poverty is less concentrated and therefore less obvious; remote rural areas are little visited by television camera crews and journalists until struck hard by a hazard such as drought. The values in Figure 2b for South East Brazil and Kerala in India represent great declines in levels of poverty as a result of urban economic developments and state investments. In contrast the backward, over-populated rural North East of Brazil remains one of South America's poorest regions.

	Urban population (%) (as a percentage of the total)		Average annual growth rates (%) of the urban population	
	1960	2000	1960-941	994-2000
World	34	47	3.3	2.5
MEDCs	61	75	1.4	0.8
LEDCs	22	41	3.9	3.7

◀ **Figure 1** Urban population and urban growth

▼ **Figure 2b**

Differences in human poverty within Brazil and India in the 1990s. (Based upon an index which took into account life expectancy, adult literacy, access to health services and safe water, and malnourishment among children. The higher the index, the greater the poverty.)

▼ **Figure 2a** Results of a survey of poverty in South America in the 1990s

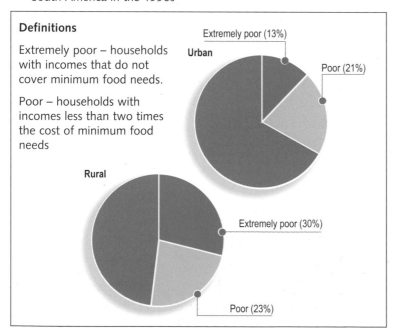

Definitions

Extremely poor – households with incomes that do not cover minimum food needs.

Poor – households with incomes less than two times the cost of minimum food needs

Urban: Extremely poor (13%), Poor (21%)

Rural: Extremely poor (30%), Poor (23%)

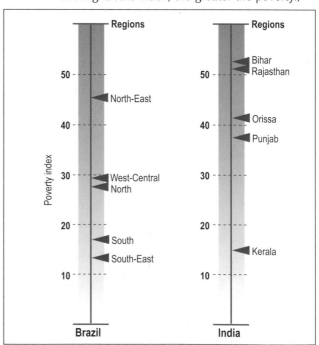

*Notice how all the words listed below end in the same way with -**ization**. This suggests increase or growth.*

Urbanization *The process which has led to an increasing proportion of a country's population living within urban areas. The inevitable consequence is a decline in the proportion (although not necessarily the total number) living in rural areas.*

Suburbanization *The process which includes the decentralization of people, industries and services from the central and inner areas of cities towards the edges of built-up areas. This results in the development of suburbs and the extension of the built-up area to take in land that was previously rural.*

Counter urbanization *The process which leads to an increased number of people living in rural areas. These are people who have moved out of the urban areas, either into the rural-urban fringe or further away into the countryside. Some businesses and other workplaces have followed. One result of the process is that some rural settlements have become suburbanized villages.*

Re-urbanization *The process whereby people, and sometimes businesses, are attracted back into inner urban areas that had been suffering from deterioration and decline. The process of gentrification is an example. Old houses and buildings are modernized and converted into homes that are attractive to the more wealthy.*

Industrialization *The growth of manufacturing industry. This, and an increasing proportion employed in the secondary sector, is a major cause of urbanization.*

Centralization *The increasing concentration of economic and other activities in one place.*

De-industrialization *The decline in numbers employed in manufacturing industry and particularly in old or heavy industries such as textiles and steel. The increasingly dominant service industries enjoy greater freedom of location and derive positive advantages from locations on the edges of urban areas. Such outward movements lead to the decentralization of economic activities.*

▲ **Figure 3a** Results of post-1950 urbanization in LEDCs: high rise in Georgetown on Penang, in Malaysia

▲ **Figure 3b** *Barriadas* climbing up the hillside on the edge of Lima, Peru

Urbanization

Characteristics and causes

Centuries ago, farming replaced nomadic ways of finding food such as hunting and settled life became possible. Improved farming techniques allowed food surpluses which freed some of the people living in the rural settlements from food production tasks. These people were then able to specialize in non-farming activities such as craft occupations and trading of goods. Some settlements, favourably placed for trading, grew into urban settlements.

Towns and cities are different from rural settlements because they depend on economic activities other than farming for their existence, prosperity and growth. It was in the cities that learning was concentrated and where breakthroughs in human knowledge occurred.

As civilizations, such as those of the Greeks and Romans in the Old World and the Aztecs and Incas in the New World, advanced, cities were built from where leaders could impose political organization and social control upon their people. Athens, Rome and Mexico City remain as capital cities of modern nations which have replaced old civilizations, showing how significant historical factors can be in explaining the present day locations and importance of settlements. Cuzco, the Inca capital located high in the Andes, is the only one of the four that has been replaced (Figure 1).

It was the Industrial Revolution in the eighteenth and nineteenth centuries, first in the UK and then in Europe and the USA, that led to a great increase in the number and size of towns and cities which quickened the pace of urbanization. In Britain, factory workers were needed in large numbers – in the textile mills of Yorkshire and Lancashire, in the iron and steel works, shipyards, metal smelting and engineering plants of Clydeside, Tyneside, the West Midlands and South Wales. Many of these were set up in new centres of industrial activity, often in coalfield regions and along the banks of navigable river estuaries. People, who moved into the rapidly growing industrial towns and cities in their thousands, needed to be housed as close to their place of work as possible, which led to the construction of rows of high density back-to-back and terraced houses. High birth rates and declining death rates in nineteenth-century Europe guaranteed the continued supply of workers. There was even a surplus who emigrated to the USA and Canada to populate the New World. In the USA the majority of immigrants stayed in the industrial cities along the eastern seaboard, on the coalfields of the north east and around the Great Lakes. Industrialization was therefore the main cause of nineteenth- and early twentieth-century urbanization. This was mainly restricted to Europe and North America.

▶ **Figure 1** View over Cuzco, the old Inca capital, from which the Spaniards first controlled their newly conquered lands in South America. Political contacts and trade with Spain soon made the location of a capital city high in the Andes unsuitable. Cuzco was replaced by Lima on the coast, which remains the capital of Peru.

▼ **Figure 2** Preston in the 1930s

Questions

Refer to **Figure 2**.

1 Draw a labelled sketch from the photograph to show layout and land uses.

2 How does the photographic evidence help to confirm that 'industrialization was the main cause of nineteenth- and early twentieth-century urbanization' in the UK?

3 Explain the likely problems caused by industrialization and urban growth in Preston in the 1930s.

Urbanization in LEDCs

During the twentieth century, mechanization and intensification of agriculture in MEDCs continued to release a stream of people looking for work in urban areas, where an increasing proportion was swallowed up by the growing service sector. However, since the 1950s there has been a dramatic shift in urbanization away from MEDCs to LEDCs. In MEDCs rates of natural increase have slowed down and in some countries have stopped. More people appreciate the advantages of rural living and have the wealth to be able to commute to work in towns and cities. Many of the services formerly only available to urban dwellers, such as electricity, piped mains water and telephone links, are now almost universally available in rural areas. Higher car ownership has increased personal mobility. Not everyone who works in an urban area needs to live there. Workplace and living place have become separated in a way that was not possible in earlier centuries.

In LEDCs the first stage of urbanization and its underlying cause is rural to urban migration. The main reason is economic - the widening wealth gap between rural and urban areas. However, from time to time numbers are topped up by environmental refugees. Although public services are inadequate in all big cities in LEDCs, their existence and availability is much greater than in rural areas. In addition there is a long tradition of centralized government in many countries, which began in colonial times when the colonial power built cities for administration and for economic control of the export of minerals and other primary products. In the colonial system wealth was focused on capital cities and main ports. Independent national governments still favour urban cores as centres of investment for scarce resources and neglect their rural areas. Investments from overseas by multinational companies are overwhelmingly directed into big cities. The economies of many LEDCs are large enough to support the growth of only one major city, which becomes the dominant primate city (see pages 222-3). Such a status increases its magnetism and pulling power for people in the countryside. In general, however, migration has not followed from the growth of industry and availability of work.

▼ **Figure 1a** The rural south of Chile. Distances between settlements are enormous and all the road surfaces are unpaved

▶ **Figure 1b**
Santiago, the urban core of Chile

Later in the urbanization process in LEDCs high rates of natural increase overtake migration as the most important factor for urban growth. Rural migrants to the city continue the tradition of having large families and, although services may be inadequate for all the new in-migrants, life expectancy increases in urban areas. The profile of the typical migrant, young and seeking work, means that the city is full of people within the reproductive age range. Currently there are such high proportions of children and young people in cities of the LEDW that natural increase is going to promote further urban growth for many years to come. This is despite the declines in urban fertility rates which are now occurring as a result of better education and improved economic circumstances.

The net result of several centuries of urbanization is shown in Figure 2. Significant spatial variations in levels of urbanization are shown particularly between the MEDW and the LEDW.

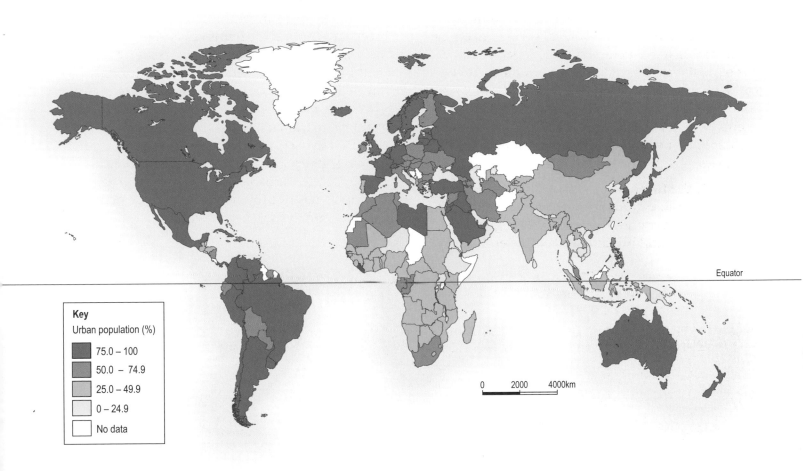

Key

Urban population (%)

- 75.0 – 100
- 50.0 – 74.9
- 25.0 – 49.9
- 0 – 24.9
- No data

0   2000   4000km

Equator

▲ **Figure 2** Urban population as a percentage of total population predicted for 2000

Questions

1 Describe and give reasons for the world pattern of urbanization in Figure 2.

2 Why might the highest rates of urbanization be expected in the continents of Asia and Africa during the next 50 years?

Results and consequences of urbanization

Accelerated world urban growth since 1950 has been the result of urbanization spreading to LEDCs. Before 1950 a millionaire city (a city with more than one million inhabitants) was considered to be something special. There were about seventy of them by 1950, which represented a tremendous increase from just two (London and Paris) in 1900. By 2000, which still represents a significant increase in number from 1990, there were about 350 of them (Figure 1). The increasing urbanization in LEDCs has reduced the average latitude of millionaire cities from 40° to close to 30° from 1950 to 2000. This reflects the tropical locations of many LEDCs.

More remarkable now is the growth of the really big city or megacity - a city with more than ten million inhabitants. It is only possible to estimate the population of most big cities, particularly when they are growing so fast, and you should not be too concerned when one source quotes a total population different from that of another. However, there were probably about 20 megacities in 2000 (Figure 3). There are at least as many megacities today as there were cities with over four million in 1960 (Figures 2, 3 and 4).

▼ **Figure 1** Millionaire cities in 1990

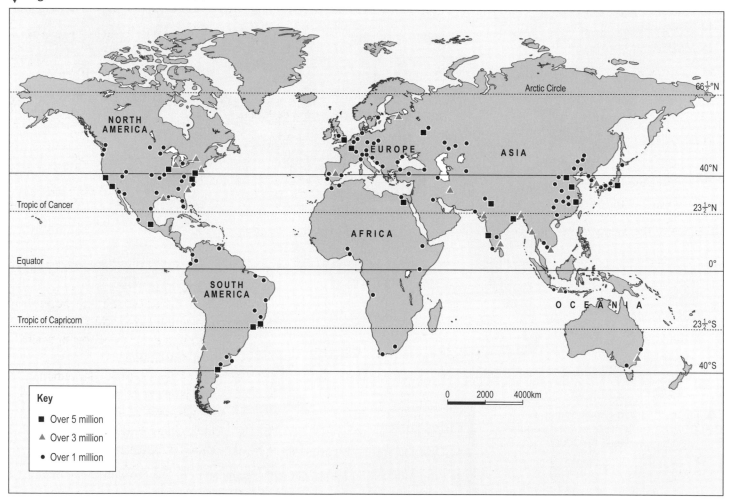

Key
■ Over 5 million
▲ Over 3 million
● Over 1 million

Rank	City	Country	Estimated population (millions)	Latitude (to nearest°)
1	New York	USA	14.2	41
2	London	UK	10.7	52
3	Tokyo	Japan	10.7	36
4	Shanghai	China	10.7	31
5	Beijing	China	7.3	40
6	Paris	France	7.2	49
7	Buenos Aires	Argentina	6.9	35
8	Los Angeles	USA	6.0	34
9	Moscow	USSR	6.3	56
10	Chicago	USA	6.0	42
11	Tianjin	China	6.0	39
12	Osaka	Japan	5.7	35
13	Calcutta	India	5.6	23
14	Mexico City	Mexico	5.2	19
15	Rio de Janeiro	Brazil	5.1	22
16	São Paulo	Brazil	4.8	22
17	Milan	Italy	4.5	45
18	Cairo	Egypt	4.5	30
19	Bombay	India	4.2	19
20	Philadelphia	USA	3.7	40

▲ **Figure 2** The twenty largest cities in 1960

Rank	City	Country	Estimated population (millions)	Latitude (to nearest°)
1	Tokyo	Japan	27.2	36
2	Mexico City	Mexico	16.9	19
3	São Paulo	Brazil	16.8	24
4	New York	USA	16.4	41
5	Bombay	India	15.7	19
6	Shanghai	China	13.7	31
7	Los Angeles	USA	12.6	34
8	Beijing	China	11.4	40
9	Calcutta	India	12.1	23
10	Buenos Aires	Argentina	11.9	35
11	Seoul	South Korea	11.8	38
12	Jakarta	Indonesia	11.5	6
13	Lagos	Nigeria	10.9	6
14	Osaka	Japan	10.7	35
15	Delhi	India	10.5	29
16	Rio de Janeiro	Brazil	10.4	22
17	Karachi	Pakistan	10.3	25
18	Cairo	Egypt	10.2	30
19	Manila	Philippines	10.1	14
20	Tianjin	China	10.1	39

▲ **Figure 3** Megacities in 2000

▲ **Figure 4** Comparisons in size between the world's twenty largest cities in 1960 and those in 2000

Questions

1 a On an outline world map, locate and name the megacities in 2000.
 b Describe the main features of their world distribution.
 c In what ways is their distribution **i** similar and **ii** different from that of the millionaire cities in Figure 1?
 d From Figures 2 and 3 calculate the mean latitude of the 20 largest cities in 1960 and 2000.

2 a Draw two dispersion diagrams placed side by side to show latitudes for the twenty biggest cities in 1960 and 2000.
 b Work out the *median* latitude for each year.

3 Give reasons for the change in *average* latitude of the world's biggest cities since 1960.

Consequences of urbanization in LEDCs

So great has been the pace of urbanization in LEDCs since 1950 that it has outstripped the capacity of the city authorities to provide essential services such as piped water, sewerage, electricity, health and education for all the inhabitants. People continue to pile into cities in such numbers that economic growth cannot generate the number of jobs needed in the formal sector. Even in cities enjoying growth in manufacturing industry, secure employment is hindered by frequent economic recessions. Increasing mechanisation also contributes to fewer jobs – a world-wide phenomenon. Would-be migrants from the countryside, however, have not been deterred by the massive economic and social problems in the rapidly growing cities. In spite of these problems, as was previously shown, most people improve their quality of life by migrating into the city. Conditions are particularly difficult for first-time migrants, who must usually earn a living in the informal sector of employment.

Employment in the informal sector implies:
- *self employment*
- *low income*
- *low productivity.*

It includes:
- *petty services, e.g. market and street sellers, shoe shiners, carriers, car guards, waste collectors*
- *small scale production, e.g. handicrafts, metal working, making replacement parts for machines and cars.*

Whereas employment in the formal sector implies:
- *permanent employment*
- *set hours of work and pay*
- *other rights, e.g. for pensions and health care.*

▼ **Figure 1** Work in the informal sector in Santiago, Chile.

a Shoe shiner in the main square. With the right pitch, a petty service can be turned into a good and regular earner.

b Moving things. Manual operations such as this survive in LEDCs because there are plenty of people to offer their services cheaply.

a

b

Shanty towns

The most visual consequence of urbanization today is the shanty town, although it is only since 1950 that they have become an important feature of cities in LEDCs. Only the upper and middle classes have the income and job security to buy or rent properly serviced houses with mains water and electricity. Formal housing is for those in formal employment. Migrants are confined at best to rented rooms in high density, grossly overcrowded slums located in and near the city centre, which have some rudimentary albeit inadequate services. At worst they live in squatter settlements and shanty towns around the edge of the urban area.

Recent arrivals from the countryside set up squatter camps on any land left unused or unoccupied. Often there is a good physical reason why the land has been left empty - a river gorge or swamp or steep slopes are some examples of the types of land that are unattractive to formal, permanent housing. The squatter settlement is characterized by illegal occupation of the land, homes of very rudimentary construction and no urban services. It is the worst kind of urban slum, plagued by open sewers and piles of fermenting rubbish and creating ideal conditions for the spread of disease, especially in hot climates. The authorities may destroy squatter settlements at any time.

However, squatter settlements are often dynamic places in which their inhabitants create conditions for change and seize any opportunities for improvements, e.g. Rocinha in Rio, Brazil where houses for 80 000 people have been upgraded with lighting and commercial services. A squatter settlement becomes a shanty town when the number of huts or simple dwellings increases with a provision, however inadequate, of some urban services. The key to further improvement is legal title to the land or at least some guarantee of permanence by the authorities. Only then is it safe for residents to build permanent homes made out of bricks and mortar. The community association can then put together a convincing case to the authorities to install water, drains and electricity and to build roads. When these services have been introduced, they may request community facilities, notably schools and clinics. It is likely that the growth of retail services will have accompanied the transition from shanty town through young township to normal urban residential district (Figure 2).

For most developing countries, public housing schemes are too expensive to contemplate on a vast scale, which leaves only this self-help route. The rate of success is heavily dependent upon attitudes of local and central governments, which in many cases are far from helpful.

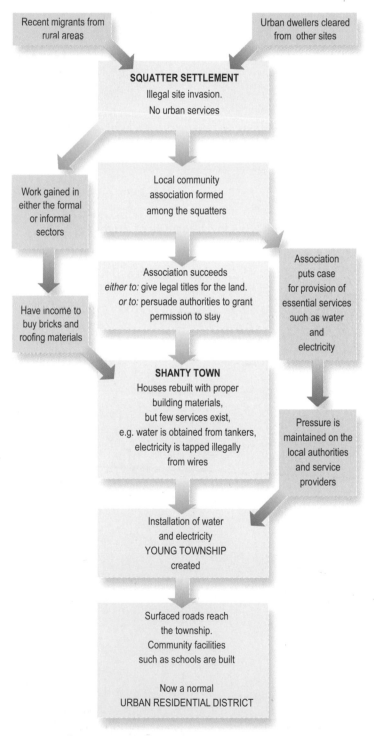

▲ **Figure 2** Shanty town change over time

Urbanization in Lima, Peru

Case Study

▼ **Figure 1** Urbanization in Peru – the proportion of the total population that is urban in Peru

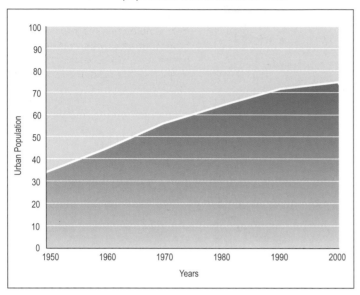

▼ **Figure 2** Lima – estimated population totals and percentages living in self-help housing

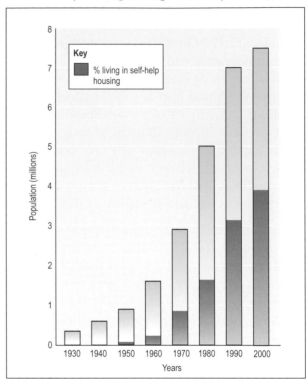

▼ **Figure 3** Lima – the distribution of shanty towns

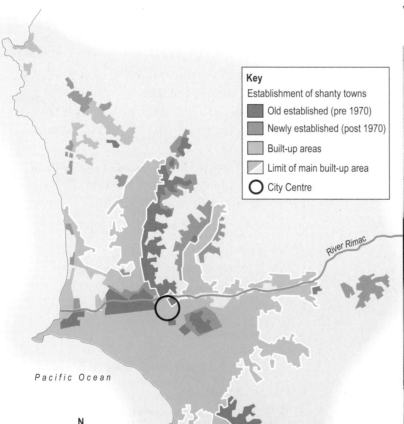

▼ **Figure 4** Lima – a squatter's home in one of the city's *barriadas*

◀ **Figure 5**

The improvement of *barriadas* into *pueblos jovenes* (young townships) close to the city centre of Lima. After having been given titles to the land by the government, some essential urban services were provided. The inhabitants felt more secure and are using money saved from employment to improve their houses and make them more permanent, at the same time upgrading the residential status of the area.

Lima houses almost one third of Peru's population. Its functions are administrative (capital and centre of government), commercial (headquarters of companies and banks), social and cultural (with the greatest concentration of artists, writers, teachers and land-owning aristocrats living in the city). There are many positive factors for Lima as it grows as an urban centre but there are negative factors for Peru as a whole.

Positive factors for Lima

- Attracts the largest amount of investment from multinational companies, e.g. 70 per cent of Peru's manufacturing industry is located here
- 70 per cent of country's doctors and best health facilities
- Inhabitants have a life expectancy of 10 years longer than in rural areas
- On average schooling lasts 11 years as opposed to 5-6 years in rural areas
- The chances of higher education are three times greater than in the rest of the country. There are no universities outside Lima and many fewer secondary schools for children over the age of 14.

Negative factors for Peru

- Wealth created by mining and farming in other parts of Peru is spent in Lima
- Taxes are collected throughout the country but mainly spent on providing hospitals, schools and paved roads in Lima
- Lima exerts a magnetic attraction upon rural dwellers so that the countryside loses its brightest and best human resources.

Questions

1 a Describe the distribution of shanty towns in Lima.

  b Suggest reasons for growth in two different types of location.

2 Describe and explain the differences in appearance between Figures 4 and 5.

3 a Define urbanization.

  b Outline what Figures 1 and 2 indicate about rates of urbanization in Peru.

  c To what extent does this case study suggest that there are grounds for hope for a better quality of life from urbanization in LEDCs?

Problems of urbanization in LEDCs

In the cities, the economic problems caused by urbanization in LEDCs are largely to do with finding employment (for the individual) and funding services (for the governments). There are too few decent jobs in the formal sector. Power cuts are commonplace, large segments of many cities have no sewage systems and water supplies are erratic and periodically polluted.

The social problems are mainly to do with housing and its effects upon the health and welfare of those living in the slums, particularly for the young. The proportion of the urban population living in squatter and shanty settlements is high and increasing, as shown in Lima (page 194 Figure 2). There is also the demographic problem of an unbalanced population structure with the dominance of young people and high rates of natural increase, which give little time or space for attempting solutions. The increase in population is too fast. There are also too many public officials and the city administrations are often incompetent and corrupt.

Some of the health problems which affect everyone come from the lack of safe water supplies, but many also result from the scarcity of fresh air. Breathing in streets clogged with cars and buses, many of which are old with inefficient exhaust systems, has been compared to 'smoking between ten and twenty cigarettes a day'. Some cities are notorious, such as Mexico City, where both relief (in a basin surrounded by mountains) and climate (dry with many days of anticyclonic conditions and stagnant air) contribute, but the great size of the city and number of cars are the main factors responsible. Traffic is undeniably the main cause of polluted air in Bangkok where it has been calculated that the average driver spends 44 days a year in gridlock, costing the local economy hundreds of millions of dollars in lost productivity. This plus the fumes from factories create a lethal cocktail. Even if pollution controls upon manufacturing companies exist, they are rarely rigorously applied.

Given the scale of the human problems, there is little time and money left to devote to the environmental problems caused by urbanization. In some cities water supplies are being used up at an alarming rate. The aquifer upon which Mexico City is built has been so depleted that the ground has sunk 7.5m over the past century. Rivers and seas are the easy dustbins for human and industrial waste so that all signs of plant and fish life are extinguished. Suburban sprawl is a destroyer of natural habitats. The houses of the poor, loosely attached to the sides of steep slopes or located on the sides of rivers, are vulnerable to mass movements and floods. One such disaster happened in Caracas in Venezuela (Figure 2).

▶ **Figure 1** Bumper to bumper traffic in the centre of Santiago in Chile. There are 400 000 cars, 40 000 taxis and 13 000 buses on the roads each working day. When readings from the smog monitoring centres are high, vehicles without catalytic converters are restricted in the city according to the last number on the licence plate.

▼ **Figure 2** Disaster in Caracas in December 1999

Floods death toll may top 10 000

As many as 10 000 people may have been killed and 150 000 left homeless by Venezuela's devastating floods, which have triggered landslides, inundated the capital, Caracas, and swept away roads, buildings and shanty towns.

The unseasonal tropical downpours that have drenched the Andes and poured down its steep valleys to the northern Caribbean coast are the worst natural disaster to have hit the country for nearly 200 years. Many of the victims had fled the countryside in the past decade as low crop prices forced them to seek work in Caracas, setting up precarious homes on isolated hillsides and river banks.

For the inhabitants of middle and upper class Caracas, last week's tropical rainfall at first seemed an inconvenience, a curious phenomemon for the dry season.

For the shanty town dwellers in the *ranchos*, it was a disaster. Caracas, a city built along a valley, is dominated by the ridge of Mount Avila, the tail-end of the Andes. Their houses were attached to the hillsides and sides of the gorges. The rains dislodged vast tracts of earth which rolled in a tide of mud down on top of the *ranchos*. The streams changed from silver trickles to muddy brown torrents cascading down mountain sides, sweeping giant boulders, trees, houses and cars with them.

Adapted from *The Guardian*, 21 December 1999

FLOOD TOLL SOARS AS APPEAL LAUNCHED

Relief workers were struggling to count the dead, the injured, the missing and the homeless yesterday as the death toll from Venezuela's worst natural catastrophe this century threatened to reach 30 000.

Near the capital Caracas, flood survivors disobeyed repeated police requests to stay away from collapsed neighbour hoods. Stepping gingerly on to the roofs of buildings half-buried under mud, they returned to guard the remains of their homes and search for relatives among the debris.

Impoverished shanty town dwellers began building precarious bridges out of zinc roofing and floating furniture to cross the rivers that now flow in and around their former homes.

Hundreds of containers carrying luxury goods into Venezuela lost their moorings in Vargas port and have been systematically looted, sometimes with the help of the army. 'Just as well Chavez is in power," said one looter, as he fled into the back streets carrying a fridge on his back. "If it were any other president we would have been shot dead by now."

An army lieutenant, looking on helplessly, complained: "We are tired, we have no electricity and we are hungry. And on top of that we are expected to deal with looters?"

Venezuela
- *Naturally rich in natural resources – oil, natural gas, iron ore, bauxite, cheap HEP and productive farmland.*
- *Some good development indicators for a LEDC: life expectancy – 73 years literary – 92% of adults urban population – 87%.*
- *Great waste of oil revenues which support the over-large government sector and the wealthy.*

Adapted from *The Guardian*, 22 December 1999

◀ **Figure 3**

President Hugo Chavez blames previous governments

Venezuela's president lambasted 'corrupt politicians and planners' for allowing precarious shanty towns to be built in steep valleys and on slopes surrounding the capital, Caracas. Officials would block new construction in the worst affected areas he warned. He promised to re-house tens of thousands of refugees in the great plains on the edge of the Amazon forests. He announced an ambitious plan to clear out poor urban districts and move unemployed shanty dwellers, relocating thousands of families outside Caracas on land suitable for farming where they would receive homes and credits for agricultural work.

Adapted from *The Guardian*, 23 December 1999

Questions

1 Describe what happened in the disaster in Caracas in December 1999.

2 To what extent were the causes and consequences physical rather than human?

3 Overseas countries were not generous with their relief aid to Venezuela. Suggest reasons why.

▲ **Figure 4**

Benefits from urbanization

Despite all the unfavourable consequences of urbanization referred to so far, LEDCs have gained some benefits from urbanization. For the economy, urban activities are generally more productive than rural ones. More value is added, for example, by processing and manufacturing goods than by exporting them as raw materials directly from the rural areas. The big city is a focus for investment from both outside the country and within, which leads to modernization. For the inhabitants of the cities there is at least a chance of increasing personal wealth. Work in the urban informal sector usually brings in more income than does farming. Many shanty towns are desperate places in which to live, but for many of their inhabitants they are seen as places in which there are opportunities for economic and social advancement. Farmers living in the rural areas close to the big city often adopt a more commercial attitude and are more likely to practise intensive farming than those farmers located beyond easy reach of an urban market.

Every big city faces problems and there are plenty of traffic and pollution nightmares for the inhabitants of big cities in MEDCs as well. However, cities don't have to be unmanageable. Tokyo, easily the world's largest city, is economically successful and its services are efficiently organised. City authorities in MEDCs are focusing more than ever on improvements in the quality of life of their citizens. Air standards in Tokyo are improving as a result of improved anti-pollution technology applied to motor vehicles and investments in public transportation. The quality of life has risen for New Yorkers as a result of a booming American economy and a street clean up which targeted both garbage and crime. Something is even being done to reduce the effects of the legendary smog of Los Angeles (page 78).

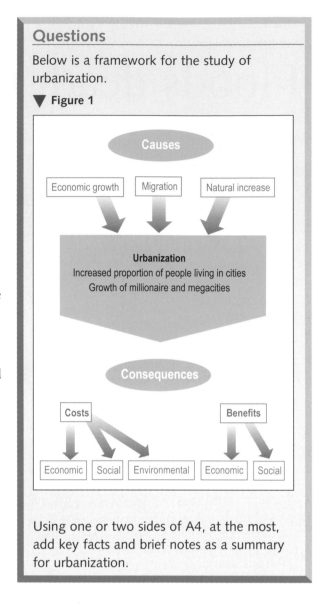

Questions

Below is a framework for the study of urbanization.

▼ Figure 1

Using one or two sides of A4, at the most, add key facts and brief notes as a summary for urbanization.

Suburbanization

To a large degree suburbanization has already been covered through the study of urbanization. Although some city growth is upwards for both commercial (page 183) and residential (Figure 3 page 185) purposes, the main effects of urbanization are spread outwards, increasing the extent of the built-up area. Rapidly growing cities in LEDCs are currently bursting at their seams as suburban sprawl swallows up farmland and destroys natural habitats. All of this typically happens in an unplanned manner. Once the inner urban areas have become so crowded that there is no more room, the sides of a main road on the fringes of the built-up area become the next most attractive location for squatters. The relentless arrival of more people from the countryside infills the areas between the main roads and extends the extent of the settled areas. The main factor responsible for suburbanization in these cities is increased numbers of people.

Cities in MEDCs show the results of past suburbanization. Their inner urban areas are small compared to the extensive suburban housing areas which surround them. In the 1930s in the UK there were fewer planning controls and urban growth typically took the form of ribbon development along the sides of main roads, which led to a distinctive style of housing which can still be seen along roads in most British cities today (Figure 3). Even by the 1940s suburbanization, which destroyed farmland and countryside, had become a source of concern to government and planners in the UK. This led to the creation of Green Belts – areas of open space and low density land use around existing urban areas where development would be strictly controlled.

▶ **Figure 2**
Self-help housing in Brasilia. Although a planned city, it is impossible to plan for the spontaneous rush of new arrivals that any development attracts in LEDCs. For most new in-migrants, the rents in formal housing are out of their reach anyway

▲ **Figure 3** The inter-war semi-detached house – one of the symbols of the beginnings of suburbanization of British cities in the 1930s

Suburbanization in the UK

Since 1950 in the UK, suburban expansion has speeded up and has been more planned. The 1950s and 60s were still the era of rented housing. Local authorities built council housing estates, for which the only places with sufficient land available were located on the suburban fringe. Since the 1970s the great move towards home ownership led to the private housing estate. To a large extent the move to the suburbs reflected a change in people's preferences for homes on the edge of countryside where more and cheaper land allowed gardens, lower density housing and greater open spaces. This became possible with improvements in transport in general, and greater private car ownership in particular, so that the typical urban inhabitant in the UK is now a suburban dweller. The rising importance and increasing dominance of road transport for moving both people and goods gave suburbanization an additional thrust. Edge of town is becoming the preferred location for many offices, factories and supermarkets where there is greater land availability, cheaper land, space for car parks and quicker access to major roads. In other words, greenfield sites, areas of open space which have not previously been built on, are being taken over for houses and businesses. This is enlarging the suburbs of most towns and cities in the UK.

Suburbanization is at its greatest where urban growth itself is greatest, which in the UK means around London and in the South East of England. The Green Belt policy was born in 1946 because of concern about the seemingly never-ending spread of Greater London. Despite great pressures upon it, the Green Belt policy has largely been upheld. However, future growth in south-east England is again a burning issue after a report published in October 1999 suggested that another 1.1 million homes in the region will be needed by 2016 (pages 262-3). Towns outside the most heavily populated and expensive parts of the south east are feeling the effects and undergoing suburbanization. One such town is Bicester set in rural Oxfordshire (pages 202-3).

Suburbanization is even taking place in those cities in the UK which are losing people. If anything the inner city areas in Liverpool, the urban area which has lost a greater proportion of its inhabitants than any other UK conurbation, are in such terminal decline that they have been deserted by people and companies to the suburbs and urban-rural fringes (page 208).

Suburbanization in the USA

However, the country which invented suburbs, and the one in which suburbanization has been taken to its extreme limits, is the USA. Henry Ford together with Detroit and assembly line car production for the mass market formed one of the pillars upon which the American dream of wealth and prosperity in the twentieth century was realized. Private car ownership arrived earlier in the USA than in Europe stifling the growth of public transport. In most cities outside of New York and Chicago, trams, trains and underground railways (metros) were not built before the car era had arrived. Without restrictive fixed rail links, roads and cars gave people choice about where to live and allowed suburbs to develop everywhere. Cheap gasoline, affluence and America's love of the car has led to cities in the suburbs. Places in which to work, shop, eat and be entertained need to be 'drive-in' or 'drive thru', which makes a suburban location essential.

▼ Figure 1

America transformed by the siren call of suburbs

A new generation of American mini-cities is rising in the suburbs. The dominant trend in American life today is not the revival of the old cities but the across-the-board decentralization of work and life to the new sprawling suburbs.

Four of the 25 fastest growing cities in America – Chandler, Scottsdale, Glendale and Mesa – are offshoots of just one city, Phoenix in Arizona. 'What we are calling cities now, we used to call suburbs.' These places are dominated by single-family homes, office parks and shopping malls.

All across America the 'burbs' are the new focus of city life. Once the typical city dwelling was multi-storey working class city apartment block – in the new cities it is a large detached house with a double garage and yard. Malls, accessible only by car, have taken the place of street corner shops and cafes. As the inner city industry has declined and the new hi-tech sector has boomed, jobs and services are increasingly moving out to the suburbs, too.

But the great unstated dimension of this suburban surge is race. The growth of the suburbs is a white phenomenon. In many of the eastern and older cities, the move to the suburbs during the 60s and 70s was characterized by 'white flight' – provoked by the fear of the black populations in the inner cities. In the 90s this is also a factor, but fuelled now by the Hispanic move to the inner cities. This helps to account for the rise of Phoenix in the sunbelt of Arizona.

Adapted from *The Guardian,* Autumn 1999

▲ **Figure 2**
Aerial view of Phoenix

▼ **Figure 3** Largest percentage increases
1996 – 1998 in cities with more
than 100 000 population

City	State	% increase
Henderson	Nevada	+21.5
Plano	Texas	+14.1
Pembroke Pines	Florida	+13.7
Cornoa	California	+13.4
Chandler	Arizona	+12.2

▶ **Figure 4**
Phoenix – now the
seventh largest city in the
USA thanks to the
numbers moving into its
'suburban cities'

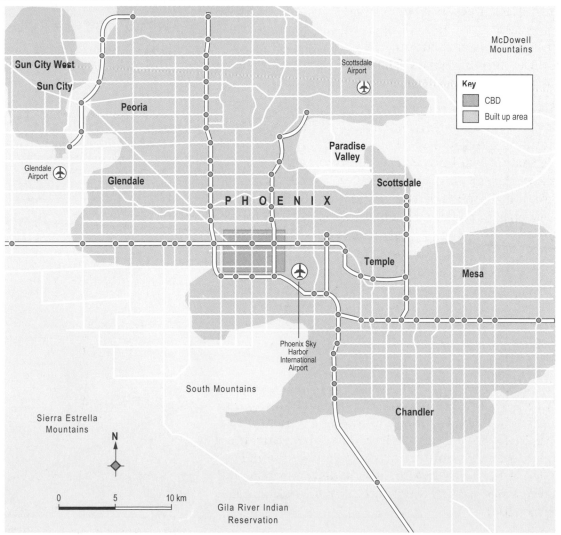

Case Study – Suburbanization in Bicester

Suburbanization

Case Study 2

in Bicester, Oxfordshire

▼ Figure 1

Suburban growth in progress in Bicester. The Bure Park development is located in the north west between Banbury Road and the railway. Between 1998 and 2001, 1 200 houses will have been built here.

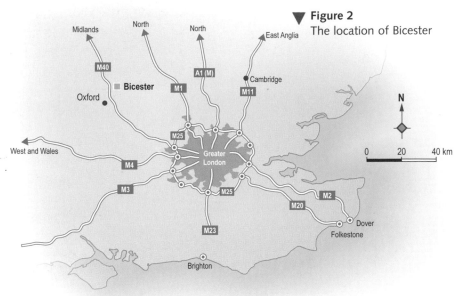

▼ Figure 2

The location of Bicester

▲ Figure 3 Ordnance Survey map of the area around Bicester. Scale 1:25 000

© Crown Copyright

Mondays to Fridays

Morning timetable

Bicester North	London Marylebone
0557	0704
0622	0730
0650	0748
0700	0808
0721	0829
0738	0832
0749	0859
0809	0905
0839	0936
0850	0954
0905	1008
0940	1045
1010	1116
1040	1146
1109	1216
1140	1240

◀ **Figure 4**
Train services from Bicester North to London Marylebone 1999

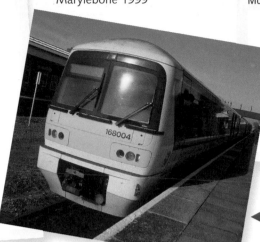

Mondays to Fridays

Morning timetable

Bicester North	London Marylebone
0606	0713
0647	0757
0708	0813
0749	0854
0854	1000
0949	1056
1049	1156
1149	1256

▲ **Figure 5**
Train services in 1994

◀ **Figure 6**
Chiltern Railways Turbo Train which can reach London in less than one hour

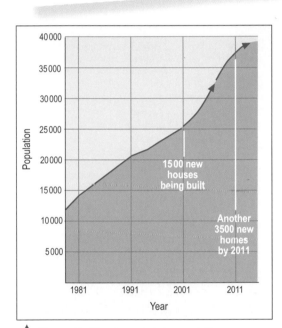

▲ **Figure 7** Bicester – total population

Text on graph:
- 1500 new houses being built
- Another 3500 new homes by 2011

OAKLAND GRANGE   BURE PARK   BICESTER

Oakland Grange is an exclusive development of 2, 3, 4 & 6 bedroom luxury homes. Situated just minutes away from the M40 Oakland Grange offers convenience in a semi-rural location.

Let the excitement begin at Bicester

2,3,4 & 6 Bedroom Homes Available from £82,995 to £273,995

For new home buyers year 2000 offers exciting times especially at Rowan Gardens in Bicester. Here you will find a brand new development of luxury detached houses just 5 minutes walk from the Market Square, and with easy access to the M40, the mainline railway station and the shopping village. Plans include the creation of a 'village green' in the centre of this exceptional location.

Visit it soon. Rowan Gardens is located just north west of the town centre between the schools and railway line west of the Banbury Road where it meets the main road from Oxford. Prices start from £93,000.

BARRATT
Britain's Premier House Builder

▲ **Figure 8** Extracts from estate agents' advertisements

Questions

1 a Describe the past and projected population growth of Bicester.

  b Identify two differences in train services from Bicester to London between 1994 and 1999.

  c i From the OS map, describe the human and physical features of the site and location of the Bure Park housing development.

  ii Suggest why this area was chosen for new house building.

2 Explain the past and projected urban growth in Bicester.

3 Two of the areas which are being studied as locations for the 3 500 new houses to be built by 2011 are named below.

  • **A** Between the village of Chesterton and the Oxford Road.
  • **B** On RAF land on the airfield, which is entirely used for pleasure flying such as gliding.

  a State some of the likely opinions of the residents of Bicester about building on each of these sites.

  b Give your views about which one may be the better choice.

4 Produce and complete a framework for the process of suburbanization as was done for urbanization on page 198.

Counter urbanization

Counter urbanization differs from suburbanization in that there is a clear break between areas of new growth and the pre-existing urban area. Suburbanization extends the size of the continuous urban area whereas counter urbanization leads to growth which is detached from it either in the rural-urban fringe or in the rural areas beyond. Of course by increasing the size of rural settlements and the numbers of people living in them, counter urbanization leads to suburbanization of the countryside. It certainly blurs the distinction between urban and rural, but it is not the growth of the city itself which is swallowing up the countryside.

In general counter urbanization occurs most in MEDCs. It first became a significant process during the 1960s in North America and Western Europe. There is a complex mix of social, economic, political and environmental factors behind its occurrence (Figure 1).

▼ **Figure 1** Factors favouring counter urbanization in MEDCs

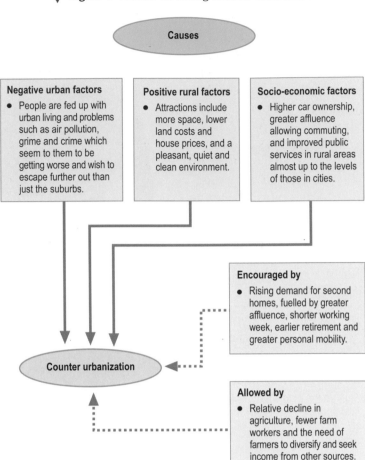

Causes

Negative urban factors
- People are fed up with urban living and problems such as air pollution, grime and crime which seem to them to be getting worse and wish to escape further out than just the suburbs.

Positive rural factors
- Attractions include more space, lower land costs and house prices, and a pleasant, quiet and clean environment.

Socio-economic factors
- Higher car ownership, greater affluence allowing commuting, and improved public services in rural areas almost up to the levels of those in cities.

Encouraged by
- Rising demand for second homes, fuelled by greater affluence, shorter working week, earlier retirement and greater personal mobility.

Counter urbanization

Allowed by
- Relative decline in agriculture, fewer farm workers and the need of farmers to diversify and seek income from other sources.

Counter urbanization is more than just the outflow of people from urban areas into the country who then commute into the city each working day. Jobs have moved as well as a result of de-industrialization. Conurbations lost over 400 000 jobs in the fifteen years between 1981 and 1996, most in manufacturing. Rural areas and small towns gained more than a million jobs in the same period (Figure 2). In some cases it was companies following their workers in to the countryside. In others, improvements in technology have allowed companies freedom of location, the like of which they have not previously known. For the first time since the Industrial Revolution technological change is allowing people working in rural areas to compete on equal terms with those in cities. A person can operate a home work-station in a village and share in global communications. In other words workplaces have been decentralized.

Counter urbanization affects the form and layout of rural settlements. Modern housing estates attach themselves to the edges of settlements and small industrial units or estates may grow up along the sides of the road leading in and out of the village.

Open areas within are infilled, old properties are modernized and some agricultural buildings such as barns are converted into homes. It also forces socio-economic changes on the village as the newcomers, whether commuters or second homers, transfer their urban wealth and attitudes with them. The interests of the newcomers often sit uncomfortably with the rural interests of the local community. What makes it worse for many locals is that village growth is actually accompanied by a reduction in village services; the newcomers have the wealth and mobility to continue using the urban services.

 Symptoms of decline in rural areas in 2000:
- *The numbers working in farming have halved since 1945*
- *Three quarters of rural parishes no longer have a daily bus*
- *Up to half of villages no longer have a school*
- *One quarter of villages are now without a post office*
- *During the last 10 years over 1000 shops, 500 post offices and 100 churches and chapels closed down in villages.*

Slowing rates of urbanization in LEDCs

While urbanization is still dominant in LEDCs, settlement processes and patterns don't remain static for any length of time because people keep moving. City migrants keep drifting back to their home villages and rural communities. Some return out of disillusionment with city life, but many others intended only to stay temporarily. Some have made money and take it back to improve the quality of rural life for themselves and their families. What happens in MEDCs has the habit of happening in LEDCs after a time lag. Rates of urbanization in many LEDCs are slowing down. As improved services and paved roads reach rural areas, a more positive view of rural areas in LEDCs may emerge promoting higher levels of counter urbanization.

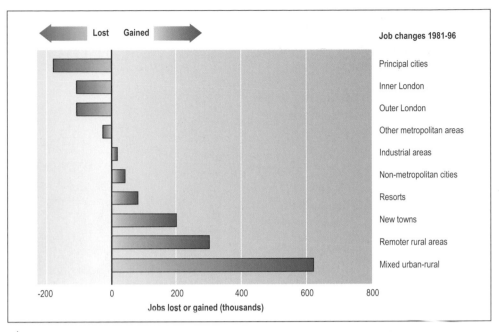

▲ **Figure 2**   Moving to the country – job changes in England 1981-96

▼ **Figure 3**   Bucknell, Shropshire
  a Villages can be pleasant places in which to live
  b However the village shop has closed. It has been converted into a house and only a small part is left to function as the post office.
  c Infilling. New houses are being built on farm land located between different parts of the village.

Village suburbanization:

Case Study

Urchfont, Wiltshire

Urchfont is an attractive village of about 1 100 inhabitants located on the edge of the rolling chalk hills of the Wiltshire Downs. In 1950 there were ten or eleven farms employing dozens of farm workers. There was no piped water in the village until 1956. Today one quarter of its population is over 65 years old compared with only 16 per cent of the population of Wiltshire as a whole.

▶ **Figure 1** The duck pond in the middle of Urchfont – just what urban dwellers would expect to find in a country village

The rural aspect of country life is currently suffering. Many farmers are facing ruin as agriculture, particularly animal farming, faces its most severe recession since the 1930s. In Urchfont the farmer at Rookery Farm finally sold his herd of dairy cattle in 1999. Knights Leaze Farm was once mainly a dairy farm but the farmer could not survive on the income from milk. Most of this farmer's income now comes from contract work such as farm construction, fencing and baling straw. This employs thirteen people, a significant number, but there has been some opposition in the village to their heavy lorries and machinery – 'We do get a bit of aggravation from the village,' says the owner. 'It's mostly the newcomers.'

The urban aspect of country life is thriving. About 7 per cent of the houses in Urchfont are second homes. One quarter of the permanent residents have arrived within the last five years. Some are self-employed and work from the village. For example, the couple renting Manor Farm House are their own bosses and can do most of their work at home. They only need to travel up to London on the high speed train a few times a week. This reflects one of the changing patterns of work. The workers have brought more young people into the village which has helped to revitalize the primary school. However, house prices have rocketed. Small cottages, which used to be within the reach of first-time local buyers, now sell for between £100 000 and £150 000. In the harsh farming climate property is becoming an increasingly significant source of income to farmers. In a dramatic turnaround farmhouses can now be worth more than the farm land. One farmhouse is rented out at nearly £2 000 per month to people from London in search of a better life.

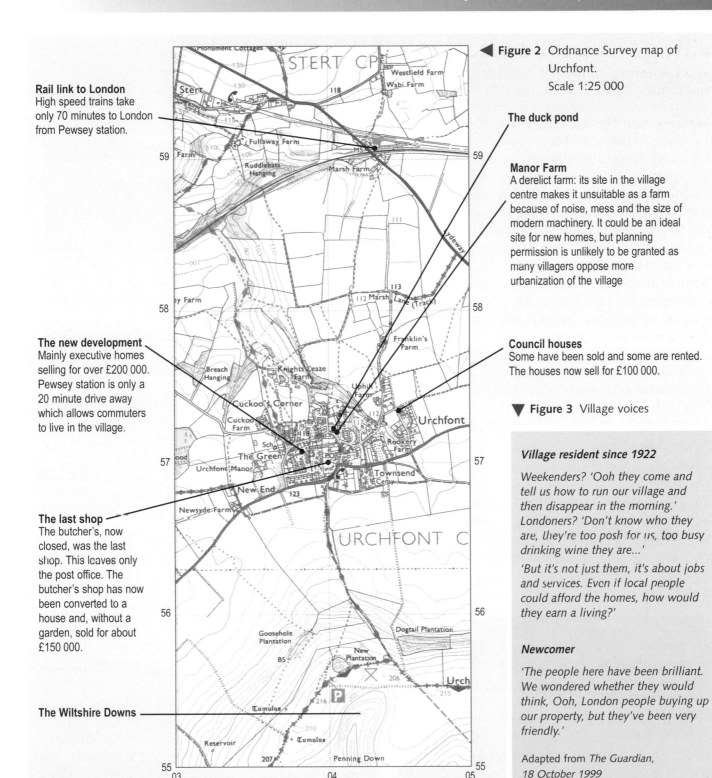

◀ **Figure 2** Ordnance Survey map of Urchfont.
Scale 1:25 000

Rail link to London
High speed trains take only 70 minutes to London from Pewsey station.

The duck pond

Manor Farm
A derelict farm: its site in the village centre makes it unsuitable as a farm because of noise, mess and the size of modern machinery. It could be an ideal site for new homes, but planning permission is unlikely to be granted as many villagers oppose more urbanization of the village

The new development
Mainly executive homes selling for over £200 000. Pewsey station is only a 20 minute drive away which allows commuters to live in the village.

Council houses
Some have been sold and some are rented. The houses now sell for £100 000.

▼ **Figure 3** Village voices

The last shop
The butcher's, now closed, was the last shop. This leaves only the post office. The butcher's shop has now been converted to a house and, without a garden, sold for about £150 000.

The Wiltshire Downs

Village resident since 1922

Weekenders? 'Ooh they come and tell us how to run our village and then disappear in the morning.' Londoners? 'Don't know who they are, they're too posh for us, too busy drinking wine they are...'

'But it's not just them, it's about jobs and services. Even if local people could afford the homes, how would they earn a living?'

Newcomer

'The people here have been brilliant. We wondered whether they would think, Ooh, London people buying up our property, but they've been very friendly.'

Adapted from *The Guardian*,
18 October 1999

Questions

1 a Describe the attractions of Urchfont that have encouraged counter urbanization there.

b Outline the changes in Urchfont as a result of it having become a suburbanized village using the headings:
i housing; **ii** employment; **iii** population structure; and **iv** social factors.

2 a Make a table of the costs and benefits for Urchfont's change from a rural to an urbanized village.

b Comment upon their relative strength and significance.

Re-urbanization

During the 1990s an average of 1 700 people a week were leaving the major cities in the UK, which means that re-urbanization is far from being the dominant process. The old northern industrial towns such as Glasgow and Liverpool are still shrinking and losing a significant proportion of their populations. However, the population in Central London is growing again after decades of falling numbers. The same trend is visible in New York. Suburbanization, counter urbanization and the transfers of jobs to the 'Sun Belt' of the south and west led to a great outflow of people and employment in the 1970s (Figure 1). The city was again threatened in the early 1990s by people moving out. In New York in 2000 life is considered to be better than it has been for decades. Murders had fallen to their lowest levels in thirty years making New York the safest large city in the USA. A 1999 survey of professionals in fast-growing industries such as marketing, advertising and finance ranked New York as the most desirable US city in which to work.

Indeed what re-urbanization is all about is the return of high status and high income groups back into the inner and central areas of cities in MEDCs. It is closely linked to the process of gentrification. (Figure 2). It is not exclusive to cities in MEDCs, but the rich have not abandoned the inner zones of cities in LEDCs to the same extent as in the UK and USA (Figure 3).

▼ **Figure 1** Employment in New York

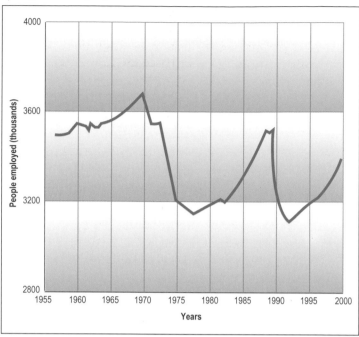

Gentrification

A process which occurs in inner city areas where old housing, dilapidated and badly in need of repair, is bought by middle class and wealthy people who have the money to modernize and improve the properties. As a result the residential status of the area increases.

▼ **Figure 3** Some of the most exclusive and expensive residential neighbourhoods are located on the edges of the city centre in Georgetown, Malayasia. They have not lost the high status established in colonial times.

▲ **Figure 2** Brooklyn Heights overlooking the East River and downtown Manhattan has become a fashionable place to live again. It is an example of gentrification.

Pockets of high status housing have continued to exist in some inner-city areas, where there is a highly favoured environment and the location has not lost its prestige. Although these include provincial locations such as the Crescent in Bath or cathedral closes in Salisbury and Lincoln, the majority are in London. Mayfair, Belgravia, Kensington and Chelsea have never lost their status. When you analyse their locations on a map, they have wonderful positions in central London, which boasts the widest range and greatest numbers of employment opportunities, of shops and stores and of cultural and sporting attractions. The closeness of large parks, such as Hyde Park, St. James's Park and Regents Park, helps to reduce the feeling of being in the middle of the UK's largest city.

Now that re-urbanization is gaining pace in London, the areas named above have become even more desirable and therefore more expensive.

In January 2000 estate agents reported that it was already difficult to find a family home for less than one million pounds in any of the four areas. Fashionable, and therefore increasingly pricey, places to live are rising close to them. One is Notting Hill (publicized by the film); another is Islington (the home of the Blair family before moving to Downing Street); a third is Primrose Hill.

One of the triggers for the current wave of re-urbanization in the UK was the total redevelopment of the London Docklands. Empty dock basins such as St. Katherine's dock were made into marinas, derelict land was occupied by national newspapers attracted by more space for building works equipped with modern technology, and decaying warehouses were gutted and converted into luxury apartments overlooking the Thames. The visual symbol is the Canary Wharf tower, an office block built as overspill for financial companies from 'the City of London'.

▼ **Figure 4** Locations in London in which re-urbanization is happening.

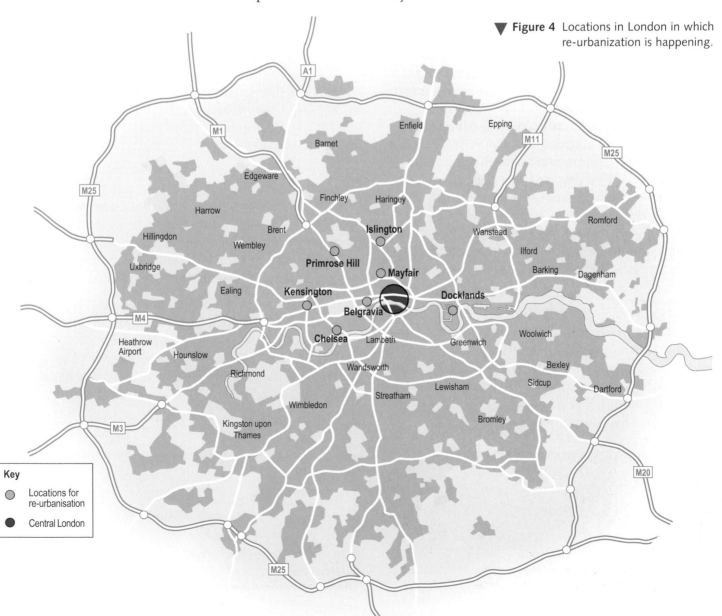

▼ **Figure 1** Two views of the inner city in the east end of London. One of the consequences of re-urbanization is that wealth and deprivation may sit uncomfortably close to each other.

The London Docklands model has been successfully copied in many other cities with defunct docks. The Albert Dock in Liverpool is perhaps the best known, but there's the Quayside in Newcastle, Salford Quays in Greater Manchester and the Marina in Hull. Waterfront locations are particularly attractive and form a focus around which the new developments can be planned. For this reason the Brindley Place redevelopment in Birmingham, without sea docks, is based upon canals. Whether by gradual gentrification (one house and one street at a time) or by total redevelopment (of potentially attractive dock and canal basins), there are two main trends supporting re-urbanization:

- Nearness to place of work, avoiding the nightmare of commuting. Although many of the lower paid occupations in retail and services have been decentralized to the urban-rural fringe, and are close to their workforce who dwell in the suburbs, the high status service sectors - notably finance and marketing, which employ well educated, highly skilled personnel - have stayed in city centres. Many are in the 20-30s age range and like the leisure and entertainment opportunities and lively atmosphere of the big city. What's more they have the money with which to enjoy it.

- Supportive attitudes of both city authorities and government. Local councils do not want to see their city centres decay and die. They perceive some of the wider advantages to be derived from multi-purpose redevelopment schemes, not only in bringing in more jobs but also promoting new types of employment, notably in tourism.

The government (and many others) prefers the use of brownfield sites (those which have previously been used for urban land uses) for new developments. This is why governments have financed Enterprise Zones and initiatives such as 'City Challenge'.

ℹ️ *Urban renaissance*
This was the government 'buzz' term of 1999. Re-urbanization is part of it because it also increases the proportion of new building on brownfield rather than greenfield sites.

Questions

Investigation

Identify an example of re-urbanization in a town or city near you using the headings:
a location; **b** original characteristics; **c** changes; and **d** consequences.

Re-urbanization of

Case Study

Greater Manchester

A Salford Quays

▲ **Figure 2** Salford quays

The dock basins and surrounding land, left vacant after the decline and final closure of the port of Manchester, have been the focus of a comprehensive inner urban re-development since the Development Plan was produced in 1985. The resulting land uses are mixed and varied:
- residential
- commercial offices
- leisure and recreation (water sports, cinemas, restaurants and eating places).

In October 1999 the tram link from the Greater Manchester system was completed which has greatly improved access. In April 2000 the Lowry Centre (named after the artist, who painted matchstick men and women in industrial scenes) opened leading to a great increase in visitors.

▼ **Figure 3** The Manchester tram

B Castlefield

During the 1970s this inner city area just to the west and north of Manchester city centre was being deserted by industries leaving behind large derelict and decaying warehouses and factories, abandoned canals, and unsightly railway viaducts. Due to the wealth of historical, industrial remains in Castlefield, Manchester City Council declared it a conservation area in 1979. Since then an investment programme, funded predominantly by Central Manchester Development Corporation, Manchester City Council and commercial investors, has turned Castlefield into a bustling area of commercial, residential and leisure developments, but with a specific focus upon tourism, which attracts over two million visitors a year. The top tourist attraction in the area is the Granada Studios Tour, but there are also museums and numerous outdoor events. The waterside offers a scenic location for restaurants, cafe bars, towpath trails and luxury apartments (Figure 4).

▲ **Figure 4** An attractive canal side, deep in the heart of Manchester

Settlement structure

- Land use patterns in suburbanized villages
- Land use patterns in urban areas

Land use patterns in suburbanized villages

The first site of a settlement was invariably well chosen, taking into account factors such as local relief, water supply, freedom from flooding, shelter, aspect and in some cases special factors such as bridging point or defence. Many different village forms (or layouts) developed, some clustered and some loose knit. Often there was a focal point such as village green, pond, crossroads or bridge and the church was built close by.

When growth occurred away from the original core, there was nothing more natural than that it should follow the sides of the roads out of the village. At first this took the form of new houses being attached to the edges of the core, which gave spaces between the roads that could then be infilled. Greater growth along the roads led to lines of houses, one deep on one or both sides of the road, known as ribbon development. This is the stage that most villages reached before being affected by suburbanization.

Suburbanization speeds up the rate of growth. The pressures from growth can be seen in the village core as old houses and cottages are renovated and modernized and, in some cases, extended. Old buildings, which have lost their rural or former uses, such as barns and chapels, are converted into houses. Small empty spaces are filled in by new houses. These changes maintain or increase the high building density in the core. Although growth by ribbon development comes next, the largest areas of new growth are inevitably around the edges where more space is available. Modern housing estates, with their typical mixture of bungalows, detached and semi-detached houses, occupy and fill up the land between the roads. These sometimes include some expensive, exclusive estates, particularly if the village is located in a scenic area within easy commuting distance of a large city. Beyond the edge of the village there may be outliers where newcomers have taken over what was formerly a working farm or gained planning permission to convert or add one or two new homes. The five land use elements (core, infills and conversions, ribbon growth along roads, housing estates and outliers) can be summarized on a model for a suburbanized village.

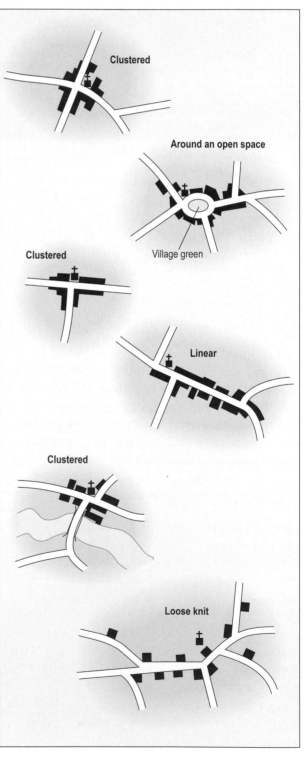

▼ **Figure 1** Examples of village forms

▼ **Figure 2** Model of land use patterns in a suburbanized village

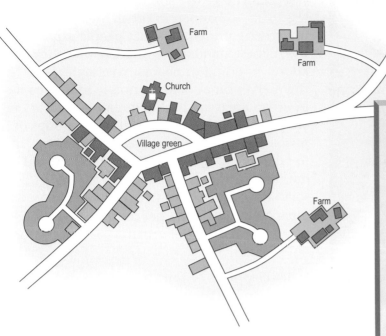

Key
- Village core
- Infills and conversions
- Ribbon growth along roads
- Housing estates
- Outlier of growth

Questions

1 From the OS map on page 207, describe **a** the form and layout and **b** the site and location of Urchfont.

2 To what extent do land uses in Urchfont match the model of a suburbanized village?

3 Suggest reasons why some villages are **a** less suburbanized and **b** more suburbanized than Urchfont.

Investigation

4 Choose a village in your region.
   a Undertake a survey of land uses.
   b Describe any characteristics which suggest suburbanization.
   c Suggest reasons for the relative amount of suburbanization discovered.

Land use patterns in urban areas

Urban land uses include productive uses such as housing, shops, offices, factories, transport, parks and other open spaces for recreation, as well as non-productive uses, such as wasteland and derelict buildings. Of these, housing covers far and away the greatest area of land; therefore, despite being places for work, shopping and leisure, the main urban function is residential. Particular land uses tend to be concentrated in different parts of the city. This means that it is possible to recognize spatial patterns of land uses within any urban area, from which urban zones can be distinguished. An urban zone is an area in which there are similarities in land uses within it which give it a common function and which make it distinctive and different from other zones which surround it.

Therefore, land uses are segregated. For example, commerce and retailing are concentrated in the CBD, because of tradition, good access, prestige and ability of businesses to afford the high rents and rates. The great height and density of its buildings gives this zone a striking appearance distinct from that of the rest of the city. Skyscrapers pinpoint its location in most big cities (Figure 3). Manufacturing industry gathers in zones where favourable factors for its location are concentrated such as around docks and canals in inner urban areas in the past and on the fringes of urban areas near motorways today.

▼ **Figure 3** 'Downtown' Chicago, the home of the city centre skyscraper

▲ **Figure 1** Substantial town houses in Harlem dating from the time when it was one of New York's most sought after residential areas for whites. Today it is a black residential district.

In villages, people of different status and wealth live together, which is still largely the case in a village the size of Urchfont. This is less likely to happen in urban areas where the underlying principle is that people aspire to the highest standard of housing that they can afford. In doing so people have segregated themselves on a socio-economic basis. People in urban areas are highly mobile so that there are processes of invasion (influx of groups of people), succession (another group moves in to take the place of those who have moved out) and segregation (people of the same socio-economic status live together in separate groups). The net result is that there is not one residential urban zone in any city but several.

Inner-city areas of the UK and the USA exemplify the trend towards segregation. Before effective methods of urban transport existed, the wealthy lived in the centre. The trend for the rich to move out to the outer suburbs and surrounding countryside began in late Victorian times in the UK. The working industrial town was not a pretty sight and offered what would now be described as a 'low quality of life' for its inhabitants (see Figure 2 page 187). The wealthy were replaced by the poor. Without the resources to keep up the properties and maintain the area's appearance, with time deterioration occurred. The arrival of concentrated cells of minority groups with shared characteristics, such as religion, culture and language, that were different from those of the majority, increased the amount of segregation in the inner cities. Ghettoes developed where particular ethnic minorities were concentrated such as blacks in Harlem. In the USA this led to the flight of whites to the suburbs already mentioned under suburbanization (page 200).

◄ **Figure 2** A view of Harlem which more people would recognize as the inner zone of a big city

Urban models

Models are attempts to summarize spatial patterns of land uses and functions within cities. While collecting data about social conditions in Chicago in the 1920s Burgess was able to identify and summarize the structure of that city. Chicago was a suitable city for study because the rapid growth of its industries was attracting migrants from within America and from the rest of the world. The more generalized Burgess model which was developed from the study of Chicago produced the familiar circular pattern of urban zones from CBD outwards, in which the residential areas, which fill most of the urban area, are differentiated mainly according to their residents' wealth.

 Advantages of models
- *Complex patterns are simplified allowing easier understanding and explanation.*
- *A framework for studies of cities in other regions and countries is provided.*
- *Comparisons (similarities and differences) between places are made possible.*

Disadvantages of models
- *Assumptions are made which may not reflect the real world, such as uniform physical and/or human conditions over wide areas.*
- *General conclusions over-emphasize the characteristics of the places where the studies are undertaken.*
- *Characteristics that are identified can change significantly with time.*

Clearly the same model does not match every city, but the Burgess model provided a starting point and proved capable of being refined and adapted. One variation was the Hoyt model in which sectors were superimposed over Burgess's concentric rings. Two slightly different ideas were incorporated within it. One was that superior transport routes pulled the growth of the city in some directions more than others. The second was that residential zones, once established, grew more and extended the zone outwards into a sector of similar residential quality.

▼ **Figure 3** The Burgess model (1924)

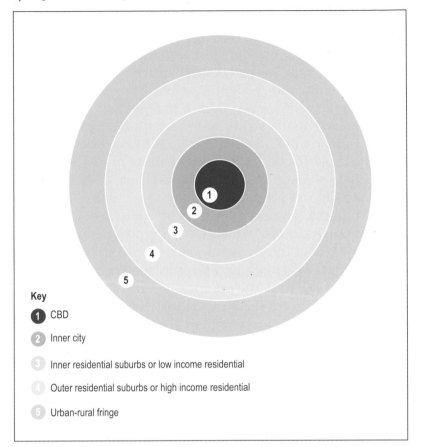

Key
1 CBD
2 Inner city
3 Inner residential suburbs or low income residential
4 Outer residential suburbs or high income residential
5 Urban-rural fringe

▼ **Figure 4** The Hoyt model (1939)

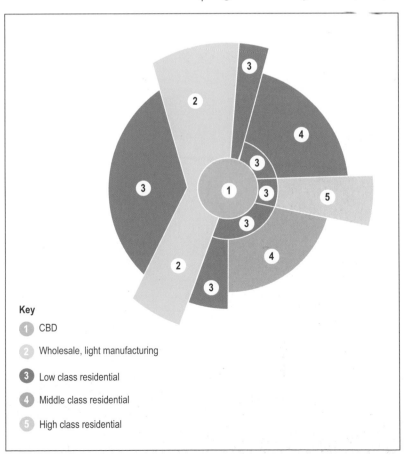

Key
1 CBD
2 Wholesale, light manufacturing
3 Low class residential
4 Middle class residential
5 High class residential

Adapting models to the UK

The models of Burgess and Hoyt were based upon North American cities. While many of the settlement processes leading to the pattern of land uses were the same in the UK, particularly suburbanization and residential segregation, there were some key differences. One of the most important was that a significant proportion of the houses in many British cities was built by councils for rent. Large council estates are a feature of the outer suburbs. Some are enormous: Wythenshawe in south Manchester was built to house more than 100 000 people. These took low-income families into the outer suburbs, which went against one of the basic ideas of the Burgess model. Mann, who used the ideas of Burgess and Hoyt to apply a model to UK cities, also took the opportunity to make an allowance for the effects of prevailing westerly winds, a physical factor which applies throughout the UK. Before Mann finalized his model, Robson tried to apply the American models to the layout and land uses found in Sunderland. Basic physical differences, coastal position and the River Wear passing through had to be taken into account. The patterns of residential segregation identified by Robson are shown in Figure 2. Robson found that a

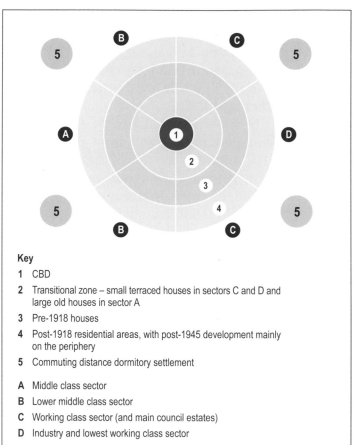

▼ **Figure 1** The Mann model (1965)

Key

1 CBD

2 Transitional zone – small terraced houses in sectors C and D and large old houses in sector A

3 Pre-1918 houses

4 Post-1918 residential areas, with post-1945 development mainly on the periphery

5 Commuting distance dormitory settlement

A Middle class sector

B Lower middle class sector

C Working class sector (and main council estates)

D Industry and lowest working class sector

mixture of concentric circles and sectors which identified the urban zones formed the framework for a land use model specific to Sunderland. One thing to note is the great dominance of areas of low and medium class housing. Heavy industries such as shipbuilding and engineering were still the big employers in 1963, hence the large areas lining the river banks and along the coast were designated as industrial. For many years Sunderland had the highest proportion of its population living in council houses in all English towns. This serves to remind us that all places are unique, which is why generalized models need to be adapted to suit individual cases.

Sometimes it is the town's function which exerts a powerful influence over its form. An example of this is the coastal tourist resort in the UK. Look at the shape of Bournemouth's built-up area (Figure 3). Its greatest length is along the shoreline because the beach, sea and coastal scenery are the main reasons why visitors go there. Human additions, such as the promenade which runs right along the sea front and piers, serve to enhance the natural attractions. The CBD, mainly in square 0891, extends down to the sea front where the main pier and international conference centre are found.

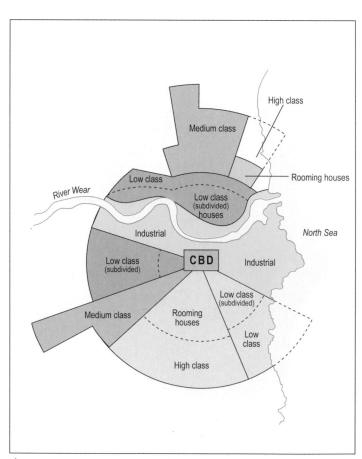

▲ **Figure 2** Robson's model for Sunderland (1963)

The area west of the centre in Westbourne and West Cliff appears to be the usual heavily built-up inner-city zone. However, here it is one of the main zones of hotels and boarding houses (Figure 4). The inner urban area east of the town centre in squares 0991 and 1091 is large hotels and expensive apartments. There is not much sign of inner-city decay and poverty here (Figure 5). Further inland in suburban Bournemouth the land use pattern is more like that of any other town in the UK.

▼ **Figure 3** Ordnance Survey map of Bournemouth. Scale 1:50 000

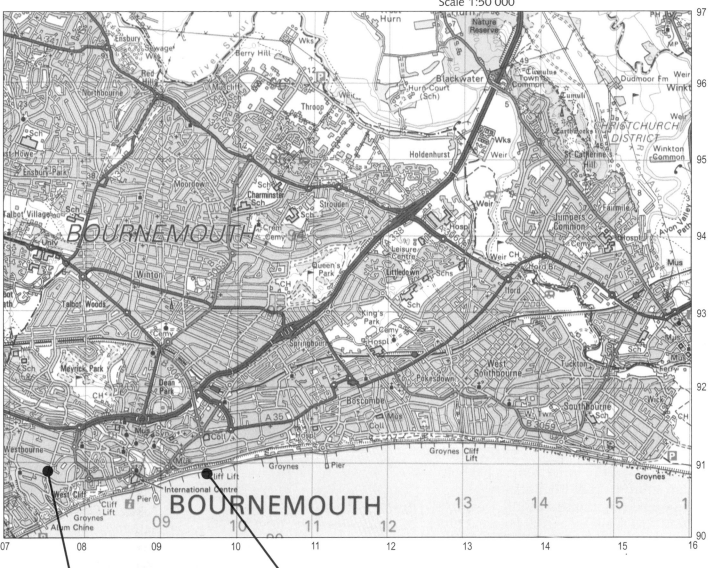

▲ **Figure 4** Inner-city zone dominated by hotels and guest houses

◀ **Figure 5** Inner-city zone of large hotels and luxury apartments enjoying good sea views from the top of East Cliff

Urban models for cities in LEDCs

Satisfactory models of city structure are less easy to create in LEDCs than for cities in the UK and USA for two main reasons:

1 Settlement histories are more varied. In many cities in LEDCs a colonial power attached its own ideas and styles to a pre-existing city so that there are many more combinations of city design. The walled *Medina* within North African cities is a maze of narrow streets and alleys in contrast to the spacious streets laid out by French colonists in the European zone outside the walls. Latin American cities have a different appearance. There the Spaniards imposed grid-iron plans irrespective of relief and layout of the pre-colonial settlement, as in the centre of Lima (Figure 4).

2 Recent city growth has been rapid and unplanned. There are large areas of informal housing in and around many large cities due to the inability of governments to provide sufficient services and housing. Although at its most extensive on the city edges, it occurs throughout the urban area.

Those who have attempted to create models for cities in LEDCs have done so for particular world regions, such as West Africa or South East Asia. A model can be put together based upon Burgess and Hoyt but has to take into account the two main ways in which the distribution of land uses is most frequently different. Firstly the inner zone is likely to contain some areas of high quality accommodation occupied by the wealthy. Much of this is a legacy from colonial times when the zone housed the wealthy landowners, traders and administrators. Instead of having fled in face of the mass urban invasions of the poor, they have built high wire fences around their properties and have employed security guards. Secondly the general rule is that the quality of housing decreases with distance from the centre, which is the exact opposite of the situation in many cities in MEDCs. The most primitive of shacks built by the most recent arrivals in the city are found on the outer edge of the built-up area; further inside the city, the greater age of the housing areas may have allowed for better services and more permanent buildings (see page 193).

Figure 1 Model for a city in a LEDC

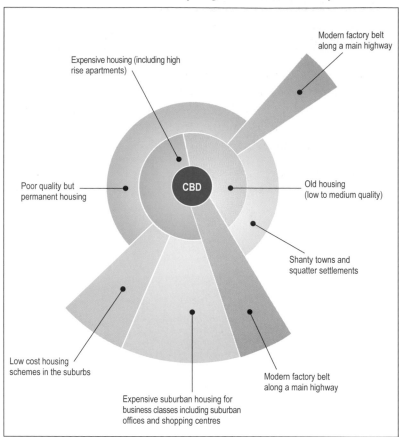

Expensive housing (including high rise apartments)

Modern factory belt along a main highway

Poor quality but permanent housing

CBD

Old housing (low to medium quality)

Shanty towns and squatter settlements

Low cost housing schemes in the suburbs

Expensive suburban housing for business classes including suburban offices and shopping centres

Modern factory belt along a main highway

Figure 2 The cathedral occupying one side of the main square, the Plaza de Armas, in Lima. The CBD is the easiest zone to identify in all cities, whether in MEDCs or LEDCs.

Settlement structure

Case Study of a city in the LEDW: Lima, Peru

Examining the map summarizing Lima's land use zones (Figure 3), you can see that it bears only a passing resemblance to the model in Figure 1. The grid-iron street plan in the centre (Figure 4) was laid out by the Spaniards who founded Lima as the capital for the whole of their empire within South America. Callao was the chief port on the coast. Urban growth in recent decades has produced one continuous built-up area. The houses of the rich are concentrated in the southern suburbs, near to the coast, particularly in San Isidro and Miraflores. Here the mansions and greenery form a stark contrast to the gloomy greyness in central Lima, where most buildings, whether publicly or privately owned, convey the feeling of having seen better days.

▼ **Figure 3** Urban land use zones in Lima

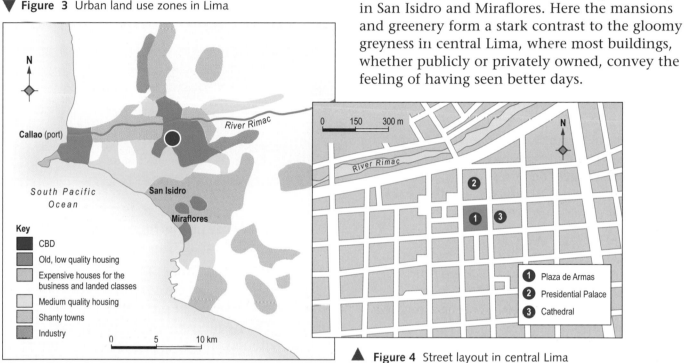

Figure 4 Street layout in central Lima

Questions

1 Refer to the OS map of Bicester on page 202.
a In a frame, **i** mark on key locators such as the railway line and main roads; **ii** divide Bicester up into its urban zones – town centre, industry, older residential and newer residential.
b Justify the divisions you have made.
c Identify and comment upon the land uses in Bicester's urban-rural fringe.

2 Refer to the OS map of Sunderland on page 265.
a Using this and Figure 2 on page 216, draw a sketch map showing the main urban zones in Sunderland.
b What are **i** the similarities and **ii** the differences between the pattern of urban zones in Sunderland and that of the urban models of Burgess and Hoyt?
c To what extent are the land uses shown in Sunderland's urban-rural fringe on the OS map typical of those expected to be found in this zone in a British city?

3 Refer to the OS map of Bournemouth on page 217.

a Outline how physical factors have influenced the site and the shape of the built up area of Bournemouth.
b In what ways is the settlement structure of a coastal tourist resort in the UK **i** similar and **ii** different compared with other towns and cities in the UK?

4 a State and suggest reasons for the distinctive features of the settlement structure of Lima.

Investigation

b **i** Outline the settlement structure of another city in a different LEDC.
ii Compare your city with Lima.

Extended prose

5 Write a comparative account of inner cities in MEDCs and shanty towns in LEDCs.

Size and spacing
of settlements

- Central places and the spacing of settlements
- Rank-size rule and urban primacy

Central places and the spacing of settlements

The geography of settlement can be viewed in another way by looking at settlements as central places. A central place provides goods and services to the area around it. This forms the settlement's sphere of influence. The range of a good or service is the maximum distance that people are prepared to travel in order to obtain it. How far people are prepared to travel largely depends upon the nature of the good or service – whether it is high order or low order.

Settlements or central places are organized in a hierarchy. It is easiest to base this on population size, although the population values used on Figure 1 are only approximate. Figure 1 shows a positive correlation between settlement size and the number of goods and services provided (i.e. the bigger the settlement the greater the number of functions). There is also an increased proportion of high order retail outlets. The sphere of influence of London is the whole of the UK. Some goods and services are only available in London such as central

ⓘ High and low order

	Goods	Service providers
High order ↑	Cars Furniture	Major shopping centre University
Low order	Newspapers Bread and milk	Primary school Corner shop

government services or sporting events like Wimbledon and football Cup Finals.

The threshold for an outlet selling goods or services in a central place is the minimum number of people needed to buy or use it in order to make the outlet profitable. The frequency with which a good or service is required and its cost mainly determine threshold. For example, many items of furniture are expensive and are only bought occasionally. Therefore the threshold population for a furniture store needs to be large to ensure profitability.

▶ **Figure 1**
Settlement hierarchy

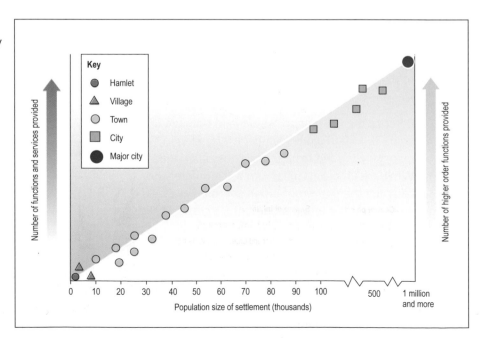

In MEDCs there have been many changes in consumer patterns for buying goods in recent years. Local and low order service centres are being used less and less so that the number of these outlets is decreasing. The number of places offering higher order functions have increased. There has been a marked rise in numbers of large out-of-town and regional shopping centres, encouraged by increased personal mobility and social changes in patterns of work and lifestyle. These are referred to in greater detail on pages 258 and 259.

ⓘ *Cristaller's theory of spacing of settlements*
The theoretical background for a study of the spacing of settlements, or central places, was provided by Christaller. He recognized that the ideal size for the trading area of a central place was circular, but this led to overlap. Therefore he modified the shape into a hexagon. Figure 2 shows the pattern of trading areas which he called k = 3, where k is the number of places dependent on the central place of the next highest order. In Figure 2 the trade area of the town, which is the one and only third order central place shown, is three times larger than that of each village, which is a second order central place. Six villages are shown within the trade area of the town. Then the trade area of each village is three times larger than that of each hamlet, which is only a first order central place. Twenty four hamlets are shown within the trade area of the town. As with all model makers, Christaller made assumptions, which may not apply in many parts in the real world. Christaller's model works best in rural areas of low lying and uniform relief.

ⓘ *Reilly's breaking point between two settlements*
Reilly's law of retail gravitation is a theoretical way of estimating the number of people likely to use a central place, such as a shopping centre. The breaking point between two towns (A and B) can be estimated by using the following formula:

$$Db = \frac{Dab}{1 + \sqrt{\dfrac{Pa}{Pb}}}$$

where Db = the breaking point between towns A and B
Dab = the distance between towns A and B
Pa = the population of town A (the larger town) and
Pb = the population of town B.

Reilly assumes that the larger the town, the stronger the attraction, which may well be safer than assuming people shop logically and use the centre closest to them to obtain the goods they want.

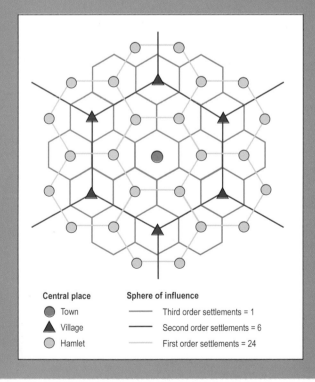

Central place
🔴 Town
🔺 Village
⚪ Hamlet

Sphere of influence
—— Third order settlements = 1
—— Second order settlements = 6
—— First order settlements = 24

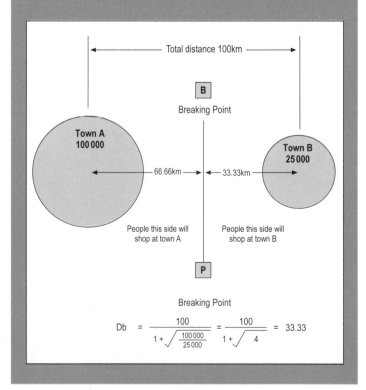

$$Db = \frac{100}{1 + \sqrt{\dfrac{100\,000}{25\,000}}} = \frac{100}{1 + \sqrt{4}} = 33.33$$

▲ **Figure 2** Central places and spheres of influence according to Christaller

▲ **Figure 3** Reilly's breaking-point between two settlements of different sizes

Rank-size rule and urban primacy

These are concerned with relationships between sizes of settlements and not their spacing. Zipf's rank-size rule states: 'If all the settlements of a country are ranked according to population size, the sizes of settlements will be inversely proportional to their rank.'

Therefore when all settlements in a country are placed in order of size from largest to smallest, the settlement placed second will have a population half the size of that of the largest. The third largest settlement will have a population one third the size of the largest ... and so on.

The rank sizes of settlements are usually plotted on a logarithmic scale. If there is a perfect negative correlation, such that the one ranked second is half the size of the one ranked first and that the one ranked third is indeed one third the size of the one ranked first etc., the graph will show a straight line. The usefulness of the rank-size rule is that it shows whether a primate or binary distribution of settlements occurs within a country.

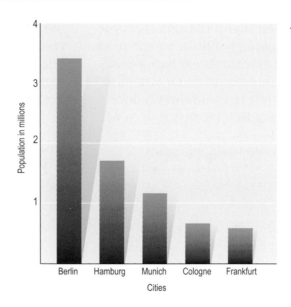

◀ **Figure 1a**
Relative sizes of the top five cities in Germany

▼ **Figure 1b** Germany: rank-size graph showing a close agreement with the rank-size rule

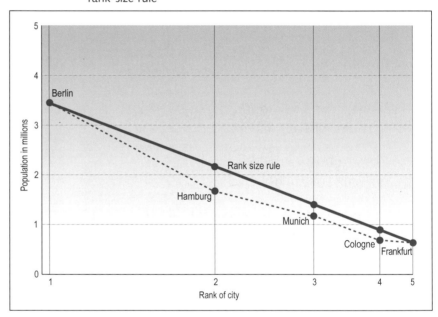

ⓘ *Urban primacy*
*Urban primacy or a **primate** distribution exists where the largest settlement is well over twice as large as the second largest. It may be many times larger. Not only does a primate city dominate a country in size, but it is likely to dominate in commerce, industry, services and wealth as well. London is six times and Paris is ten times larger than the next largest city.*

*A **binary** distribution occurs where there are two large cities of almost equal size within a country. It is likely that they have important but different functions.*
For example, Amsterdam is the main administrative centre of the Netherlands and Rotterdam is the chief port.

▼ **Figure 1c** Argentina: rank-size graph showing a high degree of urban primacy

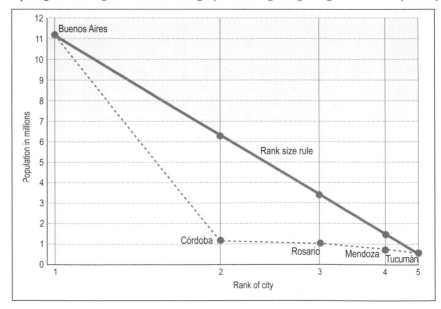

A primate pattern showing high urban primacy for the largest (usually capital) city is more common in LEDCs, although it is far from unknown in MEDCs, as the examples of London and Paris show. Of the ten main countries in South America, seven have primate patterns, including four examples of very high levels of national dominance by the capital cities of Argentina, Chile, Peru and Uruguay (Figure 2). In those that do not there are competing cities such as São Paulo (the industrial centre) and Rio de Janeiro (the port) in Brazil.

Some of the factors encouraging primacy are summarized in the flow chart below.

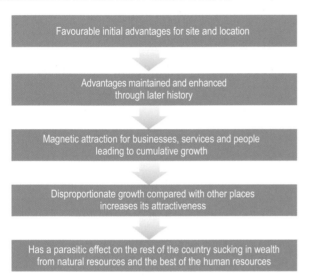

Low levels of economic development and the continuing importance of farming mean that the modern industries and services, that would promote urban growth, are not widely distributed in LEDCs. Colonial rulers favoured centralized government which promoted the importance of the chosen capital city, a tradition which has been continued in most after independence.

There are two opposing views of primate cities in LEDCs.

1 As dynamic growth points, capable of attracting investment from overseas in a way that no other city or region in the country could. They generate economic growth which will eventually benefit the whole country by diffusion from the central point.

2 As ever-increasing, unstoppable monsters with serious problems created by excessive and rapid growth. Severe traffic congestion and air pollution, serious shortages of essential services and housing, and escalating land prices are making them less attractive to investors and outsiders.

Despite this the world's largest and most continuous urban areas are in MEDCs. They are known as

megalopolises. One is Boswash down the eastern seaboard of the USA from Boston to Washington. The other is Tokkaido formed by the spread of Tokyo along the Pacific belt of Japan to join up with Nagoya and Osaka.

▼ **Figure 2** The extent of urban primacy in South America

Questions

1 Leeds (400 000 people) is 100 km from Darlington (80 000). Calculate the breaking point between them.

2 a Using the same sort of graph paper as in Figure 1b, plot the population totals and ranks for cities in Spain and Chile.

Spain		Chile	
Madrid	3 041 000	Santiago	5 343 000
Barcelona	1 631 000	Concepcion	312 000
Valencia	764 000	Vina del Mar	312 000
Seville	714 000	Valparaiso	296 000
Zaragosa	607 000	Temuco	250 000

   b Comment on the distributions shown.

3 Explain the factors which affect
   a the spacing of settlements in a region
   b the degree of urban primacy in a country.

Chapter 5 Questions

1 a Study the graph which shows past and projected urban population.

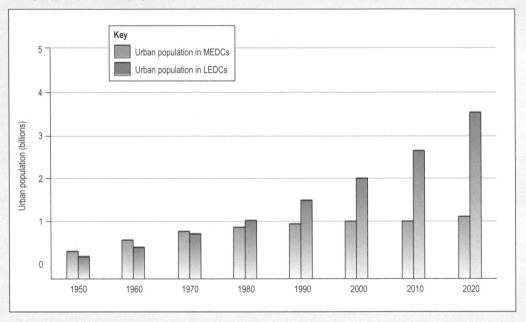

i In what way were the years between 1970 and 1980 significant? (2 marks)

ii Describe what has happened and is expected to happen to the world distribution of urban populations from 1980 onwards. (2 marks)

iii Outline two reasons for the continuing urbanization in many countries of the world. (4 marks)

b Outline the conflicts caused by urban growth on and around the edges of the cities in MEDCs. (7 marks)

Total: 15 marks

2 a Explain the causes and consequences of re-urbanization.
Illustrate your answer by reference to an example. (10 marks)

b In what ways and for what reasons are shanty towns in and around cities in LEDCs areas of constant change? (10 marks)

Total: 20 marks

A note on timing
You are expected to answer question 1 in about 15 minutes. You are expected to answer question 2 in about 40 minutes, spending an equal length of time on both parts.

Chapter **6** Economic activity

Recent tertiary activity in an area otherwise dominated by primary activities in southern Italy

Components of economic activity

Primary, secondary, tertiary, quaternary and quinary activities

Characteristics and changes

Components of economic activity

- The different sectors of economic activity
- The relationship between economic sectors and levels of development

The different sectors of economic activity

Primary to tertiary literally means first to third. This classification of different sectors of economic activity does no more than give the order in which the activities grew. At first humans behaved in the same way as all the other creatures in the animal world; their main need was food for survival. This was achieved by hunting and fishing and by gathering and collecting, i.e. using the free food supply provided by nature. A few indigenous peoples, such as tribes in remote parts of the rainforests or groups in Arctic Canada, still depend largely or entirely upon local natural resources for their existence.

One of the characteristics of the human race, however, is its inventiveness. The first of many economic revolutions was the development of agriculture – growing crops and domesticating animals – to give greater food output and more control over its supply. This happened only gradually over thousands of years in prehistoric times in the Old World, centred in the Middle East and adjacent areas of Africa and Asia, as humans learnt how to take more control over the natural environment. Food surpluses meant that some people did not have to farm or hunt and allowed them to specialize in crafts, such as metal working, pottery, leather and textiles. These were the origins of manufacturing – the secondary economic activity, i.e. the activity that developed second.

ⓘ *Classification and definitions of sectors of economic activity*

	Sector	Examples	Characteristics
1	Primary	Farming, fishing, forestry, mining and quarrying.	Any activity in which natural resources are acquired from land and sea. Raw materials are collected but not physically changed in any way.
2	Secondary	Manufacturing (making products), building and construction.	Raw materials undergo change and are made into other products. Power, whether human or from natural energy sources, is needed.
3	Tertiary	Transport and distribution, wholesale and retail, office and administration.	Services which support primary and secondary. They form a link between primary and secondary industries, and between them and their customers (the market). The movement of goods is often involved.

Tertiary may be further sub-divided into

		Examples	Characteristics
a)	**Quaternary**	Finance such as banking and insurance.	Services of a more personal nature – some are provided for companies, some are more for individuals
b)	**Quinary**	Education, health, research and development.	Some, such as research, are for both. Generally higher levels of skills, expertise and specialization are needed.

The great revolution in manufacturing happened around 1750 in the UK with the invention of the steam engine, using coal, and its application as a power source to drive a wide range of newly invented machinery. The Industrial Revolution, which allowed the growth of manufacturing on a scale never previously envisaged, was centred around the presence of coal. Land transport was so poorly developed that movement of a bulky commodity, required in large quantities, was at the best expensive and at the worst impracticable. From coalfield regions in the UK, large-scale manufacturing spread to coalfields in western and central Europe and then across to coalfields in North America. The Industrial Revolution was accompanied by other changes, both economic and social, notably improvements in transport, the growth of cities, a population explosion and an increasing need for supporting service industries. Companies and workers, specializing in particular branches of economic activity, needed to buy in services from others. This fed the growth of a tertiary sector, which was concentrated in urban areas where its customers, both factory owners and individuals, were found.

In the UK, increasing mechanization over time, both in agriculture and manufacturing industry, reduced the need for workers. Growing output, higher personal wealth and greater numbers of people all increased the demand for a growing variety of services. This has been reflected in the persistent growth of the tertiary sector (Figure 1) until the Second World War, when both the war effort and the post-war recovery boosted heavy industry and manufacturing, temporarily halting the latter's decline in relative importance.

▼ **Figure 1** The relative importance of different economic activities in the UK (% employed)

Date	Primary (%)	Secondary (%)	Tertiary (%)
1841	25	48	27
1871	17	52	31
1891	12	53	35
1911	9	55	36
1931	6	45	49
1951	5	49	4
1971	3	44	53
1991	2	27	71

▼ **Figure 2** Changes in relative importance of economic activities in the UK (1841–1991)

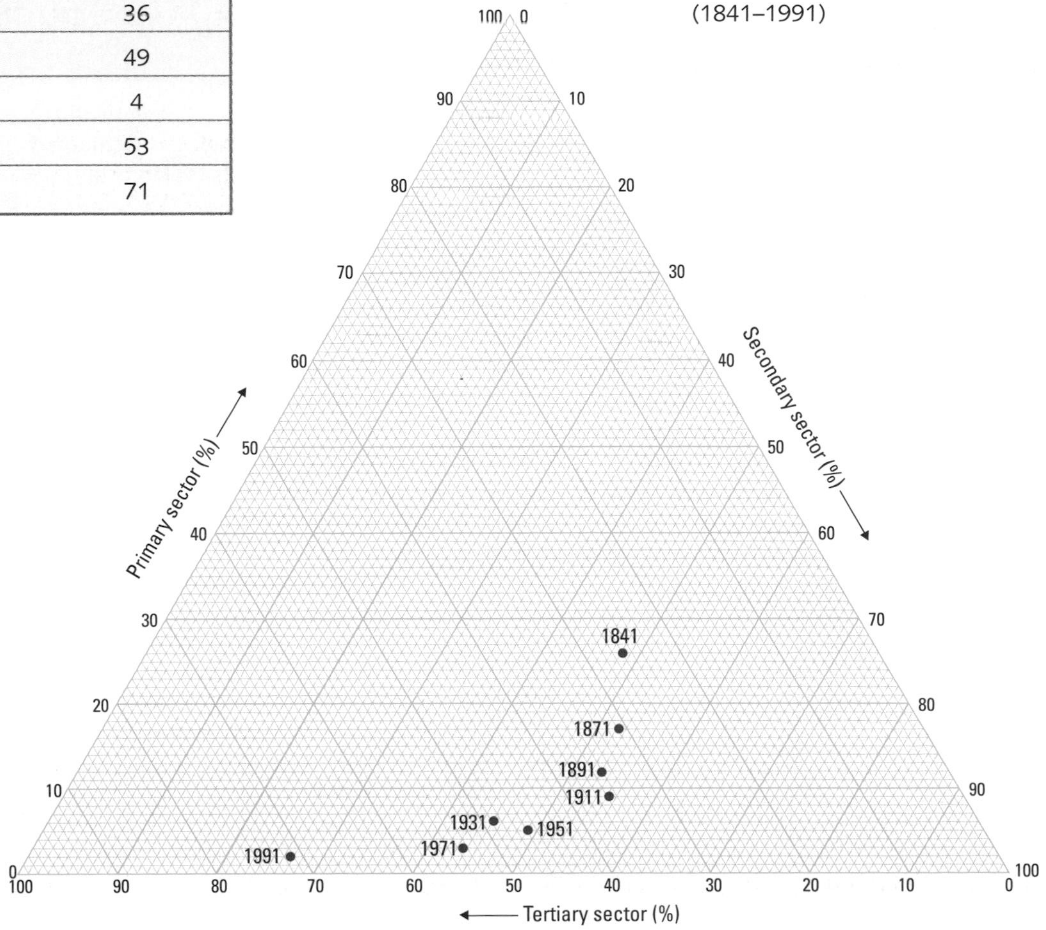

▲ **Figure 1** Problems of definition – a computer company on a business park in Coventry. Is it secondary – are computers assembled here? Is it tertiary – are computers distributed from here? Is it quaternary/quinary – is it a base for research and development?

Growth of tertiary sector

It was only in the last half of the twentieth century that coal and associated heavy industries lost their dominance. In the world's most developed countries, great increases in personal wealth have fuelled the demand for consumer goods and personal services. This has led to fundamental changes in the nature and location of manufacturing industries. At the same time a Technological Revolution has occurred and it is speeding up all the time. In an economic environment increasingly dominated by computers, global communications and worldwide competition, companies which invest in research and development, and have the financial backing to do this, are the ones with the best chance of survival and success. Economic activity is so varied, and so increasingly specialized, that it cannot be adequately covered by the one label of tertiary. The

title quaternary is the one generally used for the sector which encompasses high technology and information services, although some sub-divide it further to make a fifth (quinary) sector as well.

Although the classification of economic activity into four or five sectors has many uses, it is only a simple, and therefore crude, way of summarizing the great complexities of modern economic life. Within a manufacturing company, there are managers and office staff as well as production-line workers; many companies have a research and development unit as well. When the company which employs them is engaged in manufacturing industry, all its workers are classified in the secondary sector, even though the type of work being done by some of them belongs to the tertiary or quaternary sectors.

When compiling economic data of world countries for comparative purposes, international organizations such as the UN use only the three-fold classification of primary, secondary and tertiary, or often more simply agriculture, industry and services. The quaternary sector is new, without a fully agreed definition and is small or non-existent in many countries. Obtaining reliable employment data from LEDCs is particularly difficult as so many people work in the informal sector and are not included in any official government statistics. Informal jobs include not only those of the self-employed selling goods and offering petty services but also those who work for individuals or small enterprises with no employment contract or other benefits. Up to 60 per cent of the workers in urban areas of Latin America fall into the informal category (Figure 2), where they keep the official unemployment figures down to levels which cannot easily be believed.

▼ **Figure 2** Employment details for Latin America and the Caribbean

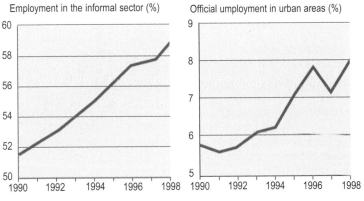

The relationship between economic sectors and levels of development

Despite the problems and limitations of defining different sectors, the relative importance of the three sectors of economic activity within a country is a good indicator of that country's level of development. Sometimes the data used is for the percentage of the workforce employed in each sector, sometimes it is the percentage contribution of each sector to a country's GDP (Gross Domestic Product).

Questions

1 a State with examples and explain the three-fold classification of economic activity into primary, secondary and tertiary.

b Outline two difficulties for making a classification of economic activities.

c Why has increased specialization in economic activities led to an increase in the number of classifications used?

2 a Using Figure 3:

  i state the percentage difference for each of the three sectors between the least developed and most developed LEDCs

  ii describe the changes in the size of the primary sector associated with greater economic development.

3 a Name another method, other than the triangular graph, for displaying the data in Figure 1 on page 227.

b Explain why the method named by you is suitable.

c Comment on the relative merits of the triangular graph and your named method as ways for showing this data.

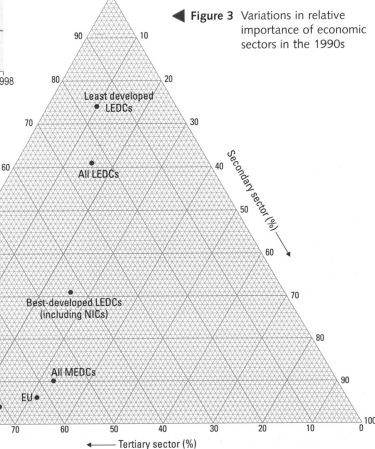

◀ **Figure 3** Variations in relative importance of economic sectors in the 1990s

Models of economic development

There are several models of economic development. One that is widely used is that first proposed by Rostow in the late 1950s, who identified five stages (Figure 1). It was based on a study of fifteen countries, mainly from Europe.

MEDCs

As the Rostow model was based upon what happened in Europe, it is easier to apply it to MEDCs. In the UK from 1750 onwards there were further improvements in farming, such as enclosure of the open fields and crop rotation. There were also several industrial developments, the key one of which was the invention of the steam engine. These provided the preconditions for take-off which happened around 1800. Such was the speed of industrial growth, supported by inventions of new machinery for industry and transport, that by the middle of the nineteenth century already half the workforce was employed in manufacturing, a remarkably high proportion (page 227). The UK in the late Victorian period was the classic example of an industrialized society. Stage 4 in Rostow's model was reached some fifty years ahead of any other country. By 1900 the UK had achieved an industrial dominance in the world out of all proportion to its size and resources.

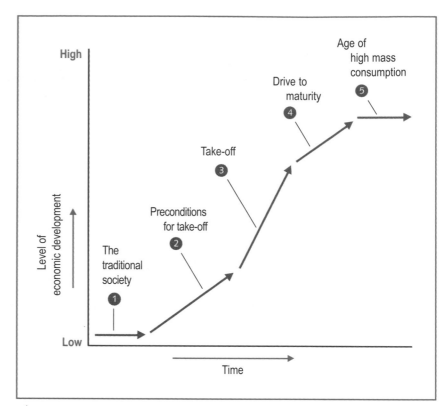

▲ **Figure 1** Rostow's model of economic development

▲ **Figure 2**
Kuala Lumpur, capital of Malaysia.
What stage in the Rostow model is suggested? There are plenty of signs that it is a modern city, but the large number of motorcyclists show that car ownership is not as widespread as would be expected in an economy which has reached the stage of high mass consumption.

Stage 1 The traditional society
Backward economy in which little change is occurring.

Employment – mainly primary, especially subsistence farming.

Stage 2 Preconditions for take-off
There are signs of economic growth such as mineral resources being developed, farming becoming more commercialized and some home industries growing, such as textiles.

Employment – mainly primary but with slight increases in secondary and tertiary.

Stage 3 Take-off
This is a time of great economic growth and change. Manufacturing growth is rapid, although it may be overwhelmingly concentrated in just one or two growth poles. The country is transformed into a modern industrialized society, which brings other changes (social and political) in its wake.

Employment – primary declines, secondary increases greatly, and some increase in tertiary takes place.

Stage 4 The drive to maturity
The now industrialized society continues to generate overall economic growth, leading to greater variety and complexity of economic activities, although some industries and regions fade as others expand.

Employment – a low percentage in primary, stable or slight decline in the percentage in secondary and a noticeable rise in tertiary.

Stage 5 High mass consumption
Manufacturing industries producing consumer durables grow, encouraged by the growth in wealth, which also stimulates more growth of services and allows more resources to be allocated to social welfare.

Employment – few left in primary, a declining number in secondary and an increase in the dominance of tertiary.

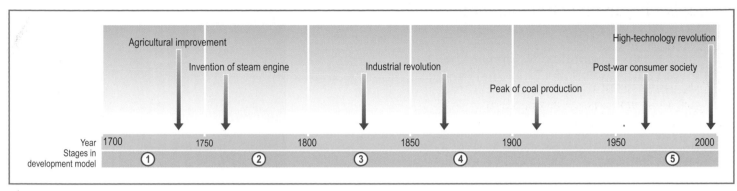

▲ **Figure 3** Timeline for economic development in the UK

Knowledge of industrial inventions spread to continental Europe and those countries with their own coalfields adopted them, although with some delay, partly caused by political instability. In North America, the flood of immigrants from Europe provided the preconditions for take-off there. The greater size and resource base of the USA, allied to its remoteness from war and political turmoil, allowed it to overtake countries in Europe and reach stage 5 first (Figure 5).

▶ **Figure 4** The Statue of Liberty, erected in 1886, was the symbol of freedom for immigrants to the New World. America was the land of opportunity for immigrants. Their energy, resourcefulness and varied skills were welcomed. These fuelled the economic growth which created the world's first consumer society.

LEDCs

Can the model be applied to LEDCs? The least developed LEDCs, many of which are located in sub-Saharan Africa, can be placed in stage 1. Many factors are present which restrict economic development – political instability, poverty, lack of education, and inadequate infrastructure in transport, energy supplies and public services. Any injection of funds into these countries tends to be in the form of aid, which is more likely to be used for survival than development. Some LEDCs, however, have managed to progress to stage 3. In Brazil and Mexico much of the stimulus for economic growth has been generated by investment from multinational companies attracted to the larger and more populous LEDCs such as these with their greater market potential. Until interrupted (temporarily) by the financial crises of the late 1990s, the quickest progress ever through stage 3 was being made by the NICs (newly industrializing countries) in eastern Asia, notably Singapore, Hong Kong, South Korea and Taiwan (from page 250). The first two of these are of great commercial as well as industrial importance and had reached at least stage 4 in the model by the mid 1990s.

▼ **Figure 5** The Rostow model applied to selected countries

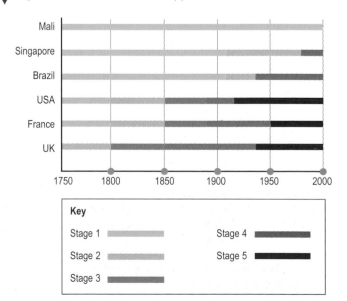

Regional variations within countries

Rostow's model provides a framework through which economic development in different countries can be better understood; however, its application to particular countries needs to take local or current conditions into account. For example, where do the small oil-rich states of the Middle East fit? They have high incomes per head, but their populations are too small to support much industry. The experiences of NICs suggests that improved communications, globalization of companies and the information revolution are speeding up the rate at which countries can progress through the different stages. What took one hundred years to achieve in nineteenth-century Britain has been squashed into thirty to forty years in some Asian countries since 1950. However, real growth within these countries may be highly concentrated in just one or two locations and its effects may be slow to spread to all parts. It is easier to achieve a balanced development within small countries, such as Singapore and Hong Kong, which are 'city states'. Neither physical appearance nor employment statistics support their continued inclusion among the list of LEDCs.

Figure 1 ▶

The commercial centre of Hong Kong reflects its rapid economic development from 1960

Mid-1990s	Primary (%)	Secondary (%)	Tertiary (%)	GDP per head ($US)
Hong Kong	1	37	62	22 310
Singapore	0	36	64	20 987

In all except the smallest countries there are regional variations in the levels of economic development. The less economically developed a country, the more likely that it can be sub-divided simply into two regions – core and periphery. The core attracts into it most of the new investments in industry, commerce and infrastructure; this increases its attractiveness to investors from both home and overseas; in turn this means further growth and economic development. Often this is achieved at the expense of the rest of the country, which remains unattractive to investors. The core can be said to behave 'like a parasite' on the rest of the country. In many LEDCs this leads to the dominance of one primary city, often the capital city, which is many times larger than the next urban area.

Regional variations within the UK are shown in Figure 3. Wealth is based upon GDP per head in the regions and has been converted into a percentage of the EU average. East Anglia at 100 per cent is on the EU average. South East England (including London) at 117 per cent is the only UK region that exceeds the EU average. What is hidden by the use of standard regions are local concentrations of wealth and poverty (such as Thanet in Kent, p.249).

▼ Figure 2 Core and periphery

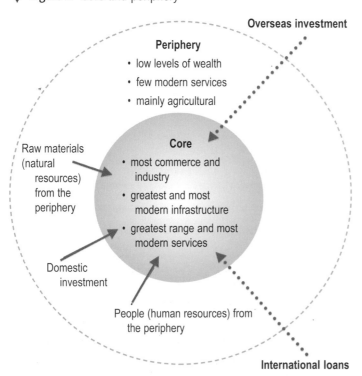

Overseas investment

Periphery
- low levels of wealth
- few modern services
- mainly agricultural

Raw materials (natural resources) from the periphery

Core
- most commerce and industry
- greatest and most modern infrastructure
- greatest range and most modern services

Domestic investment

People (human resources) from the periphery

International loans

Statistically the UK is more equal than most of its EU neighbours (Figure 4). The presence of wealthy core regions around the capital cities of Paris and Madrid reflect long histories of centralized administration in both countries. The agricultural, commercial and industrial wealth of the plain of Lombardy in northern Italy compared with the agricultural poverty and economic backwardness of the South can be explained by a combination of factors, both physical and human, such as relief and climate, political and economic history, and position within the EU. Some of the natural ruggedness of the South of Italy shows up in the photograph on page 215. The widest gap of all in Germany reflects the difficulties experienced in trying to integrate regions welcomed back after the collapse of communism in East Germany. However, there is a statistical reason as well because Hamburg is a city-region which is much smaller in size than those normally used for the collection of regional statistics.

▼ **Figure 3** Regional variations in prosperity in the UK (mid-1990s)

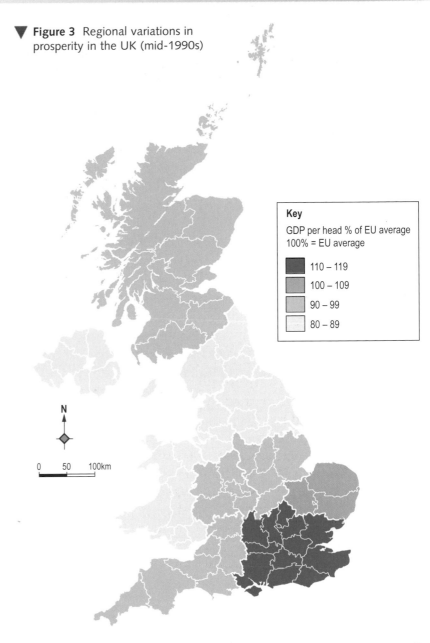

Key

GDP per head % of EU average
100% = EU average

- 110 – 119
- 100 – 109
- 90 – 99
- 80 – 89

▼ **Figure 4** Gaps in wealth between richest and poorest within selected EU countries

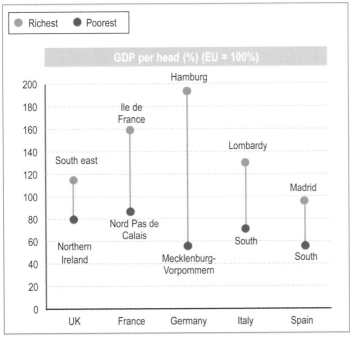

Questions

1   Explain the variations in the gradient of the line which illustrates Rostow's model.

2 a Why has 'take-off' occurred at different times in different countries?

   b Why have many countries not yet reached the stage of 'take-off'?

Investigation

Choose one country in the EU, other than the UK.

3 a i   Identify and locate its core region.

      ii Describe and explain its geographical characteristics.

   b i   Name and locate one of its peripheral regions.

      ii Describe its geographical characteristics.

      iii Why is it less economically developed than the core?

Primary activities

- Characteristics and types
- Changes in the UK's coal-mining industry

Characteristics and types

Farming

The most widespread and global of primary activities is farming. This reflects the importance of food supply to human survival and the rapid increase in numbers of people during the twentieth century (6 billion in 1999). Few people live in those areas of the world where it is either too dry or too cold or too high and too steep to farm. In some areas fishing is of equal, or even greater importance, in the local diet, but since these areas are restricted to certain coastal, river or lakeside locations, its overall importance is less.

The percentage of a country's population working in agriculture is a very reliable indicator of that country's level of development. Both the triangular graphs (pages 227 and 229) clearly show how the relative importance of the primary sector has declined as levels of development have increased. When the percentage employed in agriculture is plotted on a world map (Figure 1), the differences between the more economically developed North and the less economically developed South are clear, as also is the very low level of economic development of many countries in sub-Saharan Africa compared with LEDCs in other continents.

▼ **Figure 1** Percentages of the workforce employed in agriculture

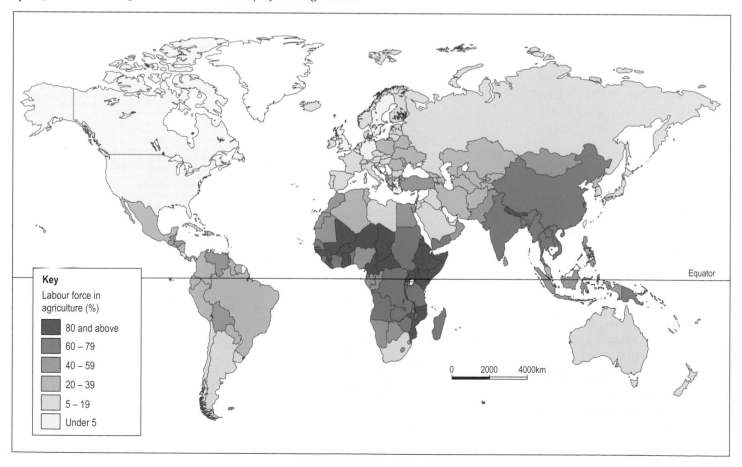

Key

Labour force in agriculture (%)

- 80 and above
- 60 – 79
- 40 – 59
- 20 – 39
- 5 – 19
- Under 5

Equator

0   2000   4000km

Farming employs so many people in LEDCs because it has not been mechanized and labour is plentiful and either free (the family) or cheap to employ at busy times such as harvesting. Also it is non-specialized, which is clear from the number and variety of crops grown (Figure 2). In contrast, wherever possible in MEDCs machines have replaced people, who have long migrated into urban areas. Farming is commercial which leads to specialization, to the point where it is not unusual for farmers to grow only one crop (Figure 3).

Forestry and mining

The other primary activities – forestry and mining of metals and minerals – are usually commercial activities, although a lot of wood is gathered for personal use in LEDCs. Capital investment and organization are needed not only for the logging and mining operations themselves, but also for the infrastructure (mainly roads) to allow access to sites, which may be in remote locations. These activities are not as widespread as farming. They have a more uneven spatial distribution depending upon where and in what quantities the natural resource is found (Figure 4).

Sub-Saharan Africa
- *This includes all African countries, except for the five in the north which border the Mediterranean Sea.*
- *Among them are many of the world's least developed and poorest countries.*
- *The majority of Africans are subsistence cultivators and/or pastoralists.*
- *Some of the problems for development are physical, for example unreliable and low rainfall – hot deserts cover large areas.*
- *Many of the problems are human – political instability, military governments, corruption, wars and tribal conflicts, high rates of population increase, diseases such as AIDS.*

▼ **Figure 2** Polyculture in Egypt

▶ **Figure 3** Monoculture of vines in Germany

Questions

1 a Describe the main features of the world pattern of the percentages employed in agriculture shown in Figure 1.
  b Choose two continents and explain the differences.

Investigation

2 Choose one country from sub-Saharan Africa.
  a State a variety of statistics which indicate its low level of economic development (such as GNP, birth rate, natural increase, life expectancy, employment).
  b Use economic, social and political factors to give a brief explanation for its low level of economic development.
  c Are there any prospects for improvement in the short term?

▼ **Figure 4** Major areas of fishing, forestry and crude oil production

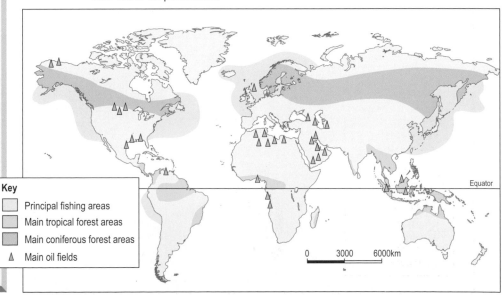

Key
- Principal fishing areas
- Main tropical forest areas
- Main coniferous forest areas
- △ Main oil fields

0   3000   6000km

Equator

Oil

To justify the costs of commercial exploitation a substantial amount of any resource needs to be present. Take crude oil, a vital ingredient of economic development. Many countries may have some commercial deposits of oil, but almost two thirds of known world reserves are in the Middle East, mainly under and around the Persian Gulf (Figure 1). Reserves of oil in Africa are almost as great as those in North America, which might suggest that Africa's current low level of economic development can be improved. However, because the oil is limited to certain areas, only four African countries make significant contributions to world oil production – Algeria and Libya in the north, Nigeria and Angola in the central zone.

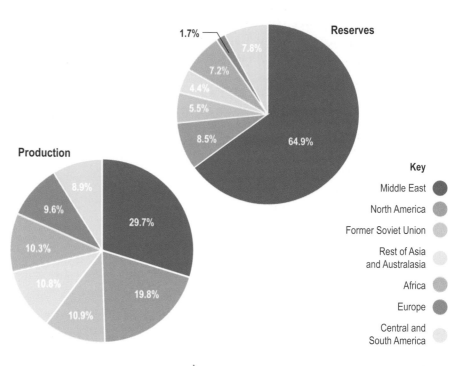

Key

Middle East
North America
Former Soviet Union
Rest of Asia and Australasia
Africa
Europe
Central and South America

▲ **Figure 1** Production and reserves of crude oil

The effects of mechanization

Even where the output of primary products is increasing, the number of people working in the primary sector is falling. The main reason is mechanization. The larger the scale of an enterprise, the greater the savings to be gained from replacing people by machines. Such economies of scale have led to the amalgamation of farm-holdings and increased farm sizes. Large logging companies, deploying giant machines, work through vast areas of forest. Mining companies close down mines not because they are exhausted but because they want to concentrate their operations where the amount of metals or minerals present justifies or allows the use of machinery. Large factory ships, fitted with sophisticated equipment to detect where the shoals are, fish wider and more distant areas of oceans. Closure of a mine or exhaustion of fish stocks can cause great hardship to local communities because these activities are often long established and carried out in locations without obvious alternative employment opportunities.

▲ **Figure 2** Above 4000m in the Andes. What employment possibilities are there once the mine closes?

Problems for primary producers

With the exception of mining, the other primary activities should be sustainable – trees can be replanted and fish stocks can be left to replenish themselves. However, soil erosion, total clearance of tropical forests and over-fishing mean that economic opportunities are declining in many areas. As a general rule, people working in the primary sector receive lower wages or have lower incomes than those of people working in the other sectors. This is one of the causes of rural to urban migration. In the same way, countries which depend for most of their earnings on the export of crops, minerals or other primary products need to export great quantities to achieve even a modest income. This is because raw materials are the bottom end of the production process. In the raw form no value has been added: value is added at each stage of the refining and production process and does not go to the producer. The price of the final product is many times the value of the raw material from which it is derived (Figure 3) as the traders, transporters, manufacturers and retailers take their cut.

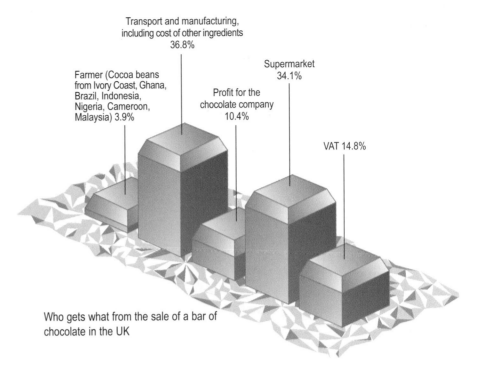

▼ **Figure 3** Chocolate – vital to many people in MEDCs, but who makes the money? Not the producer of the cocoa beans

Transport and manufacturing, including cost of other ingredients 36.8%

Farmer (Cocoa beans from Ivory Coast, Ghana, Brazil, Indonesia, Nigeria, Cameroon, Malaysia) 3.9%

Profit for the chocolate company 10.4%

Supermarket 34.1%

VAT 14.8%

Who gets what from the sale of a bar of chocolate in the UK

The primary producers are at the mercy of external physical and human factors over which they have little or no control. Crop harvests can be reduced by bad weather and disease; fish stocks can disappear if ocean currents carrying the plankton change course; a profitable mining seam can be broken by faulting. World prices for crops and minerals are set in major financial centres, such as London and New York, not in their countries of origin, leaving the producer with no control over market prices.

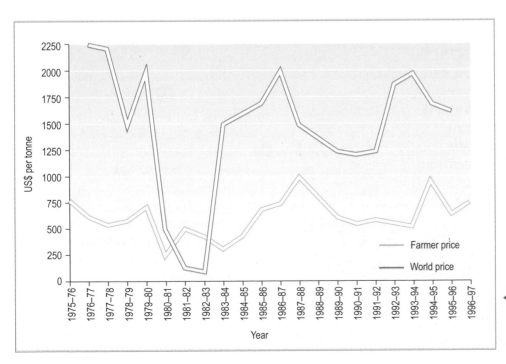

◄ **Figure 4** Price paid to farmers in Ghana for cocoa beans and world price

Questions

1 a Describe what Figure 4 shows about cocoa prices.
  b Suggest reasons for what is shown.

2   'Wealth in primary resources has allowed some countries to develop economically, but they form the minority.' Explain this statement.

Changes in the UK's coal-mining industry

It used to be called 'King Coal' because it was the economic ruler of the UK. Once geography students studied maps of coalfield areas like Figure 1A; now on a map of the same size it is possible to name all the deep mines still working in 1999 (Figure 1B). RJB mining operates the seventeen left and by the time you read this there are likely to be fewer still. The concept of a coalfield is dead. Yet there are enormous reserves of coal still left in the UK.

Coal output and use peaked between 1900 and 1913 when almost 300 million tonnes were mined per year by up to a million men. Coal accounted for an incredible 99 per cent of the UK's primary energy consumption. Durham was a county built almost entirely on coal. It was peppered with pits (Figure 2A). After the Second World War there were over 100 pits employing 90,000 men. Villages and towns grew because of coal mining and for no other reason. Virtually all the men in the village worked in the mine, living close together in rows of terraced houses which created tight-knit communities. In coal-mining areas all over the UK, the working mens' club was the focus of social life; cultivating allotments, competing in leek shows, playing in brass bands and racing pigeons and whippets were the main recreational pursuits.

However, the life of every mine is finite and closures of small mines were frequent in the 1950s and 60s. By the end of the miners' strike in 1985 there were only ten working mines left in the county of Durham with the youngest mines located near the coast (Figure 2B). As elsewhere, they had been closed by a mixture of physical problems (exhaustion of seams, geological problems such as faulting, too much water present) and economic problems (competition from oil and gas, lower costs of coal production elsewhere). Mechanization meant fewer miners were needed anyway. Investment was concentrated in the Yorkshire and Nottingham coalfields where thicker seams were more suited to the use of machines. Deep mining ended in the county of Durham in 1993. Durham's case, however, was not unique as underground mining ended in most of the other coalfields shown in Figure 1A at around the same time.

▼ **Figure 1a** The UK coalfields

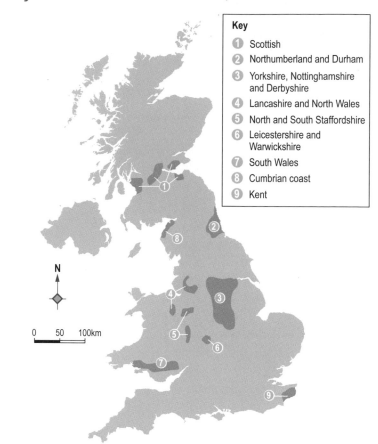

Key
1 Scottish
2 Northumberland and Durham
3 Yorkshire, Nottinghamshire and Derbyshire
4 Lancashire and North Wales
5 North and South Staffordshire
6 Leicestershire and Warwickshire
7 South Wales
8 Cumbrian coast
9 Kent

▼ **Figure 1b** The UK coal mines in mid-1999

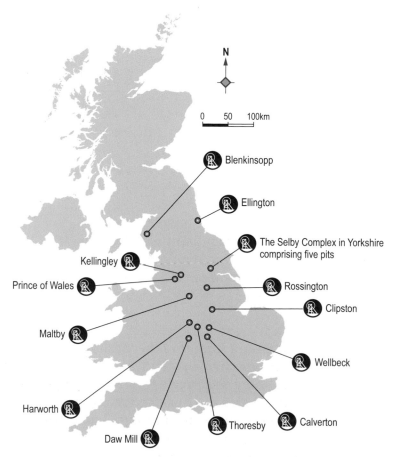

▼ **Figure 2** Working mines in the county of Durham

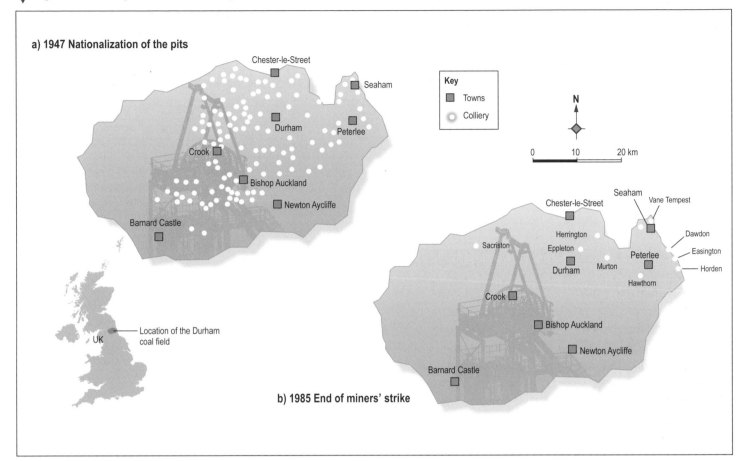

a) 1947 Nationalization of the pits

b) 1985 End of miners' strike

The competitors, oil and gas, are cheaper to mine and easier to transport and to use. Mining costs were going up due to wage pressures and narrow seams unsuited to mechanization. Imports from Australia, USA and Poland were cheaper. Fifty years of decline, largely for economic reasons, was speeded up by political decisions and environmental considerations in the early 1990s. There were no more loyal supporters of the old Labour party than the miners; many of the safest Labour seats are in mining areas. Miners were unloved by the Conservatives. One victorious miners' strike in the early 1970s contributed to the downfall of the Heath Conservative government. A much more bitter year-long strike in 1984–5 ended in defeat for the miners. From then on the Conservative government showed even less sympathy towards an industry which they believed had no place in a modern economy. The fatal blow was delivered in 1992/3 when the government decided to close more than half of the remaining fifty deep mines in preparation for the privatization of the coal industry. In the three years between 1992 and 1995 fifty deep mines employing 50,000 men were reduced to sixteen employing 10,000 men. The economic justification was lack of markets for coal. However, the government had been promoting the 'dash to gas' to make power stations burn a cleaner fuel. Without the switch to gas, the UK government was going to struggle to meet EU targets on reductions in emissions of carbon and sulphur dioxide. Another political decision was to privatize electricity generation, the main consumer for coal, which by 2000 had given the generating companies a free hand to choose which fuel and from where.

▼ **Figure 3** A plea from the coal communities which was of no interest to the government

Impact of mine closures

▼ **Figure 1** Changes in the UK coal industry 1950–2000

a Number of mines

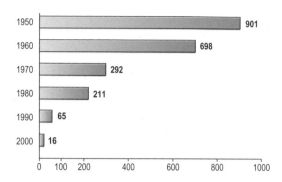

b Number of miners

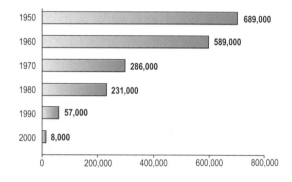

c Coal production in the UK (million tonnes)

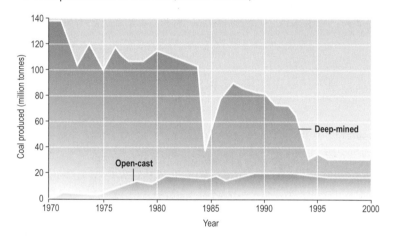

What made the impact of closing mines so great was that it affected mono-economic communities, i.e. settlements that had come into existence for mining and mining alone. Any service industries present were dependent upon the wages of the miners. They were often located away from the main routes, on the edge of uplands such as in the valleys of South Wales or on the slopes of the Pennines in Yorkshire and in the more peripheral western and northern parts of the country. Add to this pit heaps, stagnant water, black beaches and other scars of mining, and one could not imagine more unattractive locations for new industries. One of the few positive impacts of closure is that all signs of mining can be removed and the waste heaps reclaimed for great environmental improvement.

▼ **Figure 2**

Final insult for pit villages as open-cast blight spreads

It is three in the afternoon and an eerie silence has settled over the village of Sharlston, near Wakefield. In the small terraced houses, dozens of miners are sleeping off an imaginary early morning shift.

At 6am, many of them had been walking their dogs in the dawn light. The village colliery – the mainstay of this West Yorkshire community since 1885 – closed last year with a loss of 650 jobs. The former employees find it impossible to change body clocks that have been running for a quarter of a century.

When the pit closed there was first bitterness and then resignation. Now the 2,000 villagers have united in anger as a rash of prospecting for open-cast coal mines – cheaper and much less labour intensive than deep mining – threatens the Green Belt land around Sharlston.

An application to extract 196,000 tonnes of coal by tearing up the fields surrounding 150 homes and the village church and cemetery will be considered by Wakefield Council planners next month. It would bring in only 30 temporary jobs.

Anxious villagers, concerned about noise and dust pollution, fear other applications would soon follow. Meanwhile, the bulldozers are busily dismantling the Sharlston pithead, next to huge piles of unsold deep mined coal.

'This is the final betrayal,' says a miner who spent 35 years working at Sharlston. 'We were told there was no market for our coal, now they want to rip it out of the ground before our eyes. It's becoming like Klondyke country around here.'

Adapted from *The Observer,* Sunday 23 October 1994

Why the dash for gas is the pits

As the last pit in the region, the 400 miners at Ellington colliery in Northumberland know their jobs are always on the line, along with several thousand others in mines that stretch from the ultra-modern Selby complex in North Yorkshire to Nottinghamshire and beyond.

In Britain, the legacy of King Coal is everywhere; partly abandoned pit villages and towns from South Wales to Durham, with their crumbling terraces, boarded up shops and thousands without work. Men, relatively highly paid until recently – if £20,000 per year is highly paid for 10-hour shifts below ground – have been consigned to enforced idleness. In its turn, high unemployment has brought a range of social problems, from poor health to high crime, that now puts inner cities in the shade.

Yet the miners in Ellington, surveying the pock-marked landscape of surrounding Northumberland, know that someone still wants the coal from their county if not from their pit. It is being ripped from the surface by giant excavators on five huge open-cast sites – quarrying on a huge scale which blights villages, towns and large tracts of countryside.

Britain is facing a pit survival crisis. Five thousand miners' jobs are certainly on the line. The immediate problem stems from gas-fired power stations. Nineteen are now operating and ten are under construction. The gas-fired stations are cheaper and quicker to build. As a result of the so called 'dash for gas', natural gas from the North Sea fields last year accounted for a third of total power generation, as against less than 2 per cent of the market in 1992. Coal, by contrast, last year took 43 per cent compared with about 80 per cent at the start of the decade.

At the coalface the impact is and will be devastating. With gas forcing down the demand for coal, RJB mining, which took over the bulk of British Coal's collieries, could be forced to cut production by about 40 per cent. There is the prospect of a further 5,000 looming job losses. Companies like RJB will find it considerably cheaper to extract coal from huge, ugly open-cast sites rather than from deep mines. All of which poses a further threat to the survival of those battered pit communities.

Adapted from *The Guardian,*
Tuesday 2 December 1997

▲ Figure 3

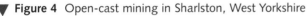

▼ **Figure 4** Open-cast mining in Sharlston, West Yorkshire

▼ Figure 5

Last deep pit in NE faces closure

The last deep coal mine in the north-east of England is to close with the loss of 400 jobs. The Ellington pit is the region's last deep mine, with shafts as deep as 800 metres and workings that extend under the North Sea, as far as 15 miles in places. RJB, the owners, have explored new reserves at the site in the past 18 months, but the coal found was not of a high enough quality for its customers.

The Confederation of UK Coal Producers alleges that the jobs are being put at risk by Polish exports being sold at a quarter of the cost of production. Competition was unfair when it meant competing against suppliers receiving unlimited state aid.

Adapted from *The Guardian,* Monday 1 November 1999

Questions

1 a Describe the evidence which
      i   shows 50 years of decline in the UK's coal industry
      ii suggests that the industry is in terminal decline.
   b Explain the causes of coal's decline using the headings
      i economic, ii political and iii environmental.

2 a Describe the distinctive features of a mining community.
   b Why does closing a coal mine have such a severe socio-economic impact at a local level?

3   Discuss the economic, social and environmental costs and benefits of open-cast mining.

Secondary activities

- Industrial change in MEDCs
- Industrial change in LEDCs
- Globalization and global interdependence

Industrial change in MEDCs

There was a significant decline in the relative importance of the manufacturing industry in the last thirty years of the twentieth century in MEDCs both in terms of employment and in its contribution to the national economy. These countries are moving through stage 5 in the Rostow model, the time of high mass consumption. What has happened in the UK (Figure 1) has been repeated in countries in North America and the EU as well. Figure 2 shows the persistent fall in numbers employed in manufacturing in the UK – the main indicator of the process of de-industrialization.

▼ **Figure 1** The decline of manufacturing in the UK (% employed)

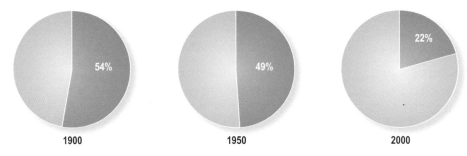

1900 — 54%

1950 — 49%

2000 — 22%

De-industrialization in the UK

Two main factors caused the general decline of manufacturing industry in the UK.

1 Increased mechanization – automation, robots and computers have reduced the numbers of workers needed along a production line. Manufacturing has become less labour intensive. The tasks done by unskilled labour were the easiest, and therefore the first, to be replaced by machines.

2 Loss of competitiveness – overseas competition, particularly from the newly industrializing countries in eastern Asia, where costs of production were lower. Many UK companies had become high-cost producers due to historical locations, outdated factory buildings, old machinery, inflexible working practices and high wages. Overseas markets were lost first and then imports from the 'Tiger economies' of Hong Kong, Singapore, Taiwan and South Korea penetrated deeper and deeper into the British market.

▼ **Figure 2** Numbers employed in manufacturing in the UK

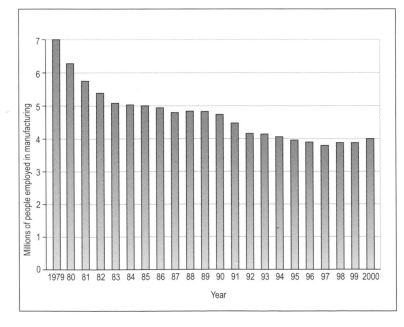

Other factors combined with these to explain why the most rapid rate of decline was around 1980 in the UK. There was a world economic recession and a 30 per cent increase in the value of sterling compared with other currencies. This was a double blow for manufacturing, i.e. at the time when overseas demand for goods was low, the cost of buying British manufactured goods increased by almost a third. Conservative government policy was that industry should become competitive rather than relying upon protection and government help. Efficient industries rationalized by concentrating production in a smaller number of larger, more modern, highly mechanized factories so that they remained internationally competitive (British Steel provides a good example – page 245). Uncompetitive industries closed. Both contributed to job losses in the manufacturing industry.

Although it is possible to view de-industrialization as part of a natural progression towards a post-industrial society as MEDCs move away from an economy based on manufacturing to one based upon services, it is a selective process. What this means is that it targets certain industries and certain industrial areas while leaving others untouched. Indeed during the main period of de-industrialization since 1979 the output from the manufacturing industry in the UK has actually increased (Figure 3). This is due to the expansion of factories manufacturing electrical and optical equipment, including computers. These factories have different needs and therefore occupy different locations to those of the more traditional textile and engineering factories.

▼ **Figure 3** Changes in manufacturing industry in the UK

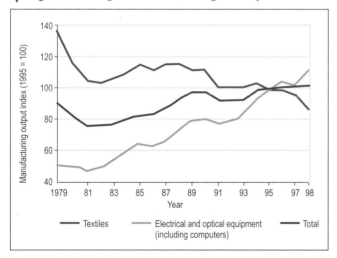

▼ **Figure 4** Traditional industrial areas in the UK

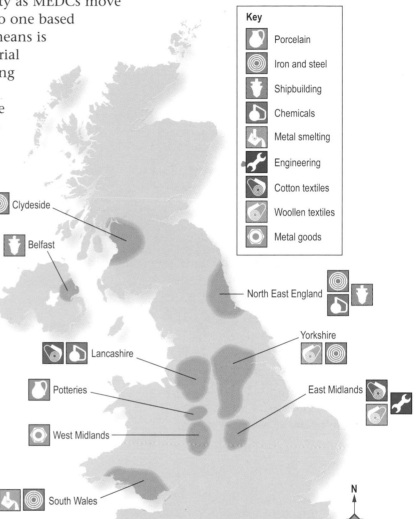

The greatest job losses have been in iron and steel, heavy engineering, shipbuilding and textiles, which were the staple industries upon which 'take off' during the Industrial Revolution had been built. They are dubbed 'smokestack' or 'sunset' industries. Many were heavy industries employing thousands. Although widely distributed, there was a strong correlation between their locations and those of the coalfields. The worst period of job losses from manufacturing coincided with the closure of the mines which increased the severity of the blow from de-industrialization in the areas named in Figure 4. Thousands were thrown out of work with minimal prospects of immediate alternative employment.

Questions

1 a Define de-industrialization.
   b i Describe how the Figures 2 and 3 show that it was at its peak in the early 1980s.
     ii Give the reasons for this.

Investigation

2 a For one of the industrial areas in Figure 4, outline the nature of industries and explain their past growth.
   b Give reasons for the absence of traditional industrial areas from the South East.

▼ **Figure 1** Population change in England and Wales 1991–98 (%)

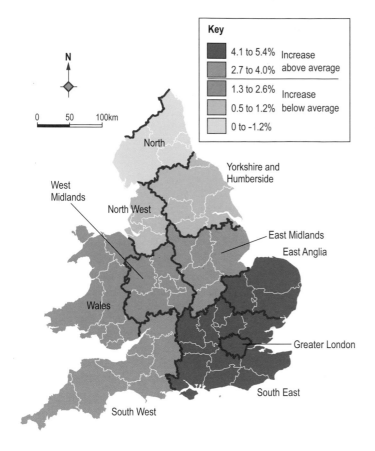

Continuing effects of de-industrialization

At the beginning of the new millennium there are still news headlines about jobs being lost, plants being shut, British goods being priced out of world markets by the high value of sterling and people migrating from north to south. They are all symptoms of continuing de-industrialization, the effects of which are most keenly felt in the North and Midlands. Despite many years of financial assistance from British governments, as well as help from the EU's regional fund, and despite a multitude of different labels used for areas eligible for aid (which include Development Areas, Enterprise Zones and Assisted Areas), the North–South divide stubbornly refuses to go away. If anything, the dividing line has crept further south to include the West Midlands as an honorary member of the North. In April 1999 the government set up eight Regional Development Agencies (RDAs) for England. Will they be able to narrow the gap?

Out-migration from north to south remains strong. Between 1991 and 1998 the population of England and Wales increased by 2.6 per cent, but the increase in North West England was negligible (0.1 per cent) and actually fell in the North of England by 0.5 per cent (Figure 1).

▶ **Figure 2** Unemployment in October 1999. This is a snapshot of the time when the government reported that the buoyant state of the labour market had led to the highest number of people in work ever recorded – 29.2 million.

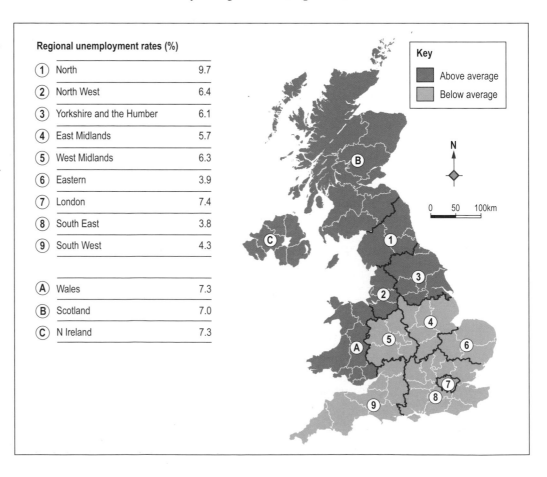

Regional unemployment rates (%)	
① North	9.7
② North West	6.4
③ Yorkshire and the Humber	6.1
④ East Midlands	5.7
⑤ West Midlands	6.3
⑥ Eastern	3.9
⑦ London	7.4
⑧ South East	3.8
⑨ South West	4.3
Ⓐ Wales	7.3
Ⓑ Scotland	7.0
Ⓒ N Ireland	7.3

▼ **Figure 3** No work, but it is cheap to live up North

Areas with significant numbers of house sales below £20,000

Questions

Investigation

1 **a** State the characteristics shown for the region you live in.
   b Outline the employment patterns in your area and any changes that may be occurring.

2   The North–South divide – myth or reality?
      Give your view and support it with geographical evidence.

What this means is that since 1991 almost a quarter of a million people have left old industrial communities in the North and Midlands, such as Tyneside, Merseyside and the Black Country. Jobs are still disappearing and unemployment rates are high (Figure 2). This has led to houses being boarded up and abandoned in northern cities and mining settlements (Figure 3). In contrast, councils in the South East are furiously searching for space to build the one million extra homes that the government forecasts are going to be needed there in the next few years. Companies in the South are suffering from acute labour shortages as potential workers can't afford the booming house prices.

Industrial change –
Case Study   ## The steel industry

British Steel, now called Corus, is one of the UK's most productive and competitive manufacturing companies. However, 20 years ago it was a high cost and notoriously inefficient steel producer. The change was achieved by:

- losing three-quarters of its workers
- increasing productivity by 350% (Figure 4)
- concentrating steel production in just four locations (Figure 5).

It produces about 17 million tonnes of steel a year, almost the same as in 1980, but with a quarter of the workforce – a clear example of de-industrialization. In 2000 it still faces formidable problems trying to remain internationally competitive, which it must do, because about half the output is exported. The company sees the high exchange rate as the number one problem. Its response is further re-structuring and cost cutting. It plans to cut the workforce by a further 12,500 over five years. Instead of production line workers, office workers and managers are the ones most likely to be targeted with some of their responsibilities taken over by the steel workers for higher rates of pay.

▼ **Figure 4** UK steel production per employee (tonnes)

Year	Tonnes
1977	114
1987	317
1997	521

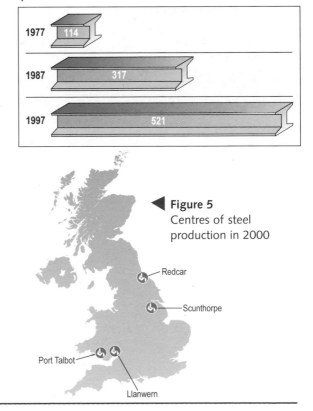

◀ **Figure 5**
Centres of steel production in 2000

Redcar
Scunthorpe
Port Talbot
Llanwern

De-industrialization in the EU

The process of de-industrialization is not unique to the UK. It affects the USA and the industrialized countries of the EU. Figure 1 shows the locations of the major industrial areas for part of the EU in 1980. The greatest concentration was within the heavy industrial triangle in northern France, Belgium and Germany, based upon the presence of coalfields, which included iron and steel, metal smelting, heavy engineering and textile industries, just as in the UK. The Nord (North) coalfield around Lille had all the usual symptoms of de-industrialization. In 1960, over 300,000 people, more than half the region's workforce, were employed in three staple industries – coal, steel and engineering and textiles. By 1985 all the coal mines had closed, steel production had moved to the coast at Dunkirk, and engineering and textile plants had closed through foreign competition and the failure to introduce modern machinery and modernize.

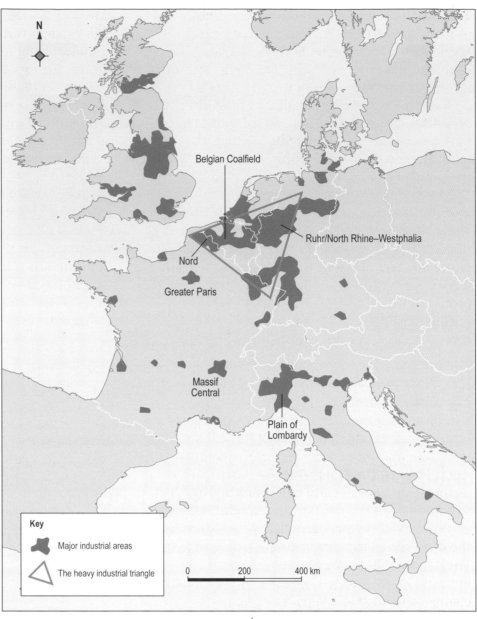

Key

▮ Major industrial areas

△ The heavy industrial triangle

0   200   400 km

▲ **Figure 1** Major industrial areas in 1980

Industrial change in the EU

Case Study

North Rhine–Westphalia, Germany

▲ **Figure 2** Location of North Rhine–Westphalia

▲ **Figure 3** Cologne – commercial, industrial and tourist centre on the banks of the busy Rhine waterway

The EU's industrial giant is Germany. The industrial heartland of Germany is North Rhine–Westphalia where Europe's largest coalfield, the Ruhr, is found. This state accounts for one–fifth of Germany's total exports by value. Despite the amount and quality of the Ruhr's coal, over 400,000 miners were made redundant in the forty years since the mid-1950s. Mining has received more political support than in the UK, but the number of mines has still fallen from about 150 to 25 during the same period. The state government has pursued a policy of diversification and a shift away from heavy industry. During the ten-year period up to 1995 state support helped to create 800,000 new jobs through investments in services, conservation and recycling industries (note not manufacturing industries). Where possible, manufacturing companies have diversified into non-manufacturing activities.

The company Mannesmann, which once specialized in steel and engineering, successfully moved into electronics and then into telecommunications. In late 1999 its industrial business employed 75 per cent of its staff but accounted for only 10 per cent of the company's value. Many other enterprises are moving into sectors such as media and communications, switching from stagnant or declining nineteenth- and early twentieth-century heavy industries into the dynamic twenty-first century service industries. The details of industries and companies in the Ruhr in Figure 4 suggest the scale of the structural changes since 1950. The pattern of change is similar to other coalfield regions in the EU, but the extent of the decline has not been as great. The region remains the largest concentration of manufacturing industry in Europe. There are good reasons for this. North Rhine-Westphalia occupies a prime position within the economic core of the EU. It is well served by a varied and dense communications network. The disadvantage of an inland location for heavy industries is offset by having the navigable Rhine pass through the middle of it. Many small industrial enterprises in Germany, called *mittelstand*, continue to be very successful in world markets. However, within the state not all locations have fared equally; mining settlements and centres of heavy industry away from the Rhine such as Essen have suffered while growth has been concentrated in cities on the banks of the Rhine such as Dusseldorf, Cologne and Bonn.

Questions

1. What are the similarities and differences between the EU and UK for:
   i the process of de-industrialization
   ii the responses of governments.
2. a Describe the evidence that the economy of North Rhine–Westphalia has diversified since 1950.
   b Explain why North Rhine–Westphalia is better placed for economic growth than many of the old industrial regions in the UK.

▼ **Figure 4** North Rhine–Westphalia industrial information

A Industry – in terms of turnover

Mid-1990s		1950
1	Chemicals	5
2	Machinery	7
3	Food	3
4	Electronics	8
5	Vehicle production	16
6	Construction	6
7	Steel and metal	4
8	Petroleum	20
9	Mining	2
10	Synthetic materials	29
11	Textiles	1

B The ten largest enterprises in 1995 (by turnover)

Name	Location	Industries
1 Veba AG	Essen	Chemicals (and telecommunications)
2 RWE	Essen	Energy (and telecommunications)
3 Telekom	Bonn	Telecommunications
4 Bayer	Leverkusen	Chemicals
5 Thyssen AG	Duisberg	Steel and machinery
6 Metro-Gruppe	Dusseldorf	Retailing and trading
7 Rewe-Gruppe	Cologne	Retailing
8 Aldi-Gruppe	Muhlheim	Retailing and trade
9 Ruhrkohle AG	Essen	Mining
10 Mannesmann AG	Dusseldorf	Engineering, automotive, electronics and telecommunications

New industrial growth in the UK

Although the contribution of manufacturing to the UK economy has fallen from one–third in 1950 to less than a quarter in 2000, it still has an important role in a modern economy as it employs four million people and includes some of the UK's leading export companies. In the 1990s advances in technology and greater personal wealth led to the growth of desired consumer goods which has led to a trebling in the production of computers and office machinery and a significant increase in the output of communications equipment. What is significant for location is the high proportion of new industries which have chosen sites within 100km of London – over 75 per cent for example in the case of those in the micro-electronics industry.

> *Six industries are shaping the economy of the future:*
> - *micro-electronics*
> - *computers*
> - *telecommunications*
> - *designer clothes*
> - *robots*
> - *biotechnology.*
>
> *These are the areas in which rapid manufacturing growth is expected.*
>
> *Definition*
> **Biotechnology** *Medical research including the study of genes and genetic engineering.*

South East England and adjacent areas

Case Study

Reasons for growth

Lighter consumer-orientated industries do not need to assemble large quantities of bulky raw materials. The main energy source is now electricity, which also means they have greater freedom of location than the industry did in the past – hence the label 'footloose' which is often applied to them. Since they are more market- orientated than heavy industries, it is natural that they decide to locate in places where there are lots of people. Some, such as companies manufacturing food and drink, are widely distributed to be close to their customers. Others, such as those making machinery, cars and domestic appliances, tend to be present in greatest numbers in the West Midlands and South Wales, reflecting the industrial history of these regions. However, all of these are well represented in the South East while many others, such as printing and publishing, are overwhelmingly concentrated here because the South East is where the largest and most wealthy market exists. The majority of light industries seek sites next to the motorways and main roads to increase speed and ease of distribution. For many the most sought-after location of all is next to a motorway junction.

Figure 1 Growth corridors along the motorways out of London

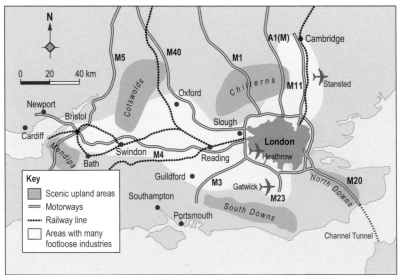

Key
- Scenic upland areas
- Motorways
- Railway line
- Areas with many footloose industries

▲ **Figure 2** Reading – one of the preferred locations for high-technology companies

The growth industries of the 1990s, many of which are at the cutting face of technology, require specialists and highly skilled workers. For these industries a location near to a source of skilled workers, such as a university or research establishment, is critical. Also important is a location where workers are happy to live, which often means having easy access to pleasant countryside for recreation as well as to London or another large urban centre with a wide range of shopping, sporting and cultural attractions and services. Their clients and customers come from many countries so the convenience of having an international airport nearby is also important.

The result is that natural new industrial growth has occurred most in corridors radiating from London, mainly following the line of the motorways past and towards university cities, notably up the M11 northwards to Cambridge, along the M4 westwards via Reading to Bristol and down the M3 towards Southampton and Portsmouth (Figure 1).

Problems

The main problem is great people pressure which will be examined later on pages 262–3. Another problem is unequal prosperity – not everywhere within the South East has shared in the growthboom. There are pockets of unemployment that are as bad as those in the North. One of these is Thanet on the eastern tip of Kent (Figure 3).

Investor prescribes medicine to prevent east Kent impotence

Pfizer, the US healthcare company, is creating drugs for the 21st century at Sandwich, east Kent, where it invented Viagra. In contrast, some rail services to London, 100 kilometres away, are slower than they were in Victorian times.

Little wonder the company, one of south east England's most important inward investors, is warning that future expansion at Sandwich is in doubt unless the infrastructure improves – not just railways, but roads, homes, schools, hotels and cultural facilities.

The loss of further investment by Pfizer would be a serious setback for the area, which has had problems in recent decades, including the closure of the Kent coalfield, a fall in agricultural employment and a decline in tourism caused by the rise in popularity of foreign package holidays. But east Kent is recovering. Even in Thanet, the worst hit district which includes Ramsgate and Margate, the count of those out of work and claiming benefit has fallen from 15 per cent to 8.7 per cent in five years. In Dover, boosted by the ferry port, the number has dropped from double figures to 4.6 per cent. Canterbury's total is 3.5 per cent – still above the 2.3 per cent south-east average.

Progress depends on Pfizer – the 'money pump' at the region's heart. Its staff have grown by 2,000 to 4,500 in three years. It is building a research facility with space for 1,000 more, dramatically raising the area's skill levels.

The Financial Times, 11 October 1999

▲ **Figure 3** The Pfizer works at Sandwich. Too much dependence upon one company?

Industrial change in LEDCs

In some LEDCs manufacturing industry has not progressed beyond the stages of domestic crafts and basic processing of raw materials. These countries can be identified in Figure 1 on page 234 by having high percentages of their workforces employed in farming. They include many countries in sub-Saharan Africa where the preconditions needed for industrial growth do not exist (see the information box on page 235). Other countries with small population totals, say less than five million, have home markets that are too small to support profitable manufacturing. However, there are exceptions to every rule and small countries can industrialize; the classic example is Singapore with under three million people, but it was helped by being a great trading country with worldwide markets. Countries which have industrialized sufficiently to be classified as NICs usually have less than 30 per cent of the workforce in agriculture, a figure which is falling all the time. Figure 1 highlights the uneven distribution of manufacturing activity between the regions of the less economically developed world. East Asia stands out. Although the forecasts for 2005 were made before the Asian financial crisis of 1997–8, the evidence from 1999 is that many Asian countries are making a rapid recovery and growth has resumed. At the other extreme, the tiny proportion of world manufacturing contributed by African countries is if anything going down, mainly as a result of continuing political instability and poverty.

What a country needs for successful economic growth, according to Lee Kuan Yew (Prime Minister 1959–90) who converted Singapore into one of the Asian 'tigers'.
- *clean (non-corrupt) government*
- *national solidarity*
- *universal education*
- *family planning*
- *leaving foreigners and entrepreneurs alone to get on with their business.*

▼ **Figure 1** Shares of world manufacturing production (%)

The changing map of world industry					
	1970	**1980**	**1990**	**1995**	**2005** (est)
MEDCs	88.0	82.8	84.2	80.3	71.0
LEDCs	12.0	17.2	15.8	19.7	29.0
LEDCs:					
Latin America	4.7	6.5	4.6	4.6	4.4
N Africa and W Asia	0.9	1.6	1.8	1.9	2.4
S Asia	1.2	1.3	1.3	1.5	1.7
E Asia (incl. China)	4.2	6.8	7.4	11.1	20.0
Sub-Saharan Africa	0.6	0.5	0.3	0.3	0.3

Multinationals

The advantage for manufacturers that all LEDCs can offer over MEDCs is cheap labour. This is an increasingly important asset now that a large proportion of the world's manufacturing output is in the hands of multinational companies, who operate on the world stage. Global operations have been greatly facilitated by improvements in telecommunications and the electronic transmission of data for administrative purposes and by use of container ships as a cheap means for transporting the finished products to world markets. Countries in East Asia remain the first choice for many multinationals; it is the favoured location for having electrical and electronic goods assembled or clothes and shoes made. Asian workers tend to be better educated and more reliable and willing than anywhere else in the developing world.

▲ **Figure 2** Siemens of Germany – in Penang (Malaysia) making semi-conductors

Wage rates are less than a quarter of those in Europe and the USA. As wage rates have increased with economic development in countries such as Singapore, Hong Kong and South Korea, companies have switched production to other countries, usually in the same region. Some of the lowest wage rates, well under US$1 per hour, are in China. Much manufacturing has already been transferred from Hong Kong across the border into mainland China.

However, to attract multinationals governments must be supportive. The great push towards industrialization from 1960 onwards in Mexico, Brazil and the Asian tigers (Singapore, Hong Kong, South Korea and Taiwan), as well as in Thailand, Malaysia, Indonesia and the Philippines, would not have been possible without government backing and a commitment to economic development. The non-existence of a local market did not matter because production was aimed at the markets of the developed world. However, East Asian countries are becoming more attractive as their living standards and consumption are rising fast. Big companies like to be where markets are expanding. This is why so many invested in Brazil in the 1960s and continue to invest there, despite bouts of financial turmoil; with 170 million people it is the fifth most populous country in the world and a market that cannot be ignored.

Multinational companies
Companies with business interests in many different countries, such as BP, Nestle, and Ford.
This makes them global companies operating in MEDCs and LEDCs alike, although the majority of the headquarters of these companies are in the USA, Europe and Japan.

Advantages of multinationals to LEDCs
- *inward investment of capital, skills, expertise and technology*
- *infrastructure (e.g. transport and energy supply) is improved for or by them*
- *jobs created which increases spending power and the home market*
- *more types of goods exported reducing dependence on low value primary products*
- *broader economic development can follow.*

Disadvantages to LEDCs
- *investment is for multinational's profits which are taken out of the country*
- *jobs are often low paid with working conditions inferior to those in MEDCs*
- *bring water and air pollution because local pollution controls are weak or ignored*
- *industries selling exports are vulnerable to global changes in demand.*

◀ **Figure 3** Hewlett Packard – one of the pioneering multinationals in Penang in 1972

Questions

1 Display the information in Figure 1 on a graph.

2 Describe what Figure 1 shows about manufacturing industry in the LEDW.

3 Explain why some LEDCs have industrialized more than others.

Industrial growth

Case Study   in Malaysia

▼ **Figure 1** Malaysian exports in 1970

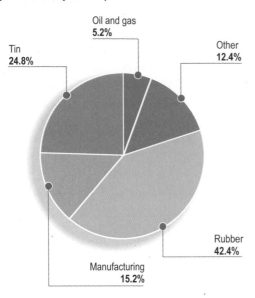

Total **M\$4 billion**

The breakdown of exports from Malaysia in 1970 shows that its economy had many of the typical features of LEDCs – an overwhelming reliance upon the export of primary products from farming and mining and a low total value.

However, things were changing. Following a severe depression in the 1960s, the local authority on the island of Penang worked with the national government to actively encourage investment from multinationals for labour-intensive work. Within a few years, the island of Penang off the north-west coast of Malaysia had become a giant assembly line for the great manufacturers of the world – Hewlett Packard, Intel, Bosch, Siemens, Fairchild, Hitachi, Motorola etc. By 1990 there were 430 factories on the industrial parks run by the Penang Development Corporation employing 100,000 workers. The reasons for this great success include:

- a long history of commerce (Penang was a colonial trading post)
- plenty of labour, well educated by LEDC standards
- supportive and stable national and local governments
- a designated industrial zone in Bayan Lepas set up in 1972.

Success bred success. Rapid growth in the 1970s and 1980s exhausted the supplies of low-cost labour. Living standards improved, costs were pushed up and overseas companies began to look for lower wage alternatives elsewhere in Malaysia and Asia. Since 1990 Penang has attempted to change direction from a haven of low-skilled cheap labour production to a regional high-technology industrial centre. The electronics industry was founded upon the semiconductor plants which sprung up in the 1970s. From this came the successful development of disk drive production, in which, since the 1990s, Penang has become one of the world leaders. In 1990 the Penang Skills Development Corporation began training workers in the skills that companies in the region found to be lacking. This has encouraged some companies to introduce research and development units.

Local industries have benefited from the technology transfer from overseas. There are many SMIs (Small and Medium-sized Indigenous companies) which support and supply parts, particularly printed circuit boards, to the multinationals. Over 400 of the factories on the industrial parks are locally owned and there are 2,000 smaller factories outside the parks. Many began making nuts and bolts before they expanded to supply a wider range of parts and components of increasing technological sophistication.

The government of Malaysia had grandiose plans for a 'Multimedia Super Corridor' south of Kuala Lumpur, the capital, but they have been put on hold as a result of Asia's financial problems in 1998. The expansion is regarded as essential to the intended transformation of Malaysia from assembly manufacturing to information technology. Tax breaks have already attracted investment from Microsoft, Sun Microsystems, Nippon Telegraph and IBM.

 Business is still booming on the industrial parks in Penang.
In 1997 there were
- *743 factories – up 73% from 1990*
- *191,000 workers – up 90% from 1990*

Main industries
1 *Electronics and electrical*
2 *Machinery, metal and equipment*
3 *Textiles*

Bill Gates, head of Microsoft, sits on the international advisory panel. However, despite changes in the 1990s, much of the work of the multinationals is still essentially assembly line manufacturing. There are still some problems with the transport infrastructure and power cuts occur frequently. However, it has led to great changes in the Malaysian economy (Figures 4 and 5), unlike many LEDCs which still depend on primary products, whose real prices have been declining for decades.

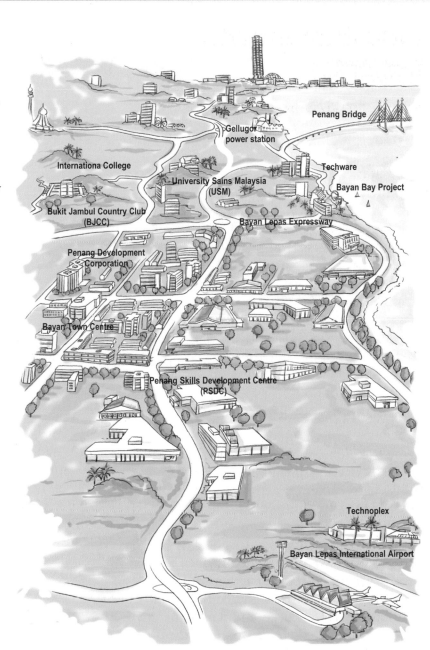

▶ **Figure 3** The Bayan Lepas Industrial Park (BLIP) in Penang, strategically located between the airport and road bridge to the mainland

Case Study – Industrial growth in Malaysia

▼ **Figure 5** Employment in Malaysia 1990 and 2000 (estimated)

Industry	1990 (%)	2000 (%)
Agriculture, forestry, livestock and fishing	26.0	13.0
Mining and quarrying	0.6	0.5
Manufacturing	19.9	28.9
Construction	6.3	9.3
Electricity, gas and water	0.7	0.9
Transport, storage and communications	4.5	5.6
Wholesale and retail trade, hotels and restaurants	18.2	16.2
Finance, insurance, real estate, business services	3.9	5.3
Government services	12.7	9.9
Other services	7.2	10.4

▼ **Figure 4** Malaysian exports in 1997

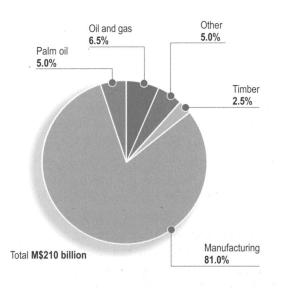

Palm oil 5.0%
Oil and gas 6.5%
Other 5.0%
Timber 2.5%
Manufacturing 81.0%
Total **M$210 billion**

Globalization and global interdependence

The pace of industrial growth in the UK during the Industrial Revolution, supported by the number of new inventions, soon outstripped the UK's own sources of raw materials; only coal supplies remained adequate for needs. Rapid population growth in urban industrial areas also exceeded the UK's food capacity. The search for colonies was largely driven by the need for raw materials and food supplies. Thus began a trading pattern which has persisted up to the present, i.e. LEDCs exporting raw materials and food supplies (primary products) and MEDCs exporting manufactured goods. It could be argued that LEDCs and MEDCs are interdependent because each depends upon what the other supplies. In practice the terms of trade are unequal because primary products have little added value and most LEDCs remain poor.

Since the 1960s there have been some major modifications to this simple pattern of trading. First came the globalization of manufacturing industry associated with the rise of multinational companies. Attracted principally by low wage rates, multinationals set up assembly lines in LEDCs. The growth of factories and the transfer of technology through them has since encouraged and allowed wider industrial growth and economic development, particularly in Mexico, Brazil and countries of East Asia. The result has been an increase in the export of manufactured goods from certain LEDCs. 'Going global' is what has allowed major Japanese companies, such as Sony, Canon and Toyota, to become industrial giants. Increasingly the big multinationals such as Ford are thinking globally and planning their operations internationally. Ford no longer has separate American and European operations. Companies make decisions globally rather than nationally. A car like the Mondeo is produced for both European and American markets. The engines for it are made in Bridgend and Cologne in Europe as well as in Cleveland (USA) and Chihuana (Mexico). The cars are assembled in Belgium, Mexico and Kansas City (USA). If you are wearing Nike shoes and shirt, they could have been manufactured in any one of a dozen countries in different parts of the world.

 Globalization

Definition The increasingly international manner in which both manufacturing and service companies are operating. They make planet-wide decisions.
Companies 'act global' – they have a presence in many countries in many different parts of the world.
Companies 'think global' – they take decisions breaking down national barriers.

What is supporting globalization?
- *improving global communications*
  - *containers for moving goods by sea and crates by air*
  - *aircraft for visiting executives, managers and skilled personnel*
  - *e-mail, fax, phone and audio/video conferencing*
- *some liberalization of world trade*
  - *trade agreements from the GATT and WTO rounds of talks*
  - *free trade organizations such as NAFTA (North American Free Trade Association between the USA, Canada and Mexico).*

Decisions affecting employment in one country may be taken in another thousands of kilometres away. People working on the assembly lines are affected by changes in the global demand for what they are making and are powerless to influence it. Although most of the headquarters of multinational companies remain in the MEDW, industrial expansion in the LEDW has spawned some large companies. Industrial growth in South Korea was achieved largely through the activities of four giant companies – Samsung, Hyundai, LG and Daewoo – whose global activities have turned them into household names. Their proposed investments in the UK were greatly welcomed in the early 1990s.

The examples on page 255 show that people in MEDCs do not always reap the benefits of globalization, even if the economic grip of the MEDW is dominant.

Questions

1 a What is meant by **i** globalization, **ii** interdependence?
   b Why are both increasing?

2   How does globalization **i** help and **ii** hinder the economic development of LEDCs?

Investigation

3   Choose one region in the UK (your own region or another).
   a Identify the multinational companies present.
   b Why were they attracted into the region?

Case Study – LG in South Wales

Case Study

increasing employment

When in July 1996 LG chose Newport in south-east Wales for a £1.7 billion project for a consumer electronics factory and semiconductor plant, directly employing over 6,000 people, there was great rejoicing. Researchers forecast a multiplier effect of over 8,000 indirect jobs in the region (Figure 1). It looked like a jackpot prize. Sadly the East Asian financial crisis of 1997/8 meant that LG had to put the project on hold. This is a reminder that being part of the global community means being at the mercy of events on the other side of the world.

Estimated employment impact in Wales of the LG project		
Number of jobs	Sector	
	LG Electronics	LG Semicon
LG Direct employment	4 410	1 696
Knock-on effects		
Agriculture	167	73
Energy	154	109
Manufacturing	1 821	781
Construction	164	115
Distribution	1 638	839
Transport	211	123
Other services	1 463	750
Total	**10 028**	**4 486**

▲ **Figure 1** LG's direct and forecast multiplier effect upon south east Wales.

'Making all the right connections'

Korean team chose region after closely examining all the options

WELSH STEEL TOWN FORCES 'GREEN' FUTURE'

Port Talbot's £230m regeneration plan could create more than 3,000 jobs

Case Study – Mexico

Case Study

a base for manufacturing

In North America, local politicians and workers are complaining as companies transfer more and more of their manufacturing to Mexico where wage rates are at least five times lower than in the USA. Over one million Mexicans now work in what are known as the maquiladora plants – factories which line the USA border assembling imported products for export. The industries range from cars to plastics, and from textiles to computers. Constant inflows of new foreign investment maintain the pace of growth. It has all been made possible by trade liberalization and the setting up of NAFTA. Whereas in 1990 Mexico relied upon the export of oil for over 50 per cent of its revenues, by 1999 manufactured goods were contributing 90 per cent.

▶ **Figure 1** Men and Women working inone of the many maquiladora plants in Tijuana, Baja California, on the USA-Mexico border

Tertiary, quaternary and quinary activities

- Different types of service industries
- Changing patterns of retailing
- The location of service industries and the development of business parks
- The globalization of services

Different types of service industries

Classification of services is difficult, mainly because of their diversity and the way one overlaps with another. Also new ones are constantly being added to the list as the more complex demands of people and businesses in post-industrial societies are met by specialized services (Figure 1). There can be no doubting the importance of services in all economically developed countries. Increasing importance reflects rising real incomes leading to increased consumer spending on personal, financial and leisure services.

The definitions in Figure 2 do not fit the idea of progression through time from third to fourth to fifth. An alternative definition is one in which tertiary is regarded as a very broad sector within which all personal, clerical, professional, business and financial services are included. Quaternary is viewed more as services rendered by those engaged in research, development and information processing. Quinary (the most recent) is reserved for those in high levels of management in all types of large organizations, whether public or private, who have more influence and power than ever before.

Quaternary	Quinary
Finance and insurance	Education, government, health, research and development
Professions:	**Professions:**
Solicitors, accountants, consultants	Civil servants, doctors, management, nurses, academics, teachers

▲ **Figure 2** Isolating different types of services in the quarternary and quinary sectors

Given these problems of definition, the best solution is to call all of them services. For purposes of official data collection, the National Office of Statistics in the UK splits the commercial service sector into financial and other services. The top five sectors are shown in Figure 3. Other sectors include rental services (renting to individuals and leasing heavy equipment, office equipment and cars to businesses) and computing services. There are equally large employment areas within the non-commercial service sector. Local authorities in the UK employ almost two million in a wide range of jobs, which include administrators, teachers, fire-fighters and street cleaners. The NHS employs almost a million; staff costs account for 70 per cent of the spending on hospitals and community health care, which indicates how labour intensive the service sector tends to be.

▲ **Figure 1** Teleport in Sunderland – call centres employed a quarter of a million people in the UK in 1999, but had barely been invented at the beginning of the decade.

▼ **Figure 3** Snapshot of commercial services in the UK at the new millennium

Type of service	What is included	Numbers employed (millions)
1 Financial services	Banks and Building Societies, insurance, Stock Exchange, investment and financial services.	Over 1m
Other services **2** Wholesaling	Distribution of goods (including food and drink) to points of sale.	1.1m
3 Retailing	Selling goods to people.	2.4m
4 Hotels and catering	Hotel and restaurant trades, including public houses and wine bars.	1.9m
5 Travel, tourism and leisure	Travel agents and businesses related to leisure and tourism.	1.8m

Associated with the growth of services have been major changes in employment characteristics in the UK. There are now many more women in the workforce (45 per cent of the employment total) and increased levels of part-time work.

Coal mining and those manufacturing industries which suffered the greatest decline (with the exception of textiles) were bastions of male employment. The new types of work in the tertiary sector are often equally suited to both men and women. Some of the new services such as telephone call centres attract a high proportion of female labour for reasons which include flexible working hours and locations near to residential areas. However, old established service industries such as retailing have witnessed great changes as well. The traditional hierarchy of retailing shown in Figure 4 has greatly changed in many urban areas today.

▼ **Figure 4** The hierarchy of retailing in the UK (pre-1970)

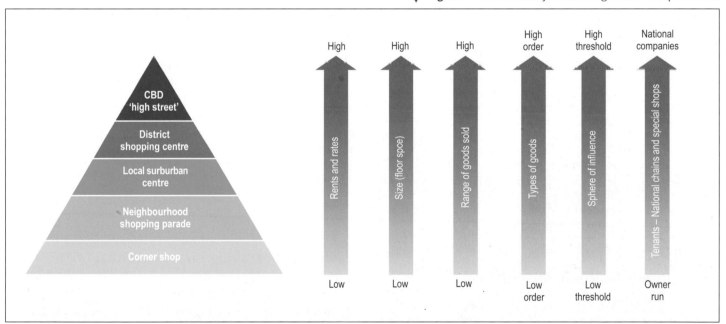

 The importance of services in the UK in 1998

- Services contributed 66% by value added to the UK's domestic economy

- 75% of the workforce employed in the service sector

- Total workers in services 20.8 million

- 800,000 workers added to the total in the previous two years.

Questions

1   Make and justify one classification of service industries.

2   Why is classification of the service sector difficult?

Changing patterns of retailing

The traditional pattern of retailing is based upon two elements:

1 Access locally to goods which are purchased regularly, often on a daily basis, particularly if perishable such as bread, milk and newspapers.

2 People's willingness to travel to a shopping centre for higher value goods purchased less often such as household and electrical goods and clothes and shoes.

In the UK local needs in areas of terraced housing are met by the corner shop and suburban shopping centres along the sides of a main road. On suburban housing estates a parade of shops, which was included in the building plans, fulfils the same function. Travelling to purchase higher order (comparison) goods means a visit to the town centre (CBD).

This pattern developed in the days of low private car ownership and reliance upon public transport, at a time when married women were unlikely to go out to work. The Americans have always been ahead of Europeans in car ownership. Many of the trends in retailing observed in the USA in the 1960s and 1970s have been adopted in the UK and Europe from the late 1970s, none more so than the switch to out-of-town shopping centres and malls. Nearly all the changes in patterns of retailing in the UK, which are summarized in Figure 1, are a response to increased mobility allowed by higher private car ownership and use. An alternative hierarchy of retailing may better reflect shopping habits of many car lovers (Figure 2).

▼ **Figure 1** Timeline of changes in UK retailing

Growth of superstores (in towns) and hypermarkets	Non-food retail parks (DIY, carpets, furniture)	Larger out-of-town shopping centres including eight major centres	E-retailers and e-commerce

1970   1980   1990   2000

Hierarchy on page 247

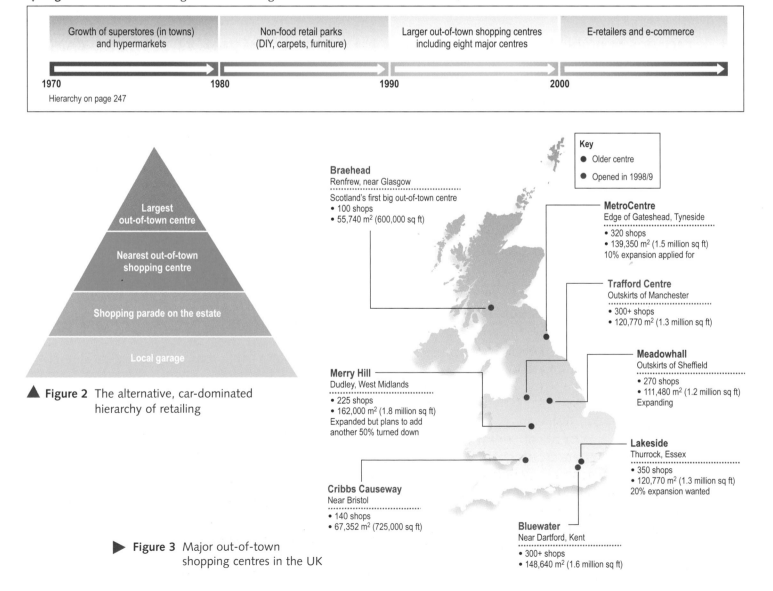

▲ **Figure 2** The alternative, car-dominated hierarchy of retailing

Largest out-of-town centre

Nearest out-of-town shopping centre

Shopping parade on the estate

Local garage

Key
- Older centre
- Opened in 1998/9

Braehead
Renfrew, near Glasgow
Scotland's first big out-of-town centre
• 100 shops
• 55,740 m² (600,000 sq ft)

MetroCentre
Edge of Gateshead, Tyneside
• 320 shops
• 139,350 m² (1.5 million sq ft)
10% expansion applied for

Trafford Centre
Outskirts of Manchester
• 300+ shops
• 120,770 m² (1.3 million sq ft)

Meadowhall
Outskirts of Sheffield
• 270 shops
• 111,480 m² (1.2 million sq ft)
Expanding

Merry Hill
Dudley, West Midlands
• 225 shops
• 162,000 m² (1.8 million sq ft)
Expanded but plans to add another 50% turned down

Lakeside
Thurrock, Essex
• 350 shops
• 120,770 m² (1.3 million sq ft)
20% expansion wanted

Cribbs Causeway
Near Bristol
• 140 shops
• 67,352 m² (725,000 sq ft)

Bluewater
Near Dartford, Kent
• 300+ shops
• 148,640 m² (1.6 million sq ft)

▶ **Figure 3** Major out-of-town shopping centres in the UK

▶ **Figure 4** An out-of-town shopping centre in Durham but, it could be anywhere in the UK.

While the private car has been the catalyst for the retailing revolution, there are other factors that explain the changes shown in Figure 1:

1 Mobility allowed by the private car
Car parking is expensive and restricted in city centres; access in and out on congested roads is slow and stressful. Out-of-town retailing offers large and free car parks. Locations next to motorways speed up access. At the local level it is easier to pull off the road into a garage shop rather than stop at a corner shop or suburban shopping centre on a busy main road.

2 Shopping habits of people
Shopping for food and essentials has become a weekly or fortnightly habit. A lot can be packed into a car boot. Freezers allow food to be stored at home. Working women cannot go out and shop every day.

3 Expectation from the shopping environment
A more pleasant shopping experience is desired, which has encouraged the growth of covered and indoor shopping centres. Fast food outlets and cinemas are an attraction to some.

4 Organization of the retail industry
Only a few large supermarket companies remain and they are very competitive. Land is cheaper out of town and business rates are lower. Large units benefit from economies of scale, but the only way to attract lots of customers is to have good road access and large car parks.

5 Attitude of planners and politicians
Government policy is now to focus new retail development in existing centres. Most of the eight major out-of-town shopping centres (Figure 3) want to build upon their success and expand. Some have been allowed a more modest expansion than they applied for, but the days of gaining easy planning permission to build on greenfield sites, as in the 1970s and 1980s, seem to be over for the moment. Some of the supermarkets are turning their attention back to inner urban areas. A chain of Tesco 'Metros' is being followed by J. Sainsbury 'Central' and 'Local' stores. They cannot sell the full range but what they stock is targeted at local needs, such as sandwiches and snacks for workers' lunches.

Questions

1 a Name the different types of outlets at the neighbourhood level.
  b Explain why many are declining and a few are growing.

2 Study Figure 3 which gives information about the UK's major out-of-town shopping centres.
  a Describe and suggest reasons for their distribution.
  b What are the common features of out-of-town shopping centres?
  c Explain why they are so popular with people.
  d Give some of the arguments against them using the headings **i** economic **ii** environmental and **iii** social.

Investigation

1 a For your own area:
  i outline the nature and location of neighbourhood stores,
  ii summarize the hierarchy of retailing by giving brief, but essential, details of shopping areas.
  b Compile information about one of the major out-of-town shopping centres on Figure 3 as a short case study.

The location of service industries and the development of business parks

Nationally there is a close relationship between the number of service sector jobs and the number of people in an area. Certain service industries are more specialized and less evenly distributed throughout the country, notably financial services. The historical heart is the 'City' of London, which houses the Bank of England, Stock Exchange and Lloyd's insurance within its square mile. The 'City' remains one of the world's top three financial centres (New York and Frankfurt are the others). Within all urban areas, the greatest concentration of services is in the CBD. As in retailing and for many of the same reasons, there has been the drift of office employment from the city centre to suburbs and rural fringes. In the UK, factories, suffering from poor access and limited space in inner urban locations, began the trend by moving into trading and industrial estates as early as the 1930s. The early estates, such as Slough west of London (known as the home of the Mars bar if for nothing else) and Team Valley south of Newcastle-upon-Tyne, were developed as large concentrations of manufacturing industry. However, if you visit Team Valley today, the first thing you will see on leaving the A1 road is a Retail Park, to be followed by distribution centres, cash and carry outlets and the Royal Mail sorting office among the factories. On the industrial estate nearest to you, it is unlikely that all of its tenants are engaged in manufacturing. This is one of the reasons why the term business park is more commonly used now.

The rise of out-of-town office parks in the USA in the 1970s coincided with the decline of the CBDs of big cities into ugly and unsafe places populated only by the poor, the ones left behind by the flight of the middle classes to the suburbs. As middle-class Americans moved further away from town centres, they became less willing to commute long distances to work to what was becoming an increasingly unfriendly and alien environment. The idea of the office park was born when developers began placing large, modern office buildings in leafy, landscaped surroundings, complete with ample car parking. One of their targets was a well-educated female workforce, whose skills would require higher salaries to be attracted to work in the CBDs every day. In the UK, although they are more likely to be called business parks, they have the same features – a pleasant, modern and secure environment allowing room for expansion. Nearness to a main road, almost certainly a dual carriageway or motorway, is considered to be a critical factor for a successful location.

A business park,

Case Study   Doxford, Sunderland

▼ **Figure 1** Doxford International Business and Technology Park near Sunderland, but it could have been a business park anywhere in the UK. Marketing people for business parks talk about 'creating a destination' and 'creating an environment for businesses'. (Location – square 3652, south of the roundabout on the B1286 OS map page 265.)

Companies include:
One 2 One and
  BT call centres
HQ of Nike (UK)
HQ of London Electric
HQ of Arriva –
  buses and cars

Special features:
Extra security systems so that it is safe for female staff to come and go at night.
Minibus service direct to Sunderland University making it easier for students to come and work part time.

Science parks

Similar, but with a slightly different focus, is the science park. There are over fifty of these in the UK employing almost 30,000 people. These are more specialist destinations dedicated to the start up and growth of technology-based industries. They tend to be attached to a university or major research centre because of the great importance of highly skilled personnel. Although the majority are among landscaped grounds on the edges of cities, a few have brownfield inner urban locations such as Aston and Wolverhampton Science Parks in the West Midlands which are located on land disfigured by the region's heavy industrial past. Of over-riding importance is the university link.

The first and biggest science park in the UK is Cambridge Science Park located on the northern edge of the university city. Already a successful growth region with some 1,200 hi-tech companies and dubbed 'Silicon Fen', it received a massive boost in 1999 when Bill Gates and Microsoft chose Cambridge as the hub of its European operations and pledged £50 million to build its first European computer research centre there. Billion-dollar companies and brand new start-ups are expected to rush into the region showing that the multiplier effect and benefits of agglomeration can apply to services as much as to manufacturing industries.

▼ **Figure 2** UK Science Parks

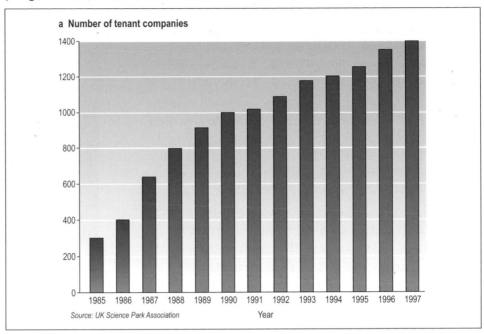

a **Number of tenant companies**

Source: UK Science Park Association

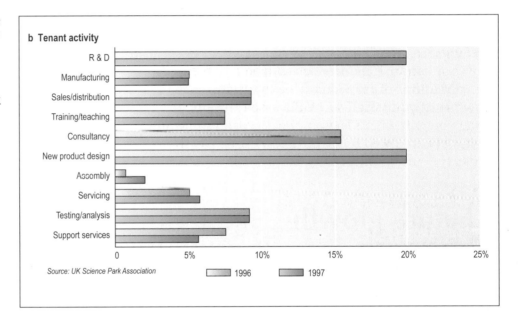

b **Tenant activity**

Source: UK Science Park Association   1996   1997

Questions

1 a Outline the features common to most business parks.
   b Explain their growth.

2   A newspaper headline after Microsoft chose Cambridge read: 'The e-volcano at the end of the M11 is about to erupt'. Why can business and science parks become growth points?

Investigation

3   Make a short case study for a business park near to you.

The globalization of services

Since the 1980s international trade within commercial services has grown. The greatest expansion has been in what are termed **producer services** to meet the needs of businesses. These include:

- finance, banking and insurance
- marketing and advertising
- research and design
- warehousing and freighting.

Most of these services form part of the quaternary sector. Without expertise in these areas, it is difficult for any manufacturing company to enter and to compete in world markets. LEDCs in particular are at a disadvantage because:

- they first have to buy these services at great expense from providers in the world's major financial and trading centres, such as London and New York
- if later available as the country develops economically, they are likely to be concentrated in the capital city or core region which does not help the country as a whole. (Manufacturing industry has the advantage of being more likely to be dispersed throughout.)

▼ **Figure 1** Downtown Manhattan houses the world's greatest concentration of financial institutions.

The world's most powerful economy is the USA. The world's largest financial centre is New York. In the second half of the 1990s the American economy was very strong and led growth in the high technology sector. This had a beneficial worldwide effect upon economic growth. However, there was a slow down in 1997 and 1998 as a result of the financial crises in East Asia, which cut demand for services in a region that had witnessed tremendous economic growth. This shows that what happens in LEDCs can have a worldwide effect, despite the smaller size of their economies. As with manufacturing, there is a global interdependence for the service sector.

Future growth

Case Study

in South East England?

For manufacturing, the South East is the preferred location for the majority of growth industries. It is often the only location that companies operating in the profitable financial and high-tech research sectors are willing to consider.

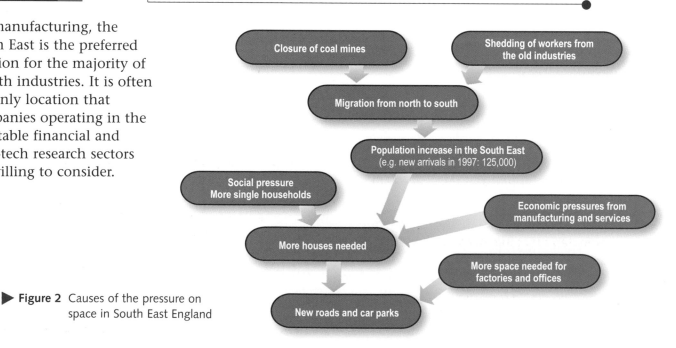

▶ **Figure 2** Causes of the pressure on space in South East England

Closure of coal mines

Shedding of workers from the old industries

Migration from north to south

Population increase in the South East (e.g. new arrivals in 1997: 125,000)

Social pressure More single households

Economic pressures from manufacturing and services

More houses needed

More space needed for factories and offices

New roads and car parks

A report published in October 1999 suggested that another 1.1 million homes will need to be built in the region by 2016 to satisfy demands. The report proposes massive developments in four areas shown in Figure 3.

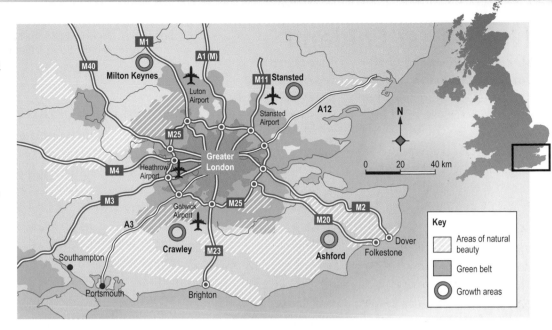

▶ **Figure 3**
Proposals put forward in 1999 for accommodating growth in South East England.

The four suggested growth areas are:

- at Stansted in Essex – based upon a new town on a greenfield site, although the location is not specified.

- at Ashford in Kent –expanded from 50,000 to 150,000 inhabitants.

- at Crawley in West Sussex – a new town created in 1947, which has been boosted by the presence of Gatwick Airport, will have a major expansion.

- at Milton Keynes in Buckinghamshire – growth mainly in the town or extension to the east of the M1.

In addition a new town outside Cambridge for about 20,000 is being considered.

Comments from Local Authorities in the South East.

- 'You would be desecrating the most beautiful part of Essex'

- '99% of residents would oppose the scheme'

- 'It will put more pressure on the road network, schools, hospitals and social services. Large swathes of countryside would be swallowed up'

Comments from local politicians in other regions of the UK.

- 'You will make the north-south divide worse and it would devastate the North of England'

- 'You would polarize investment in a way that would be bad for the North East and other regions'

- 'There has to be a strategy worked out to stop people from migrating'

- 'Encouraging people to move into the South East is obviously unsustainable'

Questions

1   Explain why the pressure for space is much greater in the South East than in any other region.

2 a   Draw a sketch map to summarize the main proposals for accommodating growth in the South East.

   b   Explain why some areas within the South East are considered more suitable for growth than others.

3   Should growth on this scale be allowed in the South East?
Identify the costs and benefits to the UK and give your own opinion about future planning policies for the UK.

North East England

Case Study

▼ **Figure 1** The old North East

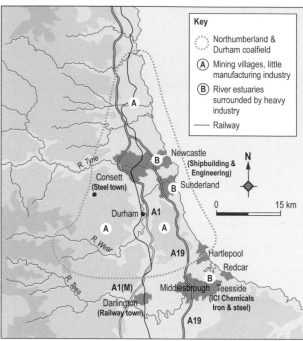

▼ **Figure 2** The North East in 2000

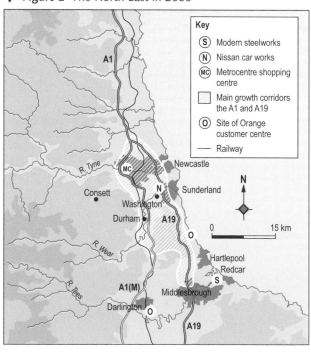

▼ **Figure 3** 1998 – a bad year for jobs in the North East

Company	Product	Size of job loss
Siemens	Semi-conductors	1000
Fujitsu	Microchips	600
Grove cranes	Cranes	600
Wilkinson	Razor blades	350

Decline of heavy industry

The regional identity of the North East was based upon coal and heavy industry. A large area was underlain by coal. The lower courses of the rivers Tyne and Wear were lined by shipyards and engineering works. As late as 1950 half the world's ships were built in the UK. In 2000, it is less than 1 per cent. The flat banks of the River Tees housed chemical works on the north bank and steel and petro-chemical works on the south bank. Many settlements had a mono-economic structure, i.e. they were dominated by a single industry, such as the coal-mining villages. The town of Consett was a classic example. In the 1970s its steelworks employed 7,500 workers out of a total population of 30,000. The work opportunities were male dominated and many men spent all their working lives with one employer.

Deep coal mining has virtually finished; all that is left is some unpopular open-cast mining. The tiny remnants of the once mighty shipbuilding industry is on the edge of survival awaiting new orders. The successful British Steel (Corus) produces approximately 70,000 tonnes of steel a week from its Redcar works on Teesside, compared with 50,000 tonnes in 1971. In 1971 the workforce was 25,000; today it is about 4,000. At first great hope was placed on the arrival of multinational companies to re-structure and modernize the region's economy. The Nissan car works near Sunderland employing over 4,500 has been a success story, officially proclaimed as the world's most productive car plant in 1998. But the arrival of others has not lived up to expectations. Microchips, one of the region's first sightings of high technology, came with Fujitsu in 1991 and Siemens in 1996. By the end of 1998, both had already gone (Figure 3). The old problems – image of the region, peripheral location within the UK and EU, and absence of a motorway link to the rest of the country – are formidable barriers to economic growth. Part-time, low-paid, female-orientated jobs, with high annual turnover rates in staff, such as working in call centres which employs over 12,000 in the region, are regarded as poor substitutes for losses in manufacturing. Orange, the mobile phone people, is one of the great job creators in the region, employing over 3,000 in its customer centres. It has even taken over the empty Siemens factory on a temporary basis. The future may be with Orange, but it does not look bright for the North East in 2000.

▼ **Figure 4** Ordnance Survey map of Sunderland. Scale 1:50 000

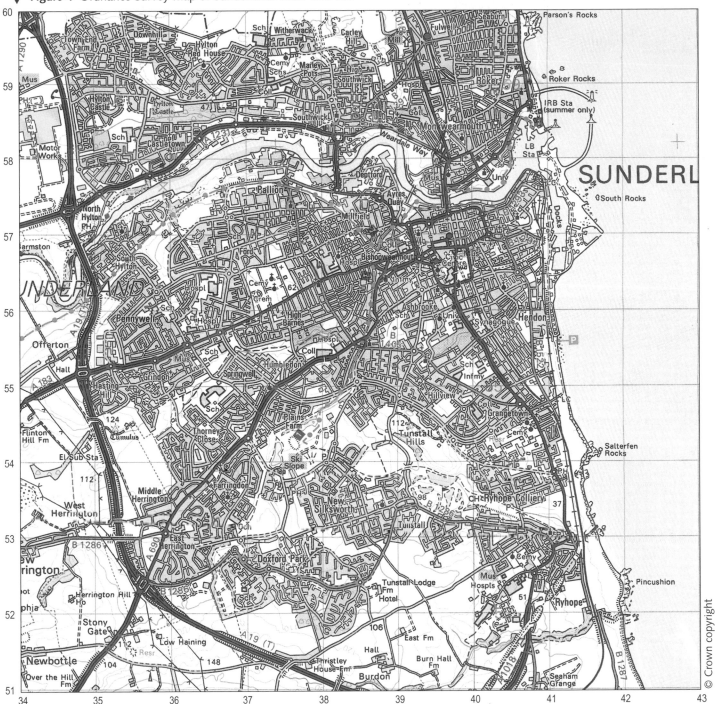

© Crown copyright

Questions

1   On a sketch map of the area covered by the OS map (so far as map evidence allows):

   a   show the distribution of industrial areas

   b   label other signs of the area's mining and industrial past.

2   a   Describe the site and location of
       i   the Nissan motor works (named in square 3458);
       ii Doxford International Business and Technology Park (south of the B1286 in square 3652).

   b   In what ways are they i similar and ii different?

3   a   Why has the switch in employment from shipbuilding to call centres occurred in the North East?

   b   Outline some of the advantages and disadvantages of this change.

4   Describe the old industrial patterns in North East England and explain how they have changed with time.

Chapter 6 Questions

1 a   Explain why coal mining is an example of a primary economic activity. (2 marks)
   b   Figure 1 shows numbers employed in coal mining in the UK.
       Describe what Figure 1 shows. (3 marks)
   c   Figure 2 shows the average price of coal since 1991.
       Outline how the information in Figure 2 can be used
       to explain what is shown in Figure 1 from 1991 onwards. (3 marks)
   d   What advantages can mining bring to an area compared with other
       primary activities such as farming and forestry? (7 marks)

Total: 15 marks

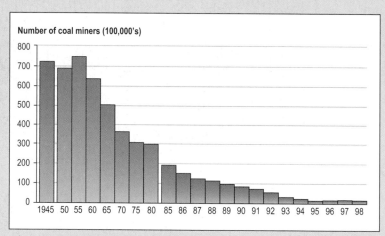

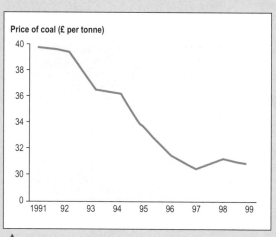

▲ **Figure 1** – The number of miners employed in the UK in there 1000's

▲ **Figure 2** – The average price of coal since 1991.

2 a   Give a classification of tertiary activities and explain why the range of
       activities included in the tertiary sector is expanding. (10 marks)
   b   How and why can the percentage of a country's population working in the tertiary sector
       be an indicator of the stage of economic development reached by that country?
       Illustrate your answer by referring to examples of countries. (10 marks)

Total: 20 marks

A note on timing

You are expected to answer question 1 in about 15 minutes. You are expected to
answer question 2 in about 40 minutes, spending an equal length of time on both parts.

Chapter **7** Geographical skills and techniques

Figure 1 Sixth-formers undertaking river fieldwork on the Isle of Arran.

Fieldwork opportunities

Geographical skills

Examination technique

Mark schemes

Fieldwork opportunities

- Water on the land
- Climatic hazards and change
- Energy and life
- Population dynamics
- Settlement processes and patterns
- Economic activity

Opportunities for primary data collection vary greatly depending on where you live. To meet the needs of Paper 3, the experience of undertaking primary data collection by a variety of methods is perhaps more important than that of undertaking work from the six separate topic areas in the specification. This will also make it easier to use opportunities that exist in the local area.

Water on the land

Fieldwork

Stream measurements
- width, depth, cross-section and channel area
- velocity, discharge, gradient and bedload size

Stream observations
- landforms such as meanders and ox-bow lakes
- channel features such as waterfalls, rapids, potholes and braided sections

Comparisons
- changes downstream between different stretches of the same stream
- changes over time in one stream, e.g. relating discharge to precipitation at different times of the year
- between two streams of different sizes (or stream orders)
- between two streams flowing through catchment areas with different land uses
- between managed and unmanaged sections of one stream

Secondary sources
- official discharge measurements taken by the Environment Agency or Water Boards
- historical records of flooding and newspaper reports of damage
- purpose of river management work and an evaluation of its success

Climatic hazards and change

Fieldwork

Weather observations
- daily recordings of temperature, precipitation etc. at a school weather station
- group survey of temperatures at the same time at different sites within and on the edges of an urban area
- group survey of other weather elements at different sites at the same time

Secondary sources
- use of national and regional weather data in the UK for comparison with locally-collected data
- study of national and regional weather maps and patterns
- monitoring records of urban air quality in relation to weather conditions
- investigation through newspapers and website information of the cause and characteristics of a climatic hazard as it develops
- a study of the short-term and long-term consequences of a climatic hazard

▲ **Figure 1** Group primary data collection in a stream

Energy and life

Fieldwork

Vegetation

- undertaking a vegetation transect over an area with varied physical conditions or across an area partly affected by human land uses
- undertaking a transect through a small area to show changes in vegetation in a plant succession (such as a psammosere or hydrosere)
- using quadrats within which the number of different species, percentage cover of each plant species and the frequency of each plant species can be measured
- examining human impact on vegetation such as footpath erosion

Soils

- undertaking a soil survey along a line of transect with physical variations such as from top to bottom of a steep valley slope
- undertaking soil surveys below deciduous woodland and coniferous forest and comparing the results
- using a soil auger to collect soil samples to analyze them for colour, texture and pH and to look for different horizons
- analyzing the differences in soil characteristics between woodland and farm land

Secondary sources

- visit websites to find data and information about some of the adverse effects of human activities upon soil such as soil erosion and salinization
- follow debates and newspaper reports of the results of trials of GM crops and other developments in modern intensive farming and people's responses to them

▲ **Figure 2** Measuring footpath erosion in the Lake District. The quadrats shown are frequently used in investigations of ground vegetation

Population dynamics

Fieldwork

- using questionnaires with people who have recently moved into a new housing estate or expanded settlement to establish small-scale patterns of migration
- using questionnaires to ascertain demographic differences, such as number in the household and their age groups, either between the old and new parts of a village or between different urban housing areas

Secondary sources

- variations in population structure and other local or regional demographic variations can be studied by using the data in national censuses. The UK census data for 1991 is available on CD-ROM. By visiting www.census.gov. there is access to US census data. Once the 2001 census in the UK has been completed and the results published, great new opportunities for more up-to-date population studies than any printed in a book will become available.

Settlement processes and patterns

Fieldwork

Urban areas

- making urban transects to determine degree of fit between actual land use patterns and those of urban models
- study of a particular urban zone, such as the CBD, to investigate its unique features, or changes, or variations within it such as between core and periphery in the example of the CBD
- study of areas of change within inner urban areas such as a waterside regeneration scheme or an example of gentrification
- study of changes occurring in an area on the edge of the city where out-of-town developments are happening
- environmental surveys or socio-economic studies based on questionnaires delivered in two contrasting housing areas
- surveys to determine an urban area's sphere of influence

Rural areas

- evidence of land use and environmental changes in a village which is growing and becoming suburbanized
- socio-economic survey by questioning to determine differences between old and new residential areas
- journey to work survey in a village to determine whether or not it can be labelled as a commuter village
- nature and provision of services in rural settlements within an area
- identifying the break-point between the spheres of influence of two market towns

Secondary sources

- using census data to identify and map variations in housing and socio-economic characteristics of residents between different urban wards
- changes in land uses and services over recent years in the CBD based upon use of Goad maps for different dates
- studying educational materials produced by private and public organizations responsible for urban regeneration and change
- the study of parish records to examine recent historical changes which help to explain current village features
- using articles in local weekly newspapers to investigate issues for people living in villages and rural areas

Economic activity

Fieldwork

- study of a business park or industrial estate examining factors such as location, characteristics and changes
- comparative study between old and new areas of industrial activity
- using questionnaires to investigate the effects of the presence of a quarry upon residents
- land use, environmental and socio-economic surveys in a former coal mining settlement
- small-scale study of a local primary or secondary activity
- small-scale study of retailing within walking distance of the home area
- establishing the hierarchy of shopping centres in all or part of an urban area (depending upon size) and their spheres of influence
- studies of out-of-town developments and their impacts upon established businesses in the area

Secondary sources

- use council and other local records to establish the relative importance of different economic activities for employment in the local area
- use international data from organizations such as the UN to examine variations in employment structure between countries at different levels of economic development

▲ **Figure 3** The renovated dock basin in Castlefields in Manchester, next to which is the education office. The staff provide packs of information and organize guided tours of an area which is an example of inner city regeneration.

▲ **Figure 4** An English tourist being questioned in Costa Rica by students from a local school.

Geographical skills

- Map skills
- Visual skills
- Graphical skills
- Statistical skills

Map skills

Ordnance Survey maps

Ordnance Survey maps, especially at 1:50 000 and 1:25 000, are basic geographical tools. They can appear anywhere in AS examinations, but are most likely to be used in questions on Paper 3. The questions for which the OS maps need to be used will be based upon the syllabus content. This is why examples of OS maps have been included within topic areas in the book, such as rivers, settlements and economic activity. Some other types of maps are more likely to be encountered during fieldwork investigations. These include soil maps for a local area of study and Goad maps for a local CBD study.

Choropleth and isoline maps

You may be required to interpret and, in some cases, draw choropleth and isoline maps. Choropleth maps are shading maps based upon data which has been refined, such as numbers per square kilometre or percentages. The denser the shading, the higher the data represented. One of their most frequent uses is for showing variations in population densities within a town, region or country. For an isoline map, lines are used to link places of equal value. The contours used on OS maps are isolines which join up places of the same height. Otherwise, one of their most frequent uses is in the study of weather and climate for showing patterns of pressure (isobars), temperature (isotherms) and rainfall (isohyets). They can be used in work in human geography, such as for plotting pedestrian counts in and around a CBD.

Visual skills

Observation and geography are inseparable. The spatial nature of the subject is given by its focus upon variations between places on the Earth's surface. The expectation is that a good geographer is also a good observer.

Observation in fieldwork has an important role and it is an important skill. Well-drawn and labelled field sketches are useful descriptive and analytical geographical tools. For those lacking in artistic skills, annotated photographs are a partial substitute. In examinations, observation and geographical understanding are tested by the inclusion of photographs (both ground and aerial) and satellite images. The usual style of question is to ask for description first and comment second. On occasions you will be required either to add labels to the photograph itself or draw a labelled (annotated) sketch of the main geographical features shown on the photograph or image. It is vital in answering these questions based upon visual resources that you describe in the detail required for all the available marks. Don't digress into explanation when the questions only asked you to describe. When observing, look for both the specific, small-scale features and the larger, more general features that are present.

Graphical skills

These are useful in every topic area in geography. You cannot study geography at any level without encountering line, bar and pie graphs.

Line graphs

Line graphs are used to plot continuous data. This is why they are always used for showing the temperature of a place. They are also suitable for showing stream discharge, population change and how the price of a commodity, such as crude oil, changes with time. When interpreting a graph which includes several lines on it showing different items, check whether it is a simple line graph (the value of each line is its total) or a compound line graph (the amount between each line is to be added up, or compounded, and is included within the total shown by the top line). As a general rule, if there is shading between the lines, accompanied by a key to the shading, it is a compound graph. Otherwise it is the more usual line graph.

Bar graphs

Lines are replaced by bars when total numbers or amounts for different places or times are plotted. Monthly rainfall, for instance, is always shown by bars. It is obtained by adding up the separate amounts of rain that fall on the different days of the month. Bars are the most versatile of all graphical techniques. The length of each bar always indicates a total, but this may be sub-divided into its component parts in a divided (or compound) bar graph. Bars placed either above or to the right of a line can be used to show positive values while those below or to the left show negative values. Bar graphs can be drawn either vertically or horizontally. Often the choice is left to the drawer, but in a population pyramid the bars must always be horizontal.

Pie charts

The pie chart is a direct alternative to the divided bar graph. In other words, whatever data can be shown on one can also be shown in the other. The resulting visual appearance should be the controlling factor for the choice.

Scatter graphs

Some other types of graphs are in more widespread use at AS and A levels than at earlier levels of study. One example is the scatter graph in which the relationship between two variables is shown visually. The independent variable is plotted on the horizontal x-axis and the variable which depends on it goes on the vertical y-axis. It is possible that plotting the values will reveal no relationship; however, often either a positive (as the value of one increases so also does the other) or a negative (as the value one increases the other decreases) relationship is indicated. Even though it is unlikely to be perfect, a straight summary line, known as the 'best fit' line, can be drawn on the graph to summarize the relationship. Note that the best fit line must always be a straight line.

Triangular graphs

Another example is the triangular graph (page 227). Always keep going in the same direction around the graph following the direction indicated by the arrows. When reading off the third value, check that it makes the total add up to 100 per cent; if it doesn't, one or more of your values is wrong.

Logarithmic scale graphs

You are also more likely to meet graphs with uneven logarithmic scales. Instead of the uniform arithmetic scale that you are used to, one or both of the scales on the graph may be uneven because they are based upon logarithms (and drawn on logarithmic graph paper). For example, there may be the same spacing for 1 to 10 as there is for 10 to 100, as there is for 100 to 1000 and so on. This is done either when the range and concentration of values is too great for a uniform scale or when it is the rate of change that matters, as for the rank-size rule (page 222). If a logarithmic scale is used on only one axis, it is called a semi-log graph; if it is used on both axes, it is a log-log graph.

Other types of graph are more specialized and therefore more restricted in their uses. The storm hydrograph shows stream discharge and has its own terminology such as rising limb, falling limb and lag time (page 14). A kite diagram is useful for showing different percentages of vegetation cover and percentages of surface cover for other types of plants measured along a transect line (page 105). A Lorenz curve is used in population studies to compare the actual numbers of people in relation to an even distribution (page 139).

Statistical skills

These are of much lower significance at AS than for A level itself. The emphasis should be placed upon geographical understanding. You will be required to comment upon what the averages and measures of dispersion around them show rather than to calculate the statistical values themselves.

Examination technique

- Understanding AS level examination questions
- Structured questions
- Extended prose questions

Understanding AS level examination questions

An examination question is composed of at least two elements. One is the command word or words. The second is the geographical theme of the question. For example, consider the following question, which is based upon the first part of question 1 on page 48.

From the photograph, describe the channel features shown which suggest river deposition.

There is only one command word in this question – 'describe'. This command word indicates that statements are needed about what can be seen on the photograph. You are not being asked to explain; all that is required for a full answer can be gained from observation of the photograph through geographical eyes. The geographical theme is 'channel features which suggest river deposition'. You don't have to write about all the river features that can be seen in the photograph; instead you are required to focus upon those related to river deposition.

In some examination questions a third element is present, namely 'where' – to where in the world your answer refers. Areas most frequently specified in questions are the UK, MEDCs and LEDCs. When the 'where' element is present in a question, this is a major restriction. If MEDCs are named in the question, and the answer you give is for LEDCs, you cannot gain any marks no matter how good geographically your answer may be.

 Examination advice
Before you begin to write the answer to a question:
- *identify and underline the command word(s)*
- *identify the geographical theme*
- *highlight any mention of where in the world or named places (if present)*
- *read the whole question again.*

Command words
A list of the command words used in the questions placed at the end of each chapter is given below. They are arranged (roughly) according to increasing complexity of expected responses.
- *Name / give*
- *Describe*
- *Describe how / how? / in what ways?*
- *Make a comparative study*
- *Outline*
- *Comment upon*
- *Justify your answer*
- *Explain / explain how / explain why / suggest why / why? / why do? / for what reasons?*
- *To what extent?*

Some longer questions have two separate command words, such as 'describe and explain' or 'how and why'.

The meaning of command words

Describe
- Make statements only and do not give reasons.
- Use information provided with the question on maps, photographs and graphs etc.

Outline
- This includes description as well.
- You are expected to elaborate further with comment and interpretation, although not in any detail.

Comment on
- There can be still some reward for description.
- It is expected that the answer will be taken further with interpretation or discussion.

Explain
- Now there is no reward for description.
- Giving reasons is needed.

The question papers for AS level Geography include a mixture of short, structured questions and longer questions requiring extended prose. A slightly different technique is needed for answering each of these two types of question.

Structured questions

For the structured questions, short but precise answers are needed. There is no time for repeating the question or stating background information in your answer. Give a direct answer to the question set. You should be starting to answer the question from the first word you write down. While it may be acceptable to write the answer down in note- or list-form for some questions worth only one or two marks, it is always better to write in sentences for questions worth three marks or more. Even in short questions, for example in those which ask you to give a definition, it matters a great deal how well the answer is expressed. Clear English expression and geographical understanding go together.

Be strongly guided by the number of marks for the question. This is a really important consideration when answering structured questions. On occasions you will know a lot more about the topic than is needed for the answer. You may feel able to answer a ten-mark question because you understand the topic so well, but if there are just four marks available for the answer, then you can gain no more than four marks for the answer no matter how much you write and how good it is. You will be penalising yourself by writing more because it is taking out time needed for answering other questions. However, the reverse problem is more common – that the answer is not extended sufficiently to claim all the marks set aside for it. An example of this is given in Figure 5.

▼ **Figure 5** Giving a definition

Question –   **'What is an ecosystem?'**   (4 marks)

Answer 1 –   An ecosystem comprises all the living communities in an area together with its non-living environment.

Mark = 1.   It is an accurate basic definition of an ecosystem, good enough for a 1 mark question, but clearly insufficient for a question worth 4 marks.

Answer 2 –   An ecosystem comprises all living things (vegetation and animals) in an area together with its non-living environment (climate, rocks and soil).

Mark = 2.   Some extension to the definition has been given by identifying the living, or biotic, factors and the non-living, or abiotic, factors.

Answer 3 –   An ecosystem comprises all living things (vegetation and animals) in an area together with its non-living environment (climate, rocks and soil). They are linked together as a functioning unit, or system, and interact with one another. For example, climatic factors such as heat and rainfall have a great influence on the type of vegetation; the decay and decomposition of vegetation affects the characteristics of the soil. This is just one example of interaction between the components of an ecosystem shown in the diagram.

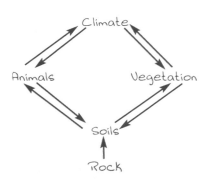

Mark = 4.   Another important aspect of the ecosystem idea is present in this answer which the other two answers didn't have. The links which make it a functioning system are referred to. The student giving the answer is erring on the right side by adding the diagram, which helps to ensure that there is more than sufficient in the answer to earn all four marks.

Therefore in short, structured questions the number of marks is the key indicator of what is expected for the answer. When asked to describe what a table of data, graph or diagram shows, you need to quote data or information which supports the descriptive points being made. The more you can use the values the better. An example of this is given in Figure 6.

▼ **Figure 6** Answering a question based upon information provided

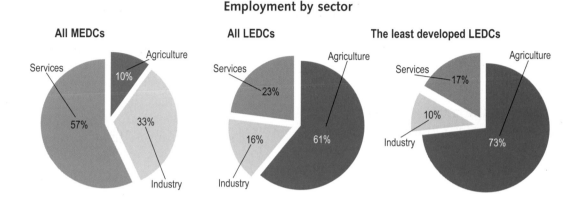

Question – 'Describe the differences in employment between countries at the various levels of economic development shown in the graphs'. **(4 marks)**

Employment by sector

Answer 1 – The percentage working in agriculture becomes less as a country becomes economically more developed whilst the percentages working in industry and services both increase. In MEDCs most are employed in services whereas in LEDCs most work in farming.

Mark = 2. The two basic differences required in a good answer have been stated. Unfortunately they have not been described, either by elaboration or by the use of values, in the manner needed for a full answer to a 4 mark question.

Answer 2 – In MEDCs 10% work in agriculture, 33% work in industry and 57% work in services. In LEDCs 61% work in agriculture, 16% in industry and 23% in services. In least developed LEDCs 73% work in agriculture, 10% in industry and 17% in services. Therefore there are great differences between them.

Mark = 0. Only the values stated on the graphs have been written out. No differences have been stated in this answer.

Answer 3 – With higher levels of development, fewer work in agriculture because it pays less than working in industry or services. The percentage working in agriculture is at least 6 times greater in LEDCs than in MEDCs. In MEDCs more than half of the employment is in services whereas in both groups of LEDCs more than half work in agriculture. In the least developed LEDCs there are 13% more working in agriculture than the average for LEDCs and 6% less in both industry and services, showing that the percentages in industry and services increase with development as those in agriculture decrease.

Mark = 4. The answer is focused upon differences. Values are used rather than stated, either by quoting percentage differences or by stating how many times larger or smaller. Can you identify the one irrelevant part of the answer which went beyond description?

Extended prose questions

For questions worth ten marks requiring extended prose, more thought and planning about the form of the answer is needed. It is also important to have good organization when writing the answers. Quality of written communication skills, appropriate to geographical studies, is built into the assessment objectives in the AS level examination. This means that the examiners must take into account quality of expression and degree of organization when deciding how many marks to award to an extended prose answer.

You are expected to do the following:
- select geographical information relevant to the question
- organize this information in a coherent way for the question
- use specialist geographical terms in your answer
- ensure that the text is legible, and English expression accurate, so that the meaning is clear.

In the extended prose answers, as in all the others, geographical content is the most important element. A superb, brilliantly-written answer, but without any geographical relevance to the question set, will gain no marks; whereas a poorly-expressed answer including relevant geographical content will gain some marks. However, you must realise that the examiner will not be allowed to give you all the marks in an extended prose answer if the quality of your written communication is poor. This will stop you from reaching the top of the level three mark band (see pages 277).

For assessment within the top level three band, examiners are looking for the two features elaborated upon below, supported by good organization and English expression.

1 Detailed and precise geographical knowledge

Supply this by answering in as much detail as your knowledge and time will allow. Support your answer whenever possible by references to places or case studies, which will add depth and weight to your answer. Include some key facts from your case study so that you are doing more than just making passing references to places and events. Take every opportunity to be precise.

Two examples of being precise
- Every time you refer to a climatic characteristic, such as temperature or precipitation, under any of

the topic headings, get into the habit of always quoting a value. 'The world's greatest biodiversity is in the tropical rainforests where it is constantly hot and wet'. The statement is accurate and uses geographical knowledge, but if you add '27°C' after hot, and 'over 2000mm' after wet, it does wonders for increasing the precision.

- Answers given by candidates to population density questions are notorious for being vague. 'Low densities of population are found where it is mountainous, dry and cold' is a typical statement that is usually left without further elaboration or use of example. References to climatic characteristics can be made more precise in the manner suggested above, and also by giving the names of areas to which they apply. 'Mountainous' can be made more precise by referring in more detail to relief and soil features such as steep slopes and thin, stony soils with frequent bare rock outcrops. Even more useful is information about a named mountain range such as mention of the extreme heights of peaks in the Himalayas where Mount Everest and others rise to over 8000 metres above sea level, which make permanent human inhabitation there impossible.

 Local examples / findings from having undertaken fieldwork
- *Never be afraid to use local information in examination answers.*
- *Use knowledge of relevant local examples even if these have not been studied in class.*
- *Don't worry that the examiner is unlikely to have direct knowledge of your local area. The broader general geographical knowledge of examiners will still allow them to assess the accuracy and value of the information quoted.*

2 Depth of understanding

One way of showing this is through the care with which you have selected the geographical information. The presence of irrelevant sections in any answer suggests to the examiner that understanding is incomplete. Whilst the examiner ignores irrelevant information, unless it contradicts the relevant points made elsewhere, it is an indicator of weakness; it also reduces the amount of relevant information you can write down in the time available for the answer. You have only about 20 minutes in which to answer each of the 10 mark extended prose questions and even that is dependent upon you having organized your examination time well. You can't afford to edge out other information more relevant to the question.

Another good way of showing understanding is to make comments back to the main theme of the question. This can be done at any stage of the answer, but it is essential that it is done at the end to round off the answer and to pin it down to the question set. It doesn't matter if you have nothing new to say. What is important is that you summarize briefly how your answer matches the question. This is also the place where it is appropriate to make comments of a more general or broader nature.

Two examples

- If the question is 'Explain the factors which have caused the de-industrialization in the UK' you should have concentrated on manufacturing industry and the reasons why it has declined in the main part of the answer. Then in the final part, you can briefly refer to the growth in tertiary industries (services) which has made manufacturing industry relatively less important in the UK.

- If the question is 'Explain the effects upon people of large variations from the average precipitation' you can show understanding in the main part of the answer if you realise that effects on people can be both good and bad, and that variations from average precipitation can include both a lot of rain and none at all. Understanding in the final few sentences can be shown by comment upon, for example, the relative strength of the different effects, or why the effects are often greater in some places than others.

Mark schemes

Introduction

Shorter questions, typically up to four marks, are either point marked or marked upon the amount of understanding shown. Within each of the 15 mark answers, there are some questions which require responses to geographical information, whether supplied in tables, graphs, diagrams, maps or photographs. Even when an answer is being point marked, precise and clear answers are still needed. You must always try to make more points than there are marks available for the answer, in case one or more of the points you make is not considered to have sufficient validity to be worth a mark by the examiner, who had not included it in the mark scheme. Therefore if the question is 'Describe the channel features shown' (3 marks), referring to the photograph in Figure 1, make reference to what you would consider to be four or five different features. Don't think that it is enough just to mention the waterfall.

Answers worth seven or more marks are assessed by what is called 'levels' marking. There are three levels and the examiner decides into which level the answer falls before assigning a mark to it. In the mark scheme, some of the likely, expected or possible answers are stated first, followed by descriptions of the different ways in which the candidates might attempt to answer and what each answer is likely to be worth. Certain general characteristics of answers at levels 1, 2 and 3 can be recognized and these are summarized below.

Level 1
The answer is inadequate for one or more of the following reasons.

- Only general points relevant to the question are made, unsupported by the use of precise information or worthwhile references to places or geographical data. In other words, the student doesn't seem to possess the knowledge and understanding needed for a good answer. This often leads to answers which are badly organized and poorly expressed.

- Only one aspect of the answer is covered. If asked to give advantages or factors or ways, only one of these will be given whereas in a good answer references to three or four of these can be expected.

- A lot of information may be given but without it having been selected for question needs. In other words, the candidate writes down all that is known about the topic so that much of the answer is irrelevant.

- The answer may be based on one case study and includes no comment of a more general nature, which is needed to make the case study information relevant for the question set.

Level 2
The answer must clearly match the main needs of the question to reach this level. Expressed another way, the answer must contain some relevant geographical information and comment. Equally it must also be inadequate in some way; otherwise it would have been placed within the Level 3 band. One of the commonest weaknesses is an unbalanced answer. For example, the question may ask for advantages and disadvantages, but the answer concentrates only on advantages with little worthwhile mention of disadvantages. In another example, the question may ask for impacts on people. Impacts can be good and bad, positive and negative. In many Level 2 answers, candidates take impacts to mean either good or bad, but not both. However, both aspects need coverage if the answer is to reach Level 3. The candidate who gives this type of answer has taken too narrow a view of the question set.

Level 3
These are strong answers to the question set. Some of the characteristic features of these good answers are set out below.

- All the stated geographical information is precise and selected to match question needs.

- The full breadth of the question is recognized and covered in a reasonably balanced manner (unlike in Level 2).

- Whenever possible references to places are made to exemplify the general points and case study knowledge is brought in to give some depth to the answer.

- Every opportunity is taken to include comment which relates back to the theme of the question.

- Some thought has gone into the answer so that it is well organized and well written.

Advice for using the mark schemes
- *By all means study the mark schemes to familiarize yourself with layout and to identify what examiners look for.*
- *But do not look at the detail in a mark scheme for a particular question until you have answered the question yourself, unseen.*
- *To gain maximum benefit for yourself, answer the questions first and check them later against the mark scheme.*
- *You are not expected to have covered all the points in a mark scheme to gain full marks for an answer.*

Water on the land (page 48)

Question 1

(a) (i)
- Boulders and stones are present in the middle of the channel.
- These form islands of deposited materials between the flowing water.
- The river flows in separate channels around these.
- This is called a braided river channel.

Any three points such as these 3 @ 1 mark   *(3 marks)*

(ii)
- Glaciers are present in the mountains from which the river is flowing.
- Water will be stored as ice and snow in the winter leading to low discharge.
- Snow and ice will melt in summer leading to high discharges.

Good understanding along the lines indicated = 2 marks. Some understanding, e.g. that the presence of the ice and snow is responsible, but without this being fully related to variations in discharge = 1 mark.   *(2 marks)*

(iii)
- During high discharge the river can transport a large load (it has a high competence / carrying capacity).
- Also the river at that time has greater powers of erosion so that more will be eroded to become load.
- During low discharge the river is over-loaded as its carrying capacity is reduced and it begins to deposit.
- Fuller reference to reasons why deposition occurs in the channel such as greater friction.

Three points made of the type suggested above.
      (3 marks)

(b) Possible channel landforms of deposition which may be referred to:

- delta or braided channels in extuaries are most likely
- references to floodplain deposition and levées could also be relevant as they are channel landforms when formed during times of flooding

Explanation could include references to:
- large river load and the reasons for it
- low gradient
- slow flow as the tidal part is reached and higher density sea water is met
- why a river is more likely to flood and to form floodplains and levées near its mouth.

Mark according to levels of response

Level 1 Basic answer (1-3 marks)
One or more of the relevant channel landforms are named, but only a little explanation about formation is given. The answer may be for one landform only, such as the delta, without explanation that is sufficiently detailed to raise it into the next level. Alternatively a more general answer about river deposition may be given which does not have deposition at or near the mouth of the river as its main focus.

Level 2 Clear answer (4-5 marks)
The answer is focused upon landforms of deposition formed at or near the mouth of the river and worthwhile explanation is given for at least one of them. This level is the limit for an answer which does not include reference to a delta or estuary.

Level 3 Detailed answer (6-7 marks)
Accurate explanation is given for deposition and channel landform formation, expressed effectively in an organized manner. If the answer is mainly concentrated upon delta formation, some explanation for other related channel features such as deposition within the channels is also included.   *(7 marks)*

Total: 15 marks

Question 2

(a) Explanation can be expected for why flooding occurs:
- melting snow / ice in summer
- periods of heavy or continuous rain
- removal of natural stores in drainage basins such as forest clearances which allows faster run off.

Explanation can be expected for what makes some rivers very likely to flood and why the severity of the hazard may be greater in some river basins:
- size and nature of the drainage basin
- climate of the area through which river passes (e.g. if heavy seasonal rains are a feature such as in tropical monsoon regions)
- references to magnitude and frequency of flooding

events could be relevant
- whether or not attempts have been made to manage the drainage basin
- the density of people and amount of economic activity in the basins affected.

Level 1 Basic answer (1 – 4 marks)
There is mention of one or more of the causes of flooding, but without explanation in any detail being attempted. Alternatively much of the answer may not meet the direct needs of the question by dealing with the effects of flooding upon people rather than why flooding is likely to be a severe hazard.

Level 2 Clear answer (5 – 7 marks)
Fuller explanation is given for why flooding is a severe hazard. The most likely answer is one in which detailed explanation is given for why flooding occurs. This may be illustrated by valid references to a particular drainage basin, which will increase the likelihood of the answer being placed at or towards the top of this level. In other answers, less detailed explanation may be offset by broader references to one or more of the other factors which make flooding a severe hazard.

Level 3 Detailed (8-10 marks)
A well-organized answer showing good understanding and full of valid explanation, so that an answer to the question is effectively communicated. A range of points is covered. References made to named river basins to exemplify the explanatory points being made increase the value of the answer. *(10 marks)*

(b) Many river basin management schemes are multi-purpose.
- Possible purposes – flood control, water supply for people and industries, irrigation, navigation.
- Reasons – to justify the high cost, to take maximum benefits and make it worthwhile, because one factor affects another, to encourage broader economic development of a country or region.
- Examples – although local river management schemes can often be dual purpose, and may be cited to support the answer, large schemes such as those on the Colorado and Nile are the best ones to use to illustrate this answer.

Mark according to levels of response
Level 1 Basic answer (1-4 marks)
The weakest answer may be almost list-like stating the reasons or purposes for undertaking large schemes. Towards the top of the range, the multi-purpose characteristics may be better stated but with only a limited explanation for why. Alternatively the answer may be developed around one named example and a lot of detail

given, but the stated information is not clearly directed towards the question set.

Level 2 Clear answer (5-7 marks)
The multi-purpose nature of many large schemes is understood and the answer is focused upon reasons for this. There may be no more than passing references to an example or examples, which stops the answer going into level three. Alternatively the whole answer may be based upon one example; although focused upon the question set, it is lacking in broader comment towards the question as a whole, which makes it too narrow a response for the next level.

Level 3 Detailed answer (8-10 marks)
A well-organized answer showing good understanding about why large river management schemes are usually undertaken for a variety of reasons. The example or examples used to illustrate the answer are well chosen and the details given include precise information about it or them, which supports the theme of the question. Overall, the answer to the question is communicated in an effective way. *(10 marks)*
Total: 20 marks

Climatic hazards and change (page 90)

Question 1
(a)(i)
- Deaths have decreased whilst cost of damage has increased = 1 mark;
- supported by more detailed description or use of values from Figure 1 = 2nd mark. *(2 marks)*

(ii)
- Deaths down as a result of better / more reliable forecasting of hurricanes.
- Further details about why, such as use of weather satellites.
- People are better prepared and know what needs to be done.
Up to 2 marks for two points made along these lines.
- Damage costs are up as the value of people's possessions and property have increased.
- Same damage as previously will cost more.
- People can move after storm warnings, but impossible to remove possessions and property.
Up to 2 marks for two points made along these lines.
2 + 1 mark or 1 + 2 marks *(3 marks)*

(iii)
- One answer might be the same changes but on a

reduced scale (i.e. reduction in lives lost but less dramatic, rise in costs of damage but not by as much).
- Another answer might be little change in loss of life (still at the mercy of the intensity of the storm), and little change in cost (although it is likely that value put on damage will increase with time).
- Or a mixture of both answers could be used.

Both aspects (loss of life and cost) explained well = 3 marks.

One aspect explained well or some explanation for both = 2 marks.

Some explanation for either loss of life or cost = 1 mark.

(3 marks)

(b) Origins of tropical revolving storms such as hurricanes / cyclones:
- above oceans when sea water temperatures are high (above 27°C) e.g. after the hottest time of year when the sun was overhead
- heated air rises high into the atmosphere
- deep centre of low pressure created which sucks in air to replace that which is rising
- wind speeds increase to 150-200kph because of the great pressure gradient
- torrential rain falls from towering cumulo-nimbus clouds formed by the rising air cooling and its moisture condensing
- occur a few degrees away from the Equator where wind deflection is possible.

Mark according to levels of response
Level 1 Basic answer (1-3 marks)
Only one or two valid points of an explanatory nature are made. Either there may be more emphasis upon the weather which results from tropical storms without explaining why it occurs or the worth of the answer may be reduced by inaccurate explanation which shows that the origins of tropical storms is not fully understood.

Level 2 Clear answer (4-5 marks)
The origins are explained in an accurate manner but the explanation falls short of that expected for a full answer.

Level 3 Detailed answer (6-7 marks)
Accurate explanation for the origins of tropical revolving storms is given, expressed effectively in an organized manner. The total explanation is reasonably complete.
(7 marks)
Total: 15 marks

Question 2
(a) Precipitation characteristics of tropical monsoon:

- wet season in summer, typically between June and October in many parts of India
- heavy downpours and great totals of rain along onshore coasts and in mountainous areas
- dry for most of the rest of the year
- precipitation totals vary greatly from under 500mm to 2500mm or more.

Precipitation characteristics of cool temperate western margin:
- wet in all seasons, typically with a maximum of rainfall in winter
- higher totals along onshore coasts and in mountainous areas
- precipitation totals vary greatly from about 500mm to 2000mm.

Comparisons - similar variations between places and similar annual totals of precipitation, but differences in seasonal occurrence and intensity of the rain, as well as the characteristics and reasons for the origins of the low pressure areas which cause the precipitation.

Mark according to levels of response
Level 1 Basic answer (1-4 marks)
Useful information is given for only one the two types of climate so that no comparisons are made. Even when comparisons are included, knowledge about only one of the climates is secure. Only one or two differences may be established without any attempt to look for similarities.

Level 2 Clear answer (5-7 marks)
To reach this level, comparisons must be made even if it clear that knowledge and understanding for just one of the two climates is greater. The answer may still concentrate on differences without any similarities being noted. Having identified comparisons, some attempted explanations are expected for answers placed at or towards the top of this level.

Level 3 Detailed (8-10 marks)
The answer is well ordered so that it includes both similarities and differences, although the concentration on differences may be greater because there are more of them. Clear identification of key characteristics is supported by some of the reasons for them. Overall the answer to the question is effectively communicated although total coverage of content is not expected.   *(10 marks)*

(b) Variations in precipitation (from those expected in an area) may lead to drought or flood.

Possible problems from drought:
- water supply shortages, crop failure, loss of pastures, over-cultivation and over-grazing leading to possible soil erosion and desertification, famine, migration and death

Possible problems from flood:
- lives lost, people made homeless, property damaged or destroyed, crops ruined, other economic activities disrupted.

Both MEDCs and LEDCs can be affected. Suffering and loss of life may be greater in LEDCs while the cost of damage may be more in MEDCs. MEDCs are not immune, especially if the variation from the average precipitation is large and greater than previously experienced. MEDCs, however, are more likely to have the money and expertise to predict and plan ahead of the event and to put emergency measures in place to alleviate the after-effects.

Mark according to levels of response
Level 1 Basic answer (1-4 marks)
One or two problems are identified, but they are little elaborated upon or explained. The answer may be devoted entirely to the effects of either too much or too little rain; if so, any explanation given for the problems caused is too weak to allow assessment above this level. One particular problem may be explained at some length but without any broader coverage which gives only a partial, unbalanced answer.

Level 2 Clear answer (5-7 marks)
The emphasis in the answer is placed upon why both less and more rainfall cause problems for people. Both aspects will be covered, although not necessarily in a totally balanced manner. The answer includes some references to the MEDC / LEDC element in the question, more likely towards the top of the range.

Level 3 Detailed answer (8-10 marks)
An organized answer which is clearly focused upon why variations in precipitation cause problems, including explanation as to why this applies to both MEDCs and LEDCs. Some meaningful comment upon likely similar and different effects between the two groups of countries may be included as well. Overall good understanding of the question theme is communicated through the well-written answer. *(10 marks)*

Total: 20 marks

Energy and life (page 136)

Question 1

(a) (i) Description of the vegetation cover which can be seen and of the soils, followed by comment about the causes of the surface erosion and / or the damage to the soil which is happening.
1 mark for limited description and comment, not well related to what can be seen on photograph A.

2 or 3 marks for some description and comment.
4 marks for either full description and some comment, or for some description and fuller comment. *(4 marks)*

(ii) Political factors means influence of governments. Governments may be in favour of deforestation for a variety of reasons such as:
- political, such as popular with voters and can distract people from other problems
- economic, often the main reason, because the government wishes to increase the area of cultivated land and food supply for rising populations, exploit timber and other resources such as minerals, increase exports and earn foreign exchange to support more general economic development
- social, to provide otherwise landless people with land and avoid difficult problems such as land reform.

Mark on the amount of coverage; the factors can be taken from just one of the reasons, most likely economic. To be valid, however, the economic factors must be placed within the political framework for the question.
Some outlining of political factors but limited overall = 1 or 2 marks.
Good coverage, well stated = 3 or 4 marks. *(4 marks)*

(b) An answer can be expected along the following lines. The net primary productivity of tropical rainforests is 2200 grammes/m^3 because of the great size of its biomass, (height of the forest, density of vegetation cover and great biodiversity), which are mainly the result of its climate. The permanently hot (27°C) and wet (2000mm+ annual precipitation) conditions promote rapid plant growth and great plant variety, as well as rapid nutrient recycling which feeds further plant growth. In other biomes, there is either less heat or less moisture or both which means lower primary productivity. Also the natural rainforests which remain have been left to grow as competitive communities for thousands of years without climatic interruptions.

Mark according to levels of response
Level 1 Basic answer (1-3 marks)
Information about rainforests is given which doesn't fit or isn't adapted towards the high productivity theme of the question so that references that could be relevant, such as those to climate, are only made incidentally. Key factors such as features of climate may be stated in an over-generalised way.

Level 2 Clear answer (4-5 marks)
Information is used and stated so that it supports the high productivity theme of the question. Perhaps the coverage is insufficiently complete to allow the answer to be placed in the next level.

Level 3 Detailed answer (6-7 marks)
Accurate and complete explanation is given so that it is clear from the answer why primary productivity in tropical rainforests is higher than that in any other biome.

(7 marks)

Total: 15 marks

Question 2

(a) Different soil characteristics on a global scale are mainly the result of differences in climate. Podsols and brown earths (or other soil types) may be used to show how and why. Much depends upon whether the movement of water in the soil is up or down and how strongly this occurs. Local differences occur due to small-scale factors such as relief, rock type, drainage and land use. Soils studied in a small area may be used to illustrate these differences.

Mark according to levels of response

Level 1 Basic answer (1-4 marks)
Some differences between soils may be stated, but the emphasis may be more upon description rather than explanation. A lot of information may be given about soil characteristics which is little adapted towards the question set. Alternatively the answer may be built up mainly around reference to one soil type with little broader comment towards the main theme of the question.

Level 2 Clear answer (5-7 marks)
The answer is focused upon different soil characteristics and why they develop. Breadth of coverage may be restricted by concentration only upon soils either at the global scale or the local scale rather than both.

Level 3 Detailed answer (8-10 marks)
Accurate explanation is given about why soils develop different characteristics. The use of well-chosen examples at both global and local scales means that a variety of factors are referred to which increases the effectiveness with which the answer is communicated.   (10 marks)

(b) Arresting factors for a plant community include:
- local physical factors, such as ground conditions e.g. rock surfaces or the presence of fresh and salt water or sand dunes are important
- these may be extended over wider areas, e.g. where there is extensive flooding in coastal areas or where volcanic eruptions have covered the surface with lava and ash
- human factors may result from deliberate clearance of the natural vegetation for settlement, logging or farming
- human arresting factors may be more accidental such as burning the vegetation in the dry season and grazing by animals, both of which prevent new tree growth

Mark according to levels of response

Level 1 Basic answer (1-4 marks)
Some of the factors that can arrest a plant succession are mentioned, but are little elaborated upon and explained. Alternatively, one example of a plant community which has been arrested, such as a hydrosere or psammosere, is used which gives limited overall coverage and doesn't lead to broader comment.

Level 2 Clear answer (5-7 marks)
Broader response, well focused upon question need. What is meant by an arresting factor is clearly understood so that several factors are referred to, even if there remains some imbalance in the answer between references to the physical and human factors.

Level 3 Detailed answer (8-10 marks)
Accurate and complete answer supported by varied references to valid physical and human factors which can arrest the progress of a plant succession towards climatic climax. Some comment can be expected about the physical and human aspects of the question, such as where one is more likely to apply or where they combine, to increase the effectiveness with which the overall answer is communicated.   (10 marks)

Total: 20 marks

Population dynamics (page 182)

Question 1

(a)(i) Germany, Italy and Sweden.
1 or 2 of these countries named (without any others) = 1 mark.
All 3 and no others = 2 marks.   *(2 marks)*

(ii) Reasons for the fall in the birth rate or why it is very low can be used e.g.
- education on birth control widely available, supported by the existence of a variety of methods through which it can be achieved
- social factors apply, such as more women work and have careers and it is no longer unusual for married couples to choose not to have children
- economic factors apply as well, such as high living standards being dependent upon two wages and not diluting income on children.

Also reasons why death rates are relatively high (compared with many LEDCs) can be used e.g.
- that the ageing population structure means that there are higher proportions of elderly people. A certain proportion will die per 1000 people each year despite high medical standards.

One or a combination of both lines of reasoning can be used. Some understanding, but only a limited number of valid points made = 1 or 2 marks.
Good understanding shown and reasons well stated = 3 or 4 marks.   *(4 marks)*

(iii) Even in those countries with a natural decrease there is a higher level of in-migration shown by the new immigrants column in the table.
Basic understanding of this = 1 mark.
Use of values from the table to support this, or a reason suggested for the high in-migration (e.g. economic migrations) = 2nd mark.   *(2 marks)*

(b) Most in stage 4, but those without natural increases can be better placed in stage 5.
- The levels of the BRs (all below 15) and DRs (all below 11) prevent inclusion in stages 1-3.
- Features of stages 4 and 5 in the demographic transition model should be explained as part of the justification.
- Examples of countries from the table in stages 4 and 5 can be used to strengthen the justification.

Mark according to levels of response
Level 1 Basic answer (1-3 marks)
Stage 4 may be used, but without mention of stage 5 it narrows the opportunities for comment on justification. Alternatively, references to stages in the model may be imprecise and / or include wrong placings (such as if stage 3 is used). Wider general information about the demographic transition model may not be applied to this particular question.

Level 2 Clear answer (4-5 marks)
References are made to countries in both stages 4 and 5. Some valid supporting justification is given without giving the complete picture.

Level 3 Detailed answer (6-7 marks)
Having clearly placed examples of different countries from the table in stages 4 and 5, the justification is thorough and displays a full understanding. All is effectively expressed.
                      (7 marks)
                      Total: 15 marks

Question 2

(a) Possible impacts of an ageing population which may be referred to:
Negative:
- elderly people are dependent upon the state and working populations for their pensions
- the pensions bill is increasing as the proportion of elderly people increases
- it may need to be financed by higher taxes on the working population
- the standard of living of those in work may be threatened
- there is increased spending on health and care services which are consumed more by elderly people
- less government money is left to spend elsewhere on education for the young or support for economic activities
- concentrations of elderly people in certain places puts a greater strain on local services.

Positive:
- some elderly people with private pensions have high

spending power which supports holiday companies and recreational activities all year around

- some companies make products targeted at the elderly such as stair lifts
- considerable amounts of local employment may be created in towns popular for retirement.

Mark according to levels of response

Level 1 Basic answer (1-4 marks)
Some impacts are described but there is little progress into explanation. Alternatively one impact such as increased pensions may be referred to in detail with only minimal references to any other impact.

Level 2 Clear answer (5-7 marks)
Several socio-economic impacts are identified and explained. It is likely that there is total concentration upon those that are negative so that the full picture is not covered.

Level 3 Detailed answer (8-10 marks)
A range of factors are accurately explained and organized in a manner which makes for an effective overall answer. There is some reference to one or more of the positive impacts which increases coverage and makes it more likely that a balanced answer is communicated.

(10 marks)

(b) In both MEDCs and LEDCs the most mobile age group is the 15-30 age range who move for work (mainly internally but in some cases overseas as well). This group are the most mobile because they need income and may not be tied down by family commitments.
In some LEDCs there are few people over 65; they are more likely to stay in the place where they have always lived, which is almost always the case for those living in rural areas. In MEDCs there is more movement as people retire; they are no longer tied to nearness to their place of work, but there aren't the same numbers of them as in the under 30 range.
There is less mobility within the 0-15 group (tied to parents and, in some cases, schools as well) and in the above 75 group when moving becomes more of a hassle.

Mark according to levels of response.

Level 1 Basic answer (1-4 marks)
The answer may be concentrated upon the migration of just one group, such as the young for work, or upon one example of migration, such as Turks into Germany or Mexicans into the USA, which leaves the broader question largely untouched. Alternatively there may be general comment about age groups migrating left unsupported by any information that is precise.

Level 2 Clear answer (5-8 marks)

Meaningful references are included to both the under 30 and over 65 age groups, supported by precise comment about why they may or may not migrate and about the extent of these movements. However, there may be little attempt to answer the 'to what extent' part of the question or to deal with variations within age groups under 30 and over 65.

Level 3 Detailed answer (8-10 marks)
A well-organized answer in which likely migrations for the age groups are commented upon in relation to the extent of these movements. The answer may be supported by reference to the differences between MEDCs and LEDCs or to located examples of migrations. The net result is that a direct answer to the question is effectively communicated, supported by relevant information on migrations.

(10 marks)

Total: 20 marks

Settlement processes and patterns (page 224)

Question 1

(a) (i) For the first time there was a greater number of people living in cities in LEDCs than in MEDCs.
Basic statement = 1 mark.
Supported by use of values from the graph or broader references to preceding and subsequent years = 2nd mark.

(2 marks)

(ii) Only a slow / minimal growth is expected in MEDCs compared with a rapid increase in the urban population in LEDCs.
Basic statement = 1 mark.
Supported by further written description or the use of values from the graph = 2nd mark.

(2 marks)

(iii) The main two reasons for continuing urbanization in many countries are continuing rural to urban migration and high natural increases of population both in LEDCs as a whole and in urban areas in particular where there are high concentrations of people of child-bearing age. But reasons within these can be separated out by the candidate to make two reasons that are distinctive such as stagnation / decline in rural areas and economic growth concentrated in urban areas.
Valid reason used = 1 mark.
Well outlined = 2nd or 3rd marks.
Allow 2 + 2 marks for the two reasons or 3 + 1 marks if one reason is really well outlined and a second is clearly identified.

(4 marks)

(b) Possible conflicts in MEDCs that can be referred to:

Environmental:

- loss of woodlands, countryside, habitats etc.
- extension of the continuous urban sprawl / concrete jungles.

Socio-economic:

- villages lose their rural character and traditions
- rural residents may be swamped by urban types with different interests and much higher income levels
- property prices increase to put them out of the range of most rural dwellers.

Economic:

- development fosters more development and a greater scramble for land, which may lead to conflicts between land users.

Mark according to levels of response

Level 1 Basic answer (1-3 marks)
Only one conflict may be referred to which gives very limited coverage. Some of the content may read as if more for appropriate for problems than conflicts.

Level 2 Clear answer (4-5 marks)
Two or more conflicts are covered in an answer which clearly relates to conflicts around the edges of cities in MEDCs. Restricted coverage or weak expression / organization limit movement up into the next level.

Level 3 Detailed answer (6-7 marks)
Several conflicts are outlined in an organized manner which demonstrate good understanding of the nature of the conflict and its cause.   *(7 marks)*

Total: 15 marks

Question 2

(a) The answer may begin with a definition of re-urbanization.

Causes:

- some large-scale, prestigious examples of schemes to attract people back into inner urban areas such as London Docklands, and smaller-scale dock basin, river and canal side locations in other UK cities
- inner urban area can have attractions for living there such as near work, shops, restaurants and places of recreation, avoiding traffic congestion associated with commuting, often attractive to the 20-30 age group
- avoids the need to move further away from the city centre as the urban area spreads.

Consequences:

- positive in bringing wealthier people back into inner urban areas and in increasing the residential function which had been declining for decades
- negative in creating small islands of wealth within a sea of poverty, creating huge environmental and social contrasts there.

Mark according to levels of response

Level 1 Basic answer (1-4 marks)
Some indication is given that re-urbanization is understood, but supporting detail about either its causes or its consequences is in limited supply. Alternatively the answer may be based upon reference to one example such as London Docklands in which information is stated without adaptation to the needs of the question.

Level 2 Clear answer (5-7 marks)
Re-urbanization is known and forms the clear focus of the answer. Towards the bottom of the range there may be worthwhile information only for causes or consequences. If an example is referred to, it may only be mentioned in passing or not applied in the best way to meet the needs of the question. Alternatively if the whole answer is example-based, this level is the limit without the inclusion of broader content and comment.

Level 3 (8-10 marks)
A well-organized answer which includes valid references to causes, consequences and an example. The focus is upon explanation which allows an effective response to be communicated.   *(10 marks)*

(b) Possible changes in shanty towns that can be referred to:

- physical appearance of the houses
- changes in the urban environment after the provision of services / infrastructure
- increased number, extent and new locations for shanty towns
- changes in socio-economic characteristics as newcomers become long-established city residents
- changes brought by economic decline / growth in the economy of the country / city.

Mark according to levels of response

Level 1 Basic answer (1-4 marks)
Only one valid change may be covered with the level of supporting detail determining its position within the mark range. Alternatively two or three changes may be identified but without much elaboration or many supporting details. Another alternative is that the answer is based upon one city but the limited amount of accurate content and the lack of wider comment restrict the answer to this level.

Level 2 Clear answer (5-7 marks)
Several ways in which change is occurring are identified and reasons are suggested for them. A good answer may have weaknesses which stop it going into the next level, such as any attempt to use an example may lack detail that is specific to the city chosen or, more likely, little notice is taken of the question's 'constant change' theme.

Level 3 Detailed answer (8-10 marks)
In a well-organized answer, ways are identified and explained in a manner that leads to comment towards the theme of constant change. The dynamic nature of many shanty towns is well communicated in the answer. Successful use of an appropriate example will increase the chance of assessment within this level.   *(10 marks)*
Total: 20 marks

Economic activity (page 266)

Question 1

(a) A primary activity is one in which a natural resource is obtained, without changing its nature or making it into other products. Mining for a mineral such as coal fits this definition.
Some understanding or weakly expressed = 1 mark.
Understood and well expressed = 2 marks.   *(2 marks)*

(b) Some description = 1 mark
Some description of the decline supported by quoting of values = 2 marks.
Detailed description of the decline supported by the use of values = 3 marks.   *(3 marks)*

(c) The price coal attained in 1991 has not been reached since then. Despite a slight rise in the late 1990s, the price was still almost £10 per tonne less than it had been in 1991. The price of coal went down while, in general, the expectation is that costs and prices go up with time. There is some association between the severity of job losses in mining in Figure 1 and the fall in coal prices in Figure 2, which can be illustrated by the use of values from the graphs.

An answer along the lines given above is expected, but the way it is expressed will vary greatly.
A little understanding or some reference to significant values = 1 mark.
Some understanding and reasonable coverage = 2 marks.
Good understanding and a well-expressed answer = 3 marks.   *(3 marks)*

(d) Possible advantages:
• a productive mine can employ much larger numbers of people than other activities which need larger areas of land, such as farming or forestry
• wages in mining tend to be higher than those in farming
• whole settlements, sometimes even towns, can grow up around a mine
• the infrastructure such as transport, power supply, water etc. is improved
• processing or mineral-using industries may grow up next to the mine increasing the employment opportunities.

Mark according to levels of response
Level 1 Basic answer (1-3 marks)
Only one advantage is used in an effective manner. Or else several advantages may be stated or hinted at without being developed.

Level 2 Clear answer (4-5 marks)
Two or three advantages are identified and elaborated upon.

Level 3 Detailed answer (6-7 marks)
Three or more advantages precisely stated in an organized answer.   *(7 marks)*
Total: 15 marks

Question 2

(a) Any type of classification is acceptable either a narrow one for tertiary activities by employment sectors such as retailing, offices, transport etc. or a broader one which includes all services, some of which could also be included under headings such as quaternary or quinary. The broader the classification used, the more opportunities are created when it comes to explaining the range.

Some of the possible points that can be made for expansion:
• the general point is that the service sector grows and expands in range and variety as economic development takes place
• rising levels of economic activity promote the need for companies to purchase specialized services
• rising personal incomes usually mean a greater proportion of earnings is spent on services such as shopping, travel and tourism, recreation and eating out
• administration, such as in local authorities, increases in order to supply the range of services expected
• there has been massive growth in financial and business services, telecommunications and the high technology sectors in recent years in MEDCs.

Mark according to levels of response

Level 1 Basic answer (1-4 marks)
There is some idea of a classification of tertiary activities even though it may not be a very well ordered one. Outline understanding of the reasons for growth without being able to explain why the range is expanding.

Level 2 Clear answer (5-7 marks)
A fuller and clearer classification of activities can be expected which includes the range needed for the explanation, accompanied by a greater emphasis upon the reasons for the increase in the range of activities. In some answers, one part will be much better developed and expressed than the other.

Level 3 Detailed answer (8-10 marks)
A well-expressed answer which covers the needs of both parts of the question in an effective manner. A valid and complete classification is followed by an explanation clearly focused on expansion in the range of tertiary sector activities.   *(10 marks)*

(b) The general point, picking up one of the themes from part (a), is that the higher the proportion of a country's population employed in the tertiary sector, the higher its stage of economic development. This can be illustrated by giving some idea of percentages for a MEDC compared with a LEDC. It can involve the use of proportions in other sectors, notably primary, which are also relevant to determining the stage of economic development reached by a country. The differences between countries can be explained by showing how activities become more specialized and varied in a country in line with higher economic development.

A candidate may wish to answer in relation to one of the models of development, such as that of Rostow, which can be helpful to both the how and why parts of the question.

Mark according to levels of response

Level 1 Basic answer (1-4 marks)
Some progress is made with the how part of the question, especially if percentage values for two or more countries are used to support the general statements, but little explanation for why is given. Alternatively there may be an attempt to deal with both aspects of the question but in only a generalized manner.

Level 2 Clear answer (5-7 marks)
An answer supported by the use of precise percentages linked in a valid way to countries in different stages of economic development. In this type of answer, one aspect, such as why, may not be sufficiently well covered to allow progress into the next level. In another style of answer, broad references may be made, showing good understanding, but the lack of sufficiently precise references keeps the answer within Level 2.

Level 3 Detailed answer (8-10 marks)
A well-organized answer in which a strong understanding of the relationships between percentages in the tertiary sector and the stages of economic development is shown, supported by a well chosen range of references to different countries. Overall, an effective answer to both the how and why parts of the question is communicated.   *(10 marks)*

Total: 20 marks

Glossary

Ageing population

One in which the proportion of old people, usually defined as aged 65 and older, is increasing.

Air mass

A body of air with similar characteristics of temperature and humidity at the surface. Tropical air masses are warm; polar air masses are cold. Maritime air masses are humid; continental ones are dry.

Air quality

This is measured by the levels of non-natural substances in the atmosphere produced by human activities, such as the burning of fossil fuels which produce carbon, hydrocarbons, sulphur dioxide and oxides of nitrogen.

Antecedent moisture

Moisture that was already being stored in the soil prior to more rain falling.

Anticyclone

An area of higher than average surface pressure formed by air descending from higher levels in the atmosphere. Sinking air leads to generally dry and sunny weather.

Binary pattern of settlement

This distribution exists in a country when the two largest cities are of almost equal size. They may be of almost equal importance although their functions may be different, such as capital city and chief port.

Braided stream

A type of stream made up of many small interconnecting channels, separated by small islands of deposited material.

Brownfield site

Places within the built-up area which have already been built on once for urban uses and which are available to be re-used again for new buildings or developments (after demolition or clearance).

Business park

This is an area mainly of offices, usually located on out-of-town, greenfield sites on the edges of the urban area. The development is usually landscaped with plentiful parking spaces.

Cap rock

The hard, resistant rock forming the top of a waterfall.

Central place

A settlement that supplies goods and services to the area around it. The larger the central place, the larger the area that it serves.

Christaller's theory

This gives the theory behind the spacing of settlements and the different sizes of the trade areas around them. Lower order settlements are closer together and serve smaller trade areas.

Climatic climax vegetation

The tallest and richest plant community that can be supported by the climate of an area. It is reaches only after a plant succession has been completed. Deciduous woodland is the climax vegetation for the UK.

Cold front

This separates warm air ahead from cold air behind, and is so called because as it moves over a place it brings colder air with it. Along the front, rapidly rising air leads to the formation of cloud, often cumulus and cumulo-nimbus, from which heavy precipitation may fall.

Condensation

The process whereby water vapour is turned into water droplets by cooling.

Conurbation

A large urban area, formed by the merging together of two or more cities, engulfing smaller towns and villages.

Convection

Rising currents of air caused by great surface heating. Air heated by the Sun at the surface becomes less dense, and therefore lighter than the air above, which encourages it to rise. The result is often cumulo-nimbus clouds from which heavy precipitation may fall.

Core and periphery

For a country or region, the core is where investments in modern industry, commerce and services are concentrated, with the greatest levels of economic activity. The periphery is the remainder of the country or region, which has been starved of investment. For an area, the core is the CBD. The periphery may include the edge (frame) of the CBD, the rest of the built-up area or the rural-urban fringe.

Counter urbanization

his occurs when increasing numbers of people move out of urban areas into the rural-urban fringe or further away into rural villages.

Crude birth rate

The number of live births per thousand people in a year.

Crude death rate

The number of deaths per thousand people in a year.

Cyclone

A deep area of low pressure in the tropics (a tropical revolving storm) that forms over warm sea surfaces and brings strong, violent winds and heavy rain to adjacent land areas, particularly at the edges of the Indian Ocean.

Decentralization

For an urban area, it is the increasing movement of industries and businesses out of the central areas (usually the CBD) towards the edges of the built-up area and into the rural-urban fringe. For a country, it is the increasing movement of people and businesses away from the core region, often around the capital city.

De-industrialization

This is the continued decline in the relative importance of manufacturing industry, resulting in a sharp reduction in its percentage share of the total workforce. Manufacturing industries such as shipbuilding, heavy engineering, steel and textiles have suffered most in the UK.

Density of population

The number of people per unit of area, usually measured as number of people per square kilometre.

Depression

An area of lower than average pressure formed by air rising from the surface into the upper atmosphere.

Distributary

A small river channel which leaves the larger main river and makes its own way to the sea in a delta.

Distribution of population

The way in which people are dispersed or spread across an area. In most countries there is an uneven distribution with high and low concentrations of people.

Drip

Water which is intercepted by leaves and branches of trees which 'drips' to the ground.

Drought

Periods of unexpectedly dry weather which cause great problems for people living in the areas affected. They can last for weeks, months or even years. The term is not used for areas which are permanently dry.

Ecosystem

The links which exist in an area between living things and their environment. Biotic elements such as vegetation and animal life are linked to abiotic elements such as climate and soils.

Eddies

Fast-moving circular currents of water in the river flow.

El Niño

This is an irregular event which occurs every three to eight years when warm water from the western Pacific replaces the usual cold water in the eastern Pacific, off the coast of Peru. This effects the tropical atmospheric circulation and results in major climatic anomalies such as heavy rain along the usually dry coast of Peru.

ENSO

The letters stand for El Niño Southern Oscillation. This happens when there is a change (or oscillation) in the distribution of warm seawater in the Pacific Ocean south of the Equator (hence southern). This creates unusual patterns of dry and wet weather in tropical areas, called an 'El Niño' weather event.

Evaporation

The process of water droplets being turned into water vapour by heating.

Evapotranspiration

The loss of moisture from a drainage basin by the processes of evaporation and transpiration.

Falling (or receding) limb

The drop in river discharge shown in the hydrograph as overland flow ceases and throughflow decreases.

Fertility rate

The average number of children born to a woman in her lifetime

Flocculation

A process in which particles carried by a river join together on contact with the salt in seawater, thus increasing the resulting particles' weight and causing them to be more readily deposited.

Footloose industries

These are light manufacturing industries, producing consumer goods, which have relative freedom in choosing where to locate their factories. As they do not use bulky raw materials they are not tied to places where these and fuel supplies can be assembled in the same way that heavy industries, such as steel and chemicals, still are.

Front

This is the dividing line between air masses where one air mass is being forced to rise. Much activity takes place as rising air leads to the formation of clouds and rain.

Frontal depressions

These areas of low pressure form in temperate latitudes where warm tropical air meets and rises above cold polar air, which leaves a centre of low pressure at the surface. Initially, there are separate warm and cold fronts although later they may join to form just one occluded front.

Function(s)

The purpose(s) for the establishment and growth of a settlement. Small settlements, such as a mining village, often have only one function. The larger the settlement, the greater the number and variety of functions it is likely to have.

Gentrification

This is when the status of an inner urban area, which has become unfashionable and neglected, is upgraded as wealthier people move back in. They have sufficient financial resources to improve properties and thereby increase the area's status again.

Global interdependence

As a result of globalization, almost all countries are dependent upon decisions made by governments, banks and companies in other countries. Multi-national companies based in Europe benefit from the low labour costs in Eastern Asia, while the latter countries benefit from the employment and introduced new technology. In this way, one is reliant upon the other – a simple example of the idea of interdependence.

Global warming

The slowly increasing temperature of the Earth's surface, indicated by climatic data and the recession of glaciers and ice caps. Scientists still dispute the causes of global warming.

Globalization

The increasingly international way in which companies, both in manufacturing and services, are operating and taking decisions which determine what happens in many other countries. The worldwide transfer of goods, people, ideas and technology is now taking place because of a revolution in global communications.

Gorge

The narrow, rocky, steep-sided valley recession created by the retreat of a waterfall.

Green Belt

The area of open space or low-density urban land uses around a town or city in which any new developments of an urban nature are strictly controlled or forbidden by planners and local authorities.

Greenfield site

Land which has never previously been built upon. It is occupied by rural land uses such as fields, woodlands or heath so that any building upon it would lead to major changes in appearance and function.

Greenhouse gases

Molecules of certain gases such as carbon dioxide, methane, CFCs and nitrous oxide detain outgoing heat radiation from the Earth's surface for a while thereby warming up the surface. Because these gases are acting in the same way as glass in a greenhouse, they are known as the greenhouse gases.

Groundwater

Water stored in rocks, usually permeable, in the saturated zone below the water table.

Hazard

This is a short-term event that brings severe variations from normal conditions, which causes great problems for the people affected by it. Drought, heavy rain and hurricane force winds are examples of climatic hazards.

Helicoidal flow

A type of water flow associated with meandering rivers in which the fastest current spirals across the channel and downstream in a corkscrew motion.

Hierarchy of retailing

This forms the shape of a pyramid with a large number of small shops, such as corner shops and garage outlets, at the base and a smaller number of 'high street' shopping centres in CBDs at the top. Changes to the traditional hierarchy are occurring as a result of out-of-town shopping centres being built.

Hierarchy of settlement

This is when settlements are placed in order according to size or to the number of goods and services supplied by them. A hierarchy always has a pyramid shape because there are more small settlements than large ones.

High order goods and services

These are consumed relatively infrequently and therefore need a large number of people living within their trade area to make them commercially profitable. They are most frequently located in retail areas at or near the top of the retail hierarchy. In less densely populated areas, their trade area, or sphere of influence, covers a large area. Examples are carpets and furniture.

Hurricane

A deep area of low pressure in the topics (a tropical revolving storm) that forms over warm sea surfaces and brings strong, violent winds and heavy rain to adjacent land areas, particularly islands in the Caribbean and neighbouring mainland coasts.

Infant mortality rate

The number of deaths per year among infants less than one year old per thousand live births.

Infrastructure

Essential services which need to be provided, often by governments, to create an environment in which commercial activities can be successfully established. This includes the provision of reliable power and water supplies and good transport links such as roads, airports and port facilities.

Insolation

Heating of the Earth's surface by the Sun's rays. These rays are more direct in the tropics, consequently heating there is greater than in temperate latitudes where the Sun's rays strike the surface at a more oblique angle.

ITCZ

The Inter-Tropical Convergence Zone is an area of low pressure near the Equator, where hot air meets and rises as a result of great surface heating from the overhead Sun.

Jet streams

Winds blowing at high levels in the atmosphere, transferring air and heat from the Equator towards the Poles. However, they have erratic speeds and patterns of flow.

La Niña

This is the normal condition (i.e. what happens most of the time) in the Pacific Ocean when the coastal seawater off Peru in the eastern Pacific is some 5∞C cooler than that in the western Pacific off Indonesia. The occurrence of cold water contributes to the desert conditions along most of the coast of Peru.

Lag time (period)

The length of time between peak precipitation and peak discharge.

Land uses in urban areas

The ways in which the land is used in towns and cities. There is a great mixture of land uses including houses, shops and factories, open spaces such as parks and sports grounds, and non-productive areas such as waste land and derelict buildings.

Load

The material carried by a stream, glacier or the sea. It varies according to carrying power and availability.

Low order goods and services

These are consumed frequently and regularly so that retail outlets specializing in these can have small trade areas and still be commercially viable. They include newspapers and magazines, and food and drink.

Maritime

The influence of the sea upon the weather and climate of adjacent land areas: increasing precipitation, lowering temperatures in summer and making land areas less cold than they would otherwise be in winter.

Megacity

A city with more than ten million inhabitants.

Migration

The movement of people both within and between countries.

Millionaire city

A city of more than one million people.

Monsoon

Seasonal reversal in wind direction on a large-scale which leads to a wet season (the wet monsoon) and a dry season (the dry monsoon).

Multi-national companies

These are businesses which have interests in more than one country. The big companies such as Ford, Nestle, Shell and Coca-Cola have operations in numerous countries, although the headquarters of the majority of these companies are located in North America, Europe and Japan. They take decisions in global terms and they can have global impacts.

Newly Industrializing Countries (NICs)

These are LEDCs which have made good progress in increasing their output of manufactured goods with an accompanying increase in the proportion of the work force employed in the secondary sector. The four countries which made the earliest and most rapid progress, Hong Kong, Singapore, Taiwan and South Korea, were given the label 'tiger economies' because of their rapid speed of growth.

Ocean current

Surface movement of seawater, driven by winds. If the water moves from tropical to temperate latitudes, as in the Gulf Stream and North Atlantic Drift, the current is warm. If it moves from polar to temperate and tropical latitudes, as in the Peruvian current, the current is cold.

Organic farming
A type of farming in which fertilizers and pest control methods are organic (based on plants and animals) rather than chemical. It may also be called biological farming, sustainable farming or regenerative farming.

Ozone
At low levels near the ground it is a toxic gas, produced in a chemical reaction of car exhaust emissions under strong sunlight, which irritates breathing. It is not to be confused with the high-level ozone layer, which offers vital protection against the Sun's dangerous ultra-violet rays.

Peak discharge
The maximum flow of the river during a rainstorm.

Peak rainfall
The time when the maximum amount of rain was falling.

Peat
Poorly-decayed plant remains found in areas where waterlogging is common. Water fills up the pore spaces in the soil so that there is a lack of oxygen which prevents soil organisms breaking down the organic matter.

Pedogenesis
The process by which soils are formed.

Photochemical smog
This is a dense haze in urban areas which restricts visibility and affects people who have breathing difficulties. It is formed by strong sunlight acting on vehicle exhaust fumes when dry, calm weather conditions allow them to accumulate.

Polar
This refers to areas north and south of latitude 60∞ where the climate is noted for its coldness.

Population structure
The make-up of a population by age and by sex. It is shown by a population pyramid.

Potential evapotranspiration
The maximum amount of evaporation and transpiration that would take place assuming a constant supply of water. If it is greater than the amount of precipitation then all water is evaporated and surface and soil moisture stores are depleted.

Precipitation
All forms of moisture that reach the Earth's surface in different forms such as snow, rain, hail and sleet.

Pressure
The weight of the atmosphere pressing down on the Earth's surface. In places where the air is sinking the pressure is greater which forms areas of high pressure. Where the air is rising the weight is reduced and low pressure forms.

Pressure gradient
The difference in pressure between centres of high and low pressure. The steeper the gradient, the greater the speed of air flow from high to low pressure and the stronger the wind.

Primary activity
Any activity which obtains a natural resource from land or sea. Raw materials are collected but not altered in any way. The principal activities are farming, fishing, forestry, mining and quarrying.

Primate pattern of settlement
This distribution exists in a country when the largest settlement is much more than twice the size of the second largest settlement. It may be many times larger and this means that the rank size rule does not apply.

Productivity
The rate of creation of living matter by photosynthesis. On this rate depend all living things (plants, animals and humans).

Quaternary sector
The definition in the examination syllabus is financial and insurance services. However, the term is generally more widely used for high technology and information services and those which involve high levels of research and development.

Quinary sector
The definition in the examination syllabus is services in education, government, health, research and development. In a broader sense it refers to services in which high skill levels and great specialization exist.

Radiation
Sunlight is short wave radiation. This heats the surface of the Earth which creates long wave radiation. This heat is lost (or radiated) into space during hours of darkness.

Range
The maximum distance that a person is prepared to travel to purchase goods or services. The range marks the limits of the area served by a settlement or central place.

Rank size rule
This rule was formulated by Zipf and states that if all settlements in a country are ranked according to population size, their sizes will be inversely proportional to their rank. Thus the second largest settlement will have a population one half the size of the largest settlement. The third largest will be one-third the size of the largest and so on.

Rationalization
Companies do this when they reduce the number of factories or offices, thereby concentrating work in a smaller number of larger, more modern and better-equipped units, with a smaller workforce, which tend to be cheaper to operate.

Regolith
The upper part of the bedrock which is broken up into loose fragments, mainly by weathering.

Reilly's Law
This law of retail gravitation uses a formula which takes population of settlements and distances between them into account in order to calculate the breaking point where the sphere of influence of one settlement ends and that of the other begins.

Retailing
Selling goods to people. Shops, stores and supermarkets are the traditional and dominant outlets, although in a rapidly changing world, selling on-line is likely to increase in importance.

Re-urbanization
This means an increasing number of people moving back into inner urban areas having previously lived in the suburbs or outside the urban area.

Rising limb
The rapid increase in river discharge as overland flow and throughflow reach the river channel, which produces a steep upward curve in the hydrograph.

River regime
The annual pattern of river discharge.

Run-off
Water flowing over the land surface, as channel flow and overland flow.

Rural settlement

A small settlement surrounded by countryside, such as a hamlet or village. A small market town would be the largest example of a rural settlement.

Rural-urban fringe

The area of countryside lying on the edges of the built-up area. Some land uses that are present, such as golf courses and water supply, are for the benefit of those living in the city. This is the area under greatest pressure from city growth, which is increasing because of the desire of many people and businesses to move out-of-town.

Science Park

These are more specialized than the business park. They are built in similar, pleasant out-of-town locations, but their primary aim is to attract technology-based industries, many of which are research oriented. This is why they are usually attached to a University or major research centre.

Secondary activity

An activity which changes raw materials and makes other products from them, using human and natural sources of energy. It principally means manufacturing industry, but building and construction are also included in this sector.

Segregation

The separation of different functions or different groups of people within cities and towns so that they are concentrated in certain areas often to the exclusion of others. Shops and offices are overwhelmingly concentrated (or segregated) into the CBD; the location of low status housing areas is separate from those of high status.

Seres

A sere is a stage in the development of plant communities towards climatic climax vegetation.

Shanty town

An area of poor, low-cost housing in or around a big city in the LEDW, often without the full provision of essential urban services. Local names are attached to them such as favelas in Brazil, barriadas in Peru and bustees in India.

Soil water

Water held in the pore spaces between soil particles.

Spatial variations

Changes over space, i.e. from place to place.

Sphere of influence

The area served by a central place, which was referred to as its trade area by Christaller. It can also be used to designate the area from within which people are attracted to buy goods and services from outlets such as shops and offices.

Squatter settlement

This is the first area of self-help housing for many newcomers into cities in LEDCs; in general they are lower in status than shanty towns.

Stemflow

Rainfall that is intercepted by vegetation and flows along branches, stems and trunks to the ground.

Structure of settlements

This is the form and lay out of settlements and includes the pattern of land uses found there. Urban models attempt to summarize these land use patterns which means they are trying to indicate settlement structure.

Suburbanization

This means the increased movement of people, services and industries from the centres and inner urban areas outwards, towards and onto the edges of the built-up area, taking over land that was previously rural.

Suburbanized village

Villages which have grown as a result of being populated by those who have moved out of urban areas. This results in conversions of old farm buildings into houses, infilling of empty spaces, the spread of ribbon development along roads and the construction of new housing estates around the edges. Both the settlement's structure and socio-economic character are changed.

Succession

A series of changes which take place in a plant community between plants colonizing a bare surface (such as rock, sand dunes or water) and reaching the climatic climax vegetation.

Sustainable development

The human use of a resource that ensures there is at least the same amount and quality of the resource after use as before for use by future generations.

Temperate

If applied to areas of the world, the term refers to latitudes between 30 and 60∞ north and south of the Equator (between the tropical and polar latitudes). If applied to weather and climate, the term implies lack of extremes of temperature, precipitation and winds.

Temporal variations

Changes over time.

Tertiary activity

An activity which provides a service. It includes transport and the distribution of goods, wholesale and retail, office and administration.

Thermal lows

Areas of low pressure which form around the Equator due to intense solar heating (hence the term thermal). They are present for most of the year and are also called the Equatorial Low.

Threshold

For a central place selling goods or offering a service, this is the minimum number of people who are needed to buy goods or use the service to make it profitable.

Throughflow

The flow of water downslope through the soil.

Tornado (twister)

A small-scale but very vigorous 'twisting' spiral of air rising high into the sky, recognizable by its long tail of dust and debris sucked in by the uplift of air.

Transpiration

The process in which water is lost to the atmosphere from the leaves of plants.

Tropical

Strictly speaking, these areas lie within 23° of the Equator. However, in climatic terms it is usually applied to all areas within 30° of the Equator, in which the weather is hot all year.

Tropical revolving storm

A circular system of very low pressure which develops over tropical oceans at the time of the year when the water is at its warmest. They are driven by the uplift of hot moist air, sucked up in a spiral as the storm system moves and is affected by the Earth's rotation (hence revolving storm).

Urban heat island

Pockets of higher temperatures coinciding with the extent of the built-up area. Quite frequently the centre of a large city will be 4-5°C warmer than the surrounding countryside.

Urban models

These represent attempts to summarize the distribution of land uses in cities and to show the general spatial pattern on a summary diagram, which might be applied in whole or in part to many other cities.

Urban settlement

This is distinguished from a rural settlement by one or more of the following: greater size, larger number of services, wider range of services, greater number of functions, larger sphere of influence.

Urban zone

A part of the town or city in which there are similarities in land uses which lead to common functions. Examples of urban zones are the CBD, inner city, low-value housing area, high-status housing area and industrial area.

Urbanization

This means an increasing proportion of a country's population living within urban areas leading to growth in population and increased extent of towns and cities. It is caused by rural to urban migration and by natural increases in population.

Warm front

This separates cold air ahead from warm air behind, and is so called because as it moves over an area it brings warmer air and higher temperatures. Along the front, the warm tropical air is forced to rise above the cold air resulting in the formation of stratus cloud. Often a period of rain is felt ahead of the front.

Water balance

The relationship between precipitation, evapotranspiration and water storage in a drainage basin.

Wind

This is the surface transfer of air from areas of high pressure towards areas of low pressure. The greater the difference in pressure between the centres of high and low, the faster the wind speeds.

Index